300 FUSS FREE | 20-MINUTE RECIPES

300 FUSS FREE | 20-MINUTE RECIPES

**FABULOUS IDEAS FOR FAST MEALS, FROM BREAKFASTS, SOUPS, APPETIZERS AND SNACKS
TO MAIN COURSES, SIDE DISHES AND DESSERTS, IN 300 PHOTOGRAPHS**

CONTRIBUTING EDITOR:
JENNI FLEETWOOD

southwater

This edition is published by Southwater, an imprint of Anness Publishing Ltd, Blaby Road, Wigston, Leicestershire LE18 4SE

Email: info@anness.com

Web: www.southwaterbooks.com; www.annesspublishing.com

If you like the images in this book and would like to investigate using them for publishing, promotions or advertising, please visit our website www.practicalpictures.com for more information.

Publisher: Joanna Lorenz
Editors: Elizabeth Woodland and Kate Eddison
Design: SMI and Diane Pullen
Cover Design: Nigel Partridge
Production Controller: Bessie Bai

Recipes: Pepita Aris, Catherine Atkinson, Mridula Baljekar, Jane Bamforth, Ghillie Basan, Judy Bastyra, Steve Baxter, Michelle Berriedale-Johnson, Angela Boggiano, Janet Brinkworth, Kathy Brown, Georgina Campbell, Carla Capalbo, Kit Chan, Jacqueline Clarke, Maxine Clarke, Carole Clements, Trish Davies, Roz Denny, Patrizia Diemling, Matthew Drennen, Coralie Dorman, Joanna Farrow, Valerie Ferguson, Rafi Fernandez, Maria Filippelli, Jenni Fleetwood, Christine France, Silvano Franco, Sarah Gates, Shirley Gill, Brian Glover, Nicola Graimes, Rosamund Grant, Carole Handslip, Juliet Harbutt, Simona Hill, Shehzad Husain, Deh-Ta Hsiung, Christine Ingram, Becky Johnson, Bridget Jones, Peter Jordan, Manisha Kanani, Soheila Kimberley, Masaki Ko, Lucy Knox, Elisabeth Lambert Ortiz, Ruby Le Bois, Clare Lewis, Sara Lewis, Gilly Love, Lesley Mackley, Norma MacMillan, Sue Maggs, Kathy Man, Sally Mansfield, Elizabeth Martin, Norma Miller, Jane Milton, Sallie Morris, Annie Nichols, Suzannah Olivier, Maggie Pannell, Katherine Richmond, Keith Richmond, Rena Salaman, Anne Sheasby, Jennie Shapter, Ysanne Spevack, Marlena Spieler, Jenny Stacey, Liz Trigg, Linda Tubby, Sunil Vijayakar, Hilaire Walden, Stuart Walton, Laura Washburn, Steven Wheeler, Kate Whiteman, Jenny White, Biddy White-Lennon, Rosemary Wilkinson, Elizabeth Wolf-Cohen, Jeni Wright, Annette Yates

Photography: Karl Adamson, Edward Allwright, Peter Anderson, David Armstrong, Tim Auty, Caroline Barty, Steve Baxter, Martin Brigdale, Nicki Dowey, James Duncan, Gus Filgate, John Freeman, Ian Garlick, Michelle Garrett, Amanda Heywood, Peter Henley, John Heseltine, Ferguson Hill, Janine Hosegood, David Jordan, Maria Kelly, Dave King, Don Last, William Lingwood, Patrick McLeavey, Michael Michaels, Norma Miller, Craig Robertson, Steve Moss, Thomas Odulate, Sam Stowell, Simon Smith and Stuart Walton.

© Anness Publishing Ltd 2011

Publisher's Note

Ethical Trading Policy

At Anness Publishing we believe that business should be conducted in an ethical and ecologically sustainable way, with respect for the environment and a proper regard to the replacement of the natural resources we employ.
As a publisher, we use a lot of wood pulp in high-quality paper for printing, and that wood commonly comes from spruce trees. We are therefore currently growing more than 750,000 trees in three Scottish forest plantations: Berrymoss (130 hectares/320 acres), West Touxhill (125 hectares/305 acres) and Deveron Forest (75 hectares/185 acres). The forests we manage contain more than 3.5 times the number of trees employed each year in making paper for the books we manufacture.
Because of this ongoing ecological investment programme, you, as our customer, can have the pleasure and reassurance of knowing that a tree is being cultivated on your behalf to naturally replace the materials used to make the book you are holding.
Our forestry programme is run in accordance with the UK Woodland Assurance Scheme (UKWAS) and will be certified by the internationally recognized Forest Stewardship Council (FSC). The FSC is a non-government organization dedicated to promoting responsible management of the world's forests. Certification ensures forests are managed in an environmentally sustainable and socially responsible way. For further information about this scheme, go to www.annesspublishing.com/trees

Main front cover image shows Chicken & Lemon Grass Curry – for recipe, see page 124

Previously published as part of a larger volume, *500 20-Minute Recipes*

Notes

Bracketed terms are intended for American readers.

For all recipes, quantities are given in both metric and imperial measures and, where appropriate, in standard cups and spoons. Follow one set of measures, but not a mixture, because they are not interchangeable.

Standard spoon and cup measures are level. 1 tsp = 5ml, 1 tbsp = 15ml, 1 cup = 250ml/8fl oz.

Australian standard tablespoons are 20ml. Australian readers should use 3 tsp in place of 1 tbsp for measuring small quantities.

American pints are 16fl oz/2 cups. American readers should use 20fl oz/2.5 cups in place of 1 pint when measuring liquids.

Electric oven temperatures in this book are for conventional ovens. When using a fan oven, the temperature will probably need to be reduced by about 10–20°C/20–40°F. Since ovens vary, you should check with your manufacturer's instruction book for guidance.

The nutritional analysis given for each recipe is calculated per portion (i.e. serving or item), unless otherwise stated. If the recipe gives a range, such as Serves 4–6, then the nutritional analysis will be for the smaller portion size, i.e. 6 servings. The analysis does not include optional ingredients, such as salt added to taste.

Medium (US large) eggs are used unless otherwise stated.

Contents

Introduction 6

Breakfasts & Brunches 8

Soups & Appetizers 18

Snacks & Light Bites 40

Fish 50

Shellfish 76

Meat & Game 92

Poultry 118

Salads 132

Side Dishes, Dips & Sauces 138

Sweet Treats 150

Index 158

Introduction

Twenty minutes isn't very long. You can easily spend that amount of time puzzling over a difficult crossword clue, or trying to telephone a company determined to leave you on hold, or having a

cup of coffee in a busy restaurant. So can you cook a meal in twenty minutes? Yes you can, and this is the book to tell you how to do it.

Time: we never seem to have enough of it. Whether you are a student trying to balance study with a hectic social life, a single person trying to carve out a career, or a parent with a different but equally pressing set of priorities, time is a precious luxury. We're all riding the rollercoaster, rushing from home to work to home to sport to parents' evening to home to sleep. Putting good food on the table should be in there somewhere, but sometimes it is difficult to achieve. That's why this book takes a pragmatic approach. Preparing your own vegetables is ideal, but if buying a bag of shake-it-out salad or some ready-trimmed beans means you can eat well and still get to your night class, go for it. Look out for quick-cook versions of favourite ingredients such as polenta and rice, and don't be afraid of mixing bought items like pesto or tapenade with home-cooked pasta.

When you want great food fast, what you need in your repertoire are easy, no-fuss recipes: breakfasts you can blitz in a blender; lunches you can prepare and pack in next to no time; and

suppers that raise your spirits without sapping any of the energy you have left at the end of the day. If you are entertaining, you want to do so in style, but without missing more than a few moments of your guests' company.

You can achieve these aims – after a fashion – by frequenting the ready meal section of your favourite supermarket. Some days you'll do just that, but it is more rewarding and nutritious to serve something you've cooked yourself.

The aim of this book is to provide a wide-ranging selection of recipes that can be cooked in 20 minutes or less. That's assuming the cook is reasonably experienced. If you've never chopped

an onion in your life, it is likely to take you a little longer. Efficient cooking is all about organization, so do read through your chosen recipe carefully, assemble your ingredients and give some thought to strategy. Recipe methods reflect this, but you need to work within the bounds of your own ability and the confines of your own kitchen. If a recipe calls for a slotted spoon and you need to rummage under the sink for one, you could lose valuable time, so be as

well prepared as possible. If you are inexperienced, the best way to start is by choosing the shortest recipes of 10 minutes or less, or opt for something that needs no cooking at all, such as a salad. Also, enlist aid when you can. Something as simple as getting a partner to line up ingredients can be a huge help.

Some of the recipes in this book require some advance preparation – for example, marinating, soaking or chilling. The timeline at the top of the recipe will make it clear when this is required and there will probably be some mention of the fact in the recipe introduction, so do watch out for this. The recipes still won't take more than 20 minutes in all, but the preparation will be in

stages and not all at the same time. There are times when advance preparation can be a great advantage, such as when you want to get some food for a dinner party out of the way beforehand, for instance.

When you have extra time on your hands, consider making stock or a few sauces that can be frozen for later use. Then, when you are in a rush, you'll have the means to make a simple, speedy meal that tastes great.

Croque Monsieur

This classic French toastie is delicious served at any time of day, but with a double espresso or a foaming cup of milky coffee it makes a particularly enjoyable breakfast or brunch dish.

Serves 4
8 slices white bread
softened butter
4 large lean ham slices
175g/6oz Gruyère or
    mild Cheddar cheese
ground black pepper

Preparation: 5 minutes; Cooking: 5 minutes

1 Preheat the grill (broiler) to the highest setting. Arrange the bread on the grill rack and toast four slices on both sides and the other four slices on one side only.

2 Slice the cheese thinly. Butter the slices of bread that have been toasted on both sides and top with the ham, then the cheese. Season with plenty of ground black pepper. Transfer the topped bread slices to the grill pan.

3 Lay the remaining, half-toasted bread slices on top of the cheese, with the untoasted side uppermost. Grill (broil) the tops of the sandwiches until golden brown, then cut them in half using a sharp knife and serve.

Variations
Using Gruyère can make this rather an expensive dish, so look out for cheeses that are similarly tasty, but do not cost quite so much. Jarlsberg is a good alternative, or try Emmenthal.

Cook's Tip
To slice the cheese thinly, use a cheese parer, which looks like a spatula with a slot cut in the head. This stands slightly proud of the utensil, and has a cutting edge. If you draw it across the face of the cheese, it is possible to slice the cheese very thinly. For slightly thicker slices, press down harder.

Cheese Toasties

Also known as bubbly cheese toast, because of the way the egg and cheese mixture puffs up during baking, this is a nutritious and easy snack that everyone enjoys. It goes down well with children, especially if you swap the mustard for sweet pickle.

Serves 4
2 eggs
175–225g/6–8oz/1½–2 cups
    grated Cheddar cheese
5–10ml/1–2 tsp wholegrain
    mustard
4 slices bread, buttered
2–4 halved tomatoes (optional)
ground black pepper
watercress or fresh parsley,
    to serve (optional)

Preparation: 3–4 minutes; Cooking: 10–15 minutes

1 Preheat the oven to 230°C/450°F/Gas 8 (the top oven of a range-type stove is ideal for this recipe). Whisk the eggs lightly and stir in the grated cheese, mustard and pepper.

2 Lay the buttered bread face down in a shallow baking dish. Divide the cheese mixture among the slices of bread, spreading it out evenly.

3 Bake in the oven for 10–15 minutes, or until well risen and golden brown, adding the halved tomatoes for a few minutes, if using. Serve immediately, with the tomatoes, and garnish with sprigs of watercress or parsley.

Variation
Any cheese that can be grated can be used for these toasties, and this is a good way of using up leftovers from a cheeseboard.

Cook's Tips
• For the best flavour, use a mature (sharp) Cheddar cheese or a mixture of Cheddar and Leicester.
• To save time, buy packets of ready-grated cheese.

Croque Monsieur Energy 336kcal/1409kJ; Protein 20.3g; Carbohydrate 26.9g, of which sugars 1.7g; Fat 16.2g, of which saturates 9.8g; Cholesterol 57mg; Calcium 385mg; Fibre 0.8g; Sodium 897mg.
Cheese Toasties Energy 357kcal/1484kJ; Protein 16.6g; Carbohydrate 13.4g, of which sugars 0.8g; Fat 25.8g, of which saturates 15.5g; Cholesterol 159mg; Calcium 369mg; Fibre 0.4g; Sodium 552mg.

Kidney & Mushroom Toasts

Meltingly tender lamb's kidneys are a traditional breakfast treat. Cooking them with mushrooms in mustard butter flatters their flavour and they taste great on toast, making a delightful hot breakfast. Buy the kidneys from a reputable butcher and cook them as soon as possible after purchase. If they smell a bit strong, soak them in milk before cooking.

Serves 2–4
4 large flat field (portabello) mushrooms, stalks trimmed
75g/3oz/6 tbsp butter, softened
10ml/2 tsp wholegrain mustard
15ml/1 tbsp chopped fresh parsley
4 lamb's kidneys, skinned, halved and cored
4 thick slices of brown bread, cut into rounds and toasted
sprig of parsley, to garnish
tomato wedges, to serve

Preparation: 5 minutes; Cooking: 4–6 minutes

1 Wash the mushrooms, pat dry with kitchen paper and remove the stalks.

2 Mix the butter, wholegrain mustard and fresh parsley together in a small bowl.

3 Rinse the prepared lamb's kidneys well under cold running water and pat dry with kitchen paper.

4 Melt about two-thirds of the butter mixture in a large frying pan and fry the mushrooms and kidneys for 2–3 minutes on each side. Spoon the butter over occasionally.

5 When the kidneys are cooked to your liking, spread them with the remaining herb butter. Pile on the hot toast and serve with the tomato, garnished with parsley.

> **Cook's Tips**
> • *Kidneys are best served when they are still pink in the centre. If overcooked, they will become tough.*
> • *Serve the mixture on halved, warm scones, if you prefer.*

Bacon Sandwich

The secret of making the perfect bacon sandwich is to use quality bacon.

Makes 1
4 best bacon rashers (strips), dry-cured if possible
a large, soft morning roll or 2 thick slices fresh white, crusty bread
softened butter
sauce of your choice, such as tomato or brown sauce

Preparation: 2 minutes; Cooking: 6 minutes

1 Grill (broil) the bacon rashers to your liking, then put on a dinner plate, cover, and keep them warm. While the bacon is grilling, warm a bread roll, if using, underneath the grill pan.

2 Toast the bread after you have grilled the bacon. Butter both pieces of the bread or toast, or split and butter the roll. Top the bread or toast with the bacon, or fill the roll. Add the sauce and top with the remaining slice of bread or toast. Serve at once.

Panettone French Toast

Thickly sliced stale white bread is usually used for French toast, but the slightly dry texture of panettone makes a great alternative. Serve with fresh summer berries or an apricot or peach compote.

Serves 4
2 large (US extra large) eggs
50g/2oz/¼ cup butter or 30ml/2 tbsp sunflower oil
4 large slices panettone, halved
30ml/2 tbsp caster (superfine) sugar
fresh berries, to serve

Preparation: 2 minutes; Cooking: 4–6 minutes

1 Break the eggs into a bowl and whisk lightly, then tip them into a shallow dish. Heat the butter or oil in a large non-stick frying pan. Dip the panettone slices in the egg and fry for 2–3 minutes on each side, until golden brown. Drain, dust with sugar and serve with the berries.

Kidney Toasts Energy 379kcal/1580kJ; Protein 20.1g; Carbohydrate 14.9g, of which sugars 1g; Fat 27.1g, of which saturates 15.9g; Cholesterol 353mg; Calcium 59mg; Fibre 1.7g; Sodium 560mg.
Bacon Sandwich Energy 416kcal/1738kJ; Protein 21.1g; Carbohydrate 26.7g, of which sugars 1.5g; Fat 25.7g, of which saturates 11.4g; Cholesterol 74mg; Calcium 66mg; Fibre 0.8g; Sodium 1881mg.
Panettone Energy 369kcal/1550kJ; Protein 9.2g; Carbohydrate 47.4g, of which sugars 19.9g; Fat 17.3g, of which saturates 8.7g; Cholesterol 123mg; Calcium 103mg; Fibre 1.7g; Sodium 349mg.

Pancakes with Caramelized Pears

If you can find them, use Williams pears for this recipe because they are so juicy. For a really indulgent breakfast, top with a spoonful of crème fraîche or fromage frais. Or serve with yogurt – low fat or rich and creamy.

Serves 4
8 ready-made pancakes
50g/2oz/¼ cup butter
4 ripe pears, peeled, cored and
   thickly sliced
30ml/2 tbsp light muscovado
   (brown) sugar
crème fraîche or fromage frais,
   to serve

Preparation: 5 minutes; Cooking: 6 minutes

1 Preheat the oven to 150°C/300°F/Gas 2. Tightly wrap the pancakes in foil and place in the oven to warm through.

2 Meanwhile, heat the butter in a large frying pan and add the pears. Fry for 2–3 minutes, until the undersides are golden. Turn the pears over and sprinkle with sugar. Cook for a further 2–3 minutes, or until the sugar dissolves and the pan juices become sticky.

3 Remove the pancakes from the oven and take them out of the foil. Divide the pears among them, placing them in one quarter. Fold each pancake in half over the filling, then into quarters and place two folded pancakes on each plate. Drizzle the pan juices over and serve with crème fraîche or fromage frais.

Cook's Tip
Look out for ready-made pancakes in the chiller cabinet at the supermarket. They freeze well and are handy for breakfasts and desserts. Alternatively, make your own: sift 115g/4oz/1 cup plain (all-purpose) flour into a bowl and add a pinch of salt. Make a well in the centre and add 1 beaten egg and 120ml/4fl oz/½ cup each of milk and water. Beat the liquids and incorporate the flour to make a smooth batter. Cook in a greased 18cm/7in frying pan. Makes eight.

Light Pancakes

These pancakes are sweetened with sugar and should be kept small, otherwise they can be difficult to turn. They need a well-buttered or oiled surface for cooking. Aim for pancakes with one side that is smooth and golden brown, and the other full of holes and lightly browned. Eat them warm with butter, maybe with fresh soft fruit such as raspberries.

Makes 12–14
125g/4½ oz/1 cup plain
   (all-purpose) flour
1.25ml/¼ tsp bicarbonate of
   soda (baking soda)
pinch of salt
75g/3oz/⅔ cup caster
   (superfine) sugar
1 egg
about 90ml/6 tbsp buttermilk
   or milk
butter for greasing

Preparation: 3 minutes; Cooking: 12–15 minutes

1 Preheat a large bakestone or heavy frying pan over medium heat.

2 Sift the flour, bicarbonate of soda and salt into a bowl and stir in the sugar.

3 With a whisk beat the egg into the flour, and then add enough milk to make a batter.

4 Butter the hot bakestone or pan. Drop spoonfuls of batter on the surface to make pancakes about 7.5–10cm/3–4in in diameter, allowing space between.

5 Cook for a minute or two until the underside is golden brown and small bubbles have risen to the top surface and burst open. With a metal spatula, carefully flip the pancakes over and briefly cook the second side until light golden brown and set. Lift off and keep warm on a warm dish.

6 Repeat with the remaining pancake batter to make 12–14 pancakes. They are best served warm and certainly should be eaten on the day they are made.

Pear Pancakes Energy 544kcal/2274kJ; Protein 7.7g; Carbohydrate 64.9g, of which sugars 42.4g; Fat 29.9g, of which saturates 6.5g; Cholesterol 27mg; Calcium 155mg; Fibre 4.3g; Sodium 144mg.
Light Cakes Energy 60kcal/254kJ; Protein 1.5g; Carbohydrate 12.8g, of which sugars 6g; Fat 0.6g, of which saturates 0.2g; Cholesterol 14mg; Calcium 25mg; Fibre 0.3g; Sodium 8mg.

Buttermilk Pancakes

It is traditional to have these plump pancakes on their own, with honey, but they also taste good American-style, with crisp fried bacon and a generous drizzle of maple syrup. In Yorkshire, they might be enjoyed with raspberry vinegar, while South Africans would add a drizzle of golden (light corn) syrup. However you serve them, they are delicious.

Makes about 12

225g/8oz/2 cups plain (all-purpose) flour
7.5ml/1½ tsp bicarbonate of soda (baking soda)
25–50g/1–2oz/2–4 tbsp sugar
1 egg
about 300ml/½ pint/1¼ cups buttermilk
butter and oil, mixed, or white vegetable fat (shortening), for frying
honey, to serve

Preparation: 2 minutes; Cooking: 12–18 minutes

1 In a food processor or a large mixing bowl, mix together the plain flour, the bicarbonate of soda and enough sugar to taste.

2 Add the egg, blend or stir to mix, then gradually pour in just enough of the buttermilk to make a thick, smooth batter.

3 Heat a heavy pan and add the butter and oil, or fat. Place spoonfuls of the batter into the hot pan and cook for 2–3 minutes until bubbles rise to the surface.

4 Flip the pancakes over and cook for a further 2–3 minutes. You will need to cook the pancakes in batches, so keep them warm on a low oven temperature, tightly wrapped in foil. Serve warm with honey.

Variation
Buttermilk is not always easy to locate. As a substitute, use milk that has been soured by the addition of 5ml/1 tsp vinegar. Skimmed milk is better than whole or full cream milk, as it most closely resembles buttermilk. If you have time, leave the batter to stand for about an hour before using it.

Oatmeal Pancakes with Bacon

Wrap an oatmeal pancake around a crisp slice of best bacon and sample a new taste sensation with your traditional cooked breakfast. It makes a great egg dipper, too. If you don't like fried egg, serve these filled pancakes with sliced grilled (broiled) tomatoes or a home-made tomato sauce.

Makes 4 pancakes

50g/2oz/½ cup fine wholemeal (whole-wheat) flour
30ml/2 tbsp fine pinhead oatmeal
pinch of salt
1 egg
about 150ml/¼ pint/⅔ cup buttermilk or milk
butter or oil, for greasing
4 rashers (strips) bacon

Preparation: 2–3 minutes; Cooking: 12 minutes

1 Mix the flour, oatmeal and salt in a bowl, beat in the egg and add enough buttermilk or milk to make a creamy batter of the same consistency as that used for ordinary pancakes.

2 Thoroughly heat a griddle or cast-iron frying pan over a medium-hot heat. When very hot, grease the surface lightly with butter or oil.

3 Pour in the batter, about a ladleful at a time. Tilt the frying pan to spread the batter evenly and cook the pancake for about 2 minutes until set and the underside is browned. Turn over and cook for 1 minute until browned.

4 Keep the pancake warm while you cook the others and fry the bacon. Roll the pancakes around the bacon to serve.

Cook's Tip
The oatmeal in the batter gives it texture, so these pancakes are firmer than conventional crêpes. You can easily double or treble the mixture and even make it ahead of time. It will thicken on standing, though, so thin it with buttermilk or milk before use. Ladle the batter into the frying pan or – if you are good at judging the right amount to use – pour it in from a jug (pitcher).

Buttermilk Pancakes Energy 90kcal/380kJ; Protein 3.2g; Carbohydrate 18.7g, of which sugars 4.4g; Fat 0.8g, of which saturates 0.2g; Cholesterol 17mg; Calcium 61mg; Fibre 0.6g; Sodium 18mg.
Oatmeal Pancakes Energy 148kcal/621kJ; Protein 9.7g; Carbohydrate 13.1g, of which sugars 2g; Fat 6.7g, of which saturates 2.2g; Cholesterol 64mg; Calcium 62mg; Fibre 1.5g; Sodium 469mg.

American Pancakes with Bacon

These small, thick, buttery pancakes will be eaten in seconds, so make plenty. The batter can be made the night before.

Makes about 20
175g/6oz/1½ cups plain (all-purpose) flour, sifted
pinch of salt
15ml/1 tbsp caster (superfine) sugar
2 large eggs
150ml/¼ pint/⅔ cup milk
5ml/1 tsp bicarbonate of soda (baking soda)
10ml/2 tsp cream of tartar
oil, for cooking
butter
maple syrup
crisp bacon, to serve

Preparation: 3–4 minutes; Cooking: 12 minutes

1 To make the batter, mix together the flour, salt and sugar. In a separate bowl, beat the eggs and milk together, then gradually stir into the flour, beating to a smooth, thick consistency.

2 Add the bicarbonate of soda and cream of tartar, mix well, then cover and chill until ready to cook. When you are ready to cook the pancakes, beat the batter again. Heat a little oil in a heavy-based frying pan or griddle.

3 Drop dessertspoonfuls of the mixture into the pan, spaced well apart, and cook over a fairly high heat until the batter sets, bubbles appear on the surface of the pancakes and the undersides become golden brown.

4 Carefully turn the pancakes over with a fish slice or metal spatula and cook briefly until golden underneath, then transfer them to a heated serving dish.

5 Top each pancake with a little butter and drizzle with maple syrup. Serve with grilled bacon.

Cook's Tip
Make bitesize pancakes in advance and freeze for parties or children's teas.

Lox with Bagels & Cream Cheese

This sophisticated dish is perfect for a weekend breakfast or brunch with friends. Lox is the Jewish word for smoked salmon and this deli classic is so easy that anyone can make it at home.

Serves 2
2 bagels
115–175g/4–6oz/½–¾ cup full-fat cream cheese
150g/5oz sliced best smoked salmon
ground black pepper
lemon wedges, to serve

Preparation: 3 minutes; Cooking: 4–5 minutes

1 Preheat the oven to 200°C/400°F/Gas 6. Put the bagels on a large baking sheet and warm them in the oven for 4–5 minutes.

2 Remove the bagels from the oven, split them in two and spread each half generously with cream cheese. Pile the salmon on top of the bagel bases and grind over plenty of black pepper.

3 Squeeze over some lemon juice, then add the bagel tops, placing them at a jaunty angle.

4 Place on serving plates with the lemon wedges. If you have time, wrap each lemon wedge in a small square of muslin (cheesecloth), tie with fine string and put it on the plate.

Cook's Tip
It is essential to be generous with the smoked salmon and to use the best cream cheese you can find.

Eggs Benedict

Using a good-quality bought hollandaise for this recipe saves time and makes all the difference to the end result. Eggs Benedict are delicious served on toasted English muffins.

Serves 4
4 large (US extra large) eggs
4 lean ham slices
60ml/4 tbsp warm hollandaise sauce
2 English muffins, split
salt and ground black pepper

Preparation: 2–3 minutes; Cooking: 4–6 minutes

1 Pour cold water into a medium pan to a depth of about 5cm/2in and bring to a gentle simmer. Crack an egg into a saucer. Swirl the water in the pan with a spoon, then slide the egg carefully into the centre of the swirl.

2 Add the second egg to the pan. Simmer both eggs for 2–3 minutes, until the whites are set, but the yolks are still soft.

3 Meanwhile, toast the muffin halves. Place on four serving plates and arrange the ham slices on top. Remove the eggs from the pan using a slotted spoon and place on top of the ham on two of the plates. Poach two more eggs and top the remaining muffins.

Pancakes Energy 496kcal/2068kJ; Protein 25.9g; Carbohydrate 28.9g, of which sugars 3.3g; Fat 31.6g, of which saturates 17.7g; Cholesterol 81mg; Calcium 71mg; Fibre 1.2g; Sodium 1858mg.
Bagels Energy 276kcal/1154kJ; Protein 14.9g; Carbohydrate 15.9g, of which sugars 1.6g; Fat 17.7g, of which saturates 3.7g; Cholesterol 258mg; Calcium 81mg; Fibre 0.7g; Sodium 520mg.
Eggs Benedict Energy 553kcal/2304kJ; Protein 19.8g; Carbohydrate 31.6g, of which sugars 2.2g; Fat 39.7g, of which saturates 18.9g; Cholesterol 427mg; Calcium 148mg; Fibre 1.3g; Sodium 635mg.

Egg Crostini with Rouille

Crostini are extremely quick to make so are perfect for breakfast or brunch. The rouille gives them a hint of Mediterranean flavour. Traditionally, rouille is served with thick fish soup, but here it provides the perfect complement to lightly fried eggs.

Serves 4

4 slices of ciabatta bread
extra virgin olive oil
45ml/3 tbsp home-made
*   mayonnaise*
5ml/1 tsp harissa
4 eggs
4 small slices smoked ham
watercress, to serve

Preparation and cooking: 10 minutes

1 Preheat the oven to 200°C/400°F/Gas 6. Use a pastry brush to lightly brush each slice of ciabatta bread with a little olive oil.

2 Place the bread on a baking sheet and bake for 10 minutes or until crisp and turning golden brown.

3 Meanwhile, make the rouille. Mix together the mayonnaise and harissa. Then fry the eggs lightly in a very little oil in a non-stick pan.

4 Top the baked bread with the ham, eggs and a small spoonful of rouille. Serve immediately with watercress.

> **Cook's Tip**
> *Harissa is a fiery North African chilli paste made from dried red chillies, cumin, garlic, coriander, caraway and olive oil. It adds a sweet spicy taste to dips, sauces and stews, and makes a great addition to mayonnaise for serving with meat or fish dishes. It is usually sold in glass jars or tubes. In this recipe, home-made mayonnaise is specified, but if you do not have time to make your own, or are serving this to someone for whom a raw egg product is not recommended, it is perfectly acceptable to use a good quality bought mayonnaise for mixing with the harissa.*

Bacon & Egg Muffins Hollandaise

This tasty breakfast is ideal for days when you want to treat family or friends to an extra-special start to the day.

4 eggs
4 English muffins
butter, for spreading
ground black pepper

Serves 4

350g/12oz rindless back (lean)
*   bacon rashers (strips)*
dash of white wine vinegar

For the hollandaise sauce
2 egg yolks
5ml/1 tsp white wine vinegar
75g/3oz/6 tbsp butter

Preparation: 5 minutes; Cooking: 8–12 minutes

1 Preheat the grill (broiler) and cook the bacon for 5–8 minutes, turning once, or until crisp on both sides. Keep warm.

2 Fill a large frying pan with water and bring to the boil. Add the vinegar and regulate the heat so that the water simmers. Crack the eggs into the water and poach them for 3–4 minutes, or slightly longer for firm eggs.

3 Meanwhile, make the hollandaise sauce. Process the egg yolks and white wine vinegar in a blender or food processor. Melt the butter. With the motor still running, very gradually add the hot melted butter through the feeder tube. The hot butter will cook the yolks to make a thick, glossy sauce. Switch off the machine as soon as all the butter has been added and the sauce has thickened. Season to taste.

4 Split and toast the muffins. Spread with butter and place on warmed plates. Arrange the bacon on the muffins and add a poached egg to each. Top with a spoonful of sauce and grind over some black pepper. Serve immediately.

> **Variations**
> • *Replace the bacon with smoked salmon for a special treat.*
> • *Add some sliced grilled (broiled) mushrooms for a more filling breakfast or brunch.*

Egg Crostini Energy 259kcal/1083kJ; Protein 15.8g; Carbohydrate 13.6g, of which sugars 1.3g; Fat 16.3g, of which saturates 3.4g; Cholesterol 220mg; Calcium 62mg; Fibre 0.6g; Sodium 705mg.
Muffins Energy 612Kcal/2549kJ; Protein 32.6g; Carbohydrate 30.2g, of which sugars 2.4g; Fat 41.1g, of which saturates 18.3g; Cholesterol 429mg; Calcium 143mg; Fibre 1.3g; Sodium 1880mg.

Scrambled Eggs with Asparagus & Mangetout

Delightfully tender fresh asparagus and mangetout make perfect partners to lightly cooked eggs. The secret of successful scrambling is to keep the heat under the pan fairly low and serve the eggs while they are still creamy.

Serves 4
1 bunch thin asparagus
30–45ml/2–3 tbsp tiny raw mangetout (snow peas)
8 large (US extra large) eggs
30ml/2 tbsp milk
50g/2oz/¼ cup butter
salt and ground black pepper
sweet paprika, for dusting

Preparation: 3–4 minutes; Cooking: 13–15 minutes

1 Prepare the asparagus. Using a large sharp knife, cut off and discard any hard stems. Cut the stems into short lengths, keeping the tips separate. Shell some of the fatter mangetout pods, to extract the tiny peas.

2 Transfer the stems into a pan of boiling water and simmer for 4 minutes. Add the asparagus tips, and cook for 6 minutes more. If including some pea pod strips, cook them for 2 minutes.

3 Break the eggs into a bowl. Add the milk, salt and black pepper and beat with a whisk until well combined. Melt the butter in a large frying pan and pour in the eggs, scrambling them by pulling the cooked outsides to the middle with a wooden spoon.

4 When the eggs are almost cooked, drain the asparagus and pea pod strips, if using, and stir into the eggs. Sprinkle the peas over the top, and dust lightly with paprika. Serve immediately.

Variation
Replace the asparagus with thinly sliced smoked salmon for an indulgent weekend breakfast. Place the smoked salmon on the plate and top with the scrambled egg mixture.

Chive Scrambled Eggs in Brioches

These creamy scrambled eggs are delicious at any time of day, but when served with France's favourite breakfast bread, they become the ultimate breakfast or brunch treat. Set the brioches at an angle so some filling spills on to the plate.

Serves 4
4 individual brioches
6 eggs, beaten
45ml/3 tbsp chopped fresh chives, plus extra to serve
25g/1oz/2 tbsp butter
45ml/3 tbsp cottage cheese
60–75ml/4–5 tbsp double (heavy) cream
salt and ground black pepper

Preparation: 6 minutes; Cooking: 7 minutes

1 Preheat the oven to 180°C/350°F/Gas 4. Cut the tops off the brioches and set to one side. Carefully scoop out the centre of each brioche, leaving a bread case. Put the brioche cases and lids on a baking sheet and bake in the oven for 5 minutes until they are hot and crisp.

2 Meanwhile, beat the eggs lightly and season to taste. Add about one-third of the chopped chives. Heat the butter in a medium pan until it begins to foam, then add the eggs and cook, stirring constantly with a wooden spoon until semi-solid.

3 Stir in the cottage cheese, cream and half the remaining chives. Cook for 1–2 minutes more, making sure that the eggs remain soft and creamy.

4 To serve, put the crisp brioche shells on individual plates, spoon in the creamy scrambled egg and sprinkle with the remaining chives. Top with the lids.

Variation
If you do not happen to have brioches to hand, these wonderful herby eggs taste delicious on top of thick slices of toasted bread. Try them piled high on warm focaccia, or on toasted ciabatta, Granary (whole-wheat) bread or muffins.

Eggs with Asparagus Energy 252kcal/1045kJ; Protein 13.8g; Carbohydrate 1.3g, of which sugars 1.2g; Fat 21.7g, of which saturates 9.7g; Cholesterol 408mg; Calcium 78mg; Fibre 0.6g; Sodium 219mg.
Eggs in Brioches Energy 414kcal/1731kJ; Protein 16.2g; Carbohydrate 32.5g, of which sugars 10.5g; Fat 25.5g, of which saturates 12g; Cholesterol 322mg; Calcium 154mg; Fibre 1.9g; Sodium 374mg.

Scrambled Eggs with Smoked Salmon & Roe

For a luxury breakfast, or a special brunch, you can't beat this delicious combination. Serve it with Buck's Fizz: champagne mixed with equal parts of freshly squeezed orange juice.

Serves 4
4 slices of pumpernickel or
  wholemeal (whole-wheat)
bread, crusts trimmed
50g/2oz/¼ cup butter
115g/4oz thinly sliced
  smoked salmon
6 eggs
105ml/7 tbsp crème fraîche or
  sour cream
salt and ground black pepper
generous 60ml/4 tbsp salmon roe
  or lumpfish roe
sprigs of dill, to garnish

Preparation: 3 minutes; Cooking: 3–5 minutes

1 Spread the slices of pumpernickel or wholemeal bread with half of the butter and arrange the smoked salmon on top. Cut each slice in half, place two halves on each serving plate and set aside while you make the scrambled eggs.

2 Lightly beat the eggs in a bowl and season with salt and freshly ground pepper. Melt the remaining butter in a pan until sizzling, then quickly stir in the beaten eggs. Stir constantly until the eggs begin to thicken. Just before they have finished cooking, remove the pan from the heat and stir in the crème fraîche or sour cream. Return to the heat briefly to finish cooking, if required.

3 Spoon the scrambled eggs on to the smoked salmon. Top each serving with a spoonful of salmon roe or lumpfish roe and serve garnished with sprigs of dill.

Variation
If you are lucky enough to have a truffle, another treat is to grate a little into the scrambled eggs. Serve them on toast, topped with a little chopped fresh chervil.

Scrambled Eggs with Anchovies

Lifting the spirits on the dullest of days, scrambled eggs are true comfort food. This version combines with anchovies, whose salty tang is superb with the egg. The flavour of anchovies is echoed in the paste.

Serves 2
2 slices bread
40g/1½ oz/3 tbsp butter, plus
  extra for spreading
anchovy paste, such as
  Gentleman's Relish, for
  spreading
2 eggs and 2 egg yolks, beaten
60–90ml/4–6 tbsp single (light)
  cream or milk
ground black pepper
anchovy fillets, cut into strips,
  and paprika, to garnish

Preparation: 2–3 minutes; Cooking: 7 minutes

1 Toast the bread, spread with butter and anchovy paste, then remove the crusts and cut into triangles. Place on a plate and keep warm under a low grill (broiler).

2 Melt the rest of the butter in a medium non-stick pan, then stir in the beaten eggs, cream or milk, and a little ground pepper. Heat very gently, stirring constantly, until the mixture begins to thicken.

3 Remove the pan from the heat and continue to stir until the mixture becomes very creamy, but do not allow it to harden.

4 Divide the scrambled eggs among the triangles of toast and garnish each one with strips of anchovy fillet and a generous sprinkling of paprika. Serve immediately, while the scrambled eggs are still hot and have not had time to set firm.

Cook's Tip
These creamy scrambled eggs are delicious in baked potatoes instead of on toast. Serve with a salad and a glass of crisp white wine for a tasty brunch or light lunch.

Eggs with Salmon Energy 369kcal/1535kJ; Protein 18.7g; Carbohydrate 13.3g, of which sugars 1.5g; Fat 27.4g, of which saturates 15.2g; Cholesterol 259mg; Calcium 78mg; Fibre 1.5g; Sodium 837mg.
Eggs with Anchovies Energy 405kcal/1680kJ; Protein 12.6g; Carbohydrate 14.1g, of which sugars 1.5g; Fat 33.7g, of which saturates 17.2g; Cholesterol 451mg; Calcium 112mg; Fibre 0.4g; Sodium 350mg.

Scrambled Eggs with Prawns

The Spanish are particular about eggs, distinguishing between a revuelto, which uses softly set scrambled eggs, and the more solid tortilla that is cooked until set. This revuelto de gambas is an economical way of using a few shellfish and tastes delicious with crusty bread or toast.

Serves 4
1 bunch spring onions (scallions)
25g/1oz/2 tbsp butter
30ml/2 tbsp oil
150g/5oz shelled prawns (shrimp)
8 large (US extra large) eggs
30ml/2 tbsp milk
45ml/3 tbsp chopped
    fresh parsley
salt and ground black pepper
crusty bread, to serve

Preparation: 3 minutes; Cooking: 4–6 minutes

1 Chop the spring onions, keeping the white section separate from the green. Put the white pieces in a bowl and 30ml/ 2 tbsp of the chopped green pieces in another bowl.

2 Heat the butter and oil in a large frying pan. Add the spring onion white and cook briefly. Add the prawns and heat through. (If the prawns are raw, cook them for 2 minutes or until they turn pink. Do not overcook them or they will toughen.)

3 In a bowl, beat the eggs with the milk and then season with plenty of salt and pepper. Turn the heat to medium-high and pour the egg mixture over the prawns. Cook for about 2 minutes, stirring with a wooden spoon.

4 Sprinkle the creamy scrambled eggs and prawn mixture with parsley and spring onion greens. Divide among four plates and serve immediately with crusty bread.

Variation
The green shoots from garlic bulbs are another very popular spring ingredient for this type of dish and can be used in place of the spring onions (scallions). Called ajetes in Spain, they lend a delicate flavour to scrambled eggs or tortillas.

Smoked Salmon & Chive Omelette

The addition of a generous portion of chopped smoked salmon gives a really luxurious finish to this simple, classic dish, which is an ideal quick lunch for two people. The chives add colour and extra flavour.

Serves 2
4 eggs
15ml/1 tbsp chopped fresh chives
    or spring onions (scallions)
a knob (pat) of butter
50g/2oz smoked salmon,
    roughly chopped
salt and ground black pepper

Preparation: 2–3 minutes; Cooking: 5–6 minutes

1 Break the eggs into a bowl. Beat with a fork until just combined, then stir in the chopped fresh chives or spring onions. Season with salt and a generous sprinkling of freshly ground black pepper, and set aside.

2 Heat the butter in a medium frying pan until foamy. Pour in the eggs and cook over a medium heat for 3–4 minutes, drawing the cooked egg from around the edge into the centre of the pan from time to time.

3 At this stage, you can either leave the top of the omelette slightly soft or finish it off under the grill (broiler), depending on how you like your omelette. Top with the smoked salmon, fold the omelette over and cut in half to serve.

Variations
• *Use smoked trout instead of smoked salmon. The colour ranges from rose pink to reddish brown and it has very good flavour, especially when it has been hot smoked over oak or birch chippings.*
• *Add a little rocket (arugula) or watercress when folding the omelette. Both have peppery leaves, so use slightly less pepper to season the scrambled egg.*
• *A little crème fraîche or fromage frais, served on the side, makes a good addition. For an extra special occasion, top this with salmon or trout roe.*

Eggs with Prawns Energy 287kcal/1191kJ; Protein 20.1g; Carbohydrate 1.9g, of which sugars 1.9g; Fat 22.4g, of which saturates 7.4g; Cholesterol 468mg; Calcium 126mg; Fibre 0.9g; Sodium 258mg.
Omelette Energy 221kcal/920kJ; Protein 19g; Carbohydrate 0.2g, of which sugars 0.2g; Fat 16.4g, of which saturates 5.9g; Cholesterol 400mg; Calcium 65mg; Fibre 0.1g; Sodium 641mg.

Sweet Breakfast Omelette

For a hearty start to a day when you know you're going to be too rushed to have much more than an apple for lunch, try this sweet omelette with a spoonful of jam or a good fruit compote.

Serves 1
3 eggs
10ml/2 tsp caster (superfine) sugar
5ml/1 tsp plain (all-purpose) flour
10g/¼ oz/½ tbsp unsalted (sweet) butter
bread and jam, to serve

Preparation: 3 minutes; Cooking: 5 minutes

1 Break the eggs into a large bowl, add the sugar and flour and beat until really frothy.

2 Heat the butter in an omelette pan until it begins to bubble, then pour in the egg mixture and cook, without stirring, until it begins to set on top and is golden brown underneath.

3 Run a wooden spatula around the edge of the omelette, then carefully turn it over and cook the second side for 1–2 minutes until golden. Serve hot or warm with thick slices of fresh bread and a bowlful of fruity jam.

Cook's Tips
• Although this recipe is stated to serve one, it is substantial enough for two not-very-hungry people. Omelettes are best eaten the moment they emerge from the pan, so if you are cooking for a crowd, get each guest to make his or her own and eat breakfast in relays.
• This tastes good with a plum or nectarine compote. Buy fruit that is ripe, but still slightly on the firm side. Cut the fruit in half and either remove the stones (pits) or cut around the stones to remove the flesh in neat slices. Mix 60ml/4 tbsp sugar with 120ml/4fl oz/½ cup water in a shallow pan. Bring to the boil, stirring until the sugar dissolves to form a syrup. Add the fruit, with a cinnamon stick and some cloves if you like, and simmer until it is tender. Serve warm or cold.

Omelette Arnold Bennett

This smoked haddock soufflé omelette is delicious.

Serves 2
175g/6oz smoked haddock fillet (preferably undyed if available)
50g/2oz/4 tbsp butter, diced
175ml/6fl oz/¾ cup whipping or double (heavy) cream
4 eggs, separated
40g/1½ oz/⅓ cup mature (sharp) Cheddar cheese, grated
ground black pepper
watercress, to garnish

Preparation: 2 minutes; Cooking: 12 minutes

1 Put the haddock in a shallow pan with water to cover and poach over a medium heat for 8–10 minutes. Drain well. Remove the skin and any bones and flake the flesh.

2 Melt half the butter with 60ml/4 tbsp of the cream in a pan, add the flaked fish and stir together. Preheat the grill (broiler).

3 Mix the egg yolks with 15ml/1 tbsp of the cream. Season with pepper, then stir into the fish. Mix the cheese and the remaining cream. Whisk the egg whites until stiff, then fold into the mixture. Heat the remaining butter in an omelette pan, add the fish mixture and cook until browned. Pour the cheese mixture over and grill (broil) until bubbling. Garnish and serve.

Jugged Kippers

The demand for naturally smoked kippers is ever increasing. They are most popular for breakfast, with butter and lemon.

Serves 4
4 kippers (smoked herrings)
25g/1oz/2 tbsp butter
ground black pepper
lemon wedges, to serve

Preparation: 2–3 minutes; Cooking: 5–6 minutes

1 If the heads are still on the kippers, remove them. Put into a jug, tails up. Cover with boiling water. Leave for 5 minutes, until tender. Drain well and serve with butter and the lemon wedges.

Omelette Energy 351kcal/1465kJ; Protein 19.3g; Carbohydrate 14.4g, of which sugars 10.6g; Fat 24.9g, of which saturates 9.9g; Cholesterol 592mg; Calcium 100mg; Fibre 0.2g; Sodium 271mg.
Arnold Bennett Energy 821kcal/3396kJ; Protein 36.1g; Carbohydrate 2.6g, of which sugars 2.6g; Fat 74g, of which saturates 42.6g; Cholesterol 577mg; Calcium 280mg; Fibre 0g; Sodium 1123mg.
Jugged Kippers Energy 248kcal/1025kJ; Protein 15.9g; Carbohydrate 0g, of which sugars 0g; Fat 20.4g, of which saturates 5.8g; Cholesterol 68mg; Calcium 49mg; Fibre 0g; Sodium 776mg.

Avgolemono

The name of this popular Greek soup means 'egg and lemon', the two key ingredients. It is a light soup made with orzo, a Greek rice-shaped pasta, but you can use any very small pasta shape in its place.

Serves 4–6

1.75 litres/3 pints/7½ cups chicken stock
115g/4oz/½ cup orzo pasta
3 eggs
juice of 1 large lemon
salt and ground black pepper
lemon slices, to garnish

Preparation: 2–3 minutes; Cooking: 7 minutes

1 Pour the stock into a large pan and bring to the boil. Add the pasta and cook for 5 minutes.

2 Beat the eggs until frothy, then add the lemon juice and 15ml/1 tbsp cold water.

3 Stir in a ladleful of the hot chicken stock, then add 1–2 more. Return this mixture to the pan, off the heat, and stir well. Season with salt and pepper, ladle into warmed bowls and serve at once, garnished with lemon slices.

Cook's Tips

• To make your own chicken stock, place a chicken carcass in a large pan with 1 onion, 1 carrot, 1 celery stick, 1 garlic clove and a bouquet garni, cover with water and bring to the boil. Simmer for 2 hours, skimming occasionally. Strain the stock and use as required. If you do not need the stock immediately, cool it quickly by pouring it into a large jug (pitcher) and standing this in a sink of iced water. As soon as it is cold, put the jug in the refrigerator (or, briefly, in the freezer), until the fat solidifies on the surface and can be lifted off. Defatted stock freezes well and can be thawed at room temperature or in the microwave for use in soups and stews and for making risotto.
• Do not allow the soup to boil once the eggs have been added or they will curdle.

Avocado Soup

This delicious soup has a fresh, delicate flavour and a wonderful colour. For added zest, add a squeeze of lime or lemon juice just before serving. Serve the soup in white bowls if possible, to show off the pretty green hue to best advantage.

Serves 4

2 large ripe avocados
300ml/½ pint/1¼ cups sour cream
1 litre/1¾ pints/4 cups well-flavoured chicken stock
a small bunch of fresh coriander (cilantro) or flat leaf parsley, chopped
salt and ground black pepper

Preparation: 3 minutes; Cooking: 3–4 minutes

1 Cut the avocados in half, remove the peel and lift out the stones (pits). Chop the flesh coarsely and place it in a food processor with 45–60ml/3–4 tbsp of the sour cream. Process until smooth.

2 Heat the chicken stock in a pan. When it is hot, but still below simmering point, add the rest of the sour cream and stir gently to mix.

3 Gradually stir the avocado mixture into the hot stock. Heat gently but do not let the mixture approach boiling point. Add salt to taste.

4 Ladle the soup into heated bowls and sprinkle each portion with chopped coriander or flat leaf parsley and black pepper. Serve immediately, as it will discolour on standing.

Cook's Tip

Choose ripe avocados for this soup – they should feel soft when gently pressed. Keep very firm avocados at room temperature for 3–4 days until they soften. To speed ripening, place the avocados in a brown paper bag with a ripe banana or an apple. Look out for 'ready to eat' avocados at the supermarket – expensive but handy for dishes like these.

Avgolemono Energy 104kcal/440kJ; Protein 5.6g; Carbohydrate 14.3g, of which sugars 0.7g; Fat 3.3g, of which saturates 0.8g; Cholesterol 95mg; Calcium 20mg; Fibre 0.6g; Sodium 171mg.
Avocado Soup Energy 343kcal/1416kJ; Protein 4.4g; Carbohydrate 5.1g, of which sugars 3.6g; Fat 33.9g, of which saturates 13.4g; Cholesterol 45mg; Calcium 106mg; Fibre 4g; Sodium 41mg.

Butter Bean & Tomato Soup

This soup is quick and easy to make. The key is to use a good-quality home-made or bought fresh stock with plenty of pesto and sun-dried tomato purée. Only partly blending the soup gives it great texture.

Serves 4

2 x 400g/14oz cans butter (lima) beans, drained and rinsed
900ml/1½ pints/3¾ cups chicken or vegetable stock
60ml/4 tbsp sun-dried tomato purée (paste)
75ml/5 tbsp pesto

Preparation: 2 minutes; Cooking: 12 minutes

1 Put the butter beans in a pan. Pour in the chicken or vegetable stock and bring to the boil over a medium heat, stirring once or twice.

2 Stir in the tomato purée and pesto. Lower the heat and cook gently for 5 minutes.

3 Transfer six ladlefuls of the soup to a blender or food processor, scooping up plenty of the beans. Process until smooth, then return the purée to the pan.

4 Heat gently, stirring frequently, for 5 minutes. Season to taste.

5 Ladle into four warmed soup bowls and serve with warm crusty bread or breadsticks.

> **Cook's Tips**
> • For the busy cook, good-quality bought stocks are a blessing. Most large supermarkets now sell fresh stock in tubs or packets. Another good product is concentrated liquid stock, sold in bottles. Varieties include beef, chicken and vegetable. However, if you cannot find any of the above, a good-quality stock cube will do the job.
> • Swirl a little extra pesto on top of each portion of soup for an attractive finish, or garnish with one or two small fresh basil leaves to echo the pesto flavour.

Pea Soup with Garlic

This delicious green pea and garlic soup has a wonderfully sweet taste and smooth texture, and is great served with crusty bread and garnished with fresh garden mint.

Serves 4

25g/1oz/2 tbsp butter
1 garlic clove, crushed
900g/2lb/8 cups frozen peas
1.2 litres/2 pints/5 cups chicken stock
salt and ground black pepper

Preparation: 3–4 minutes; Cooking: 8–10 minutes

1 Heat the butter in a large pan and add the garlic. Fry gently for 2–3 minutes, until softened, then add the peas. Cook for 1–2 minutes more, then pour in the stock.

2 Bring the soup to the boil, then reduce the heat to a simmer. Cover and cook for 5–6 minutes, until the peas are tender.

3 Leave to cool slightly, then transfer the mixture to a food processor and process until smooth (you may have to do this in two batches).

4 Return the soup to the pan and heat through gently. Season with salt and pepper to taste.

> **Variation**
> To make Pea and Leek Soup with Garlic, slice a leek in half, then slice it thinly. Add to the pan with the garlic. Cook over low heat for about 5 minutes until softened, then add the peas and proceed as in the recipe.

> **Cook's Tip**
> If you keep a bag of frozen peas in the freezer, you can rustle up this soup at very short notice. When processing the peas cooked in the soup, keep a few back and float them on each portion as an additional garnish.

Butter Bean Energy 269kcal/1130kJ; Protein 15.6g; Carbohydrate 28.3g, of which sugars 4.5g; Fat 11.2g, of which saturates 2.5g; Cholesterol 6mg; Calcium 111mg; Fibre 9.7g; Sodium 944mg.
Pea Soup Energy 233Kcal/965kJ; Protein 15.6g; Carbohydrate 25.5g, of which sugars 5.2g; Fat 8.5g, of which saturates 3.9g; Cholesterol 13mg; Calcium 49mg; Fibre 10.6g; Sodium 40mg.

Egg & Cheese Soup

In this classic Roman soup, eggs and cheese are beaten into hot soup, producing the slightly scrambled texture that is characteristic of this dish. The texture isn't to everyone's taste, but aficionados rave about it. The trick is to remove the soup from the heat when the eggs have thickened but not curdled it.

Serves 6

3 eggs
45ml/3 tbsp fine semolina
90ml/6 tbsp freshly grated
    Parmesan cheese
pinch of nutmeg
1.5 litres/2½ pints/6¼ cups cold
    meat or chicken stock
salt and ground black pepper
12 rounds of country bread or
    ciabatta, to serve

Preparation: 2–3 minutes; Cooking: 6–7 minutes

1 Beat the eggs in a bowl, then beat in the semolina and the cheese. Add the nutmeg and beat in 250ml/8fl oz/1 cup of the meat or chicken stock. Pour the mixture into a measuring jug (pitcher). Pour the remaining stock into a large pan, heat the stock and bring to a gentle simmer.

2 A few minutes before you are ready to serve the soup, whisk the egg mixture into the hot stock. Raise the heat slightly, and bring it barely to the boil. Season and cook for 3–4 minutes.

3 To serve, toast the rounds of country bread or ciabatta, place two in each soup plate and ladle on the hot soup. Serve at once.

> **Variation**
> If Parmesan is a bit expensive, use Pecorino Romano. It has a slightly milder flavour, which works very well in this soup.

> **Cook's Tip**
> Once added to the hot soup, the egg will begin to cook and the soup will become less smooth. Try not to overcook the soup at this stage because it may cause the egg to curdle.

Chinese Crab & Corn Soup

There's no denying the delightful combination of shellfish and corn in this Chinese favourite, but dressing the crab does increase the preparation time somewhat. Using frozen white crab meat will work just as well.

Serves 4

600ml/1 pint/2½ cups fish or
    chicken stock
2.5cm/1in piece fresh root ginger,
    peeled and very finely sliced
400g/14oz can creamed corn
150g/5oz cooked fresh white crab
    meat or frozen crab, thawed
    and drained
15ml/1 tbsp arrowroot or
    cornflour (cornstarch)
15ml/1 tbsp rice wine or
    dry sherry
15–30ml/1–2 tbsp light soy sauce
1 egg white
salt and ground white pepper
shredded spring onions (scallions)
    or finely chopped fresh chives,
    to garnish

Preparation: 6 minutes; Cooking: 10 minutes

1 Put the stock and ginger in a large pan and bring to the boil. Stir in the creamed corn and bring back to the boil.

2 Switch off the heat and add the crab meat. Put the arrowroot or cornflour in a cup and stir in the rice wine or sherry to make a smooth paste.

3 Stir the paste into the soup. Cook over a low heat for about 4 minutes until the soup has thickened and is slightly glutinous in consistency. Add soy sauce, salt and white pepper to taste.

4 In a bowl, whisk the egg white to a stiff foam. Gradually fold it into the soup. Ladle the soup into heated bowls, garnish each portion with spring onions and serve.

> **Cook's Tip**
> This soup is sometimes made with whole kernel corn, but creamed corn gives a better texture. If you can't find it in a can, use thawed frozen creamed corn.

Egg and Cheese Energy 245kcal/1030kJ; Protein 14.1g; Carbohydrate 27.5g, of which sugars 1.3g; Fat 9.4g, of which saturates 4.1g; Cholesterol 110mg; Calcium 246mg; Fibre 1.1g; Sodium 424mg.
Crab Soup Energy 194kcal/821kJ; Protein 10.5g; Carbohydrate 30.1g, of which sugars 9.7g; Fat 3.9g, of which saturates 0.6g; Cholesterol 27mg; Calcium 50mg; Fibre 1.4g; Sodium 494mg.

Malaysian Laksa

This spicy prawn and noodle soup tastes just as good when made with fresh crab meat or any flaked cooked fish. If you are short of time, buy ready-made laksa paste, which is available from most Asian stores.

Serves 2–3
15ml/1 tbsp vegetable or
  groundnut (peanut) oil
115g/4oz rice vermicelli or stir-fry
  rice noodles
600ml/1 pint/2½ cups fish stock
400ml/14fl oz/1⅔ cups thin
  coconut milk
30ml/2 tbsp Thai fish sauce
¼ lime

16–24 cooked peeled
  prawns (shrimp)
salt and cayenne pepper
60ml/4 tbsp fresh coriander
  (cilantro) sprigs and leaves,
  chopped, to garnish

For the spicy laksa paste
2 lemon grass stalks,
  finely chopped
2 fresh red chillies, seeded
  and chopped
2.5cm/1in piece fresh root ginger,
  peeled and sliced
2.5ml/½ tsp shrimp paste
2 garlic cloves, chopped
2.5ml/½ tsp ground turmeric
30ml/2 tbsp tamarind paste

Preparation: 8 minutes; Cooking: 9–10 minutes

1 To make the spicy paste, place all the ingredients in a mortar and pound with a pestle. Alternatively, use a food processor.

2 Heat the vegetable or groundnut oil in a large pan, add the spicy paste and cook, stirring occasionally, for a few moments.

3 Meanwhile, cook the rice vermicelli or noodles in a large pan of boiling salted water according to the instructions on the packet. Tip into a large colander, rinse, drain and keep warm.

4 Add the fish stock and coconut milk to the spicy paste and bring to the boil. Stir in the Thai fish sauce, then simmer for 5 minutes. Season with salt and cayenne to taste, adding a squeeze of lime. Add the prawns and heat through briefly.

5 Divide the noodles among two or three soup plates. Pour over the soup, garnish and serve piping hot.

Cucumber & Salmon Soup with Salsa

Charred salmon brings a hint of heat to the refreshing flavours of this chilled soup. Good-looking and beautifully light, it makes the perfect opener for an al fresco meal.

Serves 4
3 medium cucumbers
300ml/½ pint/1¼ cups Greek
  (US strained plain) yogurt
250ml/8fl oz/1 cup vegetable
  stock, chilled

120ml/4fl oz/½ cup crème
  fraîche
15ml/1 tbsp chopped
  fresh chervil
15ml/1 tbsp chopped fresh chives
15ml/1 tbsp chopped fresh
  flat leaf parsley
1 small fresh red chilli, seeded
  and very finely chopped
a little oil, for brushing
225g/8oz salmon fillet, skinned
  and cut into eight thin slices
salt and ground black pepper
fresh chervil or chives, to garnish

Preparation: 8–10 minutes; Cooking: 2–4 minutes

1 Peel two of the cucumbers and halve them lengthways. Scoop out and discard the seeds, then roughly chop the flesh. Purée the chopped flesh in a food processor or blender.

2 Add the yogurt, chilled vegetable stock, crème fraîche, chervil, chives and seasoning to the food processor or blender, and process until smooth. Pour the mixture into a bowl, cover and chill.

3 Peel, halve and seed the remaining cucumber. Cut the flesh into small neat dice. Mix with the chopped parsley and chilli in a bowl. Cover the salsa and chill until required.

4 Brush a griddle or frying pan with oil and heat until very hot. Add the salmon slices and sear them for 1–2 minutes, then turn over carefully and sear the other side until tender and charred.

5 Ladle the chilled soup into four soup bowls. Top each portion with two slices of salmon, then pile a portion of salsa in the centre. Garnish with the chervil or chives, and serve.

Malaysian Laksa Energy 436kcal/1830kJ; Protein 36.9g; Carbohydrate 55.2g, of which sugars 10.1g; Fat 7.6g, of which saturates 1.2g; Cholesterol 341mg; Calcium 239mg; Fibre 0.8g; Sodium 562mg.
Cucumber and Salmon Energy 314Kcal/1299kJ; Protein 17.8g; Carbohydrate 3.9g, of which sugars 3.7g; Fat 26.1g, of which saturates 13.1g; Cholesterol 62mg; Calcium 183mg; Fibre 1.2g; Sodium 92mg.

Snapper, Tamarind & Noodle Soup

Red snapper is a popular fish throughout South-east Asia, and tamarind gives this light, fragrant noodle soup a slightly sour taste.

Serves 4
2 litres/3½ pints/8 cups water
1kg/2¼lb red snapper or other red fish such as mullet
1 onion, sliced
50g/2oz tamarind pods
15ml/1 tbsp Thai fish sauce
15ml/1 tbsp sugar
30ml/2 tbsp vegetable oil
2 garlic cloves, finely chopped
2 lemon grass stalks, very finely chopped
4 ripe tomatoes, roughly chopped
30ml/2 tbsp yellow bean paste
225g/8oz rice vermicelli, soaked in warm water until soft
115g/4oz/1⅓ cups beansprouts
8–10 fresh basil or mint sprigs
25g/1oz roasted peanuts, ground
salt and ground black pepper

Preparation: 4–5 minutes; Cooking: 15 minutes

1 Bring the water to the boil in a pan. Lower the heat and add the fish and onion, with 2.5ml/½ tsp salt. Simmer gently until the fish is cooked through.

2 Remove the fish from the stock and set aside. Add the tamarind, fish sauce and sugar to the stock. Cook for 5 minutes, then strain the stock into a large jug (pitcher) or bowl. Carefully remove all of the bones from the fish, keeping the flesh in large pieces rather than small chunks. Keep hot.

3 Heat the oil in a large frying pan. Add the garlic and lemon grass and fry for a few seconds. Stir in the tomatoes and bean paste. Cook gently for 5–7 minutes, until the tomatoes are soft. Add the reserved flavoured fish stock, bring back to a simmer and adjust the seasoning.

4 Drain the vermicelli. Plunge it into a pan of boiling water for a few minutes, drain and divide among individual serving bowls. Add the beansprouts, fish, basil or mint, and sprinkle the ground peanuts on top. Top up each bowl by pouring in the hot soup. If there is any soup left over, pour it into a jug and place it on the table so guests can top up their bowls as needed.

Pork & Sichuan Pickle Noodle Soup

Noodle soup can taste a bit bland, but not when Sichuan hot pickle is one of the ingredients. This tasty soup makes a great winter warmer.

Serves 4
1 litre/1¾ pints/4 cups chicken stock
350g/12oz egg noodles
15ml/1 tbsp dried shrimp, soaked in water
30ml/2 tbsp vegetable oil
225g/8oz lean pork, such as fillet (tenderloin), finely shredded
15ml/1 tbsp yellow bean paste
15ml/1 tbsp soy sauce
115g/4oz Sichuan hot pickle, rinsed, drained and shredded
pinch of sugar
salt and ground black pepper
2 spring onions (scallions), finely sliced, to garnish

Preparation: 5 minutes; Cooking: 12 minutes

1 Bring the stock to the boil in a large pan. Add the noodles and cook until almost tender. Drain the dried shrimp, rinse them under cold water, drain again and add to the stock. Lower the heat and simmer for a further 2 minutes. Keep hot.

2 Heat the oil in a frying pan or wok. Add the pork and stir-fry over a high heat for about 3 minutes.

3 Add the bean paste and soy sauce to the pork and stir-fry the mixture for 1 minute more. Add the hot pickle with a pinch of sugar. Stir-fry for 1 minute more.

4 Divide the noodles and soup among individual serving bowls. Spoon the pork mixture on top, then sprinkle with the spring onions and serve immediately.

> **Cook's Tip**
> Sichuan hot pickle, also known as Szechuan (or Sichuan) preserved vegetables, is a pickle made from the stems of mustard cabbage, which are dried in the sun and then pickled in brine with chillies and spices.

Snapper, Tamarind Energy 495kcal/2079kJ; Protein 43.1g; Carbohydrate 55.5g, of which sugars 9.1g; Fat 11.4g, of which saturates 1.9g; Cholesterol 65mg; Calcium 108mg; Fibre 2.4g; Sodium 165mg.
Pork and Sichuan Energy 218kcal/911kJ; Protein 24.5g; Carbohydrate 7.8g, of which sugars 0.9g; Fat 9.7g, of which saturates 3g; Cholesterol 74mg; Calcium 90mg; Fibre 0.8g; Sodium 454mg.

Chiang Mai Noodle Soup

A signature dish of the Thai city of Chiang Mai, this delicious noodle soup has Burmese origins and is the Thai equivalent of the Malaysian laksa.

Serves 4–6
600ml/1 pint/2½ cups coconut milk
30ml/2 tbsp red curry paste
5ml/1 tsp ground turmeric
450g/1lb boneless chicken thighs, cut into bitesize chunks
600ml/1 pint/2½ cups chicken stock

60ml/4 tbsp Thai fish sauce
15ml/1 tbsp dark soy sauce
juice of ½–1 lime
450g/1lb fresh egg noodles
salt and ground black pepper

For the garnish
3 spring onions (scallions), chopped
4 red chillies, chopped
4 shallots, chopped
60ml/4 tbsp sliced pickled mustard leaves, rinsed
30ml/2 tbsp fried sliced garlic
coriander (cilantro) leaves
4–6 fried noodle nests (optional)

Preparation: 5–6 minutes; Cooking: 13 minutes

1 Pour about one-third of the coconut milk into a large pan and bring to the boil over medium heat, stirring frequently with a wooden spoon until it separates.

2 Add the curry paste and ground turmeric, stir to mix completely and cook until fragrant.

3 Add the chicken and stir-fry for about 2 minutes, ensuring that all the chunks are coated with the paste.

4 Add the remaining coconut milk, chicken stock, fish sauce and soy sauce. Season with salt and pepper to taste. Simmer gently for 7–10 minutes. Remove from the heat and stir in the lime juice, a little at a time.

5 Cook the noodles in a large pan of boiling water until just tender, following the directions on the packet. Drain and divide among individual bowls. Divide the chicken among the bowls and ladle in the hot soup. Serve with the garnishes in separate bowls so guests can add the toppings of their choice.

Chicken & Soba Noodle Soup

Soba noodles are widely enjoyed in Japan. They are usually served in hot seasoned broth with a mixture of chicken, fish, seafood or vegetables.

Serves 4
225g/8oz skinless, boneless chicken breast portions

120ml/4fl oz/½ cup soy sauce
15ml/1 tbsp sake
1 litre/1¾ pints/4 cups chicken stock
2 young leeks, cut into 2.5cm/1in pieces
175g/6oz spinach leaves
300g/11oz soba noodles
sesame seeds, toasted, to garnish

Preparation: 5 minutes; Cooking: 13 minutes

1 Slice the chicken diagonally into bitesize pieces. Combine the soy sauce and sake in a pan. Bring to a simmer. Add the chicken and cook gently for about 3 minutes until it is tender. Keep hot.

2 Bring the stock to the boil in a pan. Add the leek and simmer for 3 minutes, then add the spinach. Keep the mixture warm.

3 Cook the noodles in a large pan of boiling water until just tender, following the directions on the packet. Drain the noodles and divide among individual serving bowls. Ladle the hot soup into the bowls, then add a portion of chicken to each. Serve immediately, sprinkled with sesame seeds.

> **Cook's Tip**
> Home-made chicken stock makes the world of difference to noodle soup. Put about 1.3–1.6kg/3–3½lb meaty chicken bones into a large pan, add 3 litres/5 pints/12 cups water and gradually bring to the boil, skimming off any foam that rises to the top. Add 2 slices fresh root ginger, 2 garlic cloves, 2 celery sticks, 4 spring onions (scallions), a handful of coriander (cilantro) stalks and about 10 peppercorns, crushed. Reduce the heat and simmer the stock for 2–2½ hours. Remove from the heat and leave to cool, uncovered and undisturbed. Strain the stock and remove any fat that congeals on top.

Chiang Mai Energy 453kcal/1915kJ; Protein 28.8g; Carbohydrate 59.1g, of which sugars 6.7g; Fat 12.9g, of which saturates 3.7g; Cholesterol 120mg; Calcium 63mg; Fibre 2.3g; Sodium 513mg.
Chicken and Soba Energy 373kcal/1563kJ; Protein 20.1g; Carbohydrate 65.7g, of which sugars 4g; Fat 1.3g, of which saturates 0.3g; Cholesterol 39mg; Calcium 103mg; Fibre 2g; Sodium 2241mg.

Sweet & Sour Cucumber with Dill

This dish is half pickle, half salad, and totally delicious served as a brunch or appetizer. Serve with thin slices of pumpernickel or other coarse, dark, full-flavoured bread. Some people find cucumber skin indigestible, so peel them if you prefer. The dill will provide plenty of colour.

Serves 4
1 large or 2 small cucumbers, thinly sliced
3 onions, thinly sliced
45ml/3 tbsp sugar
75–90ml/5–6 tbsp white wine vinegar or cider vinegar
30–45ml/2–3 tbsp water
30–45ml/2–3 tbsp chopped fresh dill
salt

Preparation: 10–12 minutes; Cooking: 0 minutes; Chilling ahead

1 In a bowl, mix together the sliced cucumber and onion, season with salt and toss together until thoroughly combined. Leave to stand in a cool place for 5–10 minutes. Add the sugar, vinegar, water and chopped dill to the cucumber mixture. Toss together until well combined, then chill for a few hours, or until ready to serve.

Spinach & Mushroom Salad

This nutritious salad goes well with strongly flavoured dishes like chilli chicken.

Serves 4
10 baby corn cobs

2 tomatoes
115g/4oz/1½ cups mushrooms
1 onion, cut into rings
20 small spinach leaves
25g/1oz salad cress (optional)
salt and ground black pepper

Preparation: 5 minutes; Cooking: 0 minutes

1 Halve the baby corn cobs lengthwise and slice the tomatoes. Trim the mushrooms and cut them into thin slices.

2 Arrange all the salad ingredients attractively in a large bowl. Season with salt and pepper and serve.

Pears with Blue Cheese & Walnuts

Succulent pears filled with blue cheese and walnut cream look pretty on colourful leaves and make a great appetizer.

Serves 6
115g/4oz fresh cream cheese
75g/3oz Stilton or other mature blue cheese, such as Roquefort
30–45ml/2–3 tbsp single (light) cream
115g/4oz/1 cup roughly chopped walnuts

6 ripe pears
15ml/1 tbsp lemon juice
mixed salad leaves, such as frisée, oakleaf lettuce and radicchio
6 cherry tomatoes
sea salt and ground black pepper
walnut halves and sprigs of fresh flat leaf parsley, to garnish

For the dressing
juice of 1 lemon
a little finely grated lemon rind
a pinch of caster (superfine) sugar
60ml/4 tbsp olive oil

Preparation: 8–10 minutes; Cooking: 0 minutes

1 Mash the cream cheese and blue cheese together in a mixing bowl with a good grinding of black pepper, then blend in the cream to make a smooth mixture. Add 25g/1oz/¼ cup of the chopped walnuts and mix to distribute evenly.

2 Peel and halve the pears and scoop out the core from each. Put the pears into a bowl of water with the 15ml/1 tbsp lemon juice to prevent them from browning. Make the dressing by whisking the ingredients together in a small bowl, and then add salt and pepper to taste.

3 Arrange a bed of salad leaves on six plates – shallow soup plates are ideal – add a cherry tomato to each and sprinkle over the remaining chopped walnuts.

4 Drain the pears well and pat dry with kitchen paper, then turn them in the prepared dressing and arrange, hollow side up, on the salad leaves.

5 Divide the blue cheese filling among the 12 pear halves and spoon the dressing over the top. Garnish each filled pear half with a walnut half and a sprig of flat leaf parsley before serving.

Cucumber Energy 89kcal/375kJ; Protein 2g; Carbohydrate 20.7g, of which sugars 18.3g; Fat 0.4g, of which saturates 0g; Cholesterol 0mg; Calcium 63mg; Fibre 2.3g; Sodium 9mg.
Spinach Energy 21kcal/89kJ; Protein 2g; Carbohydrate 2.4g, of which sugars 2.2g; Fat 0.5g, of which saturates 0.1g; Cholesterol 0mg; Calcium 29mg; Fibre 1.5g; Sodium 309mg
Pears Energy 322kcal/1332kJ; Protein 5.1g; Carbohydrate 15.7g, of which sugars 15.7g; Fat 26.9g, of which saturates 10.2g; Cholesterol 30mg; Calcium 109mg; Fibre 3.7g; Sodium 218mg.

Salad Leaves with Gorgonzola

Crispy fried pancetta makes a tasty addition and contrasts well in texture and flavour with the softness of mixed salad leaves and the sharp taste of Gorgonzola.

Serves 4
225g/8oz pancetta rashers (strips), any rinds removed, coarsely chopped
2 large garlic cloves, roughly chopped
75g/3oz rocket (arugula) leaves
75g/3oz radicchio leaves or mixed baby salad leaves
50g/2oz/½ cup walnuts, roughly chopped
115g/4oz Gorgonzola cheese
60ml/4 tbsp olive oil
15ml/1 tbsp balsamic vinegar
salt and ground black pepper

Preparation: 5 minutes; Cooking: 5 minutes

1 Put the chopped pancetta and garlic in a non-stick or heavy frying pan and heat gently, stirring constantly, until the pancetta fat runs.

2 Increase the heat and fry until the pancetta and garlic are crisp. Try not to let the garlic brown or it will acquire a bitter flavour. Remove the pancetta and garlic with a slotted spoon and drain on kitchen paper. Leave the pancetta fat in the pan, but take it off the heat.

3 Tear the rocket and radicchio or mixed baby salad leaves into a salad bowl. Sprinkle over the walnuts, pancetta and garlic. Add salt and pepper and toss to mix. Crumble the Gorgonzola cheese on top.

4 Return the frying pan to medium heat and add the oil and balsamic vinegar to the pancetta fat. Stir until sizzling, then pour over the salad. Serve at once, to be tossed at the table.

> **Variation**
> If pancetta is not available, use unsmoked streaky (fatty) bacon instead. You could also try chorizo, cut thinly, for extra flavour.

Prawn Cocktail

There is no nicer starter than a good, fresh prawn cocktail, with firm, juicy prawns, crisp lettuce and a piquant sauce. This recipe shows just how good a prawn cocktail can be.

Serves 6
60ml/4 tbsp double (heavy) cream, lightly whipped
60ml/4 tbsp mayonnaise
60ml/4 tbsp tomato ketchup
5–10ml/1–2 tsp Worcestershire sauce
juice of 1 lemon
½ cos lettuce or other crisp lettuce
450g/1lb cooked peeled prawns (shrimp)
salt, ground black pepper and paprika
6 large whole cooked prawns (shrimp) in the shell, to garnish (optional)
thinly sliced brown bread and butter and lemon wedges, to serve

Preparation: 6–7 minutes; Cooking: 0 minutes

1 Place the lightly whipped cream, mayonnaise and tomato ketchup in a small bowl and whisk lightly to combine. Add Worcestershire sauce to taste, then whisk in enough of the lemon juice to make a really tangy sauce.

2 Finely shred the lettuce and spoon it into six individual glasses, filling them about one-third full.

3 Stir the prawns into the sauce, then check the seasoning and spoon the prawn mixture generously over the lettuce. If you like, drape a whole cooked prawn over the edge of each glass and sprinkle each of the cocktails with ground black pepper and/or paprika. Serve immediately, with thinly sliced brown bread and butter and lemon wedges.

> **Cook's Tip**
> Partly peeled prawns make a pretty garnish. To prepare, carefully peel the body shell from the prawns and leave the tail fan for decoration.

Salad Leaves Energy 448Kcal/1850kJ; Protein 17.7g; Carbohydrate 1g, of which sugars 0.9g; Fat 41.4g, of which saturates 12.4g; Cholesterol 58mg; Calcium 219mg; Fibre 1.2g; Sodium 1113mg.
Prawn Cocktail Energy 194kcal/805kJ; Protein 13.9g; Carbohydrate 4.2g, of which sugars 4g; Fat 13.6g, of which saturates 4.6g; Cholesterol 167mg; Calcium 80mg; Fibre 0.4g; Sodium 384mg.

Crab Salad with Rocket

This colourful and fresh-tasting appetizer is an interesting way to use crab meat. The capers and peppery rocket leaves add a zing to the dish.

Serves 6

white and brown meat from
   4 small fresh dressed crabs,
   about 450g/1lb
1 small red (bell) pepper, seeded
   and finely chopped
1 small red onion, finely chopped
30ml/2 tbsp drained capers
30ml/2 tbsp chopped fresh
   coriander (cilantro)
grated rind and juice of 2 lemons
Tabasco sauce, to taste
salt and ground black pepper
lemon rind strips, to garnish

For the rocket (arugula) salad

40g/1½oz rocket leaves
30ml/2 tbsp sunflower oil
15ml/1 tbsp fresh lime juice

Preparation: 6–7 minutes; Cooking: 0 minutes

1 Put the white and brown crab meat, red pepper, onion, capers and chopped coriander in a bowl. Add the lemon rind and juice and toss gently to mix together. Season with a few drops of Tabasco sauce, according to taste, and a little salt and ground black pepper.

2 Divide the rocket leaves among four plates. Mix together the oil and lime juice in a small bowl. Dress the rocket leaves, then pile the crab salad on top and serve garnished with lemon rind.

Variation

Sweet red piquant peppers in oil would make a great addition to this salad. Drain 4–6 of the peppers, chop them roughly and add with the red (bell) pepper.

Cook's Tip

If the dressed crabs are really small, pile the salad back into the shells to serve. This looks very pretty.

Amanida

This salad is simple to make, because it combines small quantities of ready-to-eat ingredients.

Serves 6

1 lolla green lettuce
50g/2oz cured, sliced chorizo or
   in a piece, skinned and diced
4 thin slices Serrano ham
130g/4½oz can sardines
   in oil, drained
130g/4½oz can albacore tuna
   steak in oil, drained
8 canned white asparagus
   spears, drained
2–3 canned palm hearts, drained
115g/4oz/⅔ cup tiny
   arbequina olives
115g/4oz/⅔ cup big gordas or
   queen olives, preferably
   purplish ones
10 medium red tomatoes
15ml/1 tbsp chopped fresh
   parsley, to garnish

For the vinaigrette

1 garlic clove, split lengthways
30ml/2 tbsp sherry vinegar
30ml/2 tbsp red wine vinegar
60ml/4 tbsp olive oil
60ml/4 tbsp extra virgin olive oil
salt and ground black pepper

Preparation: 20 minutes; Cooking: 0 minutes

1 Make the vinaigrette. Wipe the cut side of the garlic round a bowl, then discard.

2 Whisk the sherry vinegar, red wine vinegar, olive oil and extra virgin olive oil together in the bowl, then season with salt and black pepper. Tip the vinaigrette into a small jug (pitcher) and set aside.

3 Choose a large serving plate. Select eight lettuce leaves, to make small bunches round it. Break off the stem ends. Tip the leaves into the vinaigrette bowl and toss to coat in a little dressing. Arrange them around the serving plate.

4 Position the chorizo slices on one side of the plate. Roll the ham and arrange opposite. Drain and blot the canned fish and arrange the sardines and tuna across the plate, in a cross.

5 Arrange the asparagus, spears outwards, and the palm hearts (split lengthways), on opposite sides of the plate. Pile the two types of olive in the remaining spaces.

6 Put the tomatoes in a bowl and pour over boiling water. Leave to stand for 10 minutes, then drain. Peel and quarter two-thirds of the tomatoes and cut out the centres.

7 Arrange the tomatoes, round side up, in the centre of the plate, just touching all the prepared sections. Prepare more tomatoes as they are needed.

8 Arrange them in a flower shape, each new ring just overlapping the previous one. The final ring, in the centre of the pile, should make a flower shape.

9 Brush vinaigrette dressing over the tomatoes, palm hearts and asparagus spears and season lightly with salt and black pepper. Sprinkle parsley very discreetly on the tomatoes and white vegetables. Serve at room temperature. (Refrigerate if you must, while waiting to serve.)

Crab Salad Energy 106kcal/443kJ; Protein 14.2g; Carbohydrate 2.1g, of which sugars 2g; Fat 4.6g, of which saturates 0.6g; Cholesterol 54mg; Calcium 114mg; Fibre 0.7g; Sodium 431mg.
Amanida Energy 304Kcal/1264kJ; Protein 14.7g; Carbohydrate 7.5g, of which sugars 6.8g; Fat 24.2g, of which saturates 4.4g; Cholesterol 37mg; Calcium 169mg; Fibre 3.4g; Sodium 878mg.

Rice Triangles

These rice shapes – onigiri – are very popular in Japan. You can put anything you like in the rice, so you could invent your own onigiri.

Serves 4
1 salmon steak
15ml/1 tbsp salt

450g/1lb/4 cups freshly cooked sushi rice
1/4 cucumber, seeded and cut into matchsticks
1/2 sheet yaki-nori seaweed, cut into four equal strips
white and black sesame seeds, for sprinkling on the salmon onigiri before serving

Preparation: 12 minutes; Cooking: 6 minutes

1 Grill (broil) the salmon steaks on each side, until the flesh flakes easily when tested with the tip of a sharp knife. Set aside to cool while you make other onigiri. When the salmon is cold, flake it, discarding any skin and bones.

2 Put the salt in a bowl. Spoon an eighth of the warm cooked rice into a small rice bowl. Make a hole in the middle of the rice and put in a few cucumber matchsticks. Smooth the rice over to cover the cucumber completely.

3 Wet the palms of both hands with cold water, then rub the salt evenly on to your palms.

4 Empty the rice and cucumbers from the bowl onto one hand. Use both hands to shape the rice into a triangular shape, using firm but not heavy pressure, and making sure that the cucumber is encased by the rice. Make three more rice triangles the same way.

5 Mix the flaked salmon into the remaining rice, then shape it into triangles as before.

6 Wrap a strip of yaki-nori around each of the cucumber triangles. Sprinkle sesame seeds on the salmon triangles.

7 Arrange the onigiri on a plate, with alternate triangles inverted for best presentation. Serve at once.

Smoked Fish Platter

A wide variety of smoked fish is available today – trout, salmon and mackerel feature in this simple appetizer – but any smoked fish can be used.

Serves 4
1/2 Charentais melon
1/2 cantaloupe melon
50g/2oz rocket (arugula)

75g/3oz hot-smoked trout fillets
75g/3oz smoked salmon
75g/3oz smoked mackerel with peppercorns

For the dressing
75ml/5 tbsp extra virgin olive oil
15ml/1 tbsp white wine vinegar
5ml/1 tsp wholegrain mustard
5ml/1 tsp clear honey
salt and ground black pepper

Preparation: 8 minutes; Cooking: 0 minutes

1 Scoop out and discard all the seeds from the Charentais and cantaloupe melons and cut each melon into four or eight slices, leaving the skin on. Divide the melon slices among four small serving plates, placing the slices neatly to one side.

2 Add a quarter of the rocket leaves to each plate, placing them opposite the melon.

3 Make the honey dressing by combining all the ingredients in a small jug (pitcher). Add plenty of salt and black pepper and whisk with a fork until emulsified.

4 Divide the smoked fish into four portions, breaking or cutting the trout fillets and smoked salmon into bitesize pieces. Peel the skin from the mackerel, then break up the flesh.

5 Arrange the trout fillets, smoked salmon and mackerel over the rocket and melon on each platter. Drizzle the dressing over and serve immediately.

> **Variation**
> *As long as the total amount of smoked fish is 250g/9oz, any varieties can be used. Try smoked eel for a change.*

Rice Triangles Energy 342kcal/1427kJ; Protein 10.5g; Carbohydrate 29.8g, of which sugars 1.9g; Fat 20.7g, of which saturates 7.8g; Cholesterol 37mg; Calcium 140mg; Fibre 1.1g; Sodium 38mg.
Fish Platter Energy 312kcal/1298kJ; Protein 14.8g; Carbohydrate 15.2g, of which sugars 15.2g; Fat 21.7g, of which saturates 3.5g; Cholesterol 33mg; Calcium 66mg; Fibre 1.3g; Sodium 961mg.

Chilled Soba Noodles with Nori

Nori is familiar as the seaweed sheets that are used for wrapping sushi, but it is often crumbled or sliced and used as a flavourful topping for Japanese dishes. Nori is widely available in supermarkets, but you will find a greater selection in Asian supermarkets.

Serves 4

350g/12oz dried soba noodles
1 sheet nori seaweed

For the dipping sauce

300ml/½ pint/1¼ cups
  bonito stock
120ml/4fl oz/½ cup dark
  soy sauce
60ml/4 tbsp mirin
5ml/1 tsp sugar
10g/¼oz loose bonito flakes

To serve

4 spring onions (scallions),
  finely chopped
30ml/2 tbsp grated daikon
wasabi paste
4 egg yolks (optional)

Preparation: 6 minutes; Cooking: 10–12 minutes

1 Make the dipping sauce. Combine the stock, soy sauce, mirin and sugar in a pan. Bring rapidly to the boil, add the bonito flakes, then remove from the heat. When cool, strain the sauce into a bowl and cover. (This can be done in advance and the sauce kept chilled for up to a week.)

2 Cook the soba noodles in a pan of lightly salted boiling water for 6–7 minutes or until just tender, following the manufacturer's directions on the packet.

3 Drain and rinse the noodles under cold running water, agitating them gently to remove the excess starch. Drain well, tip into a bowl and set aside.

4 Toast the nori over a high gas flame or under a hot grill (broiler), then place on a board and cut into thin strips.

5 Divide the noodles among four serving dishes and top with the nori. Serve each portion with an individual bowl of dipping sauce and offer the spring onions, daikon and wasabi paste separately. An egg yolk can be added to each portion if liked.

Cheese Fritters in Wonton Wrappers

These crisp fritters owe their inspiration to Italy although the wrappers are strictly Chinese – a fine example of fusion food. A note of caution – do be careful not to burn your mouth when you take your first bite, as the soft, rich cheese filling will be very hot and the fritters are so irresistible that waiting for them to cool down is well nigh impossible.

Makes 16

115g/4oz/½ cup
  ricotta cheese
50g/2oz/½ cup grated
  fontina cheese
25g/1oz/⅓ cup finely grated
  Parmesan cheese
pinch of cayenne pepper
1 egg, beaten, plus a little extra
  to seal the wontons
16 wonton wrappers
vegetable oil, for deep-frying

Preparation: 6–8 minutes; Cooking: 12 minutes

1 Line a large baking sheet with baking parchment or sprinkle it lightly with flour. Set aside. Combine the cheeses in a bowl, then add the cayenne and beaten egg and mix well.

2 Place one wonton wrapper at a time on a board. Brush the edges with egg. Spoon a little filling in the centre. Pull the top corner down to the bottom corner, to make a triangle.

3 Transfer the filled wontons to the prepared baking sheet.

4 Heat the oil in a deep-fryer or large pan. Slip in as many wontons at one time as can be accommodated without overcrowding. Fry them for 2–3 minutes on each side or until the fritters are golden. Remove with a slotted spoon and keep warm while you make the remaining fritters. Drain well on kitchen paper and serve immediately.

Cook's Tip
The optimum temperature for frying wontons is 190°C/375°F. If you do not have a thermometer, drop a cube of stale bread into the oil; it should brown in 30–40 seconds.

Soba Noodles Energy 353kcal/1479kJ; Protein 5.5g; Carbohydrate 75.7g, of which sugars 4.1g; Fat 0.2g, of which saturates 0g; Cholesterol 0mg; Calcium 23mg; Fibre 0.2g; Sodium 2150mg.
Cheese Fritters Energy 112kcal/467kJ; Protein 3.5g; Carbohydrate 8.7g, of which sugars 0.4g; Fat 7.2g, of which saturates 2.3g; Cholesterol 20mg; Calcium 59mg; Fibre 0.3g; Sodium 44mg.

Fried Black Pudding

Spanish morcilla – black pudding – is very popular throughout Spain. It is flavoured with spices and herbs, usually including garlic and oregano, and has a wonderfully rich, spicy taste.

Serves 4

15ml/1 tbsp olive oil
1 onion, thinly sliced
2 garlic cloves, thinly sliced
5ml/1 tsp dried oregano
5ml/1 tsp paprika
225g/8oz black pudding
   (blood sausage), cut into
   12 thick slices
1 thin French stick, sliced into 12
30ml/2 tbsp fino sherry
sugar, to taste
salt and ground black pepper
chopped fresh oregano, to garnish

Preparation: 5 minutes; Cooking: 15 minutes

1 Heat the olive oil in a large frying pan and fry the sliced onion, garlic, oregano and paprika for about 7–8 minutes until the onion is softened and has turned golden brown.

2 Add the slices of black pudding, then increase the heat and cook them for 3 minutes, without stirring. Turn them over carefully with a spatula and cook for a further 3 minutes until the slices of black pudding are crisp.

3 Arrange the rounds of bread on a large serving plate and top each with a slice of black pudding.

4 Stir the sherry into the onions and add a little sugar to taste. Heat, swirling the mixture around the pan until bubbling, then season with salt and black pepper.

5 Spoon a little of the onion mixture on top of each slice of black pudding. Scatter the oregano over and serve.

> **Cook's Tip**
> *If you can find real morcilla, serve it neat: simply fry the slices in olive oil and use to top little rounds of bread. If you cannot find black pudding, you can use red chorizo instead.*

Walnut & Goat's Cheese Bruschetta

The combination of toasted walnuts and melting goat's cheese is lovely in this simple lunchtime snack, which can be served with a dressed salad if the occasion calls for it.

Serves 4

50g/2oz/½ cup walnut pieces
4 thick slices walnut bread
120ml/4fl oz/½ cup French
   dressing
200g/7oz chèvre or other
   semi-soft goat's cheese

Preparation: 5 minutes; Cooking: 3–5 minutes

1 Preheat the grill (broiler). Spread out the walnut pieces on a baking sheet. Lightly toast them, shaking the baking sheet once or twice so that they cook evenly, then remove and set them aside, leaving them to cool on the baking sheet.

2 Put the walnut bread on a foil-lined grill rack and lightly toast on one side. Turn the slices over and drizzle the untoasted side of each with 15ml/1 tbsp of the French dressing so that it soaks in a little.

3 Cut the goat's cheese into 12 slices and place three on each piece of bread. Grill (broil) under medium heat for about 3 minutes, until the cheese is melting and beginning to brown and bubble on the surface.

4 Transfer the bruschetta to serving plates, sprinkle with the toasted walnuts and drizzle with the remaining French dressing. Serve the bruschetta immediately with salad leaves.

> **Cook's Tip**
> *Walnut bread is sold in most large supermarkets and makes an interesting alternative to ordinary crusty bread, although a freshly baked loaf of the latter is fine if speciality breads are not available. If using crusty bread, try to find a slender loaf to slice, so that the portions are not too wide. If you can only buy a large loaf, cut the slices in half to make neat, chunky pieces, perfect for making bruschetta.*

Black Pudding Energy 506kcal/2137kJ; Protein 18.4g; Carbohydrate 77.8g, of which sugars 4.7g; Fat 14.8g, of which saturates 5.2g; Cholesterol 38mg; Calcium 171mg; Fibre 3.1g; Sodium 1422mg.
Bruschetta Energy 558kcal/2321kJ; Protein 16.7g; Carbohydrate 25.6g, of which sugars 2.2g; Fat 37.2g, of which saturates 12.7g; Cholesterol 47mg; Calcium 137mg; Fibre 1.2g; Sodium 841mg.

Rice Balls Stuffed with Mozzarella

These deep-fried balls are very popular snacks, which is hardly surprising as they are quite delicious.

Serves 4
1 quantity risotto with Parmesan cheese or mushroom risotto

3 eggs
breadcrumbs and plain (all-purpose) flour, to coat
115g/4oz/²/₃ cup mozzarella cheese, cut into small cubes
oil, for deep-frying
dressed curly endive and cherry tomatoes, to serve

Preparation: 5 minutes; Cooking: 6–9 minutes

1 Put the risotto in a bowl and allow it to cool completely. Beat two of the eggs, and stir them into the bowl of cold risotto until the ingredients are well mixed.

2 Use your hands to form the rice mixture into balls the size of a large egg. If the mixture is too moist to hold its shape well, stir in a few tablespoons of breadcrumbs.

3 Poke a hole in the centre of each ball with your finger, then fill it with a few small cubes of mozzarella, and close the hole over again with the rice mixture.

4 Heat the oil for deep-frying in a wok or deep-fryer to a temperature of 190°C/375°F or until a small piece of bread sizzles as soon as it is dropped in.

5 Spread some flour on a plate. Beat the remaining egg in a shallow bowl. Sprinkle another plate with breadcrumbs. Roll the balls in the flour, then in the egg, and finally in the breadcrumbs, making sure they are coated all over.

6 Fry the coated rice balls a few at a time in the hot oil until golden and crisp. Drain on kitchen paper while the remaining balls are being fried.

7 Pile the rice balls on to a serving platter and serve hot, with a simple salad of dressed curly endive leaves and cherry tomatoes.

Mozzarella & Tomato Skewers

Stacks of flavour – layers of oven-baked mozzarella, tomatoes, basil and bread. These colourful kebabs will be popular with adults and children alike.

Serves 4
12 slices white country bread, each about 1cm/¹/₂in thick

45ml/3 tbsp olive oil
225g/8oz mozzarella cheese, cut into 5mm/¹/₄ in slices
3 ripe plum tomatoes, cut into 5mm/¹/₄ in slices
15g/¹/₂oz/¹/₂ cup fresh basil leaves, plus extra to garnish
salt and ground black pepper
30ml/2 tbsp chopped fresh flat leaf parsley, to garnish

Preparation: 3 minutes; Cooking: 13–15 minutes

1 Preheat the oven to 220°C/425°F/Gas 7. Trim the crusts from the bread and cut each slice into four equal squares. Arrange on a baking sheet and brush with half the olive oil. Bake for 3–5 minutes until the squares are a pale golden colour.

2 Remove the bread squares from the oven and place them on a chopping board with the sliced mozzarella and tomatoes and the fresh basil leaves.

3 Make 16 stacks, each starting with a square of bread, then a slice of mozzarella topped with a slice of tomato and a basil leaf. Sprinkle with salt and pepper, then repeat, ending with a piece of bread. Push a skewer through each stack and place on the baking sheet.

4 Drizzle the kebabs with the remaining oil and bake for 10–12 minutes until the cheese begins to melt. Garnish with basil and flat leaf parsley.

Cook's Tips
• If you use wooden skewers, soak them in water first, to prevent them from scorching during the cooking time.
• The bread for these skewers needs to be quite robust, so don't be tempted to use slices from a soft white sandwich loaf.

Rice Balls Energy 670kcal/2792kJ; Protein 23.8g; Carbohydrate 73.8g, of which sugars 1.5g; Fat 31.2g, of which saturates 18.2g; Cholesterol 192mg; Calcium 383mg; Fibre 0.7g; Sodium 621mg.
Skewers Energy 472kcal/1981kJ; Protein 20g; Carbohydrate 47.2g, of which sugars 5g; Fat 24g, of which saturates 10g; Cholesterol 36mg; Calcium 341mg; Fibre 2.4g; Sodium 726mg.

Chinese-steamed Prawns

This is a wonderfully simple dish, widely eaten in China but equally popular in other parts of the world.

Serves 4
350–450g/12oz–1lb large raw prawns (shrimp)
soy sauce, to serve

Preparation: 0 minutes; Cooking: 2–3 minutes

1 Place the raw prawns in a large bamboo steamer. Steam over a high heat for 2–3 minutes, or until the prawns have turned pink. Pile the prawns on plates and serve immediately with the soy sauce for dipping.

Garlic Prawns

For this simple Spanish tapas dish, you really need fresh raw prawns which absorb the flavours of the garlic and chilli as they fry. Have everything ready for last-minute cooking so you can take it to the table while it is still sizzling.

Serves 4
350–450g/12oz–1lb large raw prawns (jumbo shrimp)
2 fresh red chillies
75ml/5 tbsp olive oil
3 garlic cloves, crushed
salt and ground black pepper

Preparation: 5 minutes; Cooking: 3 minutes

1 Remove the heads and shells from the prawns, leaving the tails intact. Devein the prawns.

2 Halve each chilli lengthways and discard the seeds. Heat the oil in a flameproof pan, suitable for serving. (Alternatively, use a frying pan and have a warmed serving dish ready in the oven.)

3 Add all the prawns, chilli and garlic to the pan and cook over a high heat for about 3 minutes, stirring until the prawns turn pink. Season lightly with salt and pepper and serve immediately.

Aromatic Tiger Prawns

There is no elegant way to eat these aromatic prawns – just hold them by the tails, pull them off the sticks with your fingers and pop them into your mouth.

Serves 4
16 raw tiger prawns (shrimp) or scampi (extra large shrimp) tails
2.5ml/½ tsp chilli powder
5ml/1 tsp fennel seeds
5 Sichuan or black peppercorns
1 star anise, broken into segments
1 cinnamon stick, broken into pieces
30ml/2 tbsp groundnut (peanut) or sunflower oil
2 garlic cloves, chopped
2cm/¾in piece fresh root ginger, peeled and finely chopped
1 shallot, chopped
30ml/2 tbsp water
30ml/2 tbsp rice vinegar
30ml/2 tbsp soft brown or palm (jaggery) sugar
salt and ground black pepper
lime slices and chopped spring onion (scallions), to garnish

Preparation: 5 minutes; Cooking: 15 minutes

1 Thread the prawns or scampi tails in pairs on 8 wooden cocktail sticks. Set aside.

2 Heat a frying pan over medium heat, put in all the chilli powder, fennel seeds, Sichuan or black peppercorns, star anise and cinnamon stick and dry-fry for 1–2 minutes to release the flavours. Leave to cool, then grind coarsely in a grinder or tip into a mortar and crush with a pestle.

3 Heat the groundnut or sunflower oil in a shallow pan, add the garlic, ginger and chopped shallot and then fry gently until very lightly coloured. Add the crushed spices and seasoning and cook the mixture gently for 2 minutes. Pour in the water and simmer, stirring constantly, for 5 minutes more.

4 Add the rice vinegar and soft brown or palm sugar, stir until dissolved, then add the prawns or scampi tails. Cook for about 3–5 minutes, until the seafood has turned pink, but is still very juicy. Serve hot, garnished with lime slices and spring onion.

Chinese Prawns Energy 67kcal/281kJ; Protein 15.4g; Carbohydrate 0g, of which sugars 0g; Fat 0.5g, of which saturates 0.1g; Cholesterol 171mg; Calcium 69mg; Fibre 0g; Sodium 166mg.
Garlic Prawns Energy 118kcal/495kJ; Protein 17.9g; Carbohydrate 3g, of which sugars 3g; Fat 3.9g, of which saturates 0.5g; Cholesterol 195mg; Calcium 83mg; Fibre 0.4g; Sodium 234mg.
Tiger Prawns Energy 142kcal/593kJ; Protein 13.4g; Carbohydrate 9g, of which sugars 8.7g; Fat 6g, of which saturates 0.7g; Cholesterol 146mg; Calcium 67mg; Fibre 0.2g; Sodium 144mg.

Prawn & Sesame Toasts

These attractive little toast triangles are ideal for serving with pre-dinner drinks and are always a favourite hot snack at parties. They are surprisingly easy to prepare and you can cook them in your wok for just a few minutes. Serve them with a sweet chilli sauce for dipping.

Serves 4

225g/8oz peeled raw
   prawns (shrimp)
15ml/1 tbsp sherry
15ml/1 tbsp soy sauce
30ml/2 tbsp cornflour (cornstarch)
2 egg whites
4 slices white bread
115g/4oz/½ cup sesame seeds
oil, for deep-frying
sweet chilli sauce, to serve

Preparation: 6 minutes; Cooking: 6–9 minutes

1 Put the prawns, sherry, soy sauce and cornflour in a food processor. Pulse until the ingredients are processed to a rough paste which retains some texture.

2 In a grease-free bowl, whisk the egg whites until stiff. Fold them into the prawn and cornflour mixture.

3 Cut each slice of bread into four triangular quarters. Spread out the sesame seeds on a large plate. Spread the prawn paste over one side of each bread triangle, then press the coated sides into the sesame seeds so that they stick and cover the prawn paste.

4 Heat the oil in a wok or deep-fryer, to 190°C/375°F or until a cube of bread, added to the oil, browns in about 45 seconds. Add the toasts, a few at a time, prawn side down, and deep-fry for 2–3 minutes, then turn the toasts over carefully and fry on the other side until golden.

5 Drain on kitchen paper and serve hot with sweet chilli sauce.

> **Variation**
> *Crabmeat can be used instead of peeled raw prawns (shrimp). Use fresh crab if you can get it, or thawed frozen crabmeat.*

Pumpkin & Prawn Cakes

This unusual Asian combination makes a delicious dish which needs only a fish sauce or soy sauce to dip into. Serve with noodles or fried rice for a lovely light meal.

Serves 4

200g/7oz/1⅔ cups strong white
   bread flour
2.5ml/½ tsp salt
2.5ml/½ tsp dried yeast
175ml/6fl oz/¾ cup warm water
1 egg, beaten
200g/7oz raw prawns (shrimp)
225g/8oz pumpkin, peeled,
   seeded and grated
150g/5oz sweet potato, grated
2 spring onions (scallions),
   chopped
50g/2oz water chestnuts,
   chopped
2.5ml/½ tsp chilli sauce
1 garlic clove, crushed
juice of ½ lime
vegetable oil, for deep-frying
lime wedges, to serve

Preparation: 8 minutes; Cooking: 12 minutes

1 Sift together the flour and salt into a large bowl and make a well in the centre. In a separate container dissolve the yeast in the water until creamy, then pour into the centre of the flour and salt mixture. Pour in the egg and set aside for a few minutes until bubbles appear. Mix to form a smooth batter.

2 Peel the prawns, if necessary, then place in a pan with just enough boiling water to cover. Simmer for about 2 minutes or until the prawns have turned pink. Drain, rinse in cold water and drain again well.

3 Coarsely chop the prawns, then place in a bowl with the pumpkin and sweet potato.

4 Add the spring onions, water chestnuts, chilli sauce, garlic and lime juice and mix well. Fold into the batter mixture carefully until evenly mixed.

5 Heat a 1cm/½ in layer of oil in a large frying pan until really hot. Spoon in the batter in heaps, leaving space between each one, and cook until golden on both sides. Drain on kitchen paper and serve with the lime wedges.

Sesame Toasts Energy 392Kcal/1634kJ; Protein 19.1g; Carbohydrate 21.1g, of which sugars 1.2g; Fat 25.8g, of which saturates 3.4g; Cholesterol 110mg; Calcium 270mg; Fibre 2.7g; Sodium 557mg.
Prawn Cakes Energy 317kcal/1346kJ; Protein 18.2g; Carbohydrate 57.6g, of which sugars 9.1g; Fat 3.2g, of which saturates 0.9g; Cholesterol 145mg; Calcium 216mg; Fibre 6g; Sodium 383mg.

Scallops with Bacon & Sage

Many people consider scallops the finest of all seafood, with their tender flesh and pure, sweet flavour. This dish adds bacon for a contrasting taste. Samphire, a salty asparagus-like plant that grows on sea margins around England, goes very well with the scallops. It can be obtained from fishmongers in summer.

Serves 4
15ml/1 tbsp olive oil
4 streaky (fatty) bacon rashers (strips), cut into 2.5cm/1in strips
2–3 fresh sage leaves, chopped small piece of butter
8 large or 16 small scallops
15ml/1 tbsp fresh lemon juice
100ml/3½ fl oz dry cider or white wine

Preparation: 4 minutes; Cooking: 6 minutes

1 Heat a frying pan and add the oil, bacon and sage. Cook over medium heat, stirring occasionally, until the bacon is golden brown. Lift out and keep warm.

2 Add the butter to the pan and when hot add the scallops. Cook for about 1 minute on each side until browned. Lift out and keep warm with the bacon.

3 Add the lemon juice and cider to the pan and, scraping up any sediment, bring just to the boil. Continue bubbling gently until the mixture has reduced to a few tablespoons of syrupy sauce that barely covers the bottom of the pan.

4 Serve the scallops and bacon with the sauce drizzled over.

Cook's Tips
• *Scallops that are particularly large can be sliced in half so that they form two discs before cooking (cut off the corals and cook these separately in the pan).*
• *To prepare samphire (glasswort), wash it and pick off the soft fleshy branches, discarding the thicker woody stalks. Drop it into boiling water for just 1 minute before draining and serving.*

Oysters on the Half-shell

Ireland is famous for oysters. The best native ones come from the Galway area on the west coast and, every September, festivals are held in Galway and Clarenbridge to celebrate the beginning of the new season. Whatever the source of the oysters you buy, enjoy them with freshly made brown soda bread and butter, and a cool glass of Guinness or white wine.

Serves 2–4
24 Galway oysters, in the shell crushed ice and dulse or dillisk (soaked if dried), to garnish soda bread and butter, and lemon wedges, to serve

Preparation: 14 minutes; Cooking: 0 minutes

1 Use a blunt-ended oyster knife to shuck the oysters: insert the end of the knife between the shells near the hinge and work it until you cut through the muscle that holds the shells together. Catch the oyster liquid in a bowl.

2 When the oysters are all open, discard the flat shells. Divide the oysters, in the deep halves, among four serving plates lined with crushed ice and soaked dulse. Strain the reserved liquid over the oysters. Serve immediately with the lemon wedges for squeezing over each portion.

Cook's Tips
• *Although they were once plentiful, Galway oysters are now a rare delicacy and should be eaten raw – buy them with their shells tightly clamped together, showing that they are still alive. The edible seaweed, dulse, or dillisk as it is also known, is an appropriate garnish for oysters.*
• *If you want oysters for a cooked dish, look for the widely cultivated, larger Pacific oysters, which are available all year round, unlike the native oyster which is found only when there's an 'r' in the month. In Britain, native oysters are named after their place of origin, such as the Irish Galway and the English Whitstable, Helford and Colchester; and in America the best known of the eastern and Atlantic oysters is the Blue Point.*

Scallops Energy 179kcal/745kJ; Protein 15.6g; Carbohydrate 1.9g, of which sugars 0.2g; Fat 10.4g, of which saturates 3.3g; Cholesterol 42mg; Calcium 19mg; Fibre 0g; Sodium 414mg.
Oysters Energy 78Kcal/330kJ; Protein 13g; Carbohydrate 3.3g, of which sugars 0g; Fat 1.6g, of which saturates 0.3g; Cholesterol 68mg; Calcium 168mg; Fibre 0g; Sodium 612mg.

Sautéed Mussels with Garlic & Herbs

These mussels are served without their shells, in a delicious paprika-flavoured sauce. Eat them with cocktail sticks.

Serves 4
900g/2lb fresh mussels
1 lemon slice

90ml/6 tbsp olive oil
2 shallots, finely chopped
1 garlic clove, finely chopped
15ml/1 tbsp chopped
   fresh parsley
2.5ml/½ tsp sweet paprika
1.5ml/¼ tsp dried chilli flakes
parsley sprigs, to garnish

Preparation: 4 minutes; Cooking: 4–6 minutes

1 Scrub the mussels, discarding any damaged ones as well as any that are open and which do not close when tapped with the back of a knife.

2 Put the mussels in a large pan with 250ml/8fl oz/1 cup water and the slice of lemon. Bring to the boil and cook for 3–4 minutes, removing the mussels with a slotted spoon as they open and putting them in a bowl.

3 Discard any mussels that remain closed. Using a sharp knife, cut the mussels out of the shells and drain them on kitchen paper.

4 Heat the oil in a sauté pan, add the mussels and cook, stirring, for a minute. Remove from the pan.

5 Add the shallots and garlic and cook, covered, over a low heat, for about 5 minutes, until soft and tender. Stir in the parsley, paprika and chilli, then add the mussels with any juices. Cook briefly.

6 Remove the pan from the heat, cover and leave for 1–2 minutes to let the flavours mingle.

7 Pile the mussels into a large warmed serving bowl or spoon into individual bowls, garnish with parsley sprigs and serve immediately.

Fried Squid with Salt & Pepper

Cooking squid couldn't be simpler. Salt and pepper are used to season, and that's it. A Chinese tradition for all sorts of fish and shellfish, this is a Vietnamese and Cambodian favourite, too. Ideal snack and finger food, the tender squid can be served on its own, with noodles or – as it is in the streets of Saigon – with baguette and chillies. Those who like chilli can replace the black pepper with chopped dried chilli or chilli powder. Butterflied prawns, with the shells removed, are also delicious cooked in this way. To butterfly prawns, cut down the backs and open them out.

Serves 4
450g/1lb baby or medium squid
30ml/2 tbsp coarse salt
15ml/1 tbsp ground black pepper
50g/2oz/½ cup rice flour or
   cornflour (cornstarch)
vegetable oil, for deep-frying
2 limes, halved

Preparation: 8 minutes; Cooking: 6 minutes

1 Prepare the squid by pulling the head away from the body. Sever the tentacles from the rest and trim them. Reach inside the body sac and pull out the backbone, then clean the squid inside and out, removing any skin. Rinse well in cold water.

2 Using a sharp knife, slice the squid into rings and pat them dry with kitchen paper. Put them in a dish with the tentacles.

3 Combine the salt and pepper with the rice flour or cornflour, add it to the squid and toss well, making sure that all the pieces are evenly coated.

4 Heat the oil for deep-frying in a wok or heavy pan. Cook the squid in batches, until the rings turn crisp and golden. Drain on kitchen paper and serve with limes to squeeze over.

> **Variation**
> Use chopped dried chillies or chilli powder instead of black pepper, or flavour the flour with ground coriander or cumin.

Sautéed Mussels Energy 214kcal/888kJ; Protein 12g; Carbohydrate 1.3g, of which sugars 0.9g; Fat 17.9g, of which saturates 2.6g; Cholesterol 27mg; Calcium 145mg; Fibre 0.4g; Sodium 144mg.
Fried Squid Energy 339Kcal/1405kJ; Protein 14g; Carbohydrate 5g, of which sugars 0g; Fat 29g, of which saturates 4g; Cholesterol 146mg; Calcium 70mg; Fibre 0g; Sodium 140mg.

Fish Cakes

A well-made fishcake is always a treat and they can be made with salmon or any fresh or smoked white fish. This dish makes a little fish go a long way, but don't stretch it beyond equal quantities of fish and potato. Parsley sauce is the traditional accompaniment, but for a change, try mushroom sauce or a rich tomato sauce. A cold sauce such as tzatziki would also go well with the fish cakes.

Serves 4

450g/1lb fresh salmon or smoked white fish
wedge of lemon
small bay leaf and a few fresh parsley stalks
25g/1oz/2 tbsp butter
1 onion, finely chopped
450g/1lb potatoes, cooked and mashed
30ml/2 tbsp chopped fresh parsley
pinhead oatmeal, to coat
butter and oil, for frying
ground black pepper

Preparation: 5–6 minutes; Cooking: 14 minutes

1 Rinse the fish and cut it into medium-sized pieces. Put it into a pan with the lemon, bay leaf and parsley stalks and enough cold water to cover. Bring slowly to the boil, then reduce the heat and simmer gently for 5–7 minutes. Remove the fish and drain well.

2 When cool enough to handle, flake the flesh and discard the skin and bones. Melt the butter in a large pan, add the onion and cook gently for a few minutes until softened but not coloured. Add the flaked fish, potato and parsley. Season to taste with pepper.

3 Turn the mixture on to a work surface generously covered with pinhead oatmeal. Divide in half, and then quarter each piece. Form into eight flat cakes and coat them evenly with the oatmeal on all sides.

4 Heat a little butter and an equal quantity of oil in a heavy frying pan, add the fishcakes (in batches, if necessary) and fry until golden on both sides. Drain on kitchen paper and serve immediately with your favourite sauce.

Thai-style Fish Cakes

These light fish cakes are scented with the exotic flavours of sesame, lime and ginger. They make a tempting appetizer served simply with a wedge of lime for squeezing over, but are also perfect for a light lunch or supper, served with a crunchy, refreshing salad.

Makes 25

500g/1¼lb salmon fillet, skinned and boned
45ml/3 tbsp dried breadcrumbs
30ml/2 tbsp mayonnaise
30ml/2 tbsp sesame seeds
30ml/2 tbsp light soy sauce
finely grated rind of 2 limes
10ml/2 tsp finely grated fresh root ginger
4 spring onions (scallions), finely sliced
vegetable oil, for frying
salt and ground black pepper
spring onions (scallions), to garnish
lime wedges, to serve

Preparation: 5 minutes; Cooking: 12–15 minutes; Chilling: 2 hours

1 Finely chop the salmon and place in a bowl. Add the breadcrumbs, mayonnaise, sesame seeds, soy sauce, lime rind, ginger and spring onions and use your fingers to mix well.

2 With wet hands, divide the mixture into 25 portions and shape each into a small round cake. Place the cakes on a baking sheet lined with baking parchment, cover and chill for at least two hours. They can be left overnight.

3 When you are ready to cook the fish cakes, heat about 5cm/2in vegetable oil in a wok and fry the fish cakes in batches, over a medium heat, for 2–3 minutes on each side.

4 Drain the fish cakes well on kitchen paper and serve warm or at room temperature, garnished with spring onion slivers and plenty of lime wedges for squeezing over.

Cook's Tip
When chopping the salmon, look out for stray bones and pick these out with tweezers.

Fish Cakes Energy 380Kcal/1584kJ; Protein 25.3g; Carbohydrate 20.5g, of which sugars 3.3g; Fat 22.4g, of which saturates 8.6g; Cholesterol 83mg; Calcium 49mg; Fibre 1.8g; Sodium 138mg.
Thai-style Fish Cakes Energy 83Kcal/343kJ; Protein 4.6g; Carbohydrate 1.6g, of which sugars 0.2g; Fat 6.5g, of which saturates 0.9g; Cholesterol 11mg; Calcium 16mg; Fibre 0.2g; Sodium 117mg.

Tuna & Corn Fish Cakes

Definitely one for younger members of the family who like the sweet taste of corn. The children may even enjoy helping you make some fishy-shaped cakes.

Serves 4
300g/11oz mashed potatoes
200g/7oz can tuna in soya
    oil, drained
115g/4oz/¾ cup canned or
    frozen corn
30ml/2 tbsp chopped
    fresh parsley
50g/2oz/1 cup fresh white or
    brown breadcrumbs
60ml/4 tbsp sunflower oil
salt and ground black pepper

Preparation: 6 minutes; Cooking: 12 minutes

1 Place the mashed potatoes in a large bowl. Flake the tuna with a fork and stir it into the potatoes with the corn and chopped fresh parsley.

2 Season the mixture to taste with salt and black pepper and mix together thoroughly, then shape into eight patty shapes.

3 Lightly coat the fish cakes in the breadcrumbs, pressing to adhere, then place on a baking sheet.

4 Heat the oil in a large frying pan and cook the fish cakes until crisp and golden brown on both sides, turning once. Serve hot.

> **Cook's Tip**
> *For extra colour on the plate, add peas, broad (fava) beans or lightly cooked green beans. Broccoli would also be suitable.*

> **Variation**
> *For simple variations, try using canned sardines, red or pink salmon or smoked mackerel in place of the tuna, and instant mash when you're in a real hurry.*

Fried Whitebait with Sherry Salsa

Small freshly fried fish are offered in every tapas bar in Spain. Black-backed anchovies taste the best, but whitebait are often easier to come by. They cook very quickly, in less than two minutes.

Serves 4
225g/8oz whitebait
30ml/2 tbsp seasoned plain
    (all-purpose) flour
60ml/4 tbsp olive oil
60ml/4 tbsp sunflower oil

For the salsa
1 shallot, finely chopped
2 garlic cloves, finely chopped
4 ripe tomatoes, roughly chopped
1 small red chilli, seeded and
    finely chopped
30ml/2 tbsp olive oil
60ml/4 tbsp sweet oloroso sherry
30–45ml/2–3 tbsp chopped
    mixed fresh herbs, such as
    parsley or basil
25g/1oz/½ cup stale white
    breadcrumbs
salt and ground black pepper

Preparation: 5–6 minutes; Cooking: 14 minutes

1 To make the salsa, place the chopped shallot, garlic, tomatoes, chilli and olive oil in a pan. Cover with a lid and cook gently for about 10 minutes.

2 Pour the sherry into the pan and season with salt and pepper to taste. Stir in the herbs and breadcrumbs, then cover and keep the salsa hot until the whitebait are ready.

3 Preheat the oven to 150°C/300°F/Gas 2. Wash the whitebait thoroughly, drain well and dry on kitchen paper, then dust in the seasoned flour.

4 Heat the oils together in a heavy frying pan and cook the fish in batches for 1–2 minutes until crisp and golden. Drain on kitchen paper and place in a bowl. Keep warm in the oven until all the fish are cooked. Serve at once with the salsa.

> **Cook's Tip**
> *The trick when frying whitebait is not to crowd the pan, or the fish will simply clump together in a soggy and unattractive mass.*

Fish Cakes Energy 231kcal/976kJ; Protein 17.5g; Carbohydrate 29.8g, of which sugars 4.4g; Fat 5.5g, of which saturates 0.9g; Cholesterol 25mg; Calcium 53mg; Fibre 2.1g; Sodium 330mg.
Whitebait Energy 406kcal/1683kJ; Protein 12.5g; Carbohydrate 12.4g, of which sugars 4.4g; Fat 32.6g, of which saturates 0.9g; Cholesterol 0mg; Calcium 502mg; Fibre 1.2g; Sodium 186mg.

Devilled Whitebait

This is the classic way of cooking whitebait, juvenile fish that are fried and eaten whole. In the UK whitebait are herring, but other types of fish are used elsewhere. Serve with lemon wedges and thinly sliced brown bread and butter, and eat them with your fingers.

Serves 4
oil for deep-frying
150ml/¼ pint/⅔ cup milk
115g/4oz/1 cup plain
   (all-purpose) flour
450g/1lb whitebait, thawed if
   frozen and dried thoroughly on
   kitchen paper
salt, freshly ground black pepper
   and cayenne pepper

Preparation: 3 minutes; Cooking: 6–9 minutes

1 Heat the oil in a large pan or deep-fryer. Put the milk in a shallow bowl and spoon the flour into a plastic bag. Season the flour with salt, pepper and a little cayenne.

2 Dip a handful of the whitebait into the bowl of milk, drain well, then pop them into the paper bag. Shake gently to coat them evenly in the seasoned flour. Repeat until all the fish have been coated. This is the easiest method of flouring whitebait, but don't add too many at once, or they will stick together.

3 Heat the oil to 190°C/375°F or until a cube of stale bread, dropped into the oil, browns in 20 seconds. Add a batch of whitebait, preferably in a chip basket, and fry for 2–3 minutes, until crisp and golden brown. Drain and keep hot while you fry the rest. Sprinkle with more cayenne and serve very hot.

Cook's Tip
Devilled whitebait is traditionally served with tartare sauce. To make this, press 2 hard-boiled egg yolks through a sieve (strainer) into a bowl. Stir in 2 fresh egg yolks. Season to taste, then mix in 15ml/1 tbsp white wine vinegar. Add 300ml/½ pint/ 1¼ cups olive oil, trickling it in gradually while whisking the mixture as when making mayonnaise. Flavour with capers, chopped gherkin, chopped parsley and chives.

Surtido de Pescado

The Spanish enjoy and make the most of preserved fish. This is a very pretty dish, which uses whatever is easily available, and it makes an ideal party starter.

Serves 4
6 eggs
cos or romaine lettuce leaves
75–90ml/5–6 tbsp mayonnaise
90g/3½oz jar Avruga herring roe

2 x 115g/4oz cans sardines
   in oil
2 x 115g/4oz cans mackerel
   fillets in oil
2 x 150g/5oz jars cockles (small
   clams) in brine, drained
2 x 115g/4oz cans mussels
   or scallops in tomato sauce
fresh flat leaf parsley or dill
   sprigs, to garnish
lemon or lime wedges or slices,
   to serve

Preparation: 3–4 minutes; Cooking: 12 minutes

1 Put the eggs in a pan with enough water to cover and bring to the boil. Turn down the heat and simmer for 10 minutes. Drain immediately, then cover with cold water and set aside until completely cool. Peel the eggs and slice in half.

2 Arrange the lettuce leaves on a large serving platter, with the tips pointing outwards. (You may need to break off the bottom end of each leaf if the leaves are large.)

3 Place a teaspoonful or so of mayonnaise on the flat side of each halved egg and top with a spoonful of fish caviar. Carefully arrange in the centre of the dish. Arrange the sardines and mackerel fillets at four points on the plate. Spoon the pickled cockles into two of the gaps, opposite each other, and the mussels in sauce in the remaining gaps. Garnish with parsley sprigs or dill. Serve with lemon or lime.

Cook's Tip
Smoked salmon, kippers (smoked herrings) and rollmops (pickled herring fillets) can also be included on the platter. Try to maintain a balance between fish or shellfish pickled in brine or vinegar, with those in oil or sauce.

Devilled Whitebait Energy 656kcal/2718kJ; Protein 24.4g; Carbohydrate 6.6g, of which sugars 0.1g; Fat 59.4g, of which saturates 0g; Cholesterol 0mg; Calcium 1075mg; Fibre 0.3g; Sodium 288mg.
Surtido de Pescado Energy 622kcal/2588kJ; Protein 56.1g; Carbohydrate 2.7g, of which sugars 0.7g; Fat 43.2g, of which saturates 8.8g; Cholesterol 482mg; Calcium 373mg; Fibre 0.2g; Sodium 661mg.

Smoked Mackerel Pâté

A delicious dish that is simple to make.

Serves 6
4 smoked mackerel fillets, skinned
225g/8oz/1 cup cream cheese

1–2 garlic cloves, finely chopped
juice of 1 lemon
30ml/2 tbsp chopped fresh
  chervil, parsley or chives
15ml/1 tbsp Worcestershire sauce
salt and cayenne pepper

Preparation: 3 minutes; Cooking: 0 minutes; Make ahead

1 Break up the mackerel and put it in a food processor. Add the cream cheese, garlic, lemon juice and herbs. Process the mixture. Add Worcestershire sauce, salt and cayenne pepper to taste. Whizz to mix, then spoon the pâté into a dish, cover with clear film (plastic wrap) and chill.

Chicken Liver & Brandy Pâté

This pâté tastes so much better than anything you can buy in the supermarkets.

Serves 4
50g/2oz/¼ cup butter

350g/12oz chicken livers,
  trimmed and roughly chopped
30ml/2 tbsp brandy
30ml/2 tbsp double (heavy)
  cream
salt and ground black pepper

Preparation: 3 minutes; Cooking: 5–6 minutes; Make ahead

1 Heat the butter in a large frying pan. Add the chicken livers. Cook over a medium heat for 3–4 minutes, or until browned and cooked through. Add the brandy and allow to bubble for a few minutes. Let the mixture cool slightly, then place in a food processor with the cream and some salt and pepper.

2 Process the mixture until smooth and spoon into ramekin dishes. Level the surface and chill overnight to set. If making more than 1 day ahead, seal the surface of each portion with a layer of melted butter. Serve garnished with sprigs of parsley to add a little colour.

Figs with Prosciutto & Roquefort

In this easy, stylish dish, figs and honey balance the richness of the ham and cheese. Serve with warm bread for a simple appetizer before any rich main course.

Serves 4
8 fresh figs
75g/3oz prosciutto
45ml/3 tbsp clear honey
75g/3oz Roquefort cheese
ground black pepper

Preparation: 2–3 minutes; Cooking: 4–5 minutes

1 Preheat the grill (broiler). Quarter the figs and place on a foil-lined grill rack. Tear each slice of prosciutto into two or three pieces. Crumple the pieces of prosciutto and place them on the foil beside the figs. Brush the figs with 15ml/1 tbsp of the clear honey and cook under the grill until lightly browned.

2 Crumble the Roquefort cheese and divide among four plates, setting it to one side. Add the honey-grilled figs and ham and pour over any cooking juices caught on the foil. Drizzle the remaining honey over the figs, ham and cheese, and serve seasoned with plenty of ground black pepper.

Variations
• Any thinly sliced cured ham can be used instead of prosciutto: Westphalian, Bayonne, Culatello or Serrano.
• The figs could be replaced with fresh pears. Slice 2 ripe but firm dessert pears in quarters and remove the cores. Toss in olive oil and cook on a hot ridged grill or griddle pan for 2 minutes on each side. Drizzle balsamic vinegar over and cook for 1 minute more until nicely coloured.

Cook's Tip
Fresh figs are a delicious treat, whether you choose dark purple, yellowy green or green-skinned varieties. When they are ripe, you can split them open with your fingers to reveal the soft, sweet flesh full of edible seeds. They also taste great stuffed with goat's cheese.

Mackerel Pâté Energy 344kcal/1421kJ; Protein 10.7g; Carbohydrate 0.5g, of which sugars 0.4g; Fat 33.3g, of which saturates 14.3g; Cholesterol 88mg; Calcium 57mg; Fibre 0.1g; Sodium 518mg.
Chicken Liver Pâté Energy 227kcal/942kJ; Protein 15.7g; Carbohydrate 0.2g, of which sugars 0.2g; Fat 16.3g, of which saturates 9.6g; Cholesterol 369mg; Calcium 13mg; Fibre 0g; Sodium 144mg.
Figs Energy 326kcal/1378kJ; Protein 10.7g; Carbohydrate 57.4g, of which sugars 57.4g; Fat 7.5g, of which saturates 3.8g; Cholesterol 25mg; Calcium 324mg; Fibre 6.9g; Sodium 512mg.

Chicken Lettuce Parcels

Known as sang choy in Hong Kong, this is a popular assemble-it-yourself treat. The filling is served with crisp lettuce leaves, which are used as wrappers.

Serves 6

2 chicken breast fillets, total weight about 350g/12oz
4 dried Chinese mushrooms, soaked for 30 minutes in warm water to cover
30ml/2 tbsp vegetable oil
2 garlic cloves, crushed
6 drained canned water chestnuts, thinly sliced
30ml/2 tbsp light soy sauce
5ml/1 tsp Sichuan peppercorns, dry-fried and crushed
4 spring onions (scallions), finely chopped
5ml/1 tsp sesame oil
vegetable oil, for deep-frying
50g/2oz cellophane noodles
salt and ground black pepper (optional)
1 crisp lettuce, divided into leaves, and 60ml/4 tbsp hoisin sauce, to serve

Preparation: 8 minutes; Cooking: 10 minutes

1 Remove the skin from the chicken breast fillets, pat dry and set aside. Chop the chicken into thin strips. Drain the soaked mushrooms. Cut off and discard the mushroom stems; slice the caps finely and set aside.

2 Heat the oil in a wok or large frying pan. Add the garlic, then add the chicken. Stir-fry until the pieces are cooked through. Add the sliced mushrooms, water chestnuts, soy sauce and peppercorns. Toss for 2–3 minutes, then season. Stir in half the spring onions, then the sesame oil. Set aside.

3 Cut the chicken skin into strips, deep fry in hot oil until very crisp and drain on kitchen paper. Deep fry the noodles until crisp. Drain on kitchen paper.

4 Crush the noodles and put in a serving dish. Top with the chicken skin, chicken mixture and the remaining spring onions. Arrange the lettuce leaves on a platter. Toss the chicken and noodles to mix. Invite guests to take a lettuce leaf, spread the inside with hoisin sauce and add a spoonful of filling, turning in the sides of the leaf and rolling it into a parcel before eating it.

Chorizo in Olive Oil

Spanish chorizo sausage has a deliciously pungent taste; its robust seasoning of garlic, chilli and paprika flavours the ingredients it is cooked with. Frying chorizo with onions and olive oil is one of its simplest and most delicious uses.

Serves 4

75ml/5 tbsp extra virgin olive oil
350g/12oz chorizo sausage, sliced
1 large onion, thinly sliced
roughly chopped flat leaf parsley, to garnish

Preparation: 2 minutes; Cooking: 5 minutes

1 Heat the oil in a frying pan and fry the chorizo sausage over a high heat until beginning to colour. Remove from the pan with a slotted spoon.

2 Add the onion to the pan and fry until coloured. Return the sausage slices to the pan and heat through for 1 minute.

3 Tip the mixture into a shallow serving dish and scatter with the parsley. Serve with warm bread.

Variations
• Peppers go well with chorizo. Add slices of fresh red (bell) pepper or drained canned pimiento when frying the onion.
• A little fresh chilli would be a good addition, but don't overdo it as the chorizo already contains this seasoning. Choose mild fresnos or jalapenos, and remove the seeds.
• For those who prefer not to go for the burn, substitute sun-dried tomatoes. Use the ones that come packed in oil, so that you can drain off a little of the oil for frying the chorizo.

Cook's Tip
Chorizo is usually available in large supermarkets or delicatessens. Other similarly rich, spicy sausages can be used as a substitute.

Chorizo Energy 408kcal/1689kJ; Protein 9.2g; Carbohydrate 15.2g, of which sugars 5.1g; Fat 35g, of which saturates 10.7g; Cholesterol 35mg; Calcium 58mg; Fibre 1.3g; Sodium 711mg.
Lettuce Parcels Energy 237kcal/984kJ; Protein 15.3g; Carbohydrate 7.6g, of which sugars 1.1g; Fat 16.1g, of which saturates 2g; Cholesterol 41mg; Calcium 24mg; Fibre 0.6g; Sodium 41mg.

Goat's Cheese & Trout Toasties

These little rounds are packed full of flavour – the goat's cheese and trout combine beautifully to make a delicious snack suitable for any time of the day.

Serves 4
8 thick slices of white bread
30ml/2 tbsp olive oil
5ml/1 tsp fresh thyme leaves
20ml/4 tsp pesto
50g/2oz smoked trout slices
4 round goat's cheese slices,
  each about 50g/2oz
salt and ground black pepper
cherry tomatoes and fresh basil,
  to serve

Preparation: 2 minutes; Cooking: 14 minutes

1 Preheat the oven to 200°C/400°F/Gas 6. Using a pastry cutter that is slightly larger than the goat's cheese rounds, cut a circle from each slice of bread.

2 Brush the bread rounds with a little olive oil, scatter with a few thyme leaves and season well. Place the bread rounds on a baking sheet and bake for 5 minutes or until crisp and a light golden colour, turning over once.

3 Remove the bread from the oven and spread 5ml/1 tsp pesto over half the rounds. Divide the smoked trout among the pesto-topped bread, top with the cheese rounds and season well with black pepper. Top the cheese with the remaining bread circles, sandwich-style.

4 Bake the toasties in the oven for 5 minutes more, until the cheese has just started to soften slightly. Remove from the oven, transfer to a platter and serve immediately with the cherry tomatoes and basil leaves.

> **Variation**
> *Thyme goes particularly well with goat's cheese but other strong herbs can be substituted. Try oregano, marjoram or sage for a completely different taste.*

Welsh Rarebit

The Welsh have always loved roasted cheese. In its simplest form Welsh Rarebit, Caws wedi pobi, would traditionally have consisted of a slice of bread and a large slice of hard cheese, each toasted in front of the open fire. Just before the cheese had a chance to soften too much, it was laid on top of the crisp bread and served.

Serves 2
2 thick slices bread
soft butter, for spreading
10ml/2 tsp ready-made mustard
  of your choice
100g/3¾oz Cheddar-style cheese
  such as Llanboidy, or crumbly
  cheese such as Caerphilly, sliced
ground black pepper
pinch of paprika or cayenne
  pepper
tomato wedges and basil leaves,
  to garnish (optional)

Preparation: 2 minutes; Cooking: 4–5 minutes

1 Put the bread on the rack of a grill (broiler) pan and put the pan under a hot grill until both sides are lightly toasted.

2 Spread one side of each slice of toast with butter and then a little mustard (or to taste). Top with cheese slices.

3 Put under the hot grill until the cheese is soft and bubbling and beginning to turn golden brown.

4 Sprinkle with a little black pepper and paprika or cayenne and serve immediately, garnished with tomato wedges and basil leaves (if using).

> **Variations**
> *• As an alternative method, use a mixture of cheeses, grated and stirred together with the butter and mustard before spreading them on the toast and grilling (broiling).*
> *• For another topping, melt 25g/1oz butter and stir in 15ml/1 tbsp plain (all-purpose) flour. After 1 minute, stir in 45ml/3 tbsp milk and 30ml/2 tbsp ale. Add 175g/6oz grated hard cheese and allow it to melt.*

Toasties Energy 402kcal/1685kJ; Protein 21.7g; Carbohydrate 30.1g, of which sugars 2.1g; Fat 22.6g, of which saturates 11.4g; Cholesterol 58mg; Calcium 225mg; Fibre 0.9g; Sodium 929mg.
Rarebit Energy 386kcal/1611kJ; Protein 18.4g; Carbohydrate 25.8g, of which sugars 1.4g; Fat 23.7g, of which saturates 13.5g; Cholesterol 59mg; Calcium 442mg; Fibre 0.8g; Sodium 652mg.

Grilled Aubergine

The combination of hot, spicy, sweet and fruity flavours in this Moroccan dish will have everyone asking for the recipe. Serve as an appetizer or for a light second course. This is a good dish for vegetarian guests who are bored with always being given the ubiquitous pasta with pesto.

Serves 4

2 aubergines (eggplants)
olive oil, for frying
2–3 garlic cloves, crushed
5cm/2in piece fresh root ginger,
    peeled and grated
5ml/1 tsp ground cumin
5ml/1 tsp harissa
75ml/5 tbsp clear honey
juice of 1 lemon
salt

Preparation: 2 minutes; Cooking: 15 minutes

1 Preheat the grill (broiler) or a griddle pan. Cut the aubergines lengthways into thick slices.

2 Brush each aubergine slice with olive oil and cook in a pan under the grill or in a griddle pan. Turn the slices so that they are lightly browned on both sides.

3 Meanwhile, in a wide frying pan, fry the garlic in a little olive oil for a few seconds, then stir in the ginger, cumin, harissa, honey and lemon juice.

4 Add enough water to thin the mixture, then add the aubergine slices. Cook for about 10 minutes, or until they have absorbed all the sauce.

5 Add a little extra water if necessary, season to taste with salt, and serve at room temperature, with chunks of fresh bread to mop up the juices.

Cook's Tip
Grilled (broiled) blood oranges make an excellent quick accompaniment to this dish. Dip the halves or quarters in icing (confectioners') sugar and grill until just about to blacken.

Green Curry Puffs

Shrimp paste and green curry sauce, used judiciously, give these puffs their distinctive spicy, savoury flavour, and the addition of chilli steps up the heat.

Makes 24

24 small wonton wrappers, about
    8cm/3¼in square, thawed
    if frozen
15ml/1 tbsp cornflour
    (cornstarch), mixed to a paste
    with 30ml/2 tbsp water
oil, for deep-frying

For the filling

1 small potato, about 115g/4oz,
    boiled and mashed
25g/1oz/3 tbsp cooked petits pois
    (baby peas)
25g/1oz/3 tbsp cooked corn
few sprigs fresh coriander
    (cilantro), chopped
1 small fresh red chilli, seeded
    and finely chopped
½ lemon grass stalk,
    finely chopped
15ml/1 tbsp soy sauce
5ml/1 tsp shrimp paste or
    fish sauce
5ml/1 tsp Thai green curry paste

Preparation: 3 minutes; Cooking: 17 minutes

1 Combine the mashed potato, peas, corn, coriander, chilli and lemon grass in a bowl. Stir in the soy sauce, shrimp paste or fish sauce and Thai green curry paste. Lay out one wonton wrapper on a board or clean work surface and place a teaspoon of the filling in the centre.

2 Brush a little of the cornflour paste along two sides of the square. Fold the other two sides over to meet them, then press together to make a triangular pastry and seal in the filling. Make more pastries in the same way.

3 Heat the oil in a wok to 190°C/375°F or until a cube of bread, added to the oil, browns in about 45 seconds. Add the pastries to the oil, a few at a time, and fry them for about 5 minutes, until golden brown.

4 Remove from the wok and drain on kitchen paper. If you intend serving the puffs hot, place them in a single layer on a serving plate in a low oven while cooking successive batches. The puffs also taste good cold.

Grilled Aubergine Energy 168kcal/701kJ; Protein 1g; Carbohydrate 16.5g, of which sugars 16.3g; Fat 11.4g, of which saturates 1.7g; Cholesterol 0mg; Calcium 11mg; Fibre 2g; Sodium 4mg.
Green Curry Puffs Energy 69Kcal/291kJ; Protein 1.4g; Carbohydrate 9.9g, of which sugars 0.4g; Fat 3g, of which saturates 0.4g; Cholesterol 1mg; Calcium 22mg; Fibre 0.5g; Sodium 58mg.

Thai Spring Rolls

Crunchy spring rolls are as popular in Thailand as in China. Everyone loves them.

Makes 24
4–6 Chinese dried mushrooms, soaked for 30 minutes
50g/2oz cellophane noodles
30ml/2 tbsp vegetable oil
2 garlic cloves, chopped
2 fresh red chillies, seeded and chopped
225g/8oz minced (ground) pork
50g/2oz cooked prawns (shrimp)
30ml/2 tbsp Thai fish sauce
5ml/1 tsp sugar

ground black pepper
1 carrot, grated
50g/2oz drained canned bamboo shoots, chopped
50g/2oz/1 cup beansprouts
2 spring onions (scallions), finely chopped
15ml/1 tbsp chopped fresh coriander (cilantro)
24 x 15cm/6in square spring roll wrappers
flour and water paste, for sealing rolls
vegetable oil, for deep-frying
Thai sweet chilli dipping sauce, to serve (optional)

Preparation: 10 minutes; Cooking: 10 minutes

1 Drain the mushrooms, discard the stems and chop the caps finely. Soak the noodles in boiling water for 10 minutes. Drain the noodles and chop them into 5cm/2in lengths.

2 Heat the oil in a wok, add the garlic and chillies and stir-fry for 30 seconds. Transfer to a plate. Add the pork to the wok and stir-fry until browned. Add the noodles, mushrooms and prawns. Stir in the fish sauce and sugar; season with pepper.

3 Tip the noodle mixture into a bowl and stir in the carrot, bamboo shoots, beansprouts, spring onions and chopped coriander together with the reserved chilli mixture.

4 Unwrap the spring roll wrappers. Place a spoonful of filling in the centre of each wrapper, turn up the bottom edge, fold in the sides, then roll up and seal with flour and water paste.

5 Heat the oil and fry the spring rolls until crisp and golden brown. Drain on kitchen paper and keep hot while cooking successive batches. Serve hot, with the sauce, if you like.

Breaded Sole Batons

Crisp, crumbed fish strips are almost as speedy as fish fingers, but much smarter.

Serves 4
275g/10oz lemon sole fillets, skinned
2 eggs

115g/4oz/2 cups fine fresh breadcrumbs
75g/3oz/3/4 cup plain (all-purpose) flour
salt and ground black pepper
oil, for frying
lemon wedges and tartare sauce, to serve

Preparation: 10–12 minutes; Cooking: 6–7 minutes

1 Cut the fish fillets into long diagonal strips each measuring about 2cm/3/4in wide.

2 Break the eggs into a shallow dish and beat well with a fork. Place the fresh breadcrumbs in another shallow dish. Put the flour in a large plastic bag and season with plenty of salt and ground black pepper. Shake to mix.

3 Dip the fish strips in the egg, turning to coat well. Place on a plate and then shake a few at a time in the bag of seasoned flour.

4 Dip the fish strips in the egg again and then in the breadcrumbs, turning to coat well. Place on a tray in a single layer, making sure that none of the breaded strips touches its neighbour. Let the coating set for at least 5 minutes.

5 Heat 1cm/1/2in oil in a large frying pan over medium-high heat. When the oil is hot (a cube of bread will sizzle) fry the fish strips in batches for about 2–2 1/2 minutes, turning once, taking care not to overcrowd the pan. Drain on kitchen paper and keep warm. Serve the fish on a platter, with the tartare sauce and lemon wedges.

> **Variation**
> Instead of lemon sole, use fillets of plaice (flounder) or cod. Pollock would also work well.

Thai Spring Rolls Energy 74kcal/310kJ; Protein 3.1g; Carbohydrate 7.2g, of which sugars 0.7g; Fat 3.8g, of which saturates 0.7g; Cholesterol 10mg; Calcium 13mg; Fibre 0.4g; Sodium 12mg.
Breaded Sole Batons Energy 334kcal/1405kJ; Protein 20.2g; Carbohydrate 36.9g, of which sugars 1g; Fat 12.9g, of which saturates 2.1g; Cholesterol 136mg; Calcium 90mg; Fibre 1.2g; Sodium 320mg.

Crab Dim Sum with Chinese Chives

These delectable Chinese-style dumplings have a wonderfully sticky texture and make a perfect appetizer. You can make these in advance, storing them in the refrigerator until ready to cook. Steam them just before serving, then enjoy the sensation as your teeth sink through the soft wrapper into the savoury crab filling.

Serves 4

150g/5oz fresh white crab meat
115g/4oz minced (ground) pork
30ml/2 tbsp chopped Chinese chives
15ml/1 tbsp finely chopped red (bell) pepper
30ml/2 tbsp sweet chilli sauce
30ml/2 tbsp hoisin sauce
24 fresh dumpling wrappers (available from Asian stores)
Chinese chives, to garnish
chilli oil and soy sauce, to serve

Preparation: 8 minutes; Cooking: 8–10 minutes

1 Place the crab meat, pork and chopped chives in a bowl. Add the red pepper and mix well, then pour in the sweet chilli and hoisin sauces. Stir until thoroughly combined.

2 Working with 2–3 wrappers at a time, put a spoonful of the mixture on to each wrapper. Brush the edges of a wrapper with water and fold over to form a half-moon shape. Press and pleat the edges to seal, and flatten. Cover with a clean, damp dish towel and make the rest.

3 Arrange the dumplings on three lightly oiled plates and fit inside three tiers of a bamboo steamer. Alternatively, use a stainless steel steamer or an electric steamer.

4 Cover the bamboo steamer and place over a wok of simmering water (making sure the water does not touch the steamer). Steam for 8–10 minutes, or until the dumplings are cooked through and become slightly translucent. If using an electric steamer follow the manufacturer's instructions.

5 Divide the dumplings among four plates. Garnish with Chinese chives and serve immediately with chilli oil and soy sauce for dipping.

Salmon & Scallop Brochettes

With their delicate colours and superb flavour, these salmon and scallop skewers are the perfect choice for a sophisticated al fresco lunch in the summer.

½ yellow (bell) pepper, seeded and cut into 8 squares
25g/1oz/2 tbsp butter
juice of ½ lemon
salt, ground white pepper and paprika

Serves 4

8 lemon grass stalks
225g/8oz salmon fillet, skinned
8 queen scallops, with their corals if possible
8 baby (pearl) onions, peeled and blanched

For the sauce

30ml/2 tbsp dry vermouth
50g/2oz/¼ cup butter
5ml/1 tsp chopped fresh tarragon

Preparation: 8 minutes; Cooking: 7–10 minutes

1 Preheat the grill (broiler) to medium-high. Cut off the top 7.5–10cm/3–4in of each lemon grass stalk. Reserve the bulb ends for another dish.

2 Cut the salmon into 12 x 2cm/¾in cubes. Thread the salmon, scallops, corals if available, onions and pepper squares on to the lemon grass and arrange the brochettes in a grill pan.

3 Melt the butter in a small pan, add the lemon juice and a pinch of paprika and then brush all over the brochettes. Grill (broil) the skewers for about 2–3 minutes on each side, turning and basting the brochettes every minute, until the fish and scallops are just cooked, but are still very juicy. Transfer to a platter and keep hot while you make the tarragon butter sauce.

4 Pour the dry vermouth and all the leftover cooking juices from the brochettes into a small pan and boil quite fiercely to reduce by half.

5 Add the butter and melt, stirring constantly. Stir in the chopped fresh tarragon and add salt and ground white pepper to taste. Pour the butter sauce over the brochettes and serve.

Crab Dim Sum Energy 166kcal/700kJ; Protein 14.7g; Carbohydrate 20.5g, of which sugars 1.4g; Fat 3.3g, of which saturates 1.1g; Cholesterol 46mg; Calcium 83mg; Fibre 0.8g; Sodium 287mg.
Brochettes Energy 333kcal/1384kJ; Protein 23.9g; Carbohydrate 7.4g, of which sugars 4.4g; Fat 22.5g, of which saturates 11.1g; Cholesterol 92mg; Calcium 45mg; Fibre 1.1g; Sodium 232mg.

Whitefish Salad with Toasted Bagels

A traditional deli favourite, smoked whitefish makes a superb salad. If you can't find it, use smoked halibut, but don't pass up the bagels, which are the perfect accompaniment.

Serves 4–6

1 smoked whitefish or halibut, skinned and boned
2 celery sticks, chopped
½ red, white or yellow onion or 3–5 spring onions (scallions), chopped
45ml/3 tbsp mayonnaise
45ml/3 tbsp sour cream
juice of ½–1 lemon
1 round lettuce
ground black pepper
5–10ml/1–2 tsp chopped fresh parsley, to garnish
toasted bagels, to serve

Preparation: 8–10 minutes; Cooking: 0 minutes

1 Break the smoked fish into bitesize pieces. In a bowl, combine the chopped celery, onion or spring onion, mayonnaise and sour cream, and add lemon juice to taste.

2 Fold the fish into the mixture and season with pepper. Arrange the lettuce leaves on serving plates, then spoon the smoked fish salad on top. Sprinkle with parsley and serve with the toasted bagels.

Cook's Tip
Smoked whitefish is a product you are more likely to come across in the United States or Canada than in the UK. The fish is related to char and grayling and is a member of the salmon family. The flesh is soft and oily, with a mild flavour. As the introduction to the recipe suggests, smoked halibut can be used instead, or you could substitute smoked trout. Mackerel would have too dominant a flavour and is not as suitable. If buying smoked fish direct from the smokehouse, use it as quickly as possible; if you have purchased it at the supermarket in a vacuum pack, check the use-by date. Smoked fish can be frozen in the original packaging for up to 1 month.

Tuna Melt Muffins

Take a tip from the Americans and try this delicious and nutritious snack consisting of wholemeal muffins topped with tuna and hot bubbling cheese. Use wholemeal toast in place of the muffins, if you like.

Serves 2

200g/7oz can tuna, drained and flaked
1 spring onion (scallion), chopped
1 small celery stick, chopped
15ml/1 tbsp chopped canned pimiento or 1 medium tomato, chopped
30ml/2 tbsp mayonnaise
generous pinch of dried oregano or marjoram
2 wholemeal muffins, split
65g/2½ oz mature Monterey Jack or Cheddar cheese, coarsely grated or sliced
8 pimiento- or anchovy-stuffed olives, sliced
salt and ground black pepper

Preparation: 6 minutes; Cooking: 3–4 minutes

1 Mix the tuna with the spring onion, celery, pimiento or tomato, mayonnaise and oregano or marjoram. Stir in salt and pepper to taste, then set aside.

2 Preheat the grill (broiler) and toast the cut side of the muffins until they are golden and slightly crisp.

3 Spoon a quarter of the tuna mixture on to each muffin half, then top with the cheese and stuffed olive slices. Grill (broil) until the cheese has melted and is bubbling. There is no need to brown the cheese. Serve hot, sprinkled with more pepper.

Variations
• *Melts have become increasingly popular and often feature on snack bar menus. In this version, muffins form the base, but baps or bread rolls, split in half, could be used instead.*
• *Tuna is frequently used for the topping, but cooked chicken or turkey also make a good melt. Use the white breast meat only, and cut it into bitesize pieces before mixing it with the mayonnaise and flavouring ingredients.*

Whitefish Salad Energy 108kcal/450kJ; Protein 7.8g; Carbohydrate 1.6g, of which sugars 1.3g; Fat 7.9g, of which saturates 1.9g; Cholesterol 22mg; Calcium 29mg; Fibre 0.4g; Sodium 64mg.
Tuna Muffins Energy 567kcal/2356kJ; Protein 22.3g; Carbohydrate 23.3g, of which sugars 1.6g; Fat 42.8g, of which saturates 15.5g; Cholesterol 96mg; Calcium 231mg; Fibre 3.2g; Sodium 832mg.

Salmon Tortilla Cones

Whether you're snuggling up on the sofa to watch a late-night movie or catering for a crowd, these simple yet sophisticated wraps are irresistible.

Serves 4

115g/4oz/½ cup soft white (farmer's) cheese
30ml/2 tbsp roughly chopped fresh dill
juice of 1 lemon
1 small red onion
15ml/1 tbsp drained bottled capers
30ml/2 tbsp extra virgin olive oil
30ml/2 tbsp roughly chopped fresh flat leaf parsley
115g/4oz smoked salmon
8 small or 4 large wheat flour tortillas
salt and ground black pepper
lemon wedges, for squeezing

Preparation: 8–10 minutes; Cooking: 0 minutes

1 Place the soft cheese in a small bowl and mix in half the chopped dill. Add a little salt and pepper and just a dash of the lemon juice to taste. Put the remaining lemon juice in a fairly large bowl and set it aside.

2 Finely chop the red onion. Add the chopped onion, drained capers and olive oil to the lemon juice in the bowl. Add the chopped flat leaf parsley and the remaining dill and stir gently. Set aside for 5 minutes to give the ingredients a chance to infuse. The lemon will soften the onion a little.

3 Cut the smoked salmon into short, thin strips, and add to the red onion mixture. Toss to mix. Season to taste with plenty of pepper.

4 If using small tortillas, leave them whole, but large ones need to be cut in half so that they can be rolled into cones. Spread a little of the soft cheese mixture on each piece of tortilla and top with the smoked salmon mixture.

5 Roll up the tortillas into cones and secure with wooden cocktail sticks (toothpicks). Arrange on a serving plate and add some lemon wedges, for squeezing. Serve immediately. The tortillas are eaten in the hand; supply wipes for sticky fingers.

Anchovy & Quail's Egg Bruschetta

Quail's eggs taste marvellous with the anchovies and mild red onion slices, especially when the mixture is piled on toasted ciabatta which has been rubbed with fresh garlic to add flavour.

Serves 4–6

50g/2oz anchovy fillets in salt
milk, for soaking
12 quail's eggs
2–3 garlic cloves
1 ciabatta or similar loaf
coarse salt
1 red onion, halved and thinly sliced
10–15ml/2–3 tsp cumin seeds, roasted and ground
a small bunch of flat leaf parsley, roughly chopped
30–45ml/2–3 tbsp olive oil

Preparation: 15 minutes; Cooking: 3–5 minutes

1 Soak the anchovies in a shallow bowl of milk for 15 minutes to reduce the salty flavour.

2 Meanwhile, put the quail's eggs in a pan of cold water. Bring to the boil and cook for 2 minutes, then drain and plunge into cold water.

3 Remove the skin from the garlic cloves, halve, and crush using a pestle and mortar.

4 Preheat the grill (broiler) on the hottest setting. Slice the loaf of bread horizontally in half and toast the cut sides until golden.

5 Rub the toasted bread all over with the crushed garlic and sprinkle with a little salt. Don't overdo this, as the anchovies will be quite salty.

6 Cut each piece of bread into four or six equal pieces. Drain the quail's eggs, shell them and cut them in half. Drain the anchovy fillets.

7 Pile the onion slices, quail's egg halves and anchovy fillets on the pieces of bread. Sprinkle liberally with the ground roasted cumin and chopped parsley and serve immediately.

Tortilla Cones Energy 374kcal/1576kJ; Protein 16.6g; Carbohydrate 53.2g, of which sugars 3g; Fat 12g, of which saturates 3.6g; Cholesterol 22mg; Calcium 128mg; Fibre 2.9g; Sodium 783mg.
Bruschetta Energy 181kcal/761kJ; Protein 8.8g; Carbohydrate 18.2g, of which sugars 1.7g; Fat 8.6g, of which saturates 1.6g; Cholesterol 100mg; Calcium 87mg; Fibre 1g; Sodium 543mg.

Sardines & Tomatoes on Focaccia

Fresh sardines have a lovely flavour and texture, are cheap to buy and cook quickly.

Serves 4
20 cherry tomatoes
45ml/3 tbsp herb-infused olive oil
12 fresh sardine fillets
1 focaccia loaf
salt and ground black pepper

Preparation: 3–4 minutes; Cooking: 15 minutes

1 Preheat the oven to 190°C/375°F/Gas 5. Put the cherry tomatoes in a small roasting pan and drizzle 30ml/2 tbsp of the herb-infused olive oil over the top.

2 Season the tomatoes with salt and pepper and roast for 10–15 minutes, shaking the pan gently once or twice so that the tomatoes cook evenly on all sides. When they are tender and slightly charred, remove from the oven and set aside.

3 While the tomatoes are cooking, preheat the grill (broiler) to high. Brush the sardine fillets with the remaining oil and lay them on a baking sheet. Grill (broil) for 4–5 minutes on each side, until cooked through.

4 Split the focaccia in half horizontally and cut each piece in half again to give four equal pieces. Toast the cut side under the grill.

5 Top with the sardines and tomatoes and an extra drizzle of oil. Season with black pepper and serve.

> **Variations**
> • This rather sumptuous topping tastes great on focaccia, but a split French stick would work just as well.
> • Slice some cold boiled potatoes and fry them quickly in oil while the sardines are cooking. Abandon the bread and pile the sardines and tomatoes on the potatoes.

Roast Chicken Pitta Pockets

Families often have to eat in relays: a parent is going to be home late; one child has a music lesson; another is off to the skate park. This serve-anytime snack will suit the lot.

Makes 6
1 small cucumber, peeled and diced
3 tomatoes, peeled, seeded and chopped
2 spring onions (scallions), chopped
30ml/2 tbsp olive oil
a small bunch of flat leaf parsley, finely chopped
a small bunch of mint, finely chopped
½ preserved lemon, finely chopped
45–60ml/3–4 tbsp tahini
juice of 1 lemon
2 garlic cloves, crushed
6 pitta breads
½ small roast chicken or 2 large roast chicken breasts, cut into strips
salt and ground black pepper

Preparation: 12–14 minutes; Cooking: 2 minutes

1 Place the cucumber in a sieve (strainer) over a bowl, sprinkle with a little salt and leave for 5 minutes to drain. Rinse well and drain, then place in a bowl with the tomatoes and spring onions. Stir in the olive oil, parsley, mint and preserved lemon. Season well.

2 In a small bowl, mix the tahini with the lemon juice, then thin the mixture down with a little water to the consistency of thick double (heavy) cream. Beat in the garlic and season.

3 Preheat the grill (broiler) to hot. Lightly toast the pitta breads well away from the heat source until they puff up. (Alternatively, lightly toast the breads in a toaster.) Open the breads and stuff them liberally with the chicken and salad. Drizzle tahini sauce into each one and serve with any extra salad.

> **Cook's Tip**
> The chicken in these pitta breads can be hot or cold – either roast a small bird specially or use up the leftovers from a large roast chicken.

Focaccia Energy 301kcal/1262kJ; Protein 15.8g; Carbohydrate 27.6g, of which sugars 3.1g; Fat 15g, of which saturates 2.9g; Cholesterol 0mg; Calcium 106mg; Fibre 1.7g; Sodium 334mg.
Pitta Pockets Energy 337kcal/1419kJ; Protein 21g; Carbohydrate 43.5g, of which sugars 4.4g; Fat 9.9g, of which saturates 1.5g; Cholesterol 35mg; Calcium 182mg; Fibre 3.5g; Sodium 369mg.

Dates Stuffed with Chorizo

This is a delicious combination from Spain, using fresh dates and spicy chorizo sausage, wrapped in bacon and encased in breadcrumbs so that all the flavour is sealed in. When the snacks are fried, the coating becomes crisp and crunchy; a lovely contrast to the squidgy dates inside.

Serves 4–6
50g/2oz chorizo sausage
12 fresh dates, stoned
6 streaky (fatty) bacon slices
oil, for frying
plain (all-purpose) flour, for dusting
1 egg, beaten
50g/2oz/1 cup fresh breadcrumbs

Preparation: 6 minutes; Cooking: 2–4 minutes

1 Trim the ends of the chorizo sausage and then peel away the skin. Cut into three 2cm/¾in slices. Cut these in half lengthways, then into quarters, giving 12 pieces.

2 Stuff each date with a piece of chorizo, closing the date around it. Stretch the bacon, by running the back of a knife along the rasher.

3 Cut each rasher in half, widthways. Wrap a piece of bacon around each date and hold in place securely with a wooden cocktail stick (toothpick).

4 In a deep pan, heat 1cm/½in of oil. Dust the dates with flour, dip them in the beaten egg, then coat in breadcrumbs. Fry the dates in the hot oil, turning them, until golden. Remove the dates with a draining spoon, and drain on kitchen paper. Serve at once.

> **Variation**
> *For a vegetarian version of this tasty snack, omit the chorizo and stuff the dates with pecan nuts or brazil nuts (halved lengthways if necessary). Omit the bacon – just coat the stuffed dates in egg and breadcrumbs and fry them as detailed in the recipe. This is good with pre-dinner drinks.*

Pork on Lemon Grass Sticks

These make a substantial snack, either on their own or as part of a barbecue menu. The lemon grass sticks not only add a subtle flavour but are also a good talking point.

Serves 4
300g/11oz/1½ cups minced (ground) pork
4 garlic cloves, crushed
4 fresh coriander (cilantro) roots, finely chopped
2.5ml/½ tsp granulated white sugar
15ml/1 tbsp soy sauce or kecap manis
salt and ground black pepper
8 x 10cm/4in lengths lemon grass stalk
sweet chilli sauce, to serve

Preparation: 6 minutes; Cooking: 6–8 minutes

1 Place the minced pork, crushed garlic, chopped coriander root, sugar and soy sauce or kecap manis in a large bowl. Season with salt and pepper to taste and mix well.

2 Divide into eight portions and mould each one into a ball. It may help to dampen your hands before shaping the mixture to prevent it from sticking.

3 Stick a length of lemon grass halfway into each ball, then press the meat mixture around the lemon grass to make a shape like a chicken leg.

4 Cook the pork sticks under a hot grill (broiler) for 3–4 minutes on each side, until golden and cooked through.

5 Serve with chilli sauce or sambal for dipping.

> **Variations**
> *• Slimmer versions of these pork sticks are perfect for parties. The mixture will be enough for 12 lemon grass sticks if you use it sparingly.*
> *• Sweet and sour sauce can be used instead of sweet chilli sauce, or try a peach chutney.*

Dates with Chorizo Energy 204kcal/851kJ; Protein 6g; Carbohydrate 17.9g, of which sugars 10.8g; Fat 12.6g, of which saturates 3.1g; Cholesterol 46mg; Calcium 29mg; Fibre 0.8g; Sodium 355mg.
Pork Sticks Energy 132kcal/552kJ; Protein 14.7g; Carbohydrate 2g, of which sugars 1.6g; Fat 7.3g, of which saturates 2.7g; Cholesterol 50mg; Calcium 10mg; Fibre 0.2g; Sodium 317mg.

Mexican Tortas

The greatest thing about hollowing out a bread roll is that you can pack in more filling. This Mexican snack uses roast pork and refried beans but any other fillings can be used.

Serves 4

2 fresh jalapeño chillies
juice of ½ lime
2 French bread rolls or 2 pieces French bread
75g/3oz/⅔ cup canned refried beans
150g/5oz roast pork
2 small tomatoes, sliced
115g/4oz Cheddar or Monterey Jack cheese, sliced
a small bunch of fresh coriander (cilantro)
30ml/2 tbsp crème fraîche

Preparation: 5–6 minutes; Cooking: 0 minutes

1 Cut the chillies in half, scrape out the seeds, then cut the flesh into thin strips. Put it in a bowl and pour in the lime juice.

2 If using rolls, slice them in half and remove some of the crumbs so that they are slightly hollowed. If using French bread, slice each piece in half lengthways.

3 Set the top of each piece of bread or roll aside and spread the bottom halves with a nice thick layer of the refried beans. Make sure the paste is evenly spread, as it will help to hold the next layer in place.

4 Cut the pork into thin shreds and put these on top of the refried beans. Top with the tomato slices. Drain the jalapeño strips and put them on top of the tomato slices. Add the cheese and sprinkle with coriander leaves.

5 Turn the top halves of the bread or rolls over so that the cut sides are uppermost, and spread these with crème fraîche. Sandwich back together again and serve.

> **Variation**
> Use sliced gammon or honey-glazed ham instead of roast pork.

Steak Ciabatta with Hummus

Packed with garlicky hummus and a mustard-seasoned dressing on the crunchy salad, these steak sandwiches are just right for lunch on the patio.

Serves 4

3 garlic cloves, crushed to a paste with enough salt to season the steaks
30ml/2 tbsp extra virgin olive oil
4 sirloin steaks, 2.5cm/1in thick, total weight about 900g/2lb
2 romaine lettuce hearts
4 small ciabatta breads
salt and ground black pepper

For the dressing
10ml/2 tsp Dijon mustard
5ml/1 tsp cider or white wine vinegar
15ml/1 tbsp olive oil

For the hummus
400g/14oz can chickpeas, drained and rinsed
45ml/3 tbsp tahini
2 garlic cloves, crushed
juice of 1 lemon
30ml/2 tbsp water

Preparation: 5 minutes; Cooking: 6–9 minutes

1 To make the hummus, place the chickpeas in a large bowl and mash to a paste. Add the tahini, garlic, lemon juice, salt and pepper. Stir in the water. Mash together well.

2 Make a dressing by mixing the mustard and vinegar in a jar. Add the oil and season to taste. Shake well.

3 Mix the garlic and oil in a dish. Add the steaks and rub the mixture into both surfaces.

4 Preheat the grill (broiler). Cook the steaks on a rack in a grill pan. For rare meat, allow 2 minutes on one side and 3 minutes on the second side. For medium steaks, allow 4 minutes on each side. Transfer to a plate, cover and set aside to rest for 2 minutes.

5 Dress the lettuce. Split each ciabatta and heat on the grill rack for a minute. Fill with hummus, the steaks and leaves. Cut each in half and serve immediately, just as they are.

Tortas Energy 307kcal/1285kJ; Protein 22.8g; Carbohydrate 18.2g, of which sugars 2.9g; Fat 15.8g, of which saturates 9.4g; Cholesterol 78mg; Calcium 271mg; Fibre 2g; Sodium 485mg.
Ciabatta Energy 765kcal/3210kJ; Protein 69.8g; Carbohydrate 55.2g, of which sugars 2.8g; Fat 30.8g, of which saturates 7.4g; Cholesterol 115mg; Calcium 222mg; Fibre 6.7g; Sodium 783mg.

Mexican Tacos

Ready-made taco shells make perfect edible containers for shredded salad, meat fillings, grated cheese and sour cream. This is an excellent choice for a quick supper.

Serves 4

15ml/1 tbsp olive oil
250g/9oz lean minced (ground) beef or turkey
2 garlic cloves, crushed
5ml/1 tsp ground cumin
5–10ml/1–2 tsp mild chilli powder
8 ready-made taco shells
1/2 small iceberg lettuce, shredded
1 small onion, thinly sliced
2 tomatoes, chopped in chunks
1 avocado, stoned (pitted) and sliced
60ml/4 tbsp sour cream
125g/4oz/1 cup crumbled queso blanco or anejado, or grated Cheddar or Monterey Jack cheese
salt and ground black pepper

Preparation: 8 minutes; Cooking: 8 minutes

1 Heat the oil in a frying pan. Add the meat, with the garlic and spices, and brown over medium heat, stirring frequently to break up any lumps. Season with salt and ground black pepper, cook for 5 minutes, then set aside to cool slightly.

2 Meanwhile, warm the taco shells according to the instructions on the packet. Do not let them get too crisp.

3 Spoon the lettuce, onion, tomatoes and avocado slices into the taco shells. Top with the sour cream followed by the minced beef or turkey mixture.

4 Sprinkle the crumbled or grated cheese into the tacos and serve immediately. Tacos are eaten with the fingers, so have plenty of paper napkins to hand, and wipes or finger bowls filled with warm water.

> **Cook's Tip**
> Stir-fried strips of turkey, chicken or pork are excellent instead of the minced (ground) beef or turkey.

Steak & Blue Cheese on Ciabatta

Many people prefer their steaks cooked quite rare in the centre, but they are still delicious if cooked a little longer. Add a couple of minutes to the cooking time if necessary, but do not let the meat dry out.

Serves 2

1 part-baked ciabatta bread
2 ribeye steaks, about 200g/7oz each
15ml/1 tbsp olive oil
115g/4oz Gorgonzola cheese, sliced
salt and ground black pepper

Preparation: 2–3 minutes; Cooking: 12–14 minutes

1 Bake the ciabatta according to the instructions on the packet. Remove from the oven, wrap in foil to keep warm, and leave to rest while you cook the steak.

2 Heat a griddle pan until hot. Brush the steaks with the olive oil and lay them on the griddle pan. Cook for 2–3 minutes on each side, depending on the thickness of the steaks.

3 Remove the steaks and set them aside to rest. Meanwhile, cut the loaf in half and split each half horizontally.

4 Cut the steaks in half lengthways so each is only half as thick as before. Moisten the bread with the pan juices then make into sandwiches using the steak and cheese. Season well and serve on a platter or individual plates.

> **Variation**
> Gorgonzola is particularly good in this ciabatta sandwich, but St Agur would also work well. For a milder flavour, use Cambozola.

> **Cook's Tip**
> Part-baked bread cooks in about 8 minutes in a hot oven, but if even that is too long, just warm a regular baked ciabatta or French stick.

Steak Energy 767kcal/3221kJ; Protein 66g; Carbohydrate 52g, of which sugars 3.1g; Fat 34.2g, of which saturates 15.8g; Cholesterol 161mg; Calcium 410mg; Fibre 2.3g; Sodium 1360mg.
Mexican Tacos Energy 497Kcal/2067kJ; Protein 25.4g; Carbohydrate 19.4g, of which sugars 3.8g; Fat 35.1g, of which saturates 14.3g; Cholesterol 74mg; Calcium 305mg; Fibre 3.6g; Sodium 511mg.

Grilled Swordfish Skewers

This delicious skewered and grilled swordfish dish is cooked with olive oil, garlic and oregano. In Greece it is known as souvlakia.

Serves 4

2 red onions, quartered
2 red or green (bell) peppers, quartered and seeded

20–24 thick cubes of swordfish, 675–800g/1 1/2–1 3/4lb in total
lemon wedges, to garnish

For the basting sauce
75ml/5 tbsp extra virgin olive oil
1 garlic clove, crushed
large pinch of dried oregano or marjoram
salt and ground black pepper

Preparation: 10 minutes; Cooking: 8–10 minutes

1 Carefully separate the onion quarters into pieces, each composed of two or three layers. Slice each pepper quarter in half widthways, or into thirds if you have very large peppers.

2 Make the souvlakia by threading five or six pieces of swordfish on to each of four long metal skewers, alternating with pieces of the pepper and onion. Lay the souvlakia across a grill (broiling) pan and set aside while you make the sauce.

3 Whisk the olive oil, crushed garlic and oregano or marjoram in a bowl. Add salt and pepper, and whisk again. Brush the souvlakia generously on all sides with the basting sauce.

4 Preheat the grill (broiler) to the highest setting, or prepare a barbecue. Slide the grill pan or roasting tray underneath the grill or transfer the skewers to the barbecue, making sure that they are not too close to the heat.

5 Cook for 8–10 minutes, turning the skewers several times and brushing them with the basting sauce to increase the flavours, until the fish is cooked and the peppers and onions have begun to scorch around the edges.

6 Serve the souvlakia immediately with a salad of cucumber, red onion and fresh olives and garnished with one or two wedges of lemon.

Griddled Swordfish with Tomatoes

Slow-roasting the tomatoes is a great technique when you are entertaining as they need no last-minute attention, but a much quicker way is simply to grill them instead.

Serves 4

1kg/2 1/4lb large vine or plum tomatoes, peeled, halved and seeded
5–10ml/1–2 tsp ground cinnamon

a pinch of saffron threads
15ml/1 tbsp orange flower water
60ml/4 tbsp olive oil
45–60ml/3–4 tbsp caster (superfine) sugar
4 x 225g/8oz swordfish steaks
rind of 1/2 preserved lemon, finely chopped
a small bunch of fresh coriander (cilantro), finely chopped or 15ml/1 tbsp chopped fresh dill
a handful of blanched almonds
a knob (pat) of butter
salt and ground black pepper

Preparation: 4 minutes; Cooking: 12 minutes

1 Sprinkle the halved tomatoes with the cinnamon, saffron and orange flower water. Trickle half the oil over, being sure to moisten every tomato half, and sprinkle with sugar. Place under a medium grill (broiler) for 10 minutes.

2 Brush the remaining oil over the swordfish steaks and season.

3 Lightly oil a pre-heated cast-iron griddle and cook the steaks for 3–4 minutes on each side. Sprinkle the chopped preserved lemon and chopped coriander or dill over the steaks towards the end of the cooking time. Do not let the herbs char.

4 In a separate pan, fry the almonds in the butter until golden. Sprinkle them over the tomatoes. Serve the steaks immediately with the tomatoes.

Variation
For slow-roasted tomatoes, preheat the oven to 110°C/225°F/ Gas 1/4. Place the tray in the bottom of the oven and cook the tomatoes for about 3 hours, then leave them to cool.

Skewers Energy 363Kcal/1,511kJ; Protein 32.2g; Carbohydrate 11.5g, of which sugars 9.6g; Fat 21.2g, of which saturates 3.6g; Cholesterol 69mg; Calcium 33mg; Fibre 2.5g; Sodium 225mg.
Griddled Swordfish Energy 405kcal/1696kJ; Protein 42.3g; Carbohydrate 7.8g, of which sugars 7.8g; Fat 23g, of which saturates 5.2g; Cholesterol 98mg; Calcium 27mg; Fibre 2.5g; Sodium 330mg.

Warm Swordfish & Rocket Salad

Swordfish is robust enough to take the sharp flavours of rocket and Pecorino cheese. The fish can be dry, so don't skip the marinating stage unless you're really pushed.

Serves 4
4 swordfish steaks, about 175g/6oz each

75ml/5 tbsp extra virgin olive oil, plus extra for serving
juice of 1 lemon
30ml/2 tbsp finely chopped fresh parsley
115g/4oz rocket (arugula) leaves, stalks removed
115g/4oz Pecorino cheese
salt and ground black pepper

Preparation: 7 minutes; Cooking: 8–12 minutes

1 Lay the swordfish steaks in a shallow dish. Mix 60ml/4 tbsp of the olive oil with the lemon juice. Pour over the fish. Season, sprinkle with parsley and turn the fish to coat. Cover the dish and leave to marinate for 5 minutes.

2 Heat a ridged griddle pan or the grill (broiler) until very hot. Take the fish out of the marinade and pat it dry with kitchen paper.

3 Grill (broil) two steaks at a time for 2–3 minutes on each side until the swordfish is just cooked, but still juicy.

4 Meanwhile, put the rocket leaves in a bowl and season with a little salt and plenty of pepper. Add the remaining 15ml/1 tbsp olive oil and toss well.

5 Place the swordfish steaks on four individual plates and arrange a little pile of salad on each steak. Shave the Pecorino over the top. Serve extra olive oil separately so it can be drizzled over the swordfish.

> **Variation**
> *Tuna, shark or marlin steaks would be equally good in this delicious fish salad, with its sophisticated flavours.*

Swordfish Tacos

It is important not to overcook swordfish, or it can be tough and dry. Cooked correctly, however, it is absolutely delicious and makes a great change from beef or chicken as a taco filling. The mixture is also very good in warmed pitta breads. Slit them and open them out to make pockets, place a little shredded lettuce in each and fill with the swordfish mixture.

Serves 6
3 swordfish steaks
30ml/2 tbsp vegetable oil
2 garlic cloves, crushed
1 small onion, chopped
3 fresh green chillies, seeded and chopped
3 tomatoes
small bunch of fresh coriander (cilantro), chopped
6 fresh corn tortillas
1/2 iceberg lettuce, shredded
salt and ground black pepper
lemon wedges, to serve (optional)

Preparation: 7–10 minutes; Cooking: 10–13 minutes

1 Preheat the grill (broiler). Put the swordfish on an oiled rack over a grill pan and grill (broil) for 2–3 minutes on each side. When cool enough to handle, remove the skin and flake the fish into a bowl.

2 Heat the oil in a pan. Add the garlic, onion and chillies and fry for 5 minutes or until the onion is soft and translucent. Do not let the onion burn or it will taste bitter.

3 Cut a cross in the base of each tomato and pour over boiling water. After 3 minutes lift out the tomatoes and plunge them into cold water. Remove the skins and seeds and chop the flesh into 1cm/½in dice.

4 Add the tomatoes and swordfish to the onion mixture. Cook for 5 minutes over a low heat. Add the coriander and cook for 1–2 minutes. Season to taste.

5 Wrap the tortillas in foil and steam on a plate over boiling water until pliable. Place some shredded lettuce and fish mixture on each tortilla. Fold in half and serve with lemon wedges, if you like.

Warm Salad Energy 452kcal/1880kJ; Protein 43.6g; Carbohydrate 0.5g, of which sugars 0.4g; Fat 30.6g, of which saturates 9.5g; Cholesterol 101mg; Calcium 401mg; Fibre 0.6g; Sodium 581mg.
Tacos Energy 293kcal/1236kJ; Protein 22.7g; Carbohydrate 33.2g, of which sugars 3.7g; Fat 8.6g, of which saturates 1.4g; Cholesterol 41mg; Calcium 77mg; Fibre 2.1g; Sodium 276mg.

Red Snapper Burritos

Fish makes a great filling for a tortilla, especially when it is succulent red snapper.

Serves 6

3 red snapper fillets
90g/3½ oz/½ cup long grain
  white rice
30ml/2 tbsp vegetable oil
1 small onion, finely chopped
5ml/1 tsp ground achiote seed
  (annatto powder)

1 pasilla or similar dried chilli,
  seeded and ground
75g/3oz/¾ cup slivered almonds
200g/7oz can chopped tomatoes
  in tomato juice
150g/5oz/1¼ cups grated
  Monterey Jack or mild
  Cheddar cheese
8 x 20cm/8in wheat flour tortillas
fresh flat-leaf parsley to garnish
lime wedges (optional)

Preparation: 4–5 minutes; Cooking: 14 minutes

1 Preheat the grill (broiler). Grill the fish on an oiled rack for about 5 minutes, turning once. When cool, remove the skin and flake the fish into a bowl. Set it aside.

2 Meanwhile, put the rice in a pan, cover with cold water, cover and bring to the boil. Drain, rinse and drain again.

3 Heat the oil in a pan and fry the onion until soft and translucent. Stir in the ground achiote (annatto powder) and the chilli and cook for 5 minutes.

4 Add the rice, stir well, then stir in the fish and almonds. Add the tomatoes, with their juice. Cook over a moderate heat until the juice is absorbed and the rice is tender. Stir in the cheese and remove from the heat.

5 Wrap the tortillas in foil and warm them in a low oven, or wrap them in a clean dish towel, separating the individual tortillas with clear film (plastic wrap) and warm the package in the microwave. They will take about 1 minute on High.

6 Divide the filling among the tortillas and fold them to make neat parcels. Garnish with fresh parsley and serve with lime wedges, if liked. A green salad makes a good accompaniment.

Red Snapper with Fresh Coriander & Almonds

Fried almonds are a standard accompaniment for trout but are equally good with red snapper, a fish that is very popular.

Serves 4

75g/3oz/¾ cup plain
  (all-purpose) flour
4 red snapper fillets

salt and ground black pepper
75g/3oz/6 tbsp butter
15ml/1 tbsp vegetable oil
75g/3oz/¾ cup flaked
  (sliced) almonds
grated rind and juice of 1 lime
small bunch of fresh coriander
  (cilantro), finely chopped
boiled rice and warm wheat flour
  tortillas, to serve

Preparation: 4 minutes; Cooking: 8–10 minutes

1 Preheat the oven to 140°C/275°F/Gas 1. Spread out the flour in a shallow dish and add seasoning. Dry the fish fillets with kitchen paper, then coat each fillet in the seasoned flour.

2 Heat the butter and oil in a frying pan. Add the snapper fillets, in batches if necessary, and cook for 2 minutes. Turn the fillets over carefully and cook the other side until golden.

3 Using a fish slice, carefully transfer the fillets to a shallow dish and keep them warm in the oven. Add the almonds to the fat remaining and fry them for 3–4 minutes, until golden.

4 Add the lime rind, juice and coriander to the almonds in the frying pan and stir well. Heat through for 1–2 minutes, then pour the mixture over the fish. Serve with a bowl of rice or with warm wheat flour tortillas.

Cook's Tip
Warm the tortillas by wrapping them in foil and steaming them on a plate over boiling water for a few minutes. Alternatively, wrap them in microwave-safe film and heat them in a microwave on full power for about 1 minute.

Burritos Energy 224kcal/935kJ; Protein 17.1g; Carbohydrate 11.3g, of which sugars 1.7g; Fat 11.9g, of which saturates 4.6g; Cholesterol 41mg; Calcium 172mg; Fibre 1.1g; Sodium 178mg.
Red Snapper Energy 433kcal/1803kJ; Protein 25.4g; Carbohydrate 16g, of which sugars 1.2g; Fat 30.2g, of which saturates 11.3g; Cholesterol 77mg; Calcium 115mg; Fibre 2g; Sodium 194mg.

Seared Tuna Steaks with Watercress Salad

Tuna steaks are wonderful seared and served slightly rare with a punchy sauce and watercress salad.

Serves 4
30ml/2 tbsp olive oil
5ml/1 tsp harissa
5ml/1 tsp clear honey
4 x 200g/7oz tuna steaks
salt and ground black pepper
lemon wedges, to serve

For the salad
30ml/2 tbsp olive oil
a little butter
25g/1oz fresh root ginger, peeled
    and thinly sliced
2 garlic cloves, finely sliced
2 fresh green chillies, seeded and
    thinly sliced
6 spring onions (scallions), cut into
    bitesize pieces
2 large handfuls watercress
1 lemon, cut into 4 wedges

Preparation: 6 minutes; Cooking: 10 minutes

1 Mix the olive oil, harissa, honey and salt, and rub it over the tuna steaks. Heat a frying pan, grease it with a little oil and sear the tuna steaks for about 2 minutes on each side. They should still be pink on the inside.

2 Keep the tuna warm while you quickly prepare the salad: heat the olive oil and butter in a heavy pan. Stir in the ginger, garlic, chillies and spring onions, cook until the mixture begins to colour, then add the watercress. As soon as the watercress begins to wilt, toss in the lemon juice and season well with salt and plenty of ground black pepper.

3 Tip the warm salad on to a serving dish or individual plates. Slice the tuna steaks and arrange on top of the salad. Serve immediately with lemon wedges for squeezing over.

> **Cook's Tip**
> *Harissa is a North African spice paste based on chillies, garlic, coriander and cumin seeds. It is sold in tubes, like tomato purée (paste), or jars, or can be made fresh.*

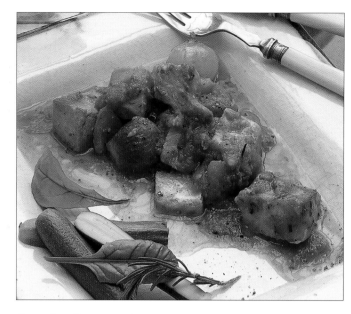

Fresh Tuna & Tomato Stew

A deliciously simple Italian recipe that relies on good basic ingredients: fresh fish, tomatoes and herbs. For an authentic flavour, serve with polenta or pasta.

Serves 4
12 baby (pearl) onions, peeled
900g/2lb ripe tomatoes
675g/1½lb tuna
45ml/3 tbsp olive oil

2 garlic cloves, crushed
45ml/3 tbsp chopped fresh herbs
2 bay leaves
2.5ml/½ tsp caster
    (superfine) sugar
30ml/2 tbsp sun-dried tomato
    purée (paste)
150ml/¼ pint/⅔ cup dry
    white wine
salt and ground black pepper
baby courgettes (zucchini) and
    fresh herbs, to garnish

Preparation: 4–5 minutes; Cooking: 15 minutes

1 Leave the onions whole and cook in a pan of boiling water for 4 minutes until softened. Drain. Plunge the tomatoes into boiling water for 30 seconds, then refresh in cold water. Peel off the skins and chop roughly.

2 Cut the tuna into 2.5cm/1in chunks. Heat the oil in a large frying or sauté pan and quickly fry the tuna until the surface has browned. Lift the chunks out of the pan and drain.

3 Stir in the onions, garlic, tomatoes, chopped herbs, bay leaves, sugar, tomato purée and wine, and bring to the boil, breaking up the tomatoes with a wooden spoon.

4 Reduce the heat and simmer the sauce gently for 5 minutes. Return the fish to the pan and cook for a further 4 minutes. Season, and serve hot, garnished with the baby courgettes and a selection of fresh herbs.

> **Variation**
> *Two large mackerel make a more readily available alternative to the tuna. Simply lay the whole fish over the sauce and cook, covered with a lid, until the mackerel is cooked through.*

Seared Tuna Energy 389kcal/1630kJ; Protein 49.2g; Carbohydrate 1.6g, of which sugars 1.6g; Fat 20.8g, of which saturates 4.2g; Cholesterol 56mg; Calcium 123mg; Fibre 1g; Sodium 120mg.
Tuna Stew Energy 393kcal/1648kJ; Protein 42.8g; Carbohydrate 13.8g, of which sugars 12.4g; Fat 16.8g, of which saturates 3.4g; Cholesterol 47mg; Calcium 64mg; Fibre 3.4g; Sodium 121mg.

Salmon & Tuna Parcels

You need fairly large smoked salmon slices for this dish, as they are wrapped around a light tuna mixture before being served on a vibrant tomato salad.

Serves 4
30ml/2 tbsp natural (plain) yogurt
15ml/1 tbsp tomato purée (paste)
5ml/1 tsp wholegrain honey mustard
grated rind and juice of 1 lime
200g/7oz can tuna in brine, drained

12–16 large slices of smoked salmon
salt and ground black pepper
fresh mint leaves, to garnish

For the salad
3 ripe vine tomatoes, sliced
2 kiwi fruit, peeled and sliced
1/4 cucumber, cut into julienne sticks
15ml/1 tbsp chopped fresh mint
7.5ml/1 1/2 tsp white wine vinegar
45ml/3 tbsp olive oil
2.5ml/1/2 tsp mustard

Preparation: 10–12 minutes; Cooking: 0 minutes

1 Put the yogurt, tomato purée and mustard in a bowl and mix well with a wooden spoon until all the tomato purée has been incorporated. Stir in the grated lime rind and juice. Add the tuna, with black pepper to taste, and mix well.

2 Spread out the salmon slices on a chopping board and spoon some of the tuna mixture on to each piece.

3 Roll up or fold the smoked salmon into neat parcels. Carefully press the edges together to seal.

4 Make the salad. Arrange the tomato and kiwi slices on four serving plates. Sprinkle over the cucumber sticks.

5 In a bowl, whisk the chopped mint, white wine vinegar, oil, mustard and a little seasoning together and spoon some over each salad to moisten.

6 Arrange 3–4 salmon parcels on each plate, placing them so that they form a rough triangle on top of the tomato and kiwi slices. Garnish with the fresh mint leaves and serve immediately.

Salmon Fish Cakes

The secret of a good fish cake is to make it with freshly prepared fish and potatoes, home-made breadcrumbs and plenty of fresh herbs, such as dill and parsley or tarragon.

Serves 4
450g/1lb cooked salmon fillet
450g/1lb freshly cooked potatoes, mashed
25g/1oz/2 tbsp butter, melted or 30ml/2 tbsp olive oil
10ml/2 tsp wholegrain mustard

15ml/1 tbsp each chopped fresh dill and chopped fresh parsley or tarragon
grated rind and juice of 1/2 lemon
15g/1/2oz/2 tbsp wholemeal (whole-wheat) flour
1 egg, lightly beaten
150g/5oz/2 cups dried breadcrumbs
60ml/4 tbsp sunflower oil
sea salt and ground black pepper
rocket (arugula) leaves and chives, to garnish
lemon wedges, to serve

Preparation: 5 minutes; Cooking: 8–10 minutes

1 Flake the cooked salmon, discarding any skin and bones. Put it in a bowl with the mashed potato, melted butter or oil and wholegrain mustard, and mix well. Stir in the herbs and the lemon rind and juice. Season to taste with plenty of sea salt and ground black pepper.

2 Divide the mixture into eight portions and shape each into a ball, then flatten into a thick disc. Dip the fish cakes first in flour, then in egg and finally in breadcrumbs, making sure that they are evenly coated with crumbs.

3 Heat the oil in a frying pan until it is very hot. Fry the fish cakes in batches until golden brown and crisp all over. As each batch is ready, drain on kitchen paper and keep hot. Garnish with rocket and chives and serve with lemon wedges.

> **Cook's Tip**
> *Any fresh white or hot-smoked fish is suitable. Always buy organically farmed fish, or sustainably caught wild fish.*

Parcels Energy 309kcal/1295kJ; Protein 38.8g; Carbohydrate 8.5g, of which sugars 8.4g; Fat 13.5g, of which saturates 2.2g; Cholesterol 61mg; Calcium 56mg; Fibre 1.6g; Sodium 2064mg.
Fish Cakes Energy 586kcal/2453kJ; Protein 29.8g; Carbohydrate 49.9g, of which sugars 3.2g; Fat 31g, of which saturates 7.2g; Cholesterol 117mg; Calcium 79mg; Fibre 1.3g; Sodium 266mg.

Salmon with Green Peppercorns

Salmon benefits from being served with a piquant accompaniment. Lemon and lime are the obvious choices, but capers and green peppercorns also serve to counter the rich taste of the fish.

Serves 4
15g/½oz/1 tbsp butter
2–3 shallots, finely chopped

15ml/1 tbsp brandy (optional)
60ml/4 tbsp white wine
90ml/6 tbsp fish or chicken stock
120ml/4fl oz/½ cup
    whipping cream
30–45ml/2–3 tbsp green
    peppercorns in brine, rinsed
15–30ml/1–2 tbsp vegetable oil
4 pieces salmon fillet, each
    about 175g/6oz
salt and ground black pepper
fresh parsley, to garnish

Preparation: 3–4 minutes; Cooking: 13–15 minutes

1 Melt the butter in a heavy pan over a medium heat. Add the shallots and cook over low to medium heat for 1–2 minutes, until just softened but not coloured.

2 Add the brandy, if using, then pour in the white wine and stock. Bring to the boil. Boil vigorously to reduce by three-quarters, stirring occasionally.

3 Reduce the heat, then add the cream and half the peppercorns, crushing them slightly against the sides of the pan with the back of a spoon. Cook very gently for 4–5 minutes, until the sauce has thickened slightly,

4 Strain the sauce into a clean pan and stir in the remaining peppercorns. Keep the sauce warm over a very low heat, stirring occasionally, while you cook the salmon fillets.

5 Heat the oil in a large, heavy frying pan over a medium-high heat. Lightly season the salmon. When the oil is very hot, add the salmon. Sear the fillets on both sides, then lower the heat and cook for 4–6 minutes, until the flesh is opaque throughout.

6 Arrange the fish on warmed plates and pour over the sauce. Garnish with parsley and serve.

Salmon with Whisky & Cream

This dish combines two of the finest flavours of Scotland – salmon and whisky. It takes very little time to make, so cook it at the last moment. Serve quite plainly.

Serves 4
4 thin pieces of salmon fillet,
    about 175g/6oz each

5ml/1 tsp chopped fresh
    thyme leaves
50g/2oz/¼ cup butter
75ml/5 tbsp whisky
150ml/¼ pint/⅔ cup double
    (heavy) cream
juice of ½ lemon (optional)
salt and ground black pepper
fresh dill sprigs, to garnish

Preparation: 2–3 minutes; Cooking: 12–16 minutes

1 Season the salmon with salt, pepper and thyme. Melt half the butter in a frying pan large enough to hold two pieces of salmon side by side.

2 When the butter is foaming, fry the first two pieces of salmon for 2–3 minutes on each side, until they are golden on the outside and just cooked through.

3 Pour in 30ml/2 tbsp of the whisky and ignite it. When the flames have died down, carefully transfer the salmon to a plate and keep it hot. Heat the remaining butter in the frying pan. Scrape the base to incorporate any sediment, and cook the second two pieces of salmon in the same way. Add them to the plate with the other pieces of salmon, cover with foil and continue to keep the fish hot while you make the sauce.

4 Pour the cream into the pan and bring to the boil, stirring constantly and scraping up the cooking juices from the base of the pan. Allow to bubble until reduced and slightly thickened, then season and add the last of the whisky and a squeeze of lemon, if you like.

5 Place the salmon pieces on individual warmed plates, pour the sauce over and garnish with dill. New potatoes and crisp green beans are good with this.

With Peppercorns Energy 526kcal/2180kJ; Protein 36.3g; Carbohydrate 2.9g, of which sugars 2.3g; Fat 40g, of which saturates 13.5g; Cholesterol 127mg; Calcium 63mg; Fibre 0.4g; Sodium 110mg.
With Whisky Energy 667kcal/2760kJ; Protein 36.1g; Carbohydrate 0.8g, of which sugars 0.8g; Fat 53g, of which saturates 24.5g; Cholesterol 174mg; Calcium 61mg; Fibre 0g; Sodium 164mg.

Salmon with Lemon & Tofu Sauce

The elegant simplicity of this dish makes it an ideal choice for a dinner party. Moreover, it is very quick and easy to prepare while looking and tasting wonderful.

Serves 2
2 salmon steaks or fillets, each weighing about 130–150g/4½–5oz
5cm/2in piece fresh root ginger, cut into thin sticks
2 garlic cloves, finely chopped

1 small red chilli, seeded and finely chopped
bunch of fresh dill, parsley or coriander (cilantro), tough stems removed
sea salt and ground black pepper
15ml/1 tbsp sesame seeds, toasted, to garnish

For the sauce
175g/6oz silken tofu
grated rind and juice of 1 lemon
50ml/3½ tbsp water

Preparation: 8 minutes; Cooking: 5–10 minutes

1 Line a bamboo steaming basket or metal steaming tray with baking parchment, then arrange the salmon steaks or fillets on top. Pile the ginger, garlic and chilli, and half of the dill, parsley or coriander on top of the fish and season with salt and pepper, then cover and steam for 5–10 minutes, or until the fish is opaque and just cooked through.

2 Meanwhile, make the sauce by blending all the ingredients and the remaining herbs in a blender or food processor until smooth. Transfer to a small pan and gently warm through, stirring frequently.

3 Serve the fish with the sauce spooned over the top and garnished with the toasted sesame seeds.

Cook's Tip
Steaming is a wonderful way of cooking fish, ensuring that the maximum flavour is retained. If you like, the water beneath the steamer can be scented by the addition of some lemon grass or a strip of pared lemon rind.

Baked Salmon with a Guava Sauce

Guavas have a creamy flesh with a citrus tang, which makes them perfect to serve with salmon.

Serves 4
6 ripe guavas
45ml/3 tbsp vegetable oil

1 small onion, finely chopped
120ml/4fl oz/½ cup well-flavoured chicken stock
10ml/2 tsp hot pepper sauce
4 salmon steaks
salt and ground black pepper
strips of red (bell) pepper to garnish

Preparation: 4 minutes; Cooking: 12–14 minutes

1 Cut each guava in half. Scoop the seeded soft flesh into a sieve (strainer) placed over a bowl. Press it through the sieve, discard the seeds and skin and set the pulp aside.

2 Heat 30ml/2 tbsp of the oil in a frying pan. Fry the chopped onion for about 4 minutes over a moderate heat until softened and translucent.

3 Stir in the guava pulp, with the chicken stock and hot pepper sauce. Cook, stirring, until the sauce thickens. Keep it warm.

4 Brush the salmon steaks on one side with a little of the remaining oil. Season them with salt and pepper. Heat a griddle or ridged grill pan until very hot and add the salmon steaks, oiled side down. Cook for 2–3 minutes, until the underside is golden, then brush the surface with oil, turn each salmon steak over and cook the other side until the fish is cooked and flakes easily when tested with the tip of a sharp knife.

5 Transfer each steak to a warmed plate. Serve, garnished with strips of red pepper on a pool of sauce. A fresh green salad is a good accompaniment.

Cook's Tip
Ripe guavas have yellow skin and succulent flesh that ranges in colour from white to deep pink or salmon red.

Filo-wrapped Salmon

Select a chunky variety of tomato sauce for this simple but delicious recipe. When working with filo pastry, keep it covered with clear film (plastic wrap) or a damp dish towel, as once it's exposed to air it dries out quickly and becomes brittle and difficult to handle.

Serves 3–4

about 130g/4¹/₂oz filo pastry
   (6–8 large sheets)
about 30ml/2 tbsp olive oil,
   for brushing
450g/1lb salmon fillets
550ml/18fl oz/2¹/₂ cups fresh
   tomato sauce

Preparation: 4–5 minutes; Cooking: 10–15 minutes

1 Preheat the oven to 200°C/400°F/Gas 6. Take a sheet of filo pastry, brush with a little olive oil and cover with a second sheet of pastry. Place a piece of fish on top of the pastry, towards the bottom edge, then top with 1–2 spoonfuls of the tomato sauce, spreading it in an even layer.

2 Roll the fish in the pastry, taking care to enclose the filling completely. Brush with a little olive oil. Place on a baking sheet and repeat with the remaining fish and pastry, placing each parcel on the baking sheet but keeping them apart. You should have about half the sauce remaining, to serve with the fish.

3 Bake for 10–15 minutes, or until golden. Meanwhile, reheat the remaining sauce. Serve the filo-wrapped salmon immediately with the remaining tomato sauce.

> **Cook's Tip**
> To save time, use a bottled tomato sauce in this dish. There is a vast selection these days and a quick trawl through the pasta sauces at the supermarket will offer a wide choice. A simple tomato and basil sauce, or one including mushrooms, would work well. Alternatively, try puttanesca sauce, which includes black olives, chilli, garlic and anchovies. It has a robust flavour but if you use it sparingly it will not overwhelm the flavour of the salmon.

Hot Smoked Salmon

This is a fantastic way of smoking salmon on a barbecue in no time at all. The mojo makes a mildly spicy companion.

Serves 6

6 salmon fillets, each about
   175g/6oz, with skin
15ml/1 tbsp sunflower oil
salt and ground black pepper
2 handfuls hickory wood chips,
   soaked in cold water for as
   much time as you have
   available, preferably 30 minutes

For the mojo

1 ripe mango, diced
4 drained canned pineapple
   slices, diced
1 small red onion, finely chopped
1 fresh long mild red chilli, seeded
   and finely chopped
15ml/1 tbsp good-quality sweet
   chilli sauce
grated rind and juice of 1 lime
leaves from 1 small lemon basil
   plant or 45ml/3 tbsp fresh
   coriander (cilantro) leaves,
   shredded or chopped

Preparation: 5 minutes; Cooking: 11–13 minutes, plus soaking

1 First, make the mojo by putting the mango and diced pineapple in a bowl. Add the chopped onion and seeded and chopped chilli, and stir to mix. Add the chilli sauce, lime rind and juice, and the herb leaves. Stir to mix well. Cover tightly with clear film (plastic wrap) and leave in a cool place until needed.

2 Rinse the salmon fillets and pat dry, then brush each with a little oil. Place the fillets skin side down on a lightly oiled grill (broiler) rack over medium-hot coals. Cover the barbecue with a lid or tented heavy-duty foil and cook the fish for 3–5 minutes.

3 Drain the hickory chips into a colander and sprinkle about a third of them as evenly as possible over the coals. Carefully drop them through the slats in the grill racks, taking care not to scatter the ash as you do so.

4 Replace the barbecue cover and continue cooking for a further 8 minutes, adding a small handful of hickory chips twice more during this time. Serve the salmon hot or cold, with the mango and pineapple mojo.

Filo-wrapped Salmon Energy 460kcal/1924kJ; Protein 28.1g; Carbohydrate 31.3g, of which sugars 5.9g; Fat 25.8g, of which saturates 5.5g; Cholesterol 70mg; Calcium 85mg; Fibre 2.7g; Sodium 519mg.
Hot Smoked Salmon Energy 364kcal/1519kJ; Protein 35.9g; Carbohydrate 7.8g, of which sugars 7.4g; Fat 21.2g, of which saturates 3.6g; Cholesterol 88mg; Calcium 58mg; Fibre 1.3g; Sodium 82mg.

Creamy Penne with Smoked Salmon

No supper dish could be simpler. Freshly cooked pasta is tossed with cream, smoked salmon and thyme to make a lovely, light dish that looks as good as it tastes and goes down well with guests of all ages.

Serves 4

350g/12oz/3 cups dried penne
115g/4oz thinly sliced
*   smoked salmon*
2–3 fresh thyme sprigs
25g/1oz/2 tbsp butter
150ml/¼ pint/⅔ cup double
*   (heavy) cream*
salt and ground black pepper

Preparation: 2 minutes; Cooking: 10–12 minutes

1 Cook the pasta in a large pan of lightly salted boiling water for 10–12 minutes, until tender but still firm to the bite.

2 Meanwhile, using kitchen scissors or a small, sharp knife, cut the smoked salmon into thin strips, each about 5mm/¼ in wide, and place on a plate. Strip the leaves from the thyme sprigs.

3 Melt the butter in a large pan. Stir in the cream with a quarter of the salmon and thyme leaves, then season with pepper. Heat gently for 3–4 minutes, stirring constantly. Do not allow the sauce to boil. Taste for seasoning.

4 Drain the pasta and toss it in the cream and salmon sauce. Divide among four warmed bowls and top with the remaining salmon and thyme leaves.

Cook's Tip
For a healthier, low-fat version of this dish, use low-fat crème fraîche in place of the double (heavy) cream.

Variation
Substitute low-fat cream cheese for half the cream in the sauce for a less rich mixture that still tastes very good.

Lemon & Salmon Pappardelle

This is a fantastic all-in-one supper dish that tastes great and is made in just a few minutes – ideal for when you're really hungry but haven't much time. Serve it with a rocket salad dressed with extra virgin olive oil, balsamic vinegar and black pepper. Add some baby plum tomatoes for extra colour, if you like, and some slices of orange or green (bell) pepper for crunch.

Serves 4

500g/1¼lb fresh pappardelle
*   or tagliatelle*
300ml/½ pint/1¼ cups single
*   (light) cream*
grated rind and juice of 2 lemons
225g/8oz smoked salmon pieces
2.5ml/½ tsp grated nutmeg
60ml/4 tbsp chopped fresh parsley
salt and ground black pepper
fresh Parmesan cheese shavings,
*   to garnish*
rocket (arugula) salad, to serve

Preparation: 2 minutes; Cooking: 6–7 minutes

1 Bring a large pan of lightly salted water to the boil and cook the pappardelle or tagliatelle for 3–5 minutes, or according to the instructions on the packet, until risen to the surface of the boiling water and just tender. Drain well.

2 Add the cream, lemon rind and juice to the pan and heat through gently until piping hot. Return the cooked pappardelle to the pan and stir thoroughly to coat the pasta with the creamy mixture.

3 Add the salmon pieces, grated nutmeg, chopped parsley and plenty of ground black pepper to the sauce in the pan and stir well to combine.

4 Divide the pasta among four warmed serving plates and top with the fresh Parmesan shavings. Serve immediately with the rocket salad.

Cook's Tip
Smoked salmon freezes well in its original packaging. It thaws quickly, ready for simple suppers and breakfasts.

Penne Energy 573kcal/2403kJ; Protein 18.5g; Carbohydrate 65.5g, of which sugars 3.6g; Fat 28.2g, of which saturates 16.2g; Cholesterol 75mg; Calcium 47mg; Fibre 2.6g; Sodium 589mg.
Pappardelle Energy 657kcal/2773kJ; Protein 32.2g; Carbohydrate 94.6g, of which sugars 6.1g; Fat 19.3g, of which saturates 9.8g; Cholesterol 61mg; Calcium 134mg; Fibre 4.3g; Sodium 1087mg.

Tagliatelle with Smoked Salmon

The light texture of the cucumber perfectly complements the smoked salmon and the pastel colours look very attractive against the creamy swirls of tagliatelle.

Serves 4

350g/12oz/3 cups dried or
  fresh tagliatelle

½ cucumber
75g/3oz/6 tbsp butter
grated rind of 1 orange
30ml/2 tbsp chopped fresh dill
300ml/½ pint/1¼ cups single
  (light) cream
15ml/1 tbsp orange juice
115g/4oz smoked salmon,
  skinned
salt and ground black pepper

Preparation: 2 minutes; Cooking: 6–16 minutes

1 Bring a large pan of lightly salted water to the boil and add the pasta. If using dried pasta, cook for about 12 minutes or for the time recommended on the packet. If using fresh pasta, cook for 2–3 minutes, or until just tender but still firm to the bite.

2 Using a sharp knife, cut the cucumber in half lengthways, then use a small spoon to scoop out and discard the cucumber seeds. Turn the cucumber on to the flat side and slice it thinly in crescent shapes.

3 Melt the butter in a heavy pan, add the grated orange rind and fresh dill and stir well. Add the cucumber and cook over a low heat for about 2 minutes, stirring from time to time with a wooden spoon.

4 Stir in the cream and orange juice, with salt and pepper to taste. Reduce the heat to the lowest setting and cook gently for 1 minute, stirring constantly with a wooden spoon.

5 Cut the salmon into thin strips. Stir these into the sauce and heat through gently. Do not let the sauce boil.

6 Drain the pasta thoroughly and return it to the pan. Add the sauce and toss to combine. Spoon into a dish or into individual shallow pasta plates and serve.

Farfalle with Smoked Salmon & Dill

This quick, luxurious sauce for pasta has become very fashionable in Italy, but wherever you have it, it will taste delicious. Dill is the classic herb for cooking with fish, but if you don't like its aniseed flavour, substitute parsley or a little fresh tarragon. The fresher the herbs, the better the taste, so it is always worth growing some in pots or in the garden.

Serves 4

6 spring onions (scallions), sliced
50g/2oz/¼ cup butter
90ml/6 tbsp dry white wine
  or vermouth
450ml/¾ pint/scant 2 cups
  double (heavy) cream
freshly grated nutmeg
225g/8oz smoked salmon
30ml/2 tbsp chopped fresh dill
freshly squeezed lemon juice
450g/1lb/4 cups fresh farfalle
salt and ground black pepper
fresh dill sprigs, to garnish

Preparation: 4 minutes; Cooking: 8–10 minutes

1 Using a sharp cook's knife, slice the spring onions finely. Melt the butter in a large pan and fry the spring onions for about 1 minute, stirring occasionally, until softened.

2 Add the wine or vermouth and boil hard to reduce to about 30ml/2 tbsp. Stir in the cream and add salt, pepper and nutmeg to taste. Bring to the boil, then simmer for 2–3 minutes until slightly thickened.

3 Cut the smoked salmon into 2.5cm/1in squares and stir into the sauce, together with the dill. Add lemon juice to taste.

4 Cook the pasta in a large pan of boiling salted water for 2–3 minutes, or until it rises to the surface of the liquid. Drain well. Toss with the sauce. Spoon into serving bowls and serve immediately, garnished with sprigs of dill.

Cook's Tip
If you can't locate fresh pasta, use dried, and cook in boiling water for 12 minutes or according to package instructions.

Tagliatelle Energy 626kcal/2624kJ; Protein 20.4g; Carbohydrate 66.9g, of which sugars 5g; Fat 32.6g, of which saturates 19.3g; Cholesterol 91mg; Calcium 98mg; Fibre 2.6g; Sodium 679mg.
Farfalle Energy 1162kcal/4846kJ; Protein 30g; Carbohydrate 86.5g, of which sugars 6.8g; Fat 77.4g, of which saturates 46.1g; Cholesterol 206mg; Calcium 104mg; Fibre 3.5g; Sodium 1180mg.

Noodles with Smoked Salmon

Young pea sprouts are available for only a short time. You can substitute watercress, mustard cress, young leeks or your favourite green vegetable or herb in this dish, but don't choose anything too robust in terms of texture or flavour. Mangetouts, sliced lengthways, pencil-thin green beans or young asparagus spears would be ideal.

Serves 4
225g/8oz buckwheat or
   soba noodles
15ml/1 tbsp oyster sauce
juice of ½ lemon
30–45ml/2–3 tbsp light olive oil
115g/4oz smoked salmon, cut
   into fine strips
115g/4oz young pea sprouts
2 ripe tomatoes, peeled, seeded
   and cut into strips
15ml/1 tbsp snipped chives
salt and ground black pepper

Preparation: 8–10 minutes; Cooking: 6–7 minutes

1 Cook the buckwheat or soba noodles in a large pan of boiling water, following the directions on the packet.

2 Drain the noodles, then tip them into a colander and rinse under cold running water. Drain well, shaking the colander to extract any remaining water.

3 Tip the noodles into a large bowl. Add the oyster sauce and lemon juice and season with pepper to taste. Moisten with the olive oil.

4 Add the smoked salmon, pea sprouts, tomatoes and chives. Mix well and serve at once.

> **Variations**
> • To keep the cost of this dish down, use a packet of smoked salmon trimmings instead of cutting up more expensive slices. It will taste just the same.
> • Instead of buckwheat or soba noodles, use fresh tagliatelle or pappardelle, cooked in salted boiling water for 2–3 minutes. The pasta is ready when it rises to the surface of the liquid.

Smoked Trout Pasta Salad

Choose hollow pasta shapes, such as shells or penne, which trap the creamy filling, creating tasty mouthfuls of trout, fennel and spring onion. The addition of dill is not only attractive, but also gives this salad a distinctive aniseed flavour.

Serves 8
15g/½oz/1 tbsp butter
1 bulb fennel, finely chopped
6 spring onions (scallions),
   2 very finely chopped and
   4 thinly sliced
225g/8oz smoked trout fillets,
   skinned and flaked
45ml/3 tbsp chopped fresh dill
120ml/4fl oz/½ cup mayonnaise
10ml/2 tsp lemon juice
30ml/2 tbsp whipping cream
450g/1lb small fresh pasta
   shapes, such as shells
salt and ground black pepper
fresh dill sprigs, to garnish

Preparation: 8–10 minutes; Cooking: 5–8 minutes

1 Melt the butter in a small frying pan. Add the fennel and finely chopped spring onions and fry over a medium heat for 3–5 minutes. Transfer to a large bowl and leave to cool.

2 Add the sliced spring onions, trout, dill, mayonnaise, lemon juice and cream to the bowl with the fennel. Season lightly with salt and pepper and mix gently until well blended.

3 Bring a large pan of lightly salted water to the boil. Add the pasta. Cook for 2–3 minutes until al dente. Drain thoroughly in a colander and leave to cool.

4 Add the pasta to the vegetable and trout mixture and toss to coat evenly. Taste for seasoning. Serve the salad lightly chilled or at room temperature. It looks good on a shallow dish, garnished with the sprigs of dill.

> **Variation**
> *This pasta salad works well with any type of fresh, cooked fish fillets, including salmon. Alternatively, you can use a 200g/7oz can of tuna in water in place of the trout.*

Noodles Energy 341kcal/1437kJ; Protein 16.2g; Carbohydrate 47.6g, of which sugars 3.6g; Fat 10.9g, of which saturates 1.2g; Cholesterol 10mg; Calcium 28mg; Fibre 3.5g; Sodium 547mg.
Pasta Salad Energy 369kcal/1548kJ; Protein 14.5g; Carbohydrate 42.7g, of which sugars 2.8g; Fat 16.8g, of which saturates 4g; Cholesterol 29mg; Calcium 31mg; Fibre 2.3g; Sodium 613mg.

Fusilli with Smoked Trout

With its creamy sauce, smoked trout blends beautifully with the crisp but tender vegetables in this classic pasta dish.

Serves 4–6

2 carrots, cut into matchsticks

I leek, cut into matchsticks

2 celery sticks, cut into matchsticks

150ml/¼ pint/⅔ cup vegetable stock

225g/8oz smoked trout fillets, skinned and cut into strips

200g/7oz cream cheese

150ml/¼ pint/⅔ cup medium sweet white wine or fish stock

15ml/1 tbsp chopped fresh dill or fennel

225g/8oz/2 cups fresh fusilli or other pasta shapes

salt and ground black pepper

fresh dill sprigs, to garnish

Preparation: 5 minutes; Cooking: 10–12 minutes

1 Put the carrot, leek and celery matchsticks into a pan and add the stock. Bring to the boil and cook quickly for 4–5 minutes, until most of the stock has evaporated. Remove from the heat and add the smoked trout.

2 Put the cream cheese and wine or fish stock into a pan over a medium heat, and whisk until smooth. Add the dill or fennel and salt and pepper.

3 Cook the fusilli in a pan of salted boiling water for 2–3 minutes, or until it rises to the surface. When the pasta is tender, but still firm to the bite, drain it thoroughly, and return to the pan.

4 Add the sauce, toss lightly and transfer to a serving bowl. Top with the cooked vegetables and trout. Serve immediately, garnished with the dill sprigs.

> **Variation**
> *Cream cheese now comes in a variety of flavours. A herb variety would be ideal in this dish, or you could use smoked salmon-flavoured cheese, and substitute salmon for the trout.*

Trout with Almonds

Some people regard this dish as a cliché, but if that's true, it's one that has endured for a long time. The reason is simple: this combination works extremely well.

Serves 2

2 trout, each about 350g/12oz, cleaned

40g/1½oz/⅓ cup plain (all-purpose) flour

50g/2oz/¼ cup butter

25g/1oz/¼ cup flaked (sliced) almonds

30ml/2 tbsp dry white wine

salt and ground black pepper

new potatoes and mixed green salad, to serve

Preparation: 2 minutes; Cooking: 14–16 minutes

1 Rinse the trout and pat dry. Put the flour in a large plastic bag and season with salt and pepper. Place the trout, one at a time, in the bag and shake to coat with flour. Shake off the excess flour from the fish and discard the remaining flour.

2 Melt half the butter in a large frying pan over a medium heat. When it is foamy, add the trout and cook for 6 minutes.

3 Turn the trout over and cook for 3 minutes more until the skin is golden brown and the flesh next to the bone is opaque. Transfer the fish to warmed plates and cover to keep warm.

4 Add the remaining butter to the pan and cook the almonds, shaking the pan frequently, until just lightly browned.

5 Add the white wine to the pan and boil for 1 minute, stirring constantly, until the sauce is slightly syrupy. Pour or spoon the sauce and almonds over each fish and serve immediately with boiled new potatoes and a green salad.

> **Variation**
> *Other nuts can be used instead of almonds. Hazelnuts are particularly good with trout. The nuts swiftly brown and go crisp, so watch them closely to prevent them burning.*

Fusilli Energy 348kcal/1455kJ; Protein 15.9g; Carbohydrate 31.4g, of which sugars 4.5g; Fat 18.5g, of which saturates 10.3g; Cholesterol 45mg; Calcium 74mg; Fibre 2.8g; Sodium 822mg.
Trout Energy 475kcal/1978kJ; Protein 39.2g; Carbohydrate 7.6g, of which sugars 0.8g; Fat 32.2g, of which saturates 12.4g; Cholesterol 187mg; Calcium 101mg; Fibre 1.2g; Sodium 249mg.

Ham-wrapped Trout

Serrano ham is used to stuff and wrap trout for this unusual recipe from Spain, ensuring a succulent flavour. One of the beauties of this method is that the skins come off in one piece, leaving the succulent, moist flesh to be eaten with the crisped, salty ham.

Serves 4

4 brown or rainbow trout, about 250g/9oz each, cleaned
16 thin slices Serrano ham, about 200g/7oz
50g/2oz/¼ cup melted butter, plus extra for greasing
salt and ground black pepper
buttered potatoes, to serve (optional)

Preparation: 10–12 minutes; Cooking: 8 minutes

1 Extend the belly cavity of each trout, cutting up one side of the backbone. Slip a knife behind the rib bones to loosen them (sometimes just flexing the fish makes them pop up). Snip these off from both sides with scissors, and season the fish well inside.

2 Fold a piece of ham into each belly. Use smaller or broken bits of ham for this, and reserve the eight best slices.

3 Prepare the barbecue. Position a lightly oiled grill (broiler) rack over the hot coals. Brush each trout with a little butter, seasoning the outside lightly with salt and pepper. Wrap two ham slices round each one, crossways, tucking the ends into the belly.

4 Put the fish into oiled hinged wire fish baskets or directly on to the grill rack. The combined grilling time should be 4 minutes on each side, though it is wise to turn the fish every 2 minutes to ensure that the ham does not become charred.

5 Serve the trout hot, with the butter spooned over the top. Diners should open the trout on their plates, and eat them from the inside, pushing the flesh off the skin.

Cook's Tip
The trout can be cooked under a conventional grill (broiler).

Classic Fish & Chips

Quintessentially English, this is fish and chips as it should be cooked, with tender flakes of fish in a crisp batter, and home-made chips.

Serves 4
450g/1lb potatoes
groundnut (peanut) oil, for deep-frying

4 x 175g/6oz cod fillets, skinned and any tiny bones removed

For the batter
75g/3oz/⅔ cup plain (all-purpose) flour
1 egg yolk
10ml/2 tsp oil
175ml/6fl oz/¾ cup water
salt

Preparation: 5 minutes; Cooking: 14–15 minutes

1 To make the chips (French fries), cut the potatoes into 5mm/¼in thick slices. Then cut the slices into 5mm/¼in fingers. Rinse thoroughly, drain well and then dry in a clean dish towel.

2 Heat the oil in a deep fat fryer to 180°C/350°F. Add the chips in the basket to the fryer and cook for 3 minutes. Lift out and shake off excess fat.

3 To make the batter, sift the flour into a bowl. Add a pinch of salt. Make a well in the middle of the flour and add the egg yolk, oil and a little of the water. Mix the yolk with the liquid, then add the remaining water and incorporate the surrounding flour to make a smooth batter. Cover and set aside.

4 Reheat the oil in the fryer and cook the chips again for about 5 minutes, until they are golden and crisp. Drain on kitchen paper and season with salt. Keep hot in a low oven.

5 Dip the pieces of fish fillet into the batter and turn them to make sure they are evenly coated. Allow any excess batter to drip off before carefully lowering the fish into the hot oil.

6 Cook the fish for 5 minutes, turning once, if necessary, so that the batter browns evenly. The batter should be crisp and golden. Drain on kitchen paper. Serve at once, with lemon wedges and the chips.

Trout Energy 369kcal/1546kJ; Protein 48g; Carbohydrate 0.6g, of which sugars 0.6g; Fat 19.4g, of which saturates 8.8g; Cholesterol 216mg; Calcium 66mg; Fibre 0g; Sodium 821mg.
Fish and Chips Energy 645kcal/2700kJ; Protein 32.6g; Carbohydrate 54.3g, of which sugars 0.7g; Fat 34.5g, of which saturates 4.2g; Cholesterol 0mg; Calcium 130mg; Fibre 3.4g; Sodium 294mg.

Roasted Cod with Tomato Sauce

Really fresh cod has a sweet, delicate flavour and a pure white flaky flesh. Served with an aromatic tomato sauce, it makes a delicious meal and is so satisfying that it is not necessary to serve potatoes alongside. Crisp green beans are the best option.

Serves 4

350g/12oz ripe plum tomatoes
75ml/5 tbsp olive oil
2.5ml/½ tsp sugar
2 strips of pared orange rind
1 fresh thyme sprig
6 fresh basil leaves
900g/2lb fresh cod fillet, skin on
salt and ground black pepper
steamed green beans, to serve

Preparation: 3–4 minutes; Cooking: 14 minutes

1 Preheat the oven to 230°C/450°F/Gas 8. Using a sharp knife, chop the tomatoes roughly.

2 Heat 15ml/1 tbsp of the olive oil in a heavy pan, add the tomatoes, sugar, orange rind, thyme and basil, and simmer for 5 minutes until the tomatoes are soft.

3 Press the mixture through a fine sieve (strainer), discarding the solids that remain in the sieve. Pour into a pan and warm.

4 Scale the cod fillet and cut on the diagonal into four pieces. Season with plenty of salt and pepper.

5 Heat the remaining oil in a heavy frying pan and fry the cod, skinside down, until the skin is crisp. Place the fish on a greased baking sheet, skinside up, and roast in the oven for 8–10 minutes until the fish is cooked through. Serve the fish on the steamed green beans with the tomato sauce.

Cook's Tip
Cod is becoming increasingly rare and expensive. You can substitute any firm white fish fillets in this dish. Try haddock, pollock, or that excellent and underrated fish, coley. When raw, coley flesh looks grey, but it turns white on cooking.

Fried Sole with Lime

Simple dishes like this one capitalize on the delicious flavour of good fish.

Serves 4

75g/3oz/¾ cup plain
  (all-purpose) flour
10ml/2 tsp garlic salt
5ml/1 tsp ground black pepper
4 sole fillets
oil, for frying
juice of 2 limes
small bunch of fresh parsley,
  chopped, plus extra sprigs,
  to garnish
fresh salsa, to serve

Preparation: 5 minutes; Cooking: 4–8 minutes

1 Mix the flour, garlic salt and pepper together. Spread out the seasoned flour mixture in a shallow dish. Pat the sole fillets dry with kitchen paper, then turn them in the seasoned flour until they are evenly coated.

2 Pour oil into a wide frying pan to a depth of 2.5cm/1in. Heat it until a cube of bread added to the oil rises to the surface and browns in 45–60 seconds.

3 Add the fish, in batches if necessary, and fry for 3–4 minutes. Lift each fillet out and drain it on kitchen paper. Transfer to a heated serving dish.

4 Squeeze the juice of half a lime over each piece of fish and sprinkle with the chopped parsley. Serve immediately, with a fresh salsa to complement the fish. Garnish with parsley sprigs. New potatoes would also go well.

Cook's Tip
A sweet pepper salsa would taste good with this dish. Roast 2 red (bell) peppers under a hot grill (broiler) until the skins blacken and blister. Put them in a plastic bag until the skin softens, then peel them and remove the seeds. Process the flesh in a food processor with 1 seeded and chopped red chilli, 30ml/2 tbsp coriander (cilantro) leaves, 30ml/2 tbsp olive oil and 15ml/1 tbsp red wine vinegar. Season to taste.

Roasted Cod Energy 294kcal/1229kJ; Protein 41.8g; Carbohydrate 2.7g, of which sugars 2.7g; Fat 12.8g, of which saturates 1.9g; Cholesterol 104mg; Calcium 26mg; Fibre 0.9g; Sodium 143mg.
Fried Sole Energy 254kcal/1066kJ; Protein 21.5g; Carbohydrate 25.6g, of which sugars 0.8g; Fat 7.9g, of which saturates 0.7g; Cholesterol 50mg; Calcium 100mg; Fibre 1.6g; Sodium 105mg.

Cajun Blackened Fish with Salsa

This is an excellent way of cooking fillets of snapper or cod, leaving the fish moist in the middle and crisp and spicy on the outside.

Serves 4

5ml/1 tsp black peppercorns
5ml/1 tsp cumin seeds
5ml/1 tsp white mustard seeds
10ml/2 tsp paprika
5ml/1 tsp chilli powder
5ml/1 tsp dried oregano
10ml/2 tsp dried thyme

4 skinned fish fillets,
    225g/8oz each
50g/2oz/¼ cup butter, melted
salt
lime wedges and coriander
    (cilantro) sprigs, to garnish

For the papaya salsa
1 papaya
1 fresh red chilli
½ small red onion, diced
45ml/3 tbsp chopped fresh
    coriander (cilantro)
grated rind and juice of 1 lime

Preparation: 8–10 minutes; Cooking: 4 minutes

1 Start by making the salsa. Cut the papaya in half and scoop out the seeds. Remove the skin, cut the flesh into small dice and place it in a bowl. Slit the chilli, remove and discard the seeds and finely chop the flesh.

2 Add the onion, chilli, coriander, lime rind and juice to the papaya. Season with salt to taste. Mix well and set aside.

3 Dry-fry the peppercorns, cumin and mustard seeds in a pan, then grind them to a fine powder. Add the paprika, chilli powder, oregano, thyme and 5ml/1 tsp salt. Grind again and spread on a plate.

4 Preheat a large heavy frying pan over a medium heat. Brush the fish fillets with the melted butter then dip them in the mixture of spices until well coated.

5 Place the fish fillets in the hot pan and cook for 1–2 minutes on each side until blackened.

6 Transfer the fish to individual heated plates and garnish with lime wedges and coriander sprigs. Serve at once, with the salsa.

Mediterranean Fish Cutlets with Aniseed Tomato Sauce

This attractive dish is perfect for a dinner party, as the white flesh of the fish contrasts with the striking red of the sauce. The pastis in the sauce adds a surprise to the range of flavours, and will give your guests a meal to remember.

Serves 4

4 white fish cutlets, about
    150g/5oz each
150ml/¼ pint/⅔ cup fish
    stock and/or dry white
    wine, for poaching
1 bay leaf

a few black peppercorns
a strip of pared lemon rind
fresh parsley and lemon wedges,
    to garnish

For the tomato sauce
400g/14oz can chopped
    tomatoes
1 garlic clove
15ml/1 tbsp sun-dried tomato
    purée (paste)
15ml/1 tbsp pastis or other
    aniseed flavoured liqueur
15ml/1 tbsp drained capers
12–16 pitted black olives
salt and ground black pepper

Preparation: 3–4 minutes; Cooking: 12 minutes

1 Make the sauce. Heat the chopped tomatoes in a pan with the whole garlic clove. Stir in the sun-dried tomato purée until it has been absorbed completely.

2 Measure the pastis or other liqueur into the pan, then add the capers and olives. Season with salt and black pepper. Heat all the ingredients together for 10 minutes, stirring occasionally, to blend the flavours.

3 Meanwhile, place the fish in a frying pan, pour over the stock and/or wine and add the flavourings. Cover and simmer for 10 minutes or until the fish flakes easily.

4 Using a slotted spoon, transfer the fish to a heated dish. Strain the stock into the sauce and boil to reduce slightly. Season the sauce, pour it over the fish and serve immediately, with parsley and lemon wedges.

Cajun Blackened Fish Energy 295kcal/1228kJ; Protein 32.7g; Carbohydrate 3g, of which sugars 2.9g; Fat 16.9g, of which saturates 10g; Cholesterol 120mg; Calcium 31mg; Fibre 0.9g; Sodium 222mg.
Mediterranean Fish Energy 187kcal/783kJ; Protein 28.7g; Carbohydrate 3.6g, of which sugars 3.6g; Fat 5.5g, of which saturates 0.9g; Cholesterol 69mg; Calcium 45mg; Fibre 2.2g; Sodium 952mg.

Fish Moolie

Choose a firm-textured fish like snapper so that the pieces stay intact during the brief cooking process.

Serves 4
500g/1¼lb firm-textured fish fillets, skinned and cut into 2.5cm/1in cubes
2.5ml/½ tsp salt
50g/2oz/⅔ cup desiccated (dry unsweetened shredded) coconut
6 shallots, roughly chopped
6 blanched almonds
2–3 garlic cloves, roughly chopped
2.5cm/1in piece fresh root ginger, peeled and sliced
2 lemon grass stalks, trimmed
10ml/2 tsp ground turmeric
45ml/3 tbsp vegetable oil
2 x 400ml/14fl oz cans coconut milk
1–3 fresh red or green chillies, seeded and sliced
salt and ground black pepper
fresh chives, to garnish

Preparation: 8 minutes; Cooking: 10 minutes

1 Spread out the pieces of fish in a shallow dish and sprinkle them with the salt. Dry-fry the coconut in a wok over medium to low heat, tip it into a food processor and process to an oily paste. Scrape into a bowl and reserve.

2 Add the shallots, almonds, garlic and ginger to the food processor. Cut off the lower 5cm/2in of the lemon grass stalks, chop them roughly and add them to the mixture. Process to a paste. Bruise the remaining lemon grass and set the stalks aside. Add the ground turmeric to the mixture in the processor and process briefly to mix.

3 Heat the oil in the clean wok. Add the onion mixture and cook for a few minutes without browning. Stir in the coconut milk and bring to the boil, stirring constantly.

4 Add the cubes of fish, most of the sliced chillies and the bruised lemon grass stalks. Cook for 3–4 minutes. Stir in the coconut paste and cook for 2 minutes. Season.

5 Remove the lemon grass stalks. Spoon the moolie on to a hot serving dish and sprinkle with the remaining slices of chilli. Garnish with chives and serve.

Poached Fish in Spicy Tomato Sauce

A selection of white fish fillets are used in this Middle Eastern dish: cod, haddock, hake or halibut are all good. Serve with flat breads, such as pitta, and serve a spicy tomato relish or some pickled lemons on the side.

Serves 8
600ml/1 pint/2½ cups fresh tomato sauce
2.5–5ml/½–1 tsp harissa
60ml/4 tbsp chopped fresh coriander (cilantro) leaves
1.5kg/3¼lb mixed white fish fillets, cut into chunks
salt and ground black pepper

Preparation: 2 minutes; Cooking: 10 minutes

1 Heat the tomato sauce with the harissa and coriander in a large pan. Add seasoning to taste and bring to the boil. Remove the pan from the heat.

2 Add the fish to the hot sauce. Return to the heat and bring the sauce to the boil again.

3 Reduce the heat and simmer very gently for about 5 minutes, or until the fish flakes easily when tested with the tip of a sharp knife. Taste the sauce and adjust the seasoning, adding more harissa if necessary. Serve hot or warm.

Cook's Tips
• Harissa is a chilli paste spiced with cumin, garlic and coriander. It is fiery and should be used with care until you are familiar with the flavour. Start by adding a small amount and then add more after tasting the sauce.
• Pickled lemons are often served with Middle Eastern dishes like this one, in the same way as fresh lemons are the classic accompaniment in the West. Look out for pickled lemons at delicatessens. It is possible – and easy – to make your own, but the ones in jars are convenient, and because very thin-skinned lemons are used, they tend to be of good quality.

Fish Moolie Energy 287kcal/1204kJ; Protein 21.3g; Carbohydrate 13g, of which sugars 12.3g; Fat 17.2g, of which saturates 8.2g; Cholesterol 18mg; Calcium 79mg; Fibre 2.1g; Sodium 493mg.
Poached Fish Energy 219kcal/923kJ; Protein 36.2g; Carbohydrate 6.7g, of which sugars 3.2g; Fat 5.5g, of which saturates 1.5g; Cholesterol 94mg; Calcium 46mg; Fibre 1.4g; Sodium 370mg.

Escabeche

This dish originated in Spain, but is now popular the world over.

Serves 6
900g/2lb white fish fillets
45–60ml/3–4 tbsp seasoned flour
vegetable oil, for shallow frying
spring onions (scallions), finely
    shredded, to garnish (optional)
boiled long grain rice, to serve

For the sauce
30ml/2 tbsp vegetable oil
2.5cm/1in piece fresh root ginger,
    peeled and thinly sliced

2–3 garlic cloves, crushed
1 onion, cut into thin rings
1/2 large green (bell) pepper,
    seeded and cut in squares
1/2 large red (bell) pepper, seeded
    and cut in squares
2 small fresh chillies, seeded and
    finely sliced
1 carrot, cut into matchsticks
25ml/1 1/2 tbsp cornflour
    (cornstarch)
450ml/3/4 pint/scant 2 cups water
45–60ml/3–4 tbsp cider vinegar
15ml/1 tbsp light soft brown sugar
5–10ml/1–2 tsp Thai fish sauce
salt and ground black pepper

Preparation: 8 minutes; Cooking: 8–10 minutes

1 Wipe the fish fillets. Leave them whole, or cut them into serving portions, if you prefer. Pat dry on kitchen paper then dust lightly with seasoned flour.

2 Heat the oil for shallow frying in a frying pan and fry the fish fillets or portions in batches until golden and almost cooked. Transfer to an ovenproof dish and keep warm.

3 Make the sauce in a wok. Heat the oil and fry the ginger, garlic and onion until the onion rings have softened. Add the pepper squares with half the chilli slices and all the carrot. Stir-fry for 1 minute. Put the cornflour in a bowl and stir in a little of the water to make a paste. Stir in the remaining water, the vinegar and the sugar. Pour the cornflour mixture over the vegetables in the wok and stir until the sauce boils and thickens a little. Season with fish sauce, and salt and pepper.

4 Add the fried fish to the sauce and reheat briefly. Transfer to a warmed platter. Garnish with the remaining chilli and shredded spring onions, if using. Serve with rice.

Hoki Stir-fry

Any firm white fish, such as monkfish, hake or cod, can be used for this stir-fry. Vary the vegetables according to what is available.

Serves 4–6
675g/1 1/2 lb hoki fillet, skinned
salt and ground black pepper
pinch of five-spice powder
115g/4oz/1 cup small
    mangetouts (snow peas)
4 spring onions (scallions)

45ml/3 tbsp groundnut
    (peanut) oil
2 garlic cloves, finely chopped
2.5cm/1in piece fresh root ginger,
    peeled and cut into thin slivers
300g/11oz beansprouts
2 carrots, cut diagonally into slices
    as thin as mangetouts
115g/4oz asparagus spears,
    trimmed and cut in half
    crossways
8–12 small baby corn cobs
15–30ml/1–2 tbsp light soy sauce

Preparation: 7–8 minutes; Cooking: 9–10 minutes

1 Cut the hoki into thin strips, removing any stray bones with tweezers. Put the salt, pepper and five-spice powder in a strong plastic bag, add the strips of fish and shake the bag gently to coat them evenly all over.

2 Trim the mangetouts. Trim the spring onions and cut the green and white parts diagonally into 2cm/3/4in pieces. Keep the green and white parts separate.

3 Heat a wok, then pour in the oil. As soon as it is hot, add the garlic and ginger. Stir-fry for 1 minute, then add the white parts of the spring onions and cook for 1 minute more.

4 Add the hoki strips and stir-fry for 2–3 minutes, until all the pieces of fish are opaque. Add the beansprouts. Toss them around to coat them in the oil, then put in the carrots, mangetouts, asparagus and corn.

5 Continue to stir-fry for 3–4 minutes, by which time the fish should be cooked, but all the vegetables will still be crunchy. Add soy sauce to taste, toss everything quickly together, then stir in the green parts of the spring onions. Spoon into a heated bowl and serve immediately.

Escabeche Energy 414kcal/1721kJ; Protein 41.9g; Carbohydrate 1.3g, of which sugars 1g; Fat 26.7g, of which saturates 3.2g; Cholesterol 104mg; Calcium 30mg; Fibre 0.2g; Sodium 137mg.
Hoki Stir-fry Energy 183kcal/764kJ; Protein 22.4g; Carbohydrate 5g, of which sugars 3.8g; Fat 8.2g, of which saturates 1.1g; Cholesterol 0mg; Calcium 49mg; Fibre 2.3g; Sodium 295mg.

Grilled Hake with Lemon & Chilli

Nothing could be simpler than perfectly grilled fish with a dusting of chilli and lemon rind. This is an ideal meal for those occasions when something light is called for.

Serves 4
4 hake fillets, each 150g/5oz
30ml/2 tbsp olive oil
finely grated rind and juice
  of 1 lemon
15ml/1 tbsp crushed chilli flakes
salt and ground black pepper

Preparation: 2 minutes; Cooking: 6–8 minutes

1 Preheat the grill (broiler) to high. Brush the hake fillets with the olive oil and place them skin side up on a baking sheet.

2 Grill (broil) the fish for 4–5 minutes, until the skin is crispy, then carefully turn the fillets over in the pan, using a metal spatula or two spoons.

3 Sprinkle the fillets with the lemon rind and chilli flakes and season with salt and ground black pepper.

4 Grill the fillets for a further 2–3 minutes, or until the hake is cooked through. (Test using the point of a sharp knife; the flesh should flake.) Transfer the fillets of hake to individual plates and squeeze over the lemon juice just before serving.

Cook's Tip
A pastry brush is the ideal implement for coating fish with oil, but keep one specifically for the purpose, unless you want your apple pie to taste slightly fishy. Draw a fish on the handle with a marker pen to distinguish it from your pastry brush.

Variation
Any firm white fish can be cooked in this simple, low-fat way. Try cod, halibut or hoki. If you haven't got any chilli flakes, brush the fish with chilli oil instead of olive oil.

Hake & Potato Salad

Hake is a meaty fish that is excellent served cold in a salad, and the flavour is enhanced here with a piquant dressing.

Serves 4
450g/1lb hake fillets
150ml/¼ pint/⅔ cup fish stock
1 onion, thinly sliced
1 bay leaf
450g/1lb cooked baby new
  potatoes, halved unless tiny
1 red (bell) pepper, seeded
  and diced
115g/4oz/1 cup petits pois
  (baby peas), cooked
2 spring onions (scallions), sliced
½ cucumber, unpeeled and diced
4 large red lettuce leaves
salt and ground black pepper

For the dressing
150ml/¼ pint/⅔ cup Greek
  (US strained plain) yogurt
30ml/2 tbsp olive oil
juice of ½ lemon
15–30ml/1–2 tbsp capers

To garnish
2 hard-boiled eggs, finely chopped
15ml/1 tbsp finely chopped fresh
  flat leaf parsley
15ml/1 tbsp finely chopped chives

Preparation: 8 minutes; Cooking: 11 minutes

1 Put the hake in a shallow pan with the fish stock, onion slices and bay leaf. Bring to the boil over a medium heat. Lower the heat and poach the fish gently for 10 minutes, until it flakes easily when tested with the tip of a sharp knife. Leave it to cool.

2 Remove and discard the skin and any remaining bones from the fish, and separate the flesh into large flakes.

3 Put the baby new potatoes in a bowl with the red pepper, petits pois, spring onions and cucumber. Gently stir in the flaked hake and season to taste with salt and pepper.

4 Make the dressing by stirring all the ingredients together in a bowl or jug (pitcher). Season and spoon or pour over the salad. Toss gently with salad servers or two spoons.

5 Place a lettuce leaf on each plate and spoon the salad over it. Mix the finely chopped hard-boiled eggs for the garnish with the parsley and chives. Sprinkle the mixture over each salad.

Grilled Hake Energy 188kcal/786kJ; Protein 27g; Carbohydrate 0.1g, of which sugars 0.1g; Fat 8.8g, of which saturates 1.2g; Cholesterol 35mg; Calcium 22mg; Fibre 0g; Sodium 150mg.
Hake Salad Energy 373kcal/1561kJ; Protein 31.2g; Carbohydrate 29.1g, of which sugars 8.8g; Fat 15.8g, of which saturates 4.2g; Cholesterol 121mg; Calcium 129mg; Fibre 4.3g; Sodium 192mg.

Kedgeree

Impress house guests by rustling up this delectable dish in less time than it takes them to take a shower. Kedgeree is an Anglo-Indian dish, made popular in England by memsahibs returning from overseas postings.

Serves 4
350g/12oz/1½ cups
   basmati rice
225g/8oz undyed smoked
   haddock fillet
4 eggs
25g/1oz/2 tbsp butter
30ml/2 tbsp garam masala
ground black pepper

Preparation: 2–3 minutes; Cooking: 16 minutes

1 Preheat the grill (broiler) to medium. Place the smoked haddock on a baking sheet and grill (broil) for 10 minutes, or until cooked through.

2 Meanwhile, place the eggs in a pan of cold water and bring to the boil. Cook for 6–7 minutes. At the same time as the eggs and haddock are cooking, cook the rice in a pan of boiling water for 10–12 minutes.

3 When the eggs are cooked, drain and place under cold running water until cool enough to handle. Shell the eggs and cut into halves or quarters.

4 Remove the baking sheet from under the grill and transfer the smoked haddock to a board. Remove the skin when cool enough to handle.

5 Using a fork, ease the flesh apart so that it separates into large flakes. Remove any remaining bones.

6 Drain the rice and tip it into a bowl. Melt the butter in a pan, stir in the garam masala and add the fish. When it has warmed through, add it to the rice with the smoked fish and eggs. Mix gently, taking care not to mash the eggs. Carefully transfer to a warmed serving dish, taste and season. The dish will probably not need much salt, since the smoked haddock will be quite salty, but be generous with the pepper. Serve immediately.

Haddock in Cider Sauce

First-class fish doesn't need elaborate treatment. The cider sauce served with the haddock is based on the poaching liquid, enriched by just a whisper of cream. If the amount of cider seems excessive, use equal parts of water and fish stock or vegetable stock.

Serves 4
675g/1½lb haddock fillet
1 medium onion, thinly sliced
1 bay leaf
2 parsley sprigs
10ml/2 tsp lemon juice
450ml/¾ pint/2 cups dry
   (hard) cider
25g/1oz/¼ cup cornflour
   (cornstarch)
30ml/2 tbsp single (light) cream
salt and ground black pepper

Preparation: 2 minutes; Cooking: 13 minutes

1 Cut the haddock fillet into four equal portions and place in a pan big enough to hold them neatly in a single layer. Add the onion, bay leaf, parsley and lemon. Season with salt.

2 Pour in most of the cider, reserving 30ml/2 tbsp for the sauce. Cover and bring to the boil, reduce the heat and simmer for 10 minutes, or until the fish is just cooked.

3 Strain 300ml/½ pint/1¼ cups of the cooking liquid into a measuring jug (cup). Cover the pan containing the fish and remove from the heat.

4 In a small pan, mix the cornflour with the 30ml/2 tbsp cider reserved earlier, then gradually whisk in the measured cooking liquid and bring to the boil. Whisk over the heat until the mixture is smooth and thick.

5 Whisk in more of the cooking liquid, if necessary, to make a pouring sauce. Remove the pan from the heat, stir in the cream and season to taste with salt and ground black pepper.

6 To serve, remove any skin from the fish, arrange on individual hot serving plates and pour the sauce over. Serve with a selection of vegetables.

Kedgeree Energy 480kcal/2006kJ; Protein 23.5g; Carbohydrate 69.9g, of which sugars 0g; Fat 11.5g, of which saturates 4.9g; Cholesterol 224mg; Calcium 59mg; Fibre 0g; Sodium 536mg.
Haddock in Cider Sauce Energy 216kcal/918kJ; Protein 32.5g; Carbohydrate 9.4g, of which sugars 3.5g; Fat 2.5g, of which saturates 1.1g; Cholesterol 65mg; Calcium 43mg; Fibre 0.1g; Sodium 127mg.

Sea Bass with Parsley & Lime Butter

The delicate but firm, sweet flesh of sea bass goes beautifully with citrus flavours. Serve with roast fennel and sautéed diced potatoes or, for a summer lunch, with new potatoes and salad.

Serves 6

50g/2oz/¼ cup butter
6 sea bass fillets, about
*   150g/5oz each*
grated rind and juice of
*   1 large lime*
30ml/2 tbsp chopped fresh parsley
salt and ground black pepper

Preparation: 2–3 minutes; Cooking: 9–10 minutes

1 Heat the butter in a large frying pan and add three of the sea bass fillets, skin side down. Cook for 3–4 minutes, or until the skin is crisp and golden. Flip the fish over and cook for a further 2–3 minutes, or until cooked through.

2 Remove the fillets from the pan with a metal spatula. Place each fillet on a serving plate and keep them warm. Cook the remaining fish in the same way and transfer to serving plates.

3 Add the lime rind and juice to the pan with the parsley, and season with salt and black pepper.

4 Allow to bubble for 1–2 minutes, then pour a little over each fish portion and serve immediately.

> **Variation**
> *Instead of serving this with sautéed diced potatoes, offer fat home-made oven chips (french fries) with fresh herbs and a little lime to echo the flavouring used in the butter for the fish. Slice 4 large waxy potatoes thickly and spread them in a single layer in a roasting pan. Sprinkle with 30ml/2 tbsp chopped fresh herbs and the finely grated rind of 1 lime. Drizzle with 30ml/2 tbsp olive oil and dot with the same quantity of butter. Cover with foil and bake at 200°C/400°F/Gas 6 for 1–1¼ hours, removing the foil after 30 minutes and stirring the chips at least twice.*

Skate with Bitter Salad Leaves

This dish is popular in Spain, which is famous for both its skate and its watercress. Skate has a delicious sweet flavour, enhanced here by orange. It contrasts well with any bitter leaves – buy a bag of mixed salad leaves for contrasting textures, colours and flavours.

Serves 4

800g/1¾lb skate wings
15ml/1 tbsp white wine vinegar
4 black peppercorns
1 fresh thyme sprig
175g/6oz bitter salad leaves,
*   such as frisée, rocket (arugula),*
*   radicchio, escarole, lamb's lettuce*
*   (mâche) and watercress*
1 orange
2 tomatoes, peeled, seeded and diced

For the dressing
15ml/1 tbsp white wine vinegar
45ml/3 tbsp extra virgin olive oil
1 bunch spring onions (scallions),
*   whites finely chopped*
salt, paprika and black pepper
crusty bread, to serve

Preparation: 5 minutes; Cooking: 8–10 minutes

1 Put the skate wings into a large shallow pan, cover with cold water and add the vinegar, peppercorns and thyme. Bring to the boil, then poach gently for 8–10 minutes, until the flesh comes away easily from the bones.

2 Make the dressing. Whisk together the vinegar, oil and spring onions and season with salt, paprika and pepper.

3 Put the salad leaves in a large bowl, pour over the dressing and toss well. Remove the rind from the orange using a zester, then peel it, removing all the pith. Slice into thin rounds.

4 Flake the fish, discarding the bones, and add to the salad. Add a pinch of zest, the orange slices and tomatoes, toss gently and serve with bread.

> **Cook's Tip**
> *Skate is a fine-flavoured fish with creamy flesh. Once it is cooked, it comes away from the bone very easily.*

Sea Bass Energy 213Kcal/890kJ; Protein 29g; Carbohydrate 0g, of which sugars 0g; Fat 11g, of which saturates 5g; Cholesterol 138mg; Calcium 199mg; Fibre 0.1g; Sodium 200mg.
Skate Energy 230kcal/965kJ; Protein 31.6g; Carbohydrate 4.8g, of which sugars 4.8g; Fat 9.5g, of which saturates 1.3g; Cholesterol 0mg; Calcium 118mg; Fibre 1.5g; Sodium 247mg.

Skate with Black Butter

Skate can be quite inexpensive and this classic dish is perfect for a family supper. The sweet flesh is easily removed from the unthreatening soft bones, and it is a good choice for children as well as senior members of the family. Serve it with steamed leeks and plain boiled potatoes.

Serves 4
4 skate wings, about
   225g/8oz each
60ml/4 tbsp red wine vinegar
   or malt vinegar
30ml/2 tbsp drained capers in
   vinegar, chopped if large
30ml/2 tbsp chopped
   fresh parsley
150g/5oz/⅔ cup butter
salt and ground black pepper

Preparation: 2 minutes; Cooking: 15–17 minutes

1 Put the skate wings in a large, shallow pan, cover with cold water and add a pinch of salt and 15ml/1 tbsp of the red wine or malt vinegar.

2 Bring to the boil, skim the surface, then lower the heat and simmer gently for about 10–12 minutes, until the skate flesh comes away from the bone easily. Carefully drain the skate and peel off the skin.

3 Transfer the skate to a warmed serving dish, season with salt and pepper and sprinkle over the capers and parsley. Keep hot.

4 In a small pan, heat the butter until it foams and turns a rich nutty brown. Pour it over the skate. Pour the remaining vinegar into the pan and boil until reduced by about two-thirds. Drizzle over the skate and serve.

Cook's Tips
• *Don't be put off by the faint ammonia smell of skate. It vanishes when the fish is cooked.*
• *Despite the title of the recipe, the butter should be a rich golden brown. It should never be allowed to blacken, or it will taste unpleasantly bitter.*

Halibut with Sauce Vierge

Sauce vierge can be served either at room temperature or, as in this popular fish dish, slightly warm.

Serves 2
3 large ripe beefsteak tomatoes, peeled, seeded and chopped
2 shallots or 1 small red onion, finely chopped
1 garlic clove, crushed
90ml/6 tbsp chopped mixed fresh herbs, such as parsley, coriander (cilantro), basil, tarragon, chervil or chives
120ml/4fl oz/½ cup extra virgin olive oil, plus extra for greasing
4 halibut fillets or steaks (175–200g/6–7oz each)
salt and ground black pepper
green salad, to serve

Preparation: 4 minutes; Cooking: 5–6 minutes

1 To make the sauce vierge, mix together the tomatoes, shallots or onion, garlic and herbs in a bowl. Stir in the oil and season with salt and ground black pepper. Cover the bowl with clear film (plastic wrap) and leave the sauce to stand at room temperature while you grill the fish.

2 Preheat the grill (broiler). Line a grill (broiling) pan with foil and brush the foil lightly with oil.

3 Season the fish with salt and pepper. Place the fish on the foil and brush with a little extra oil. Grill (broil) for 5–6 minutes until the flesh is opaque and the top lightly browned.

4 Meanwhile, transfer the sauce to a pan and heat it gently for a few minutes. Serve the fish with the sauce and a salad.

Cook's Tips
• *To peel the tomatoes, put a cross in the base of each one. Place them in a heatproof bowl and cover with boiling water. After 30 seconds, lift them out and plunge them into a bowl of cold water. Drain, then remove the skins.*
• *If time permits, leave the sauce to stand for up to an hour before heating it to serve with the fish.*

Skate Energy 411kcal/1709kJ; Protein 30.8g; Carbohydrate 0.6g, of which sugars 0.5g; Fat 31.8g, of which saturates 19.5g; Cholesterol 80mg; Calcium 112mg; Fibre 0.6g; Sodium 472mg.
Halibut Energy 791kcal/3311kJ; Protein 89.3g; Carbohydrate 10.6g, of which sugars 9.7g; Fat 43.9g, of which saturates 6.5g; Cholesterol 140mg; Calcium 230mg; Fibre 4.9g; Sodium 276mg.

Griddled Halibut

Any thick white fish fillets can be cooked in this versatile dish, but the flavoursome sauce of tomatoes, capers, anchovies and herbs also gives humbler fish such as cod, haddock or hake a real lift.

Serves 4

2.5ml/½ tsp fennel seeds
2.5ml/½ tsp celery seeds
5ml/1 tsp mixed peppercorns
105ml/7 tbsp olive oil
5ml/1 tsp chopped fresh
   thyme leaves
5ml/1 tsp chopped fresh
   rosemary leaves
5ml/1 tsp chopped fresh oregano

675–800g/1½–1¾ lb middle cut
   of halibut, about 3cm/1¼ in
   thick, cut into 4 pieces
coarse sea salt

For the sauce

105ml/7 tbsp extra virgin olive oil
juice of 1 lemon
1 garlic clove, finely chopped
2 tomatoes, peeled, seeded
   and diced
5ml/1 tsp small capers
2 drained canned anchovy
   fillets, chopped
5ml/1 tsp chopped fresh chives
15ml/1 tbsp chopped fresh
   basil leaves
15ml/1 tbsp chopped
   fresh chervil

Preparation: 7 minutes; Cooking: 6–8 minutes

1 Prepare the barbecue. Heat a griddle on the grill rack over the hot coals. Mix the fennel and celery seeds with the peppercorns in a mortar. Crush with a pestle, and then stir in coarse sea salt to taste. Spoon into a shallow dish large enough to hold the fish in one layer and stir in the herbs and oil.

2 Add the halibut pieces to the olive oil mixture, turning them to coat them thoroughly, then arrange them with the dark skin uppermost in the griddle. Cook for about 6–8 minutes, or until the fish is cooked all the way through and the skin has browned.

3 Combine all the sauce ingredients except the fresh herbs in a pan and heat gently on the grill rack until warm but not hot. Stir in the chives, basil and chervil.

4 Place the halibut on four warmed plates. Spoon the sauce around and over the fish and serve immediately.

Grilled Sole with Chive Butter

The very best way of transforming simple grilled fish into a luxury dish is by topping it with a flavoured butter, as in this recipe.

Serves 4

115g/4oz/½ cup unsalted
   (sweet) butter, softened, plus
   extra, melted
5ml/1 tsp diced lemon grass
pinch of finely grated lime rind
1 kaffir lime leaf, very finely
   shredded (optional)
45ml/3 tbsp chopped chives or
   chopped chive flowers, plus
   extra chives or chive flowers
   to garnish
2.5–5ml/½–1 tsp Thai fish sauce
4 sole, skinned
salt and ground black pepper
lemon or lime wedges, to serve

Preparation: 3–4 minutes; Cooking: 10 minutes

1 Put the butter in a bowl and cream it with a wooden spoon. Add the lemon grass, lime rind, lime leaf, if using, and chives or chive flowers. Mix well, making sure all the ingredients are thoroughly combined, then season to taste with Thai fish sauce, salt and pepper.

2 Chill the butter mixture to firm it a little, then form it into a roll and wrap in foil or clear film (plastic wrap). Chill until firm. Preheat the grill (broiler).

3 Brush the fish with melted butter. Place it on the grill rack and season. Grill (broil) for about 5 minutes, then carefully turn the pieces of fish over and grill the other side for 4–5 minutes, until firm and just cooked.

4 Meanwhile, cut the chilled butter into thin slices. Put the fish on individual plates and top with the butter. Garnish with chives and serve with lemon or lime wedges.

Cook's Tips
• Finer white fish fillets, such as plaice, can be cooked in this way, but reduce the cooking time slightly.
• The flavoured butter can be made ahead and frozen.

Griddled Halibut Energy 363kcal/1513kJ; Protein 37.4g; Carbohydrate 1.9g, of which sugars 1.8g; Fat 22.9g, of which saturates 3.3g; Cholesterol 60mg; Calcium 82mg; Fibre 1.1g; Sodium 169mg.
Grilled Sole Energy 349kcal/1447kJ; Protein 27.4g; Carbohydrate 0.5g, of which sugars 0.5g; Fat 26.3g, of which saturates 15g; Cholesterol 136mg; Calcium 49mg; Fibre 0g; Sodium 591mg.

Pan-fried Sole with Lemon Butter Sauce

The delicate flavour and texture of sole is brought out in this classic recipe, which uses just a simple sauce to complement the fish.

45ml/3 tbsp olive oil
50g/2oz/¼ cup butter
60ml/4 tbsp lemon juice
30ml/2 tbsp rinsed bottled capers
salt and ground black pepper

Serves 2
30–45ml/2–3 tbsp plain
  (all-purpose) flour
4 lemon or Dover sole fillets
  (see Cook's Tip)

For the garnish
fresh flat leaf parsley
lemon wedges

Preparation: 2–3 minutes; Cooking: 9 minutes

1 Season the flour with salt and pepper. Coat the sole fillets evenly on both sides. Heat the oil with half the butter in a large shallow pan until foaming. Add two sole fillets and fry over a medium heat for 2–3 minutes on each side.

2 Lift out the sole fillets with a fish slice or metal spatula and place on a warmed serving platter. Keep hot. Fry the remaining sole fillets in the same way, then add them to the platter.

3 Remove the pan from the heat and add the lemon juice and remaining butter. Return the pan to a high heat and stir vigorously until the pan juices are sizzling and beginning to turn golden brown. Remove from the heat and stir in the capers.

4 Arrange the sole fillets on two plates and pour the pan juices over them. Sprinkle with salt and pepper to taste. Garnish with the parsley and lemon wedges. Serve at once.

> **Cook's Tip**
> Lemon sole is used here because it is often easier to obtain and less expensive than Dover sole.

Fried Plaice with Tomato Sauce

This simple dish is perennially popular with children. It works equally well with lemon sole or dabs, which do not need skinning, or fillets of haddock or whiting.

25g/1oz/2 tbsp butter
30ml/2 tbsp sunflower oil
salt and ground black pepper
fresh basil leaves, to garnish
1 lemon, quartered, to serve

Serves 4
25g/1oz/¼ cup plain
  (all-purpose) flour
2 eggs, beaten
75g/3oz/¾ cup dried
  breadcrumbs, preferably
  home-made
4 small plaice or flounder, skinned

For the tomato sauce
30ml/2 tbsp olive oil
1 red onion, finely chopped
1 garlic clove, finely chopped
400g/14oz can chopped
  tomatoes
15ml/1 tbsp tomato
  purée (paste)
15ml/1 tbsp torn fresh
  basil leaves

Preparation: 5 minutes; Cooking: 14 minutes

1 First make the tomato sauce. Heat the olive oil in a large pan, add the finely chopped onion and garlic and cook for about 2–3 minutes, until softened. Stir in the chopped tomatoes and tomato purée and simmer for 10 minutes, or until the fish is ready to be served, stirring occasionally.

2 Spread out the flour in a shallow dish, pour the beaten eggs into another and spread out the breadcrumbs in a third.

3 Season the fish with salt and pepper. Hold a fish in your left hand and dip it first in flour, then in egg and finally in the breadcrumbs, patting the crumbs on with your dry right hand. Aim for an even coating that is not too thick. Shake off any excess crumbs and set aside while you prepare the frying pans.

4 Heat the butter and oil in two large frying pans until foaming. Fry the fish for about 5 minutes on each side, until golden brown and cooked through. Drain on kitchen paper. Season the tomato sauce, stir in the basil and serve with the fish, garnished with basil leaves. Offer lemon wedges separately.

Pan-fried Sole Energy 535kcal/2222kJ; Protein 35.9g; Carbohydrate 7.9g, of which sugars 0.3g; Fat 40.2g, of which saturates 15.8g; Cholesterol 173mg; Calcium 53mg; Fibre 0.3g; Sodium 342mg.
Fried Plaice Energy 417kcal/1738kJ; Protein 28.1g; Carbohydrate 17.7g, of which sugars 4.9g; Fat 26.4g, of which saturates 3.1g; Cholesterol 0mg; Calcium 113mg; Fibre 1.6g; Sodium 349mg.

Herring Fillets in Oatmeal with Apples

Fresh herrings make an inexpensive and tasty supper fish. Coating them in oatmeal before frying gives them a crisp outer edge that contrasts well with the tender flesh and the sweet fruitiness of the fried apples.

Serves 4
8 herring fillets
seasoned flour, for coating
1 egg, beaten
115g/4oz/1 cup fine pinhead
   oatmeal or oatflakes
oil, for frying
2 eating apples
25g/1oz/2 tbsp butter

Preparation: 3–4 minutes; Cooking: 6 minutes

1 Wash the fish and pat dry with kitchen paper. Skin the fillets and check that all bones have been removed.

2 Toss the herring fillets in the seasoned flour, then dip them in the beaten egg and roll them in the pinhead oatmeal or oatflakes until evenly coated.

3 Heat a little oil in a heavy frying pan and fry the fillets, a few at a time, until golden brown. Drain on kitchen paper, transfer to a serving platter and keep warm.

4 Core the apples, but do not peel. Slice them quite thinly. In another pan, melt the butter and fry the apple slices gently until just softened. Serve the apple with the coated fish fillets.

> **Variations**
> • Mackerel fillets can be cooked in the same way.
> • A fruit sauce – apple, gooseberry or rhubarb – could be served instead of the sliced apples. Cook 225g/8oz of your preferred fruit with 90ml/6 tbsp cold water until just softened. Purée and serve with the fish.
> • Poached nectarine slices would also be a good accompaniment.

Mackerel with Mustard & Lemon

Mackerel must be really fresh to be enjoyed. Look for bright, firm-looking fish.

Serves 4
4 fresh mackerel, about 275g/10oz
  each, gutted and cleaned
175–225g/6–8oz young
  spinach leaves

For the mustard and lemon butter
115g/4oz/½ cup butter
30ml/2 tbsp wholegrain mustard
grated rind of 1 lemon
30ml/2 tbsp lemon juice
45ml/3 tbsp chopped
  fresh parsley
salt and ground black pepper

Preparation: 5 minutes; Cooking: 10–12 minutes

1 Place the mackerel on a board. Cut off the mackerel heads just behind the gills, using a sharp knife, then slit the belly so that each fish can be opened out flat.

2 Place the fish skinside up. With the heel of your hand, press along the backbone to loosen it.

3 Turn the fish the right way up and pull the bone away. Cut off the tail and cut each fish in half lengthways. Wash all the mackerel quickly under cold running water, drain and pat dry.

4 Turn the mackerel over again. Using a sharp knife, score the skin three or four times, then season the fish with salt and ground black pepper.

5 To make the mustard and lemon butter, heat the butter in a small pan until it has melted, then stir in the wholegrain mustard, grated lemon rind and juice, with the parsley and salt and pepper to taste.

6 Place the mackerel on a grill (broiling) pan. Brush a little of the butter over the mackerel and grill (broil) for 5 minutes each side, basting occasionally, until cooked through.

7 Arrange the spinach leaves around a large plate. Place the mackerel on top. Heat the remaining flavoured butter until sizzling and pour over the mackerel. Serve at once.

Herring Energy 566kcal/2361kJ; Protein 35.6g; Carbohydrate 24.3g, of which sugars 3.4g; Fat 37g, of which saturates 9.9g; Cholesterol 146mg; Calcium 128mg; Fibre 2.6g; Sodium 270mg.
Mackerel Energy 785kcal/3253kJ; Protein 49.8g; Carbohydrate 1.2g, of which sugars 1.1g; Fat 64.5g, of which saturates 23.3g; Cholesterol 194mg; Calcium 116mg; Fibre 1.3g; Sodium 502mg.

Fillets of Brill in Red Wine Sauce

Forget the old maxim that red wine and fish do not go well together. The robust sauce adds colour and richness to this excellent and unusual fish dish.

Serves 4

4 fillets of brill, each about 175g/6oz each, skinned

150g/5oz/10 tbsp chilled butter, plus extra for greasing
115g/4oz shallots, thinly sliced
200ml/7fl oz/scant 1 cup robust red wine
200ml/7fl oz/scant 1 cup fish stock
salt and ground white pepper
fresh chervil or flat leaf parsley leaves, to garnish

Preparation: 3–4 minutes; Cooking: 12–14 minutes

1 Preheat the oven to 180°C/350°F/Gas 4. Season the fish on both sides with a little salt and plenty of pepper. Generously butter a flameproof dish, which is large enough to take all the brill fillets in a single layer without overlapping. Spread the shallots over the base and lay the fish fillets on top. Season the fish generously with salt and ground black pepper.

2 Pour in the red wine and fish stock, cover the dish and bring the liquid to just below boiling point. Transfer the dish to the oven and bake for 6–8 minutes, or until the brill is just cooked. It should flake readily if tested with the tip of a sharp knife.

3 Using a fish slice, carefully lift the fish and shallots on to a serving dish, cover with foil and keep hot.

4 Transfer the dish to the hob and bring the cooking liquid to the boil over a high heat. Cook until it has reduced by half.

5 Lower the heat and whisk in the chilled butter or margarine, one piece at a time, to make a smooth, shiny sauce. Season the sauce with salt and ground white pepper, remove from the heat and cover to keep hot.

6 Divide the shallots among four warmed plates and lay the brill fillets on top. Pour the sauce over and around the fish and garnish with the chervil or flat leaf parsley.

Monkfish with Pimiento & Cream

This recipe comes from Spain's Rioja country, where a special horned red pepper is used to make a spicy sauce. Here, red peppers are used with a little chilli, while cream makes a mellow pink sauce. To drink, choose a Marqués de Cáceres white Rioja.

Serves 4

2 large red (bell) peppers
1kg/2¼lb monkfish tail or 900g/2lb halibut

plain (all-purpose) flour, for dusting
30ml/2 tbsp olive oil
25g/1oz/2 tbsp butter
120ml/4fl oz/½ cup white Rioja or dry vermouth
½ dried chilli, seeded and chopped
8 raw prawns (shrimp), in the shell
150ml/¼ pint/⅔ cup double (heavy) cream
salt and ground black pepper
fresh flat leaf parsley, to garnish

Preparation: 4 minutes; Cooking: 12–14 minutes

1 Preheat the grill (broiler) to high and cook the peppers for 6–8 minutes, turning occasionally, until they are soft, and the skins blackened. Leave, covered, until cool enough to handle. Skin and discard the stalks and seeds. Put the flesh into a blender, strain in the juices and purée.

2 Cut the monkfish or halibut into eight steaks (freeze the bones for stock). Season well and dust with flour.

3 Heat the oil and butter in a large frying pan and fry the fish for 3 minutes on each side. Remove to a warm dish.

4 Add the wine or vermouth and chilli to the pan and stir to deglaze the pan. Add the prawns and cook them briefly, then lift out with a slotted spoon and reserve in a bowl.

5 Boil the sauce to reduce by half, then strain into a small jug (pitcher). Add the cream to the pan and boil briefly to reduce. Return the sauce to the pan, stir in the puréed peppers and check the seasonings. Pour the sauce over the fish and serve garnished with the cooked prawns and parsley.

Fillets of Brill Energy 511kcal/2123kJ; Protein 35.7g; Carbohydrate 1.3g, of which sugars 1.3g; Fat 36.7g, of which saturates 19.5g; Cholesterol 156mg; Calcium 97mg; Fibre 0.4g; Sodium 454mg.
Monkfish Energy 518kcal/2163kJ; Protein 50.2g; Carbohydrate 10.8g, of which sugars 10.3g; Fat 27.4g, of which saturates 13.7g; Cholesterol 140mg; Calcium 74mg; Fibre 2.3g; Sodium 115mg.

Spicy Squid

This aromatically spiced squid dish is simple yet delicious. Gone are the days when cleaning squid was such a chore: today they can be bought ready-cleaned from fish stores, market stalls and the fish counters of large supermarkets.

Serves 3–4
675g/1½lb squid, cleaned
45ml/3 tbsp groundnut oil
1 onion, finely chopped
2 garlic cloves, crushed
1 beefsteak tomato, peeled and chopped
15ml/1 tbsp dark soy sauce
2.5ml/½ tsp freshly grated nutmeg
6 cloves
150ml/¼ pint/⅔ cup water
juice of ½ lemon or lime
salt and ground black pepper
fresh coriander (cilantro) leaves and shredded spring onion (scallion), to garnish

Preparation: 6 minutes; Cooking: 9–11 minutes

1 Rinse and drain the squid, then slice lengthways along one side and open it out flat. Score the inside of the squid in a lattice pattern, using the blunt side of a knife blade, then cut it crossways into long thin strips.

2 Heat a wok and add 15ml/1 tbsp of the oil. When hot, toss in the squid strips and stir-fry for 2–3 minutes, by which time the squid will have curled into attractive shapes or into firm rings. Lift out and set aside.

3 Wipe out the wok, add the remaining oil and heat it. Stir-fry the onion and garlic until soft and beginning to brown. Stir in the tomato, soy sauce, nutmeg, cloves, water and lemon or lime juice. Bring to the boil, lower the heat and add the squid with seasoning to taste.

4 Cook the mixture gently for a further 3–5 minutes, stirring occasionally to prevent it from sticking. Take care not to overcook the squid.

5 Spoon the spicy squid on to warm plates. Garnish with coriander leaves and shredded spring onions and serve.

Stir-fried Squid with Ginger

There's an ancient belief that a well-loved wok holds the memory of all the dishes that have ever been cooked in it. Give yours something to think about by introducing it to this classic combination of baby squid in soy sauce, ginger and lemon juice. Chopped spring onions add a crunchy texture that is very welcome.

Serves 2
4 ready-prepared baby squid, total weight about 250g/9oz
15ml/1 tbsp vegetable oil
2 garlic cloves, finely chopped
30ml/2 tbsp soy sauce
2.5cm/1in piece fresh root ginger, peeled and finely chopped
juice of ½ lemon
5ml/1 tsp granulated (white) sugar
2 spring onions (scallions), chopped

Preparation: 2–3 minutes; Cooking: 2 minutes

1 Rinse the squid well and pat dry with kitchen paper. Place on a board and use a sharp knife to cut the bodies into rings. Halve the tentacles, if necessary.

2 Heat the oil in a wok or frying pan and cook the garlic until golden brown, but do not let it burn. Add the squid and stir-fry for 30 seconds over a high heat.

3 Add the soy sauce, ginger, lemon juice, sugar and spring onions. Stir-fry for a further 30 seconds, then spoon into individual heated bowls and serve.

Cook's Tip
Squid has an undeserved reputation for being rubbery in texture. This is always a result of overcooking it.

Variation
This dish is often prepared with fresh galangal rather than ginger and works well with most kinds of seafood, including prawns (shrimp) and scallops.

Spicy Squid Energy 310kcal/1301kJ; Protein 35.8g; Carbohydrate 8.6g, of which sugars 4.7g; Fat 15.1g, of which saturates 3g; Cholesterol 506mg; Calcium 46mg; Fibre 1.2g; Sodium 610mg.
Stir-fried Squid Energy 165Kcal/694kJ; Protein 19.7g; Carbohydrate 4.8g, of which sugars 3.2g; Fat 7.6g, of which saturates 1.2g; Cholesterol 281mg; Calcium 20mg; Fibre 0g; Sodium 1206mg.

Prawn Salad

In Mexico, this salad would form the fish course in a formal meal, but it is so good that you'll want to serve it on all sorts of occasions. It is perfect for a buffet lunch.

Serves 4

450g/1lb cooked peeled
  prawns (shrimp)
juice of 1 lime
3 tomatoes
1 ripe but firm avocado
30ml/2 tbsp hot chilli sauce
5ml/1 tsp sugar
150ml/¼ pint/⅔ cup sour cream
2 Little Gem (Bibb) lettuces,
  separated into leaves
salt and ground black pepper
fresh basil leaves and strips of
  green pepper to garnish

Preparation: 10 minutes; Cooking: 0 minutes

1 Put the prawns in a large bowl, add the lime juice and salt and pepper. Toss lightly, then cover and leave to marinate while you prepare the tomatoes and avocado.

2 Cut a cross in the base of each tomato. Place them in a heatproof bowl and pour over boiling water to cover.

3 After 3 minutes, lift the tomatoes out on a slotted spoon and plunge them into a bowl of cold water. Drain. The skins will have begun to peel back easily from the crosses.

4 Skin the tomatoes completely, then cut them in half and squeeze out the seeds. Chop the flesh into 1cm/¼ in cubes and add it to the prawns.

5 Cut the avocado in half, remove the skin and seed, then slice the flesh into 1cm/½ in chunks. Add it to the prawn and tomato mixture.

6 Mix the hot chilli sauce, sugar and soured cream in a bowl. Fold into the prawn mixture. Line a bowl with the lettuce leaves, then top with the prawn mixture. The salad can be served immediately, but will have a better flavour if covered and chilled for at least 1 hour. Garnish with fresh basil and strips of green pepper. Crusty bread makes a perfect accompaniment.

Salt & Pepper Prawns

These succulent shellfish beg to be eaten with the fingers, so provide finger bowls or hot wipes for all your guests.

Serves 3–4

15–18 large raw prawns
  (shrimp), in the shell,
  about 450g/1lb
vegetable oil, for deep-frying
3 shallots or 1 small onion,
  very finely chopped
2 garlic cloves, crushed
1cm/½in piece fresh root ginger,
  peeled and very finely grated
1–2 fresh red chillies, seeded
  and finely sliced
2.5ml/½ tsp caster (superfine)
  sugar or to taste
3–4 spring onions (scallions),
  shredded, to garnish

For the fried salt
10ml/2 tsp salt
5ml/1 tsp Sichuan peppercorns

Preparation: 7–8 minutes; Cooking: 4–5 minutes

1 Make the fried salt by dry-frying the salt and peppercorns in a heavy frying pan over medium heat until the peppercorns begin to release their aroma. Cool the mixture, then tip into a mortar and crush with a pestle.

2 Carefully remove the heads and legs from the raw prawns and discard. Leave the body shells and the tails in place. Pat the prepared prawns dry with sheets of kitchen paper.

3 Heat the oil for deep frying to 190°C/375°F. Fry the prawns for 1 minute, then lift them out and drain thoroughly on kitchen paper. Spoon 30ml/2 tbsp of the hot oil into a large frying pan, leaving the rest of the oil to one side to cool.

4 Heat the oil in the frying pan. Add the fried salt, with the shallots or onion, garlic, ginger, chillies and sugar. Toss all the ingredients in the pan together for 1 minute.

5 Add the prawns and toss them over the heat for about 1 minute more until they are coated and the shells are pleasantly impregnated with the seasonings. Spoon the shellfish mixture into heated serving bowls and garnish with the shredded spring onions.

Prawn Salad Energy 221kcal/920kJ; Protein 21.8g; Carbohydrate 3.8g, of which sugars 3.5g; Fat 13.2g, of which saturates 5.9g; Cholesterol 242mg; Calcium 141mg; Fibre 1.3g; Sodium 232mg.
Salt & Pepper Prawns Energy 122kcal/514kJ; Protein 20.1g; Carbohydrate 2.7g, of which sugars 2.4g; Fat 3.5g, of which saturates 0.5g; Cholesterol 219mg; Calcium 97mg; Fibre 0.3g; Sodium 1197mg.

Prawns in Garlic Butter

This quick and easy dish is perfect for serving to friends who don't mind getting their hands dirty. Provide a plate for the prawn shells and offer warm tortillas or chunks of crusty farmhouse bread for mopping up the delectable juices. Clean plates are guaranteed with this superb seafood recipe.

Serves 6

900g/2lb large raw tiger prawns (jumbo shrimp), in their shells, thawed if frozen
115g/4oz/½ cup butter
15ml/1 tbsp vegetable oil
6 garlic cloves, crushed
grated rind and juice of 2 limes
small bunch of fresh coriander (cilantro), chopped
warm tortillas, to serve
lemon slices, for the finger bowls

Preparation: 8 minutes; Cooking: 6–7 minutes

1 Rinse the prawns in a colander, remove their heads and leave them to drain. Heat the butter and oil in a large frying pan, add the garlic and fry over a low heat for 2–3 minutes.

2 Add the lime rind and juice. Cook, stirring constantly, for 1 minute more.

3 Add the prawns and cook them for 2–3 minutes until they turn pink. Remove from the heat, sprinkle with coriander and serve with the warm tortillas. Give each guest a finger bowl filled with water and a slice of lemon, for cleaning their fingers after shelling the prawns, and provide paper napkins.

> **Cook's Tips**
> • *Frozen prawns (shrimp) should be put in a colander and thawed for 5–8 hours in the refrigerator or 2–3 hours at room temperature. Set the colander over a bowl. For faster thawing, run cold water over the prawns or defrost them in the microwave, following the instructions in your handbook.*
> • *Cook the prawns in a large frying pan or cast iron flameproof dish that can be taken directly to the table, so that they retain their heat until they are served.*

Sizzling Prawns

When you splash out and buy a luxury item like these large prawns, you want to be sure they taste great. This recipe is swift, simple and always a sure-fire success. Serve these for a celebration lunch.

Serves 4

1–2 dried chillies (to taste)
60ml/4 tbsp olive oil
3 garlic cloves, finely chopped
16 large raw prawns (jumbo shrimp), in the shell
salt and ground black pepper
French bread, to serve

Preparation: 2–3 minutes; Cooking: 5 minutes

1 Split the chillies lengthways and discard the seeds. It is best to do this with a knife and fork, because the seeds, in particular, contain hot capsaicin, which can be very irritating to the eyes, nose and mouth.

2 Heat the oil in a large frying pan and stir-fry the garlic and chilli for 1 minute, until the garlic begins to turn brown.

3 Add the whole prawns and stir-fry for 3–4 minutes, coating them well with the flavoured oil.

4 Remove from the heat and divide the prawns among four dishes. Spoon over the flavoured oil and serve immediately. (Remember to provide a plate for the heads and shells, plus plenty of napkins for messy fingers.)

> **Variations**
> • *Another great way to serve the prawns (shrimp) is in a warm lime and sweet chilli dressing. Use garlic to flavour the oil, but remove it before frying the prawns (shrimp). Let the oil for frying cool slightly, then whisk in fresh lime juice and a little sweet chilli sauce. Spoon over the prawns.*
> • *An alternative to using fresh chillies is simply to use chilli oil for frying the garlic and prawns, or, if you prefer to avoid chillies altogether, substitute sun-dried tomatoes for the chillies and use a little of the oil from the jar for frying.*

Prawns in Garlic Energy 223kcal/924kJ; Protein 13.3g; Carbohydrate 0.3g, of which sugars 0.3g; Fat 18.8g, of which saturates 10.5g; Cholesterol 87mg; Calcium 103mg; Fibre 0.4g; Sodium 1034mg.
Sizzling Prawns Energy 124kcal/511kJ; Protein 5.7g; Carbohydrate 0g, of which sugars 0g; Fat 11.2g, of which saturates 1.6g; Cholesterol 63mg; Calcium 26mg; Fibre 0g; Sodium 62mg.

Stir-fried Prawns with Tamarind

Fresh tamarind pods can be bought, but it is much simpler and easier to use tamarind paste either in block form or packed in a jar.

Serves 4–6
6 dried red chillies
30ml/2 tbsp vegetable oil
30ml/2 tbsp chopped onion
30ml/2 tbsp palm sugar (jaggery)
  or light muscovado (brown) sugar
30ml/2 tbsp chicken stock
  or water
15ml/1 tbsp Thai fish sauce
90ml/6 tbsp tamarind juice, made
  by mixing tamarind paste with
  warm water
450g/1lb raw prawns (shrimp),
  peeled (see Cook's Tip)
15ml/1 tbsp fried chopped garlic
30ml/2 tbsp fried sliced shallots

Preparation: 8 minutes; Cooking: 10–12 minutes

1 Heat a wok or large frying pan, but do not add any oil at this stage. Add the dried chillies and dry-fry them by pressing them against the surface of the wok or pan with a spatula, turning them occasionally. Do not let them burn. Lift them out of the pan and set them aside on a plate to cool slightly.

2 Add the oil to the wok or pan and reheat. Add the chopped onion and cook over medium heat, stirring occasionally, for 2–3 minutes, until softened and golden brown.

3 Add the sugar, stock or water, fish sauce, dry-fried red chillies and the tamarind juice, stirring constantly until the sugar has dissolved. Bring to the boil over high heat, then lower the heat slightly.

4 Add the prawns, garlic and shallots to the wok or pan. Toss over the heat for 3–4 minutes, until the prawns are cooked. Transfer to a warmed dish or individual bowls.

Cook's Tip
Leave a few prawns (shrimp) in their shells for a garnish, if you like. Fry them on their own until they turn pink.

Fragrant Tiger Prawns with Dill

This elegant dish has a fresh, light flavour and is equally good served as a simple supper or for a dinner party. It takes only minutes to make, so you can spend more time with your guests. The delicate texture of fresh prawns goes really well with mild cucumber and fragrant dill, and all you need is some rice or noodles to serve.

Serves 4–6
500g/1¼lb raw tiger prawns
  (jumbo shrimp), heads and
  shells removed but tails left on
500g/1¼lb cucumber
30ml/2 tbsp butter
15ml/1 tbsp olive oil
15ml/1 tbsp finely chopped garlic
45ml/3 tbsp chopped fresh dill
juice of 1 lemon
salt and ground black pepper
steamed rice or noodles, to serve

Preparation: 3–4 minutes; Cooking: 5–7 minutes

1 Using a small, sharp knife, carefully make a shallow slit along the back of each prawn and use the point of the knife to remove the black vein. Set the prawns aside.

2 Peel the cucumber and slice in half lengthways. Using a small teaspoon, gently scoop out all the seeds and discard. Cut the cucumber into 4 x 1cm/1½ x ½in sticks.

3 Heat a wok over a high heat, then add the butter and oil. When the butter has melted, add the cucumber and garlic and fry over a high heat for 2–3 minutes, stirring continuously.

4 Add the prepared prawns to the wok and continue to stir-fry over a high heat for 3–4 minutes, or until the prawns turn pink and are just cooked through, then remove from the heat.

5 Add the fresh dill and lemon juice to the wok and toss to combine. Season well with salt and ground black pepper and serve immediately with steamed rice or noodles.

Cook's Tip
The best rice to use is jasmine, also known as Thai fragrant rice.

Stir-fried Prawns Energy 112kcal/469kJ; Protein 13.4g; Carbohydrate 5.5g, of which sugars 5.2g; Fat 4.1g, of which saturates 0.5g; Cholesterol 146mg; Calcium 65mg; Fibre 0.2g; Sodium 321mg.
Fragrant Prawns Energy 192Kcal/798kJ; Protein 23.2g; Carbohydrate 2.5g, of which sugars 1.9g; Fat 9.8g, of which saturates 4.4g; Cholesterol 260mg; Calcium 123mg; Fibre 0.9g; Sodium 287mg.

Butterflied Prawns in Hot Chocolate Sauce

This comes from Spain, where, as in Mexico, there is a long tradition of cooking savoury food – even shellfish – with chocolate.

Serves 4
8 large raw prawns (shrimp), in the shell
15ml/1 tbsp seasoned plain (all-purpose) flour

15ml/1 tbsp pale dry sherry
juice of 1 large orange
15g/¹⁄₂oz dark (bittersweet) chocolate, chopped
30ml/2 tbsp olive oil
2 garlic cloves, finely chopped
2.5cm/1in piece fresh root ginger, finely chopped
1 small dried chilli, seeded and chopped
salt and ground black pepper

Preparation: 10 minutes; Cooking: 8–9 minutes

1 Peel the prawns, leaving just the tail sections intact. Make a shallow cut down the back of each one and carefully pull out and discard the dark intestinal tract.

2 Turn the prawns over so that the undersides are uppermost, and then carefully slit them open from tail to top, using a small sharp knife, cutting them almost, but not quite, through to the central back line. Press the prawns down firmly to flatten them out. Coat with the seasoned flour and set aside.

3 Gently heat the sherry and orange juice in a small pan. When warm, remove from the heat and stir in the chopped chocolate until melted.

4 Heat the oil in a frying pan. Add the garlic, ginger and chilli and cook for 2 minutes until golden. Remove with a slotted spoon and reserve. Add the prawns, cut side down, and cook for 2–3 minutes until golden brown with pink edges. Turn the prawns and cook for a further 2 minutes.

5 Return the garlic mixture to the pan and pour the chocolate sauce over. Cook for 1 minute, turning the prawns to coat them in the glossy sauce. Season to taste and serve hot.

King Prawns in Crispy Batter

A huge range of prawns is enjoyed in Spain, each with its appropriate cooking method. Langostinos are deep-water prawns, often with tiger stripes, and can be among the biggest of the crustaceans. The best way to enjoy them is dipped in a simple batter and deep-fried.

Serves 4
120ml/4fl oz/¹⁄₂ cup water
1 large egg (US extra large)
115g/4oz/1 cup plain (all-purpose) flour
5ml/1 tsp cayenne pepper
12 raw king prawns (jumbo shrimp), in the shell
vegetable oil, for deep frying
flat leaf parsley, to garnish
lemon wedges, to serve (optional)

Preparation: 5–8 minutes; Cooking: 2–3 minutes

1 In a large bowl, whisk together the water and the egg. Whisk in the flour and cayenne pepper until smooth.

2 Peel the prawns, leaving just the tails intact. Make a shallow cut down the back of each prawn.

3 Using the tip of the knife, pull out and discard the dark intestinal tract.

4 Heat the oil in a large pan or deep-fat fryer, until a cube of bread dropped into the oil browns in 1 minute.

5 Holding the prawns by their tails, dip them into the batter, one at a time, shaking off any excess. Carefully drop each prawn into the oil and fry for 2–3 minutes until crisp and golden. Drain on kitchen paper, garnish with parsley and serve with lemon wedges, if you like.

> **Variation**
> If you have any batter left over, use it to coat thin strips of vegetables such as sweet potato, beetroot (beet), carrot or (bell) pepper, or use small broccoli florets or whole baby spinach leaves. Deep-fry the vegetables until golden.

Butterflied Prawns Energy 125kcal/520kJ; Protein 8.5g; Carbohydrate 6.5g, of which sugars 3.6g; Fat 6.9g, of which saturates 1.5g; Cholesterol 88mg; Calcium 44mg; Fibre 0.2g; Sodium 88mg.
King Prawns Energy 253kcal/1061kJ; Protein 13.1g; Carbohydrate 22.4g, of which sugars 0.4g; Fat 13.1g, of which saturates 1.8g; Cholesterol 145mg; Calcium 87mg; Fibre 0.9g; Sodium 113mg.

Hot & Spicy Prawns with Coriander

This is a quick, easy and low-fat way of preparing prawns for an appetizer. If you increase the quantities, it can be served as a main course. Scallops and mussels are also delicious cooked in this way. Serve the prawns with bread to mop up the tasty juices. Lemon is traditionally squeezed over the prawns but lime juice could be used instead. Lime juice goes well with coriander.

Serves 4
20ml/4 tsp olive oil
2–3 garlic cloves, chopped
25g/1oz fresh root ginger, peeled and grated
1 fresh chilli, seeded and chopped
5ml/1 tsp cumin seeds
5ml/1 tsp paprika
450g/1lb fresh raw king prawns (jumbo shrimp), peeled
bunch of fresh coriander (cilantro), chopped
salt, to taste
1 lemon, cut into wedges, to serve

Preparation: 3–4 minutes; Cooking: 4–6 minutes

1 In a large, heavy, non-stick frying pan, heat the oil with the garlic. Stir in the ginger, chilli and cumin seeds.

2 Cook briefly, until the ingredients give off a lovely aroma, then add the paprika and toss in the prawns.

3 Fry the prawns over a fairly high heat, turning them frequently, for 3–5 minutes, or until just cooked. Season to taste with salt and add the coriander.

4 Spoon the prawns on to a large plate and serve immediately, with lemon wedges for squeezing over the prawns.

Cook's Tip
Unless you cook Thai or Chinese dishes frequently, the chances are that you will waste a lot of root ginger through using a little and leaving the remainder in the refrigerator to soften and ultimately spoil. Freeze the root in a plastic bag instead. It can be grated from frozen and will thaw almost instantly.

Prawns on Crisp Noodle Cake

The contrast between the crisp noodle cake and the shellfish mixture works well.

Serves 4
300g/11oz thin dried egg noodles
60ml/4 tbsp vegetable oil
500g/1¼lb medium raw king prawns (jumbo shrimp), peeled and deveined
2.5ml/½ tsp ground coriander
15ml/1 tbsp ground turmeric
2 garlic cloves, finely chopped
2 slices fresh root ginger, finely chopped
tender parts of 2 lemon grass stalks, finely chopped
2 shallots, finely chopped
15ml/1 tbsp tomato purée (paste)
250ml/8fl oz/1 cup coconut milk
15–30ml/1–2 tbsp lime juice
15–30ml/1–2 tbsp Thai fish sauce
1 cucumber, peeled, seeded and cut into 5cm/2in batons
1 tomato, seeded and cut into strips
2 fresh red chillies, seeded and finely sliced in rings
salt and ground black pepper
2 spring onions (scallions), finely sliced, and a few coriander (cilantro) sprigs, to garnish

Preparation: 10 minutes; Cooking: 10 minutes

1 Cook the noodles as directed on the packet. Drain, rinse and drain well again. Heat 15ml/1 tbsp of the oil in a large frying pan. Add the noodles in an even layer. Fry for 4–5 minutes until they form a crisp, golden cake. Turn over and fry the other side.

2 In a bowl, toss the prawns with the ground coriander, garlic, ginger, turmeric, and lemon grass. Add salt and pepper to taste.

3 Heat the remaining oil in a large frying pan. Fry the shallots for 1 minute, then add the prawns and fry for 2 minutes more. Remove the prawns. Stir the tomato purée, coconut milk, lime juice and fish sauce into the pan. Bring the sauce to a simmer, gently stir in the prawns, then add the cucumber. Simmer until the prawns are cooked and the sauce has a coating consistency.

4 Add the tomato, stir until warmed, then add the chillies. Serve the prawns in the sauce on the noodle cake, and garnish with the sliced spring onions and coriander sprigs.

Hot & Spicy Prawns Energy 382kcal/1590kJ; Protein 40.8g; Carbohydrate 1g, of which sugars 0.9g; Fat 23.8g, of which saturates 3.4g; Cholesterol 439mg; Calcium 254mg; Fibre 1.9g; Sodium 440mg.
Prawns on Noodle Cake Energy 134kcal/560kJ; Protein 21.2g; Carbohydrate 2.4g, of which sugars 0.5g; Fat 4.4g, of which saturates 0.6g; Cholesterol 219mg; Calcium 116mg; Fibre 1.1g; Sodium 219mg.

Prawn Rice Vermicelli

Chillies add a hint of heat to this tasty mixture of vegetables, shellfish and rice vermicelli – perfect for a midweek supper.

Serves 4
60ml/4 tbsp vegetable oil
1 large onion, finely sliced
2–4 dried red chillies,
  finely ground
30ml/2 tbsp yellow bean paste
2 garlic cloves, finely chopped
30ml/2 tbsp soy sauce
225g/8oz cooked prawns
  (shrimp), peeled
6 fried beancurd (tofu)
  blocks, sliced
225g/8oz/2⅔ cups beansprouts
115g/4oz garlic chives, chopped
350g/12oz rice vermicelli,
  soaked in warm water
  until soft, drained
2 hard-boiled eggs, cut into
  wedges, to garnish
salt and ground black pepper

Preparation: 8–10 minutes; Cooking: 6–7 minutes

1 Heat the oil in a wok. Fry the onion with the ground chillies until soft. Stir in the yellow bean paste, garlic and soy sauce. Fry for 1–2 minutes.

2 Add the prawns, beancurd slices, beansprouts and garlic chives. Stir to mix, then fry for 1–2 minutes more.

3 Add the vermicelli to the mixture and fry, stirring gently until it is evenly heated through. Taste for seasoning, adding more soy sauce if required. Pile onto a heated platter and serve immediately, garnished with the hard-boiled egg wedges.

> **Cook's Tip**
> Rice vermicelli noodles are extremely thin, almost hair-like. It is easy to confuse them with bean thread noodles, especially as the latter are also called vermicelli noodles. The difference lies in the source: bean thread vermicelli noodles are made from ground mung beans. Both are prepared in a similar fashion, by being soaked in warm water. Rice vermicelli noodles require 5–10 minutes for this process, and can then be drained and used as indicated in recipes.

Sun-dried Tomato & Prawn Stir-fry

The Mediterranean flavour of sun-dried tomatoes combined with glossy Japanese noodles – East meets West.

Serves 4
350g/12oz somen noodles
45ml/3 tbsp olive oil
20 uncooked king prawns (jumbo
  shrimp), peeled and deveined
2 garlic cloves, finely chopped
45–60ml/3–4 tbsp sun-dried
  tomato paste
salt and ground black pepper

For the garnish
handful of fresh basil leaves
30ml/2 tbsp sun-dried
  tomatoes in oil, drained
  and cut into strips

Preparation: 4–5 minutes; Cooking: 9–11 minutes

1 Cook the noodles in a large pan of boiling water until tender, following the directions on the packet. Drain.

2 Heat half the oil in a large frying pan. Add the prawns and garlic and fry them over a medium heat for 3–5 minutes, until the prawns turn pink and are firm to the touch.

3 Stir in 15ml/1 tbsp of the sun-dried tomato paste and mix well. Using a slotted spoon, transfer to a bowl and keep hot.

4 Reheat the oil remaining in the pan. Stir in the rest of the oil with the remaining sun-dried tomato paste. You may need to add a spoonful of water if the mixture is very thick. When the mixture starts to sizzle, toss in the noodles. Add salt and pepper to taste and mix well.

5 Return the prawns to the pan and toss to combine. Serve immediately garnished with the basil and sun-dried tomatoes.

> **Cook's Tip**
> Ready-made sun-dried tomato paste is readily available, but you can make your own simply by processing bottled sun-dried tomatoes with their oil.

Vermicelli Energy 546kcal/2279kJ; Protein 25.2g; Carbohydrate 78.4g, of which sugars 6.8g; Fat 14.6g, of which saturates 1.7g; Cholesterol 110mg; Calcium 408mg; Fibre 3.3g; Sodium 665mg.
Stir-fry Energy 481kcal/2026kJ; Protein 19.2g; Carbohydrate 67.4g, of which sugars 2.9g; Fat 16.8g, of which saturates 1.6g; Cholesterol 98mg; Calcium 62mg; Fibre 2.8g; Sodium 99mg.

Seafood Pancakes

English pancakes can be traced back as far as the 15th century, when a simple batter would have been made with eggs, flour and water.

Serves 4
For the pancakes
115g/4oz/1 cup plain
    (all-purpose) flour
pinch of salt
1 egg
300ml/½ pint/1¼ cups milk
15ml/1 tbsp melted butter
oil or melted butter, for cooking

For the filling
300ml/½ pint/1¼ cups milk,
    preferably semi-skimmed
    (low-fat)
150ml/¼ pint/⅔ cup fish stock
25g/1oz/2 tbsp plain
    (all-purpose) flour
25g/1oz/2 tbsp butter
350g/12oz skinless fish fillets,
    such as haddock and salmon,
    cut into bitesize pieces
115g/4oz peeled prawns (shrimp)
large handful of baby
    spinach leaves
50g/2oz cheese, such as Cheddar
    or Lancashire, grated

Preparation: 3–4 minutes; Cooking: 15 minutes

1 To make the pancakes, sift the flour and salt into a bowl and break the egg into it. Gradually beat in the milk to make a smooth batter and then stir in 15ml/1 tbsp melted butter.

2 Put a 20cm/8in non-stick frying pan over a medium heat and brush with oil or butter. When hot, add 45ml/3 tbsp batter, tilting to cover the surface. Cook until the underside is golden brown then flip over and briefly cook the other side. Repeat with the remaining batter to make eight pancakes. Keep warm.

3 To make the filling, put the milk, stock, flour and butter into a pan. Bring to the boil, whisking continuously, until the sauce thickens. Add the fish pieces and simmer gently for 3 minutes or until the fish is just cooked. Stir in the prawns and spinach.

4 Cook until the prawns are heated through and the spinach is wilted. Stir in the cheese. Remove from the heat. Spoon the fish mixture into the centre of the pancakes and roll up or fold into triangles. Serve immediately.

Seafood Risotto

Risotto is one of Italy's most popular rice dishes and it is made with everything from pumpkin to squid ink. On the Mediterranean shores, fresh seafood is the most obvious addition.

Serves 4
60ml/4 tbsp sunflower oil
1 onion, chopped
2 garlic cloves, crushed

225g/8oz/generous 1 cup
    arborio rice
105ml/7 tbsp white wine
1.5 litres/2½ pints/6 cups hot
    fish stock
350g/12oz mixed seafood, such
    as raw prawns (shrimp),
    mussels, squid rings or clams
grated rind of ½ lemon
30ml/2 tbsp tomato purée (paste)
15ml/1 tbsp chopped
    fresh parsley
salt and ground black pepper

Preparation: 2 minutes; Cooking: 18 minutes

1 Heat the oil in a heavy-based pan, add the onion and garlic and cook until soft. Add the rice and stir to coat the grains with oil. Add the wine and cook over a moderate heat, stirring, for a few minutes until absorbed.

2 Add 150ml/¼ pint/⅔ cup of the hot stock and cook, stirring constantly, until the liquid is absorbed by the rice. Continue stirring and adding stock in 150ml/¼ pint/⅔ cup quantities, until half is left. This should take about 10 minutes.

3 Stir in the seafood and cook for 2–3 minutes. Add the remaining stock as before, until the rice is cooked. It should be quite creamy and the grains al dente.

4 Stir in the lemon rind, tomato purée and parsley. Season with salt and pepper and serve warm.

> **Cook's Tip**
> *Stirring the rice constantly produces a beautifully creamy risotto. Although this means that the cook must stand over the stove the whole time, the action is incredibly therapeutic.*

Seafood Pancakes Energy 393kcal/1647kJ; Protein 26.7g; Carbohydrate 25.4g, of which sugars 5.7g; Fat 21.2g, of which saturates 11.9g; Cholesterol 203mg; Calcium 273mg; Fibre 0.8g; Sodium 513mg.
Seafood Risotto Energy 404kcal/1693kJ; Protein 28.1g; Carbohydrate 56.3g, of which sugars 1.1g; Fat 3.9g, of which saturates 1.9g; Cholesterol 228mg; Calcium 200mg; Fibre 0.2g; Sodium 301mg.

Garlicky Scallops & Prawns

Scallops and prawns provide a healthy meal in next to no time. This particular recipe comes from France and is popular in Provence. It is very quick and easy to make and is perfect for a summer lunch or a quick meal before a trip to the theatre, as it is lovely and light, and easily digested.

Serves 2–4
6 large shelled scallops
6–8 large raw prawns (jumbo shrimp), peeled
plain (all-purpose) flour, for dusting
30–45ml/2–3 tbsp olive oil
1 garlic clove, finely chopped
15ml/1 tbsp chopped fresh basil
30–45ml/2–3 tbsp lemon juice
salt and ground black pepper

Preparation: 1 minute; Cooking: 4–5 minutes

1 Rinse the scallops under cold running water to remove any sand or grit. Drain, then pat dry using kitchen paper. Cut them in half crossways.

2 Season the scallops and prawns with salt and pepper and dust lightly with flour. Heat the oil in a large frying pan over high heat and add the scallops and prawns.

3 Reduce the heat slightly and cook for 2 minutes, then turn the scallops and prawns and add the garlic and basil, shaking the pan to distribute them evenly.

4 Cook for a further 2 minutes, until the scallops are golden and just firm to the touch. Sprinkle over the lemon juice and toss to blend. Spoon into a heated dish or on to individual plates and serve at once.

Cook's Tips
• *Like oysters, scallops are traditionally best when there is an 'r' in the month. Frozen scallops are available, but their quality is not as good as the fresh ones.*
• *Scallops should be cooked for the shortest possible time, as they become leathery when overcooked. The bright red corals require even less time than the nuggets of white flesh.*

Seafood Conchiglie

This is a very special modern dish – a warm salad composed of scallops, pasta and fresh rocket flavoured with roasted pepper, chilli and balsamic vinegar.

Serves 4
8 large fresh scallops
300g/11oz/2¾ cups dried conchiglie
15ml/1 tbsp olive oil
15g/½ oz/1 tbsp butter
120ml/4fl oz/½ cup dry white wine
90g/3½ oz rocket (arugula) leaves, stalks trimmed
salt and ground black pepper

For the vinaigrette
60ml/4 tbsp extra virgin olive oil
15ml/1 tbsp balsamic vinegar
1 piece bottled roasted pepper, drained and finely chopped
1–2 fresh red chillies, seeded and chopped
1 garlic clove, crushed
5–10ml/1–2 tsp clear honey, to taste

Preparation: 8 minutes; Cooking: 10–12 minutes

1 Cut each scallop into 2–3 pieces. If the corals are attached, pull them off and cut each piece in half. Season the scallops and corals with salt and pepper.

2 To make the vinaigrette, put all the ingredients in a measuring jug (cup) and whisk well.

3 Cook the pasta in a large pan of lightly salted boiling water for 10–12 minutes.

4 Meanwhile, heat the oil and butter in a non-stick frying pan until sizzling. Add half the scallops and toss over a high heat for 2 minutes. Remove with a slotted spoon and keep warm. Cook the remaining scallops in the same way.

5 Add the wine to the liquid remaining in the pan and stir over a high heat until the mixture has reduced to a few tablespoons. Remove from the heat and keep warm. Drain the pasta and tip it into a warmed bowl. Add the rocket, scallops, the reduced cooking juices and the vinaigrette and toss well to combine. Serve immediately.

Garlicky Scallops Energy 159kcal/664kJ; Protein 16.4g; Carbohydrate 2.9g, of which sugars 0.2g; Fat 9.2g, of which saturates 1.4g; Cholesterol 72mg; Calcium 51mg; Fibre 0.4g; Sodium 140mg.
Seafood Conchiglie Energy 485kcal/2039kJ; Protein 18.4g; Carbohydrate 59.3g, of which sugars 4.9g; Fat 18.9g, of which saturates 4.3g; Cholesterol 26mg; Calcium 72mg; Fibre 2.7g; Sodium 126mg.

Scallops with Garlic & Coriander

Shellfish is often best when cooked very simply. This recipe comes from Mexico, where hot chilli sauce and lime are popular ingredients in many fish recipes. The dish packs quite a punch, so use just enough sauce to give the intensity of flavour you prefer.

Serves 4
20 scallops
2 courgettes (zucchini)
75g/3oz/6 tbsp butter
15ml/1 tbsp vegetable oil
4 garlic cloves, chopped
30ml/2 tbsp hot chilli sauce
juice of 1 lime
small bunch of fresh coriander
    (cilantro), finely chopped

Preparation: 10 minutes; Cooking: 5–6 minutes

1 If you have bought scallops in their shells, open them. Hold a scallop shell in the palm of your hand, with the flat side uppermost. Insert the blade of a knife close to the hinge that joins the shells and prise them apart.

2 Run the blade of the knife across the inside of the flat shell to cut away the scallop. Only the white adductor muscle and the orange coral are eaten, so pull away and discard all other parts. Rinse the scallops under cold running water.

3 Cut the courgettes in half, then into four pieces. Heat the butter with the oil in a large frying pan. Add the courgettes and fry until soft. Remove from the pan. Add the garlic and fry until golden. Stir in the hot chilli sauce.

4 Add the scallops to the sauce. Cook, stirring constantly, for 1–2 minutes only. Stir in the lime juice, chopped coriander and the courgette pieces. Serve immediately on heated plates.

Cook's Tip
Hot chilli sauces vary hugely, from relatively mild mixtures to ones with paint-blistering potential. If using something like Tabasco sauce, reduce the quantity considerably unless you have a cast-iron constitution.

Herb- & Chilli-seared Scallops

Tender, succulent scallops taste simply divine when marinated in fresh chilli, fragrant mint and aromatic basil, then quickly seared in a piping hot wok. If you can't find king scallops for this recipe, use twice the quantity of smaller queen scallops or use a mixture of prawns and scallops.

Serves 4
20–24 king scallops, cleaned
120ml/4fl oz/³/₄ cup olive oil
finely grated rind and juice
    of 1 lemon
30ml/2 tbsp finely chopped mixed
    fresh mint and basil
1 fresh red chilli, seeded and
    finely chopped
salt and ground black pepper
500g/1¼lb pak choi (bok choy)

Preparation: 3 minutes; Cooking: 5 minutes

1 Place the scallops in a shallow, non-metallic bowl in a single layer. In a clean bowl, mix together half the oil, the lemon rind and juice, chopped herbs and chilli, and spoon over the scallops. Season well with salt and black pepper, cover and set aside.

2 Using a sharp knife, cut each pak choi lengthways into four pieces. Place on a plate and set aside.

3 Heat a wok over a high heat. When hot, drain the scallops (reserving the marinade) and add to the wok. Cook for 1 minute on each side, or until cooked to your liking. Don't overcook the scallops or they will toughen.

4 Pour the marinade over the scallops and remove the wok from the heat. Transfer the scallops and juices to a platter and keep warm. Wipe out the wok with a piece of kitchen paper.

5 Place the wok over a high heat. When all traces of moisture have evaporated, add the remaining oil. When the oil is hot add the pak choi and stir-fry over a high heat for 2–3 minutes, until the leaves wilt.

6 Divide the greens among four warmed serving plates, then top with the reserved scallops. Spoon the lemon, herb and chilli pan juices over the scallops and serve immediately.

Scallops with Garlic Energy 291kcal/1213kJ; Protein 24.2g; Carbohydrate 4.4g, of which sugars 1g; Fat 19.8g, of which saturates 10.5g; Cholesterol 87mg; Calcium 45mg; Fibre 0.5g; Sodium 294mg.
Chilli-seared Scallops Energy 410Kcal/1714kJ; Protein 44.5g; Carbohydrate 8.3g, of which sugars 2.1g; Fat 22.3g, of which saturates 3.5g; Cholesterol 82mg; Calcium 286mg; Fibre 3.2g; Sodium 494mg.

Scallops with Lime Butter

Chargrilling fennel releases its aniseed flavour, which tastes great with sweet and rich scallops. These wonderful shellfish are ideal for the barbecue because they have firm flesh that cooks quickly – simply toss in lime juice before cooking.

Serves 4
1 head fennel
2 limes
12 large scallops, cleaned
1 egg yolk
90ml/6 tbsp melted butter
olive oil for brushing
salt and ground black pepper

Preparation: 5 minutes; Cooking: 6–8 minutes

1 Trim any feathery leaves from the fennel and reserve them. Slice the rest lengthways into thin wedges.

2 Cut one lime into wedges. Finely grate the rind and squeeze the juice of the other lime and toss half the juice and rind on to the scallops. Season well with salt and ground black pepper to taste.

3 Place the egg yolk and remaining lime rind and juice in a small bowl and whisk until pale and smooth.

4 Gradually whisk in the melted butter and continue whisking until thick and smooth. Finely chop the reserved fennel leaves and stir them in, with seasoning.

5 Prepare the barbecue. Position a lightly oiled grill (broiler) rack over the hot coals. Brush the fennel wedges with olive oil and cook them over high heat for 3–4 minutes, turning once.

6 Add the scallops and cook for a further 3–4 minutes, turning once. Serve with the lime butter and the lime wedges.

> **Cook's Tip**
> *Thread small scallops on to metal or bamboo skewers to make turning them easier. If using bamboo, soak in water first.*

Scallops with Bacon

In the 19th century, scallops were dredged in large numbers along England's Sussex coast. Today, they are fished off the Isle of Man. Like oysters, scallops are often believed to be an aphrodisiac. They are best when cooked quickly and briefly, and go well with bacon.

Serves 4
15ml/1 tbsp olive oil
4 streaky bacon (fatty) rashers (strips), cut into 2.5cm/1in pieces
2–3 fresh sage leaves, chopped
small piece of butter
8 large or 16 small scallops
15ml/1 tbsp fresh lemon juice
100ml/3¾fl oz dry (hard) cider or dry white wine

Preparation: 3–4 minutes; Cooking: 4 minutes

1 Heat the oil in a frying pan. Add the bacon and sage and cook, stirring occasionally, until the bacon is golden brown. Lift out and keep warm.

2 Add the butter to the pan and when hot add the scallops. Cook quickly for about 1 minute on each side until browned. Lift out and keep warm.

3 Add the lemon juice and cider or wine to the pan and, scraping up any sediment remaining in the pan, bring just to the boil. Continue bubbling gently until the mixture has reduced to just a few tablespoons of syrupy sauce.

4 Serve the scallops and bacon on heated individual plates with the cider or wine sauce drizzled over.

> **Cook's Tip**
> *In summer, some fishmongers sell marsh samphire (glasswort), which grows around the coast of England and makes a good accompaniment to this dish. To prepare samphire, wash it well and pick off the soft fleshy branches, discarding the thicker woody stalks. Drop it into boiling water for just 1 minute before draining and serving.*

Scallops with Butter Energy 232kcal/961kJ; Protein 10g; Carbohydrate 2.2g, of which sugars 0.9g; Fat 20.5g, of which saturates 12.3g; Cholesterol 116mg; Calcium 31mg; Fibre 1.1g; Sodium 211mg.
Scallops with Bacon Energy 208kcal/867kJ; Protein 15.6g; Carbohydrate 2.4g, of which sugars 0.7g; Fat 14.5g, of which saturates 5.9g; Cholesterol 53mg; Calcium 19mg; Fibre 0g; Sodium 445mg.

Sautéed Scallops

Scallops go well with all sorts of sauces, but simple cooking is the best way to enjoy their delicate, fresh-from-the-sea flavour. For this recipe they are served with a vermouth sauce.

Serves 2
450g/1lb shelled scallops
25g/1oz/2 tbsp butter
30ml/2 tbsp dry white vermouth
15ml/1 tbsp finely chopped
*   fresh parsley*
salt and ground black pepper

Preparation: 1 minute; Cooking: 5 minutes

1 Rinse the scallops under cold running water to remove any sand or grit. Drain them well and pat dry using kitchen paper. Spread them out and season them lightly with salt and pepper.

2 In a frying pan large enough to hold the scallops in one layer, heat half the butter until it begins to colour.

3 Sauté the scallops for 3–5 minutes, turning until golden brown on both sides and just firm to the touch. Remove to a serving platter and cover with foil to keep hot.

4 Add the vermouth to the hot frying pan, swirl in the remaining butter, stir in the parsley and pour the sauce over the scallops. Serve immediately.

Variation

An impressive way of serving these scallops is in puff pastry boxes. It isn't necessary to make your own puff pastry as the bought product is very good. Roll out the pastry and cut out two squares, each measuring about 10cm/4in across. Then, using a sharp knife, mark out an inner square on each piece of pastry, about 2cm/¾in in from the edge and about half the depth of the pastry. Put the pastry squares on a baking sheet and bake in a preheated oven at 220°C/425°F/Gas 7 for 20 minutes until well risen and golden. Remove the inner lid from each box and scoop out the soft inside, then pile in the scallop filling and replace the lid at an angle.

Mussels in Garlic Butter

Garlic and herb butter is a classic treatment for snails in Burgundy, but became very popular in the 1960s with mussels, and makes a delicious first course.

115g/4oz/½ cup unsalted
*   (sweet) butter, softened*
2–3 garlic cloves, finely chopped
grated rind of 1 lemon
60ml/4 tbsp finely chopped mixed
*   herbs, such as parsley, chervil,*
*   tarragon and chives*
115g/4oz/1 cup fresh white
*   breadcrumbs*
salt and ground black pepper
lemon wedges, to serve

Serves 4
2kg/4½lb mussels, scrubbed
2 large shallots, finely chopped
200ml/7fl oz/scant 1 cup dry
*   white wine*

Preparation: 6–7 minutes; Cooking: 10 minutes

1 Check that all the mussels are closed after cleaning and discard any that remain open when sharply tapped. Place the shallots and wine in a large pan and bring to the boil. Throw in the mussels and cover tightly. Cook over a high heat for 4–5 minutes, shaking the pan vigorously 2–3 times.

2 The mussels should be cooked and gaping open. Discard any that do not open after 5 minutes' cooking. Drain, reserving the cooking liquid. Discard the top (empty) half of each shell. Place the mussels in a roasting pan.

3 Pour the cooking liquid into a clean pan and boil it vigorously until reduced to about 45ml/3 tbsp. Remove the pan from the heat and set it aside to cool.

4 Cream the butter with the shallots from the reduced liquid, the garlic, lemon rind and herbs. Season well and set aside.

5 Distribute the flavoured butter among the mussels. Sprinkle with the cooking liquid, then scatter the breadcrumbs over.

6 Preheat the grill (broiler) and position the shelf 10cm/4in below the heat. Grill (broil) the mussels until the butter is bubbling and the breadcrumbs are golden and crisp. Serve with lemon.

Scallops Energy 378kcal/1588kJ; Protein 52.5g; Carbohydrate 8.4g, of which sugars 0.7g; Fat 13.5g, of which saturates 7.4g; Cholesterol 132mg; Calcium 84mg; Fibre 0.4g; Sodium 485mg.
Mussels Energy 494kcal/2068kJ; Protein 26.3g; Carbohydrate 28.5g, of which sugars 2.1g; Fat 27.7g, of which saturates 15.5g; Cholesterol 141mg; Calcium 121mg; Fibre 0.9g; Sodium 875mg.

Mussels in Cider

Mussels are delicious when steamed and lifted out of their shells, and quickly fried with bacon. Here they are cooked with a broth of cider, garlic and cream. Serve the mussels in large shallow bowls with a chunk of bread to mop up the juices. Don't forget to provide finger bowls for cleaning sticky fingers.

Serves 4

1.8kg/4lb mussels in their shells
40g/1½oz/3 tbsp butter
1 leek, washed and finely chopped
1 garlic clove, finely chopped
150ml/¼ pint/⅔ cup dry
  (hard) cider
30–45ml/2–3 tbsp double
  (heavy) cream
a handful of fresh parsley,
  chopped
ground black pepper

Preparation: 5–6 minutes; Cooking: 8–10 minutes

1 Scrub the mussels and scrape off any barnacles. Discard those with broken shells or that refuse to close when given a sharp tap with a knife. Pull off the hairy beards with a sharp tug.

2 Melt the butter in a very large pan and add the leek and garlic. Cook over medium heat for about 5 minutes, stirring frequently, until very soft but not browned. Season with pepper.

3 Add the cider and immediately tip in the mussels. Cover with a lid and cook quickly, shaking the pan occasionally, until the mussels have just opened (take care not to overcook and toughen them).

4 Remove the lid, add the cream and parsley and bubble gently for a minute or two. Serve immediately in shallow bowls.

> ### Cook's Tip
> *Eat mussels the fun way! Use an empty shell as pincers to pick out the mussels from the other shells. Don't try to eat any whose shells have not opened during cooking or you risk food poisoning. Provide an empty bowl for the mussel shells.*

Thai Steamed Mussels in Coconut Milk

An ideal dish for informal entertaining, mussels steamed in coconut milk and fresh aromatic herbs are quick and easy to prepare and great for a relaxed dinner with friends.

Serves 4

1.6kg/3½lb mussels
15ml/1 tbsp sunflower oil
6 garlic cloves, roughly chopped
15ml/1 tbsp finely chopped fresh
  root ginger
2 large red chillies, seeded and
  finely sliced
6 spring onions (scallions),
  finely chopped
400ml/14fl oz/1⅔ cups
  coconut milk
45ml/3 tbsp light soy sauce
2 limes
5ml/1 tsp caster (superfine)
  sugar
a large handful of chopped
  coriander (cilantro)
salt and ground black pepper

Preparation: 10 minutes; Cooking: 6–7 minutes

1 Scrub the mussels in cold water. Scrape off any barnacles with a knife, then pull out and discard the fibrous beard visible between the hinge on any of the shells. Discard any mussels that are not tightly closed, or that fail to close when tapped sharply against the work surface.

2 Heat a wok over a high heat and then add the oil. Stir in the garlic, ginger, chillies and spring onions and stir-fry over medium to high heat for 30 seconds.

3 Grate the rind of the limes into the ginger mixture, then squeeze both fruit and add the juice to the wok with the coconut milk, soy sauce and sugar. Stir to mix.

4 Bring the mixture to the boil, then add the mussels. Return to the boil, cover and cook briskly for 5–6 minutes, or until all the mussels have opened. Discard any mussels that do not open.

5 Remove the wok from the heat and stir in the chopped coriander. Season the mussels well with salt and pepper. Ladle into warmed bowls and serve immediately.

Mussels in Cider Energy 261kcal/1092kJ; Protein 21.1g; Carbohydrate 6.5g, of which sugars 2.1g; Fat 15.6g, of which saturates 8.2g; Cholesterol 104mg; Calcium 82mg; Fibre 1g; Sodium 498mg.
Thai Steamed Mussels Energy 160kcal/679kJ; Protein 21.5g; Carbohydrate 6.7g, of which sugars 6.7g; Fat 5.5g, of which saturates 1g; Cholesterol 48mg; Calcium 272mg; Fibre 0.2g; Sodium 630mg.

Mouclade of Mussels

This recipe is quite similar to moules marinière but has the additional flavouring of fennel and mild curry. Traditionally the mussels are shelled and piled into scallop shells, but nothing beats a bowlful of steaming hot, garlicky mussels, served in their own shells.

Serves 6
1.75kg/4½lb fresh mussels
250ml/8fl oz/1 cup dry
   white wine
good pinch of grated nutmeg
3 thyme sprigs
2 bay leaves
1 small onion, finely chopped
50g/2oz/¼ cup butter
1 fennel bulb, thinly sliced
4 garlic cloves, crushed
2.5ml/½ tsp curry paste
   or powder
30ml/2 tbsp plain
   (all-purpose) flour
150ml/¼ pint/⅔ cup double
   (heavy) cream
ground black pepper
chopped fresh dill, to garnish

Preparation: 2–3 minutes; Cooking: 14 minutes

1 Scrub the mussels, discarding any that are damaged or open ones that do not close when tapped with a knife.

2 Put the wine, nutmeg, thyme, bay leaves and onion in a large pan and bring just to the boil. Tip in the mussels and cover with a lid. Cook for 4–5 minutes until the mussels have opened.

3 Drain the mussels, reserving all the juices. Discard any mussels that remain closed.

4 Melt the butter in a large clean pan and gently fry the fennel slices and garlic for about 5 minutes until softened.

5 Stir in the curry paste or powder and flour and cook for 1 minute. Remove from the heat and gradually blend in the cooking juices from the mussels. Return to the heat and cook, stirring, for 2 minutes.

6 Stir in the cream and a little pepper. Add the mussels to the pan and heat through for 2 minutes. Serve hot, garnished with chopped fresh dill.

Mussels & Clams with Lemon Grass

Fresh lemon grass has an incomparable flavour and is excellent used with seafood. If you cannot find clams, use extra mussels instead.

Serves 6
1.8–2kg/4–4½lb mussels
450g/1lb baby clams, washed
120ml/4fl oz/½ cup dry
   white wine
1 bunch spring onions
   (scallions), chopped
2 lemon grass stalks, chopped
6 kaffir lime leaves, chopped
10ml/2 tsp Thai green curry paste
200ml/7fl oz/scant 1 cup
   coconut cream
30ml/2 tbsp chopped fresh
   coriander (cilantro)
salt and ground black pepper
whole garlic chives, to garnish

Preparation: 5 minutes; Cooking: 10 minutes

1 Clean the mussels. Pull off the beards and scrub the shells. Discard any that are broken or stay open when tapped.

2 Put the wine, spring onions, lemon grass, lime leaves and curry paste in a pan. Simmer until the wine almost evaporates.

3 Add the mussels and clams to the pan, cover tightly and steam the shellfish over a high heat for 5–6 minutes, until they open. Shake the pan frequently.

4 Using a slotted spoon, transfer the mussels and clams to a warmed serving bowl and keep hot. Discard any shellfish that remain closed. Strain the cooking liquid into a clean pan and then simmer to reduce the amount to about 250ml/8fl oz/1 cup.

5 Stir in the coconut cream and coriander, with salt and pepper to taste. Heat through. Pour over the seafood and serve, garnished with garlic chives.

> **Cook's Tip**
> Buy extra mussels in case any have to be discarded because of damage or because they are permanently closed.

Mouclade of Mussels Energy 314kcal/1308kJ; Protein 16.6g; Carbohydrate 6g, of which sugars 1.9g; Fat 22.2g, of which saturates 13g; Cholesterol 87mg; Calcium 207mg; Fibre 1.1g; Sodium 246mg.
Mussels and Clams Energy 237kcal/993kJ; Protein 22.5g; Carbohydrate 2.8g, of which sugars 1.7g; Fat 13.8g, of which saturates 10.3g; Cholesterol 58mg; Calcium 238mg; Fibre 0.9g; Sodium 606mg.

Lemon & Chilli Steamed Razor Clams

Spiced Clams

Spanish clams, especially in the north, are much larger than clams found elsewhere, and have more succulent bodies. This modern recipe uses Arab spicing to make a hot dip or sauce. Serve with plenty of fresh bread to mop up the delicious juices.

Serves 3–4
1 small onion, finely chopped
1 celery stick, sliced
2 garlic cloves, finely chopped
2.5cm/1in piece fresh root
    ginger, grated
30ml/2 tbsp olive oil
1.5ml/¼ tsp chilli powder
5ml/1 tsp ground turmeric
30ml/2 tbsp chopped fresh
    parsley
500g/1¼lb small clams, in the shell
30ml/2 tbsp dry white wine
salt and ground black pepper
celery leaves, to garnish
fresh bread, to serve

Preparation: 4 minutes; Cooking: 9–12 minutes

1 Place the onion, celery, garlic and ginger in a large pan, add the olive oil, spices and chopped parsley and stir-fry for about 5 minutes. Add the clams to the pan and cook for 2 minutes.

2 Add the wine, then cover and cook gently for 2–3 minutes, shaking the pan occasionally. Season. Discard any clams whose shells remain closed. Pile the remainder on a heated platter and serve, garnished with the celery leaves.

Cook's Tips
• There are many different varieties of clam. One of the best is the almeja fina (the carpet shell clam), which is perfect used in this dish. These attractive shellfish have grooved brown shells with a yellow lattice pattern.
• Before cooking the clams, check that all the shells are closed. Any clams that do not open after cooking should be discarded.
• When buying the ginger, visit a shop or market with a rapid turnover. Much of the fresh ginger in the shops has been around for such a long time that it has dried out and developed a musty flavour. Fresh ginger should feel firm and smooth to the touch.

Razor clams have beautiful striped gold and brown tubular shells and make a wonderful and unusual appetizer. Here they are lightly steamed and tossed in a fragrant Italian-style dressing of chilli, lemon, garlic and parsley. Serve with plenty of crusty bread for mopping up the delicious pan juices. For a main course, make double the quantity.

Serves 4
12 razor clams
90–120ml/6–8 tbsp extra virgin
    olive oil
finely grated rind and juice of
    1 small lemon
2 garlic cloves, very finely grated
1 red chilli, seeded and very
    finely chopped
60ml/4 tbsp chopped flat
    leaf parsley
salt and ground black pepper
mixed salad leaves and crusty
    bread, to serve

Preparation: 5 minutes; Cooking: 3–4 minutes

1 Wash the razor clams well in plenty of cold running water. Drain and arrange half the clams in a steamer, placing them side by side, with the hinge side down.

2 Pour 5cm/2in water into a wok and bring to the boil. Carefully balance the steamer over the water and cover tightly.

3 Steam for 3–4 minutes until the clams have opened. Discard any clams that remain closed.

4 Remove the clams from the wok and keep warm while you steam the remaining clams in the same way.

5 Pour the olive oil into a small bowl. Add the grated lemon rind and juice, stir well, then add the garlic, red chilli and flat leaf parsley. Mix thoroughly.

6 Season the dressing well with salt and pepper. Spoon the steamed razor clams on to plates and spoon the dressing over.

7 Serve the razor clams immediately with a crisp mixed-leaf salad and crusty bread.

Spiced Clams Energy 126kcal/526kJ; Protein 12.5g; Carbohydrate 4.5g, of which sugars 2.2g; Fat 6g, of which saturates 0.9g; Cholesterol 50mg; Calcium 69mg; Fibre 0.6g; Sodium 906mg.
Razor Clams Energy 188Kcal/775kJ; Protein 6.1g; Carbohydrate 2.9g, of which sugars 0.5g; Fat 16.9g, of which saturates 2.4g; Cholesterol 20mg; Calcium 47mg; Fibre 1.1g; Sodium 364mg.

Oysters Rockefeller

This is the perfect dish for those who prefer to eat their oysters lightly cooked. As a cheaper alternative, for those who are not as rich as Rockefeller, give mussels or clams the same treatment; they will also taste delicious.

Serves 6
450g/1lb/3 cups coarse sea salt, plus extra to serve
24 oysters, opened
115g/4oz/½ cup butter

2 shallots, finely chopped
500g/1¼lb spinach leaves, finely chopped
60ml/4 tbsp chopped fresh parsley
60ml/4 tbsp chopped celery leaves
90ml/6 tbsp fresh white or wholemeal (whole-wheat) breadcrumbs
10–20ml/2–4 tsp vodka
cayenne pepper
sea salt and ground black pepper
lemon or lime wedges, to serve

Preparation: 6–7 minutes; Cooking: 12–13 minutes

1 Preheat the oven to 220°C/425°F/Gas 7. Make a bed of coarse salt on two large baking sheets. Set the oysters in the half-shell in the bed of salt to keep them steady. Set aside.

2 Melt the butter in a large frying pan. Add the chopped shallots and cook them over a low heat for 2–3 minutes until they are softened. Stir in the spinach and let it wilt.

3 Add the parsley, celery leaves and breadcrumbs to the pan and fry gently for 5 minutes. Season with salt, pepper and cayenne pepper.

4 Divide the stuffing among the oysters. Drizzle a few drops of vodka over each oyster, then bake for about 5 minutes until bubbling and golden brown. Serve on a heated platter on a shallow salt bed with lemon or lime wedges.

Cook's Tip
Frozen chopped spinach can be used. Thaw it in a colander over a bowl and press out as much liquid as possible.

Crab Meat in Vinegar

A refreshing summer tsumami (a Japanese dish that accompanies alcoholic drinks). For the dressing, use a Japanese or Greek cucumber, if possible – they are about one-third of the size of ordinary salad cucumbers and contain less water.

Serves 4
½ red (bell) pepper, seeded

pinch of salt
275g/10oz cooked white crab meat, or 2 x 165g/ 5½oz cans white crab meat, drained
about 300g/11oz Japanese, Greek or salad cucumber

For the vinegar mixture
15ml/1 tbsp rice vinegar
10ml/2 tsp caster (superfine) sugar
10ml/2 tsp awakuchi shoyu

Preparation: 15 minutes; Cooking: 0 minutes

1 Slice the red pepper into thin strips lengthways. Sprinkle with a little salt and leave for about 10 minutes. Rinse well and drain.

2 For the vinegar mixture, combine the rice vinegar, sugar and awakuchi shoyu in a small bowl.

3 Loosen the crab meat and mix it with the sliced red pepper in a mixing bowl. Divide among four small bowls.

4 If you use salad cucumber, scoop out the seeds. Finely grate the cucumber with a fine-toothed grater or use a food processor. Drain in a fine-meshed sieve (or strainer).

5 Mix the cucumber with the vinegar mixture, and pour a quarter on to the crab meat mixture in each bowl. Serve cold immediately, before the cucumber loses its colour.

Variation
The vinegar mixture is best made using awakuchi shoyu, but ordinary soy sauce can be used instead. It will make a darker dressing, however.

Oysters Energy 210kcal/867kJ; Protein 6.4g; Carbohydrate 3.4g, of which sugars 2.1g; Fat 17g, of which saturates 10.1g; Cholesterol 60mg; Calcium 211mg; Fibre 2.3g; Sodium 406mg.
Crab Meat in Vinegar Energy 82kcal/345kJ; Protein 13.3g; Carbohydrate 5.6g, of which sugars 5.4g; Fat 0.8g, of which saturates 0.1g; Cholesterol 50mg; Calcium 100mg; Fibre 0.9g; Sodium 560mg.

Soft-shell Crabs with Chilli & Salt

If fresh soft-shell crabs are unavailable, you can buy frozen ones in Oriental supermarkets. Allow two small crabs per serving, or one if they are large.

Serves 4

8 small soft-shell crabs, thawed
    if frozen
50g/2oz/½ cup plain
    (all-purpose) flour
60ml/4 tbsp groundnut (peanut)
    or vegetable oil

2 large fresh red chillies, or 1 green
    and 1 red chilli, seeded and
    thinly sliced
4 spring onions (scallions) or
    a small bunch of garlic
    chives, chopped
sea salt and ground black
    pepper

To serve

shredded lettuce, mooli (daikon)
    and carrot
light soy sauce, for dipping

Preparation: 6 minutes; Cooking: 6–14 minutes

1 Pat the crabs dry with kitchen paper. Season the flour with pepper and coat the crabs lightly with the mixture.

2 Heat the oil in a shallow pan until very hot, then put in the crabs (you may need to do this in two batches). Fry for 2–3 minutes on each side, until the crabs are golden brown but still juicy in the middle. Drain the cooked crabs on kitchen paper and keep hot.

3 Add the sliced chillies and spring onions or garlic chives to the oil remaining in the pan and cook gently for about 2 minutes. Sprinkle over a generous pinch of salt, then spread the chilli and onion mixture on to the crabs.

4 Mix the shredded lettuce, mooli and carrot together. Arrange on plates, top each portion with two crabs and serve, with a bowl of light soy sauce for dipping.

> **Cook's Tip**
> If you can't locate any mooli, use celeriac instead.

Stir-fried Noodles in Seafood Sauce

This Chinese-style pasta dish makes a perfect appetizer or main course, combining noodles, vegetables and crab meat in a colourful, tasty and quick dish.

Serves 4

225g/8oz Chinese egg noodles
8 spring onions (scallions),
    trimmed
8 asparagus spears, plus extra
    steamed asparagus spears,
    to serve (optional)

30ml/2 tbsp vegetable oil
5cm/2in piece fresh root
    ginger, peeled and cut into
    very fine matchsticks
3 garlic cloves, chopped
60ml/4 tbsp oyster sauce
450g/1lb cooked crab meat (all
    white, or two-thirds white and
    one-third brown)
30ml/2 tbsp rice wine vinegar
15–30ml/1–2 tbsp light soy
    sauce, to taste

Preparation: 10–12 minutes; Cooking: 6–7 minutes

1 Put the noodles in a large pan, cover with lightly salted boiling water, place a lid on top and leave for 3–4 minutes, or for the time suggested on the packet. Drain in a colander, then separate the strands with a fork. Spoon the noodles into a bowl and set aside.

2 Cut off the green spring onion tops and slice them thinly. Set aside. Cut the white parts into 2cm/¾in lengths and quarter them lengthways. Cut the asparagus spears on the diagonal into 2cm/¾in pieces.

3 Heat the oil in a pan or wok until very hot, then add the ginger, garlic and white spring onion batons. Stir-fry over high heat for 1 minute.

4 Add the oyster sauce, crab meat, rice wine vinegar and soy sauce to taste. Stir-fry over medium to high heat for about 2 minutes, until the crab and sauce are hot.

5 Add the noodles and toss until heated through. At the last moment, toss in the spring onion tops and serve with a few extra asparagus spears, if you like.

Soft-shell Crabs Energy 306kcal/1280kJ; Protein 37.6g; Carbohydrate 10g, of which sugars 0.5g; Fat 13g, of which saturates 1.5g; Cholesterol 144mg; Calcium 262mg; Fibre 0.5g; Sodium 1101mg.
Stir-fried Noodles Energy 192kcal/811kJ; Protein 14.3g; Carbohydrate 23g, of which sugars 3.2g; Fat 5.5g, of which saturates 1.1g; Cholesterol 49mg; Calcium 83mg; Fibre 1.2g; Sodium 617mg.

Thai-style Beef & Mango Salad

Rare beef and juicy
mangoes – a marriage made
in heaven. Come down to
earth by serving the salad
with a mixture of slightly
bitter salad leaves in a
lemon and oil dressing.

Serves 4
450g/1lb sirloin steak
45ml/3 tbsp garlic-infused olive oil
45ml/3 tbsp soy sauce
*2 mangoes, peeled, stoned (pitted)
    and finely sliced*
ground black pepper

Preparation: 2 minutes; Cooking: 18 minutes

1 Put the steak in a shallow, non-metallic dish and pour over
the oil and soy sauce. Season with pepper and turn the steaks
to coat them in the marinade. Marinate for at least 10 minutes;
longer if you can spare the time. Two hours in a covered bowl
in the refrigerator would be ideal.

2 Heat a griddle or ridged grill pan until hot. Remove the
steak from the marinade and place on the griddle. Cook for
3–5 minutes on each side, moving the steak halfway through
if you want a criss-cross pattern on the surface.

3 Transfer the steak to a board and leave to rest for 2 minutes.
Meanwhile, heat the marinade in a pan. Cook for a few seconds,
then remove from the heat. Slice the steak thinly and arrange on
four serving plates with the mangoes. Drizzle over the pan juices
and serve with some salad leaves dressed with lemon and oil.

Cook's Tips
• *This is a simplified version of the classic Thai beef salad,
which usually comes with a vast array of chopped vegetables.
If you want to add a complement to this delicious no-fuss
version, set out little bowls of fresh coriander (cilantro) leaves,
chopped spring onions (scallions) and peanuts, for sprinkling.*
• *Instead of using garlic-infused olive oil in the marinade for the
steak, use oil infused with basil, chilli or lemon. Flavoured oils are
readily available in bottles in most supermarkets and are useful
for adding flavour to cooked dishes and salads.*

Home-made Burgers with Relish

Making your own burgers
means you control what
goes into them. These are
full of flavour and always
prove popular. The tangy
ratatouille relish is very
easy to make.

Serves 4
2 shallots, chopped
*450g/1lb lean minced
    (ground) beef*

30ml/2 tbsp chopped parsley
30ml/2 tbsp tomato ketchup
1 garlic clove, crushed
*1 fresh green chilli, seeded and
    finely chopped*
15ml/1 tbsp olive oil
400g/14oz can ratatouille
4 burger buns
lettuce leaves
*salt and ground black pepper,
    to taste*

Preparation: 6 minutes; Cooking: 14 minutes

1 Put the shallots in a bowl with boiling water to cover. Leave for
1–2 minutes, then slip off the skins. Put the shallots on a board
and use a small sharp knife to chop them finely.

2 Mix half the shallots with the beef in a bowl. Add the
chopped parsley and tomato ketchup, with salt and pepper to
taste. Mix well with clean hands.

3 Divide the beef mixture into four. Knead each portion into a
ball, then flatten it into a burger.

4 Make a spicy relish by cooking the remaining shallots with
the garlic and green chilli in the olive oil for 2–3 minutes,
until soft.

5 Add the canned ratatouille to the pan containing the
vegetables. Bring to the boil, then lower the heat and simmer
for 5 minutes.

6 Meanwhile, preheat the grill (broiler) and cook the burgers
for about 5 minutes on each side, until browned and cooked
through. Meanwhile, split the burger buns in half. Arrange
lettuce leaves on the bun bases, add the burgers and top with
warm relish and the bun tops.

Thai-style Beef Energy 286kcal/1200kJ; Protein 27.4g; Carbohydrate 14.7g, of which sugars 14.4g; Fat 13.5g, of which saturates 3.5g; Cholesterol 57mg; Calcium 19mg; Fibre 2.6g; Sodium 615mg.
Home-made Burgers Energy 484kcal/2021kJ; Protein 27.9g; Carbohydrate 30.2g, of which sugars 7.7g; Fat 28.8g, of which saturates 9.3g; Cholesterol 68mg; Calcium 120mg; Fibre 2.2g; Sodium 473mg.

Russian Hamburgers

These tasty hamburgers can be made very quickly and yet still taste divine. Serve them solo, with a tomato sauce and vegetables, or just slide them into buns.

Serves 4
2 thick slices white bread, crusts removed
45ml/3 tbsp milk

450g/1lb finely minced (ground) beef, lamb or veal
1 egg, beaten
30ml/2 tbsp plain (all-purpose) flour
30ml/2 tbsp sunflower oil
salt and ground black pepper
tomato sauce, pickled vegetables and crispy fried onions, to serve

Preparation: 6 minutes; Cooking: 12–14 minutes

1 Cut the bread into chunks and crumb in a food processor, or by using a metal grater. Put the breadcrumbs in a bowl and spoon over the milk. Leave to soak for 3 minutes.

2 Add the minced meat, egg, salt and pepper and mix all the ingredients together thoroughly.

3 Divide the mixture into four equal portions and shape into ovals, each about 10cm/4in long and 5cm/2in wide. Coat each with the flour.

4 Heat the oil in a frying pan and fry the burgers for 6–7 minutes on each side. Serve with a tomato sauce, pickled vegetables and fried onions.

> **Variations**
> • These burgers are quite plain. For extra flavour, add freshly grated nutmeg to the mixture, or a little chopped onion fried in oil.
> • Serve with spicy corn relish. Heat 30ml/2 tbsp oil and fry 1 onion, 2 crushed garlic cloves and 1 seeded and chopped red chilli until soft. Add 10ml/2 tsp garam masala and cook for 2 minutes, then mix in 320g/11¼oz canned whole kernel corn and the grated rind and juice of 1 lime.

Corned Beef & Egg Hash

This is traditional family fare at its very best. Warm and comforting, and made in minutes, it will become a firm favourite very quickly.

Serves 4
30ml/2 tbsp vegetable oil
25g/1oz/2 tbsp butter
1 onion, finely chopped
1 green (bell) pepper, seeded and diced

2 large firm boiled potatoes, diced
350g/12oz can corned beef, cubed
1.5ml/¼ tsp grated nutmeg
1.5ml/¼ tsp paprika
4 eggs
salt and ground black pepper
parsley, deep-fried in oil, to garnish
sweet chilli sauce or tomato sauce, to serve

Preparation: 4–5 minutes; Cooking: 12–15 minutes

1 Heat the oil and butter together in a large frying pan. Add the onion and fry for 3–4 minutes until softened.

2 In a bowl, mix together the green pepper, potatoes, corned beef, nutmeg and paprika. Season well. Add to the pan and toss gently to distribute the cooked onion. Press down lightly and fry without stirring for about 3–4 minutes until a golden brown crust has formed on the underside.

3 Stir the mixture through to distribute the crust, then repeat the frying twice, until the mixture is well browned.

4 Make four wells in the hash and carefully crack an egg into each. Cover and cook gently for about 4–5 minutes until the egg whites are set.

5 Sprinkle with deep-fried parsley and cut into quarters. Serve hot with sweet chilli sauce or tomato sauce.

> **Cook's Tip**
> Put the can of corned beef into the refrigerator to chill for about half an hour before using.

Russian Hamburgers Energy 384kcal/1597kJ; Protein 26g; Carbohydrate 13g, of which sugars 1g; Fat 25.7g, of which saturates 9g; Cholesterol 116mg; Calcium 56mg; Fibre 0.4g; Sodium 183mg.
Corned Beef Hash Energy 421kcal/1758kJ; Protein 30.9g; Carbohydrate 17g, of which sugars 5.4g; Fat 26.2g, of which saturates 10.6g; Cholesterol 277mg; Calcium 65mg; Fibre 1.7g; Sodium 871mg.

Beef Stroganoff

This is one of the most famous fast meat dishes, consisting of tender strips of steak in a tangy sour cream sauce. Serve it with chips or on a bed of noodles.

Serves 4
450g/1lb fillet steak (beef tenderloin) or rump (round) steak, trimmed and tenderized with a rolling pin or meat mallet

15ml/1 tbsp sunflower oil
25g/1oz/2 tbsp butter
1 onion, sliced
15ml/1 tbsp plain (all-purpose) flour
5ml/1 tsp tomato purée (paste)
5ml/1 tsp Dijon mustard or wholegrain
5ml/1 tsp lemon juice
150ml/¼ pint/⅔ cup sour cream
salt and ground black pepper
fresh herbs, to garnish

Preparation: 3 minutes; Cooking: 12 minutes

1 Using a sharp cook's knife, cut the tenderized steak into thin strips, about 5cm/2in long.

2 Heat the oil and half the butter in a frying pan and fry the beef over a high heat for 2 minutes, or until browned. Remove with a slotted spoon, leaving any juices behind.

3 Melt the remaining butter in the pan and gently fry the onion for 8 minutes, until soft.

4 Stir in the flour, tomato purée, mustard, lemon juice and sour cream. Return the beef to the pan and stir until the sauce is bubbling. Season well and garnish with fresh herbs.

Variation
Mushrooms are often added to beef stroganoff. Buy large open-cap button (white) mushrooms or meaty field or portabello mushrooms, wipe them clean, then slice them thickly. Before cooking the steak, fry the mushrooms in butter for about 4 minutes, during which time they will yield their juice and absorb it again, becoming lovely and juicy. Set aside. Reheat them with the beef in the sauce just before serving.

Beef Strips with Orange & Ginger

Stir-frying is one of the quickest as well as one of the healthiest ways to cook.

Serves 4
450g/1lb rump (round) steak, cut into strips
grated rind and juice of 1 orange

15ml/1 tbsp soy sauce
1 tbsp cornflour (cornstarch)
2.5cm/1in fresh root ginger, finely chopped
10ml/2 tsp sesame oil
1 carrot, cut into small strips
2 spring onions (scallions), thinly sliced

Preparation: 3–4 minutes; Cooking: 6 minutes

1 Place the beef strips in a bowl and sprinkle with the orange rind and juice. Leave to marinate. Drain the liquid and reserve, then mix the meat with the soy sauce, cornflour and ginger. Heat the oil in a wok and stir-fry the beef for 1 minute. Add the carrot and stir-fry for 2–3 minutes. Stir in the spring onions and the reserved liquid, then boil, stirring, until thickened. Serve.

Steak with Pickled Walnut Sauce

This is a traditional Scottish way of cooking beef.

Serves 4
15ml/1 tbsp vegetable oil

75g/3oz/6 tbsp butter
8 slices of beef fillet (filet mignon)
4 onions, sliced
15ml/1 tbsp pickled walnut juice
salt and ground black pepper

Preparation: 2 minutes; Cooking: 15–18 minutes

1 Heat the oil and half the butter in a frying pan and cook the steaks for 4–5 minutes on each side until almost done. Keep the steaks warm while you cook the onions.

2 Melt the remaining butter then add the sliced onions. Increase the heat and stir to brown and soften the onions, scraping the base of the pan. Add the pickled walnut juice and cook for a few minutes. Season to taste with salt and ground black pepper. Serve the beef with the onions and juices on top.

Beef Stroganoff Energy 308kcal/1282kJ; Protein 26.5g; Carbohydrate 5.8g, of which sugars 2.5g; Fat 20.1g, of which saturates 10.2g; Cholesterol 102mg; Calcium 50mg; Fibre 0.4g; Sodium 124mg.
Beef Strips Energy 212kcal/885kJ; Protein 25.7g; Carbohydrate 3.8g, of which sugars 0.3g; Fat 10.5g, of which saturates 4.3g; Cholesterol 65mg; Calcium 7mg; Fibre 0g; Sodium 341mg.
Steak Energy 1960kcal/8144kJ; Protein 173.6g; Carbohydrate 24.4g, of which sugars 17.2g; Fat 130.4g, of which saturates 68g; Cholesterol 668mg; Calcium 124mg; Fibre 4.4g; Sodium 876mg.

Beef with Blue Cheese Sauce

Celebrations call for special dishes, and this one is more special than most. Roquefort cheese, cream and fillet steak is a rich combination, so keep the rest of the meal simple. Serve this with a selection of freshly roasted vegetables.

Serves 4
25g/1oz/2 tbsp butter
30ml/2 tbsp olive oil
4 fillet steaks (beef tenderloins), cut 5cm/2in thick, about 150g/5oz each

salt and coarsely ground black pepper
fresh flat leaf parsley, to garnish
roast potatoes and Mediterranean vegetables, to serve

For the blue cheese sauce
30ml/2 tbsp brandy
150ml/5fl oz/²⁄₃ cup double (heavy) cream
75g/3oz Roquefort cheese, crumbled

Preparation: 2 minutes; Cooking: 10–12 minutes

1 Heat the butter and oil together in a heavy frying pan over a high heat. Season the steaks well. Fry them for 1 minute on each side, to sear them.

2 Lower the heat slightly and cook for a further 2–3 minutes on each side, or according to your taste. Remove the steaks to a dish, cover with foil and set aside.

3 Reduce the heat and add the brandy, stirring to incorporate the pan juices.

4 Stir in the cream. Bring the sauce to the boil, then cook for 1 minute to reduce a little.

5 Add the crumbled Roquefort cheese and mash it into the sauce using a spoon. Taste for seasoning. Pour into a small sauce jug (pitcher).

6 Serve the steaks on individual heated plates, garnished with flat leaf parsley, and with a little of the Roquefort cheese sauce poured over each one. Offer the remaining sauce separately.

Steak with Warm Tomato Salsa

A tangy salsa of tomatoes, spring onions and balsamic vinegar makes a colourful topping for chunky, pan-fried steaks cooked just the way you like them.

Serves 2
2 steaks, about 2cm/¾in thick
4 large plum tomatoes
2 spring onions (scallions)
30ml/2 tbsp balsamic vinegar

Preparation: 2–3 minutes; Cooking: 8 minutes

1 Trim any excess fat from the steaks, then season on both sides with salt and pepper. Heat a non-stick frying pan and cook the steaks for about 3 minutes on each side for medium rare. Cook for a little longer if you like your steak well cooked.

2 Meanwhile, put the tomatoes in a heatproof bowl, cover with boiling water and leave for 1–2 minutes.

3 When the tomato skins start to split, drain and peel them, then halve the tomatoes and scoop out the seeds. Dice the tomato flesh.

4 When the steaks are cooked to your taste, remove from the pan with a fish slice, to drain off any excess oil, and transfer them to plates. Keep the steaks warm on a very low oven temperature while you prepare the salsa.

5 Thinly slice the spring onions and add them to the cooking juices in the frying pan with the diced tomato, balsamic vinegar, 30ml/2 tbsp water and a little seasoning. Stir briefly until warm, scraping up any meat residue. Spoon the salsa over the steaks, dividing it equally between them, and serve.

Cook's Tip
Choose rump (round), sirloin or fillet steak (beef tenderloin). If you prefer to grill (broil) the steak, the timing will be the same as the recipe, though you must take into account the thickness of the meat.

Steak with Salsa Energy 207kcal/872kJ; Protein 33.9g; Carbohydrate 3.4g, of which sugars 3.4g; Fat 6.5g, of which saturates 2.7g; Cholesterol 89mg; Calcium 17mg; Fibre 1.2g; Sodium 100mg.
With Blue Cheese Energy 573kcal/2374kJ; Protein 36.3g; Carbohydrate 0.7g, of which sugars 0.7g; Fat 45.4g, of which saturates 24.4g; Cholesterol 170mg; Calcium 117mg; Fibre 0g; Sodium 341mg.

Pan-fried Steaks with Whisky & Cream

A good steak is always a popular choice for dinner, and top quality meat plus timing are the keys to success. Choose small, thick steaks rather than large, thin ones if you can.

Serves 4
4 x 225–350g/8–12oz sirloin
   steaks, at room temperature
5ml/1 tsp oil
15g/½oz/1 tbsp butter
50ml/2fl oz/¼ cup whisky
300ml/½ pint/1¼ cups double
   (heavy) cream
salt and ground black pepper

Preparation: 0 minutes; Cooking: 10–12 minutes

1 Dry the steaks with kitchen paper and season with pepper. Heat a cast-iron frying pan, or other heavy pan, over high heat. When it is very hot, add the oil and butter. Add the steaks to the foaming butter, one at a time, and seal the meat quickly on both sides.

2 Lower the heat to moderate and continue to cook the steaks, allowing 3–4 minutes for rare, 4–5 minutes for medium or 5–6 minutes for well-done steaks.

3 When the steaks are cooked to your liking, transfer them to warmed plates and keep warm. Pour off the fat from the pan and discard. Add the whisky and stir around to scrape off all the sediment from the base of the pan.

4 Allow the liquid to reduce a little, then add the cream and simmer over a low heat for a few minutes, until the cream thickens. Season to taste, pour the sauce around or over the steaks, as you prefer, and serve immediately.

Cook's Tips
• *Turn the steaks only once during cooking to seal in the juices.*
• *Serve with fried onions and mushrooms, peas and oven chips (French fries).*

Collops of Beef with Shallots

Caramelized shallots are delicious. The time needed for cooking the steaks will depend upon how thick they are. Rare meat will feel soft to the touch; medium will have some resistance; well done will feel firm.

Serves 4
4 fillet steaks (beef tenderloin)
15ml/1 tbsp olive oil
50g/2oz/¼ cup butter
20 shallots, peeled
5ml/1 tsp caster (superfine) sugar
150ml/¼ pint/⅔ cup beef stock
salt and ground black pepper

Preparation: 0 minutes; Cooking: 10–12 minutes

1 Take the steaks out of the refrigerator well before you need them and dry with kitchen paper. Heat the oil and butter in a large frying pan then cook the steaks allowing 3–4 minutes for rare, 4–5 minutes for medium or 5–6 minutes for well-done meat.

2 Once cooked remove the steaks from the pan and keep warm. Put the shallots in the pan and brown lightly in the meat juices.

3 Add the sugar to the shallots and then stir in the stock. Reduce the heat to low and allow the liquid to evaporate, shaking the pan from time to time to stop the shallots from sticking.

4 The shallots will end up slightly soft, browned and caramelized with a shiny glaze. Season to taste with salt and ground black pepper.

5 Serve the steaks on warmed plates and spoon over the caramelized shallots and juices from the pan.

Cook's Tip
Serve with sautéed potatoes. Cook unpeeled baby potatoes in boiling salted water for about 20 minutes until just tender. Drain, cool, then remove the skins. Slice thickly. Heat a mixture of olive oil and butter in a frying pan and cook the potato slices until browned and crisp. Drain on kitchen paper and serve.

Pan-fried Steaks Energy 806kcal/3345kJ; Protein 65.9g; Carbohydrate 1.3g, of which sugars 1.3g; Fat 56.5g, of which saturates 32.6g; Cholesterol 251mg; Calcium 51mg; Fibre 0g; Sodium 232mg.
Collops of Beef Energy 424kcal/1767kJ; Protein 43.2g; Carbohydrate 6.1g, of which sugars 4.6g; Fat 25.4g, of which saturates 12.5g; Cholesterol 149mg; Calcium 27mg; Fibre 0.9g; Sodium 166mg.

Green Beef Curry

This is a very quick curry so it is essential that you use good-quality meat. Sirloin is recommended, but tender rump or even fillet steak could be used instead.

Serves 4–6

450g/1lb beef sirloin
15ml/1 tbsp vegetable oil
45ml/3 tbsp Thai green
*   curry paste*

600ml/1 pint/2½ cups
*   coconut milk*
4 kaffir lime leaves, torn
15–30ml/1–2 tbsp Thai
*   fish sauce*
5ml/1 tsp palm sugar (jaggery) or
*   light muscovado (brown) sugar*
150g/5oz small Thai aubergines
*   (eggplants), halved*
a small handful of fresh Thai basil
2 fresh green chillies, to garnish

Preparation: 2 minutes; Cooking: 16 minutes

1 Trim off any excess fat from the beef. Using a sharp knife, cut it into long, thin strips. This is easiest to do if it is well chilled, so pop it into the freezer first if you have time. Set it aside.

2 Heat the oil in a large, heavy pan or wok. Add the curry paste and cook for 1–2 minutes, until it is fragrant.

3 Stir in half the coconut milk, a little at a time. Cook, stirring frequently, for about 5–6 minutes, until an oily sheen appears on the surface of the liquid.

4 Add the beef to the pan with the kaffir lime leaves, Thai fish sauce, sugar and aubergine halves. Cook for 2–3 minutes, then stir in the remaining coconut milk.

5 Bring back to a simmer and cook until the meat and aubergines are tender. Stir in the Thai basil.

6 Prepare the garnish. Slit the fresh green chillies and scrape out the pith and seeds. Shred the chillies finely.

7 Spoon the curry into a heated serving dish or on to individual plates. Sprinkle with the finely shredded chillies and serve immediately.

Beef with Peppers & Black Bean Sauce

A spicy, rich dish with the distinctive taste of black bean sauce. This is a recipe that will quickly become a favourite because it is so easy to prepare and quick to cook.

Serves 4

350g/12oz rump (round) steak,
*   trimmed and thinly sliced*
20ml/4 tsp vegetable oil
300ml/½ pint/1¼ cups
*   beef stock*
2 garlic cloves, finely chopped

5ml/1 tsp grated (shredded) fresh
*   root ginger*
1 fresh red chilli, seeded and
*   finely chopped*
15ml/1 tbsp black bean sauce
1 green (bell) pepper, seeded and
*   cut into 2.5cm/1in squares*
15ml/1 tbsp dry sherry
5ml/1 tsp cornflour (cornstarch)
5ml/1 tsp granulated (white)
*   sugar*
45ml/3 tbsp cold water
salt
cooked rice noodles, to serve

Preparation: 6 minutes; Cooking: 7–8 minutes

1 Place the thin slices of rump steak in a bowl. Add 5ml/1 tsp of the oil and stir to coat them thoroughly.

2 Bring the stock to the boil in a pan. Add the beef and cook for 2 minutes, stirring constantly to prevent the slices from sticking together. Lift out the beef slices, put them on a plate and set aside. Strain the stock into a jug (pitcher), cool quickly and refrigerate for use in another recipe.

3 Heat the remaining oil in a wok. Stir-fry the garlic, ginger and chilli with the black bean sauce for a few seconds.

4 Add the pepper squares and a little water. Cook for about 2 minutes more, then stir in the sherry. Add the beef slices to the pan, spoon the sauce over and reheat.

5 Mix the cornflour and sugar to a cream with the water. Pour the mixture into the pan. Cook, stirring, until the sauce has thickened. Season with salt. Serve with rice noodles.

Green Beef Curry Energy 147kcal/619kJ; Protein 18.2g; Carbohydrate 6.4g, of which sugars 6.3g; Fat 5.6g, of which saturates 1.9g; Cholesterol 38mg; Calcium 36mg; Fibre 0.5g; Sodium 341mg.
Beef with Peppers Energy 146kcal/613kJ; Protein 19.3g; Carbohydrate 2.1g, of which sugars 1.1g; Fat 6.4g, of which saturates 1.8g; Cholesterol 52mg; Calcium 5mg; Fibre 0g; Sodium 115mg.

Beef with Chanterelle Mushrooms

The trick here is to use really good beef with no fat and to fry the dried pieces quickly in the hot oil so the outside is well browned and the inside very rare. Chanterelle mushrooms are the most delicious wild mushrooms, yellowy orange in colour and with a shape like inverted umbrellas.

Serves 4

115g/4oz chanterelle mushrooms
2 rump (round) steaks, 175g/6oz
  each, cut into strips
45ml/3 tbsp olive oil
1 garlic clove, crushed
1 shallot, finely chopped
60ml/4 tbsp dry white wine
60ml/4 tbsp double
  (heavy) cream
25g/1oz/2 tbsp butter
salt and ground black pepper
chopped fresh parsley, to garnish

Preparation: 2 minutes; Cooking: 7–8 minutes

1 Clean the mushrooms. If you have collected them from the wild cut off the ends where they have come from the ground and, using kitchen paper, wipe off any leaf matter or moss that may be adhering to them. Trim the mushrooms, then cut them in half through the stalk and cap.

2 Dry the beef thoroughly on kitchen paper. Heat a large frying pan over a high heat then add 30ml/2 tbsp olive oil. Working in batches add the meat to the hot oil in the pan and quickly brown the strips on all sides.

3 Remove the meat, which should still be very rare, from the pan, set aside and keep warm. Add the remaining olive oil to the pan and reduce the heat. Stir in the garlic and shallots and cook, stirring, for about 1 minute.

4 Increase the heat and add the mushrooms. Season and cook until the mushrooms just start to soften. Add the wine, bring to the boil and add the cream. As the liquid thickens, return the beef to the pan and heat through.

5 Remove the pan from the heat and swirl in the butter. Serve on warmed plates, garnished with the parsley.

Calf's Liver with Crisp Onions

Sautéed or creamy mashed potatoes go well with fried calf's liver. Serve with a salad of mixed leaves and fresh herbs, to complement the simple flavours of this main course.

Serves 4

50g/2oz/¼ cup butter

4 onions, thinly sliced
5ml/1 tsp caster (superfine) sugar
4 slices calf's liver, each weighing
  about 115g/4oz
30ml/2 tbsp plain
  (all-purpose) flour
30ml/2 tbsp olive oil
salt and ground black pepper
parsley, to garnish

Preparation: 3–4 minutes; Cooking: 16 minutes

1 Melt the butter in a large, heavy-based pan with a lid. Add the onions and mix well to coat with butter. Cover the pan with a tight-fitting lid and cook gently for 10 minutes, stirring the onions occasionally to prevent them from sticking.

2 Stir in the sugar and cover the pan. Cook the onions for 8 minutes more, or until they are soft and golden. Increase the heat, remove the lid and stir the onions over a high heat until they are deep gold and crisp. Use a slotted spoon to remove the onions from the pan, draining off the fat.

3 Meanwhile, rinse the calf's liver in cold water and pat it dry on kitchen paper. Season the flour, put it on a plate and turn the slices of liver in it until they are lightly coated in flour.

4 Heat the oil in a large frying pan, add the liver and cook for about 2 minutes on each side, or until lightly browned and just firm. Arrange the liver on warmed plates, with the crisp onions. Garnish with parsley and serve with sautéed or mashed potatoes with a little mustard, if you like.

Cook's Tip
Take care not to cook the liver for too long as this may cause it to become tough and unpalatable.

Beef Energy 415kcal/1725kJ; Protein 29.9g; Carbohydrate 0.7g, of which sugars 0.6g; Fat 31g, of which saturates 14.2g; Cholesterol 122mg; Calcium 21mg; Fibre 0.4g; Sodium 124mg.
Calf's Liver Energy 350kcal/1458kJ; Protein 23.9g; Carbohydrate 19.7g, of which sugars 8.6g; Fat 20.1g, of which saturates 8.5g; Cholesterol 452mg; Calcium 61mg; Fibre 2.4g; Sodium 162mg.

Pan-fried Veal Chops

Veal chops from the loin are an expensive cut and are best cooked quickly and simply so that their subtle flavour and tenderness can be enjoyed to the full. When a cut is costly, buy from a reputable butcher and cook with care.

Serves 2
25g/1oz/2 tbsp butter, softened
15ml/1 tbsp Dijon mustard
15ml/1 tbsp chopped fresh basil
olive oil, for brushing
2 veal loin chops, 2.5cm/1in thick
(about 225g/8oz each)
ground black pepper
fresh basil sprigs, to garnish

Preparation: 2 minutes; Cooking: 7–9 minutes

1 To make the basil butter, cream the butter with the mustard and chopped basil in a small bowl, then season with pepper.

2 Lightly oil a heavy frying pan or griddle. Set over high heat until very hot but not smoking. Brush both sides of each chop with a little oil and season with a little pepper.

3 Place the chops in the pan or griddle and reduce the heat to medium. Cook for 4–5 minutes, then turn and cook for 3–4 minutes more until done as preferred. Top each chop with half the basil butter and serve, garnished with basil.

Cook's Tip
Veal is coming back into favour in the UK, thanks to more humane farming practices than those of the past, when young, milk-fed animals were confined in crates so that their muscles atrophied to produce white veal. Today's high-welfare veal is rose pink in colour, and comes from calves that live outside for much of the year. Look for meat with the Freedom Food Label.

Variation
The flavour of basil goes well with the veal, but rosemary or parsley in the herb butter would also work well.

Veal Escalopes with Tarragon

These thin slices of veal need little cooking and the sauce is made very quickly as well, so this is the ideal dish to come home to after a busy day at the office.

Serves 4
4 veal escalopes (US scallops) about 120–150g/4–5oz each

15g/½oz/1 tbsp butter
30ml/2 tbsp brandy
250ml/8fl oz/1 cup chicken or beef stock
15ml/1 tbsp chopped fresh tarragon
salt and freshly ground black pepper
tarragon sprigs, to garnish

Preparation: 4 minutes; Cooking: 6 minutes

1 Place the veal escalopes between two sheets of clear film (plastic wrap) and pound with the flat side of a meat mallet or roll them with a rolling pin to flatten them out to about 5mm/¼in thickness. Season with salt and ground black pepper.

2 Melt the butter in a large frying pan over a medium-high heat. Add enough meat to the pan to fit easily in one layer (do not overcrowd the pan, cook in batches if necessary) and cook for 1½–2 minutes, turning once. Each escalope should be lightly browned, but must not be overcooked. Transfer to a platter.

3 Add the brandy to the pan, then pour in the stock and bring to the boil. Add the tarragon and continue boiling until the liquid is reduced by half.

4 Return the veal to the pan with any accumulated juices and heat through. Serve immediately, garnished with tarragon sprigs.

Variation
This treatment also works well with turkey escalopes. Pound them between clear film (plastic wrap) until thin and take care not to overcook them, or they will be tough. The sauce can be flavoured with tarragon, as here, or try another fresh herb, such as sage, thyme or marjoram.

Veal Chops Energy 349kcal/1459kJ; Protein 48.1g; Carbohydrate 0.8g, of which sugars 0.7g; Fat 17g, of which saturates 8.6g; Cholesterol 216mg; Calcium 26mg; Fibre 0g; Sodium 545mg.
Veal Escalopes Energy 342kcal/1436kJ; Protein 51.7g; Carbohydrate 0.8g, of which sugars 0.7g; Fat 14.7g, of which saturates 7.9g; Cholesterol 144mg; Calcium 17mg; Fibre 0g; Sodium 430mg.

Veal Escalopes with Lemon

Popular in Italian restaurants, this dish is very simple to make at home. White vermouth and lemon juice make the perfect sauce for the delicately flavoured meat.

Serves 4
4 veal escalopes (US scallops)
30–45ml/2–3 tbsp plain
 (all-purpose) flour
50g/2oz/¼ cup butter
60ml/4 tbsp olive oil
60ml/4 tbsp Italian dry white
 vermouth or dry white wine
45ml/3 tbsp lemon juice
salt and ground black pepper
lemon wedges, grated lemon rind
 and finely chopped fresh
 parsley, to garnish
salad, to serve

Preparation: 3–4 minutes; Cooking: 15 minutes

1 Put each veal escalope between two sheets of clear film (plastic wrap) and pound with the side of a rolling pin or the smooth side of a meat mallet until the slices are very thin.

2 Cut the pounded escalopes in half or quarters. Season the flour with a little salt and pepper and use it to coat the escalopes on both sides. Shake off any excess seasoned flour.

3 Melt the butter with half the oil in a large, heavy frying pan until sizzling. Add as many escalopes as the pan will hold. Cook over a medium to high heat for about 2 minutes on each side until lightly coloured. Remove with a spatula and keep hot.

4 Add the remaining oil to the pan and cook the remaining veal escalopes in the same way.

5 Remove the pan from the heat and add the vermouth or wine and the lemon juice. Stir vigorously to mix well with the pan juices, then return the pan to the heat.

6 Return all the veal escalopes to the pan. Spoon the sauce over to coat the veal. Heat through for about 2 minutes, shaking the pan occasionally. Serve immediately with a salad, garnished with lemon wedges, grated lemon rind and a sprinkling of finely chopped fresh parsley.

Escalopes of Veal with Cream Sauce

This quick, easy dish is delicious served with buttered tagliatelle and lightly steamed green vegetables. It works just as well with turkey escalopes.

Serves 4
15ml/1 tbsp plain
 (all-purpose) flour
4 veal escalopes (US scallops),
 about 75–115g/3–4oz each
30ml/2 tbsp sunflower oil
1 shallot, chopped
150g/5oz/2 cups oyster
 mushrooms, sliced
30ml/2 tbsp Marsala or
 medium-dry sherry
200ml/7fl oz/scant 1 cup crème
 fraîche or sour cream
30ml/2 tbsp chopped
 fresh tarragon
salt and ground black pepper

Preparation: 2–3 minutes; Cooking: 15–17 minutes

1 Put the flour in a strong plastic bag and season with salt and pepper. Add the veal escalopes and shake the bag to coat them. Remove from the bag and set the meat aside, taking care not to disturb the coating.

2 Heat the oil in a large frying pan and cook the shallot and mushrooms for 5 minutes. Add the escalopes and cook over a high heat for about 1½ minutes on each side. Pour in the Marsala or sherry and cook until reduced by half.

3 Remove the escalopes from the pan. Stir the crème fraîche, tarragon and seasoning into the juices in the pan and simmer gently for 3–5 minutes, or until the sauce is thick and creamy.

4 Return the escalopes to the pan and heat through for 1 minute before serving on heated individual plates with the sauce, noodles and broccoli.

Cook's Tip
If the escalopes (US scallops) are too thick, put them between pieces of clear film (plastic wrap) and flatten them with a rolling pin or meat mallet. This will help to cut down the cooking time.

Veal with Lemon Energy 360kcal/1498kJ; Protein 29g; Carbohydrate 4.8g, of which sugars 0.6g; Fat 23.5g, of which saturates 8.9g; Cholesterol 92mg; Calcium 16mg; Fibre 0.2g; Sodium 151mg.
Veal with Cream Energy 377kcal/1567kJ; Protein 25.1g; Carbohydrate 5.9g, of which sugars 2.5g; Fat 27.5g, of which saturates 14.9g; Cholesterol 108mg; Calcium 45mg; Fibre 0.8g; Sodium 75mg.

Cantonese Fried Noodles

Chow mein is hugely popular with the Chinese, who believe in turning leftovers into tasty dishes.

Serves 2–3

225g/8oz lean beef steak
    or pork fillet (tenderloin)
225g/8oz can bamboo
    shoots, drained
1 leek
25g/1oz Chinese dried
    mushrooms, soaked for
    30 minutes in 120ml/4fl oz/
    ½ cup warm water
150g/5oz Chinese leaves
    (Chinese cabbage)
450g/1lb cooked egg noodles
    (255g/8oz dried), drained well
90ml/6 tbsp vegetable oil
30ml/2 tbsp dark soy sauce
15ml/1 tbsp cornflour
    (cornstarch)
15ml/1 tbsp rice wine or
    medium-dry sherry
5ml/1 tsp sesame oil
5ml/1 tsp caster (superfine) sugar
salt and ground black pepper

Preparation: 5 minutes; Cooking: 12 minutes

1 Slice the beef or pork, bamboo shoots and leek into matchsticks. Drain the mushrooms, reserving 90ml/6 tbsp of the soaking water.

2 Cut off and discard the mushroom stems, then thinly slice the caps. Cut the Chinese leaves into diamond-shaped pieces and sprinkle with salt. Pat the noodles dry with kitchen paper.

3 Heat a third of the oil in a large wok or frying pan and sauté the noodles. After turning them over once, press the noodles evenly against the bottom of the pan with a wooden spatula until they form a flat, even cake.

4 Cook over medium heat for about 4 minutes or until the noodles at the bottom have become crisp.

5 Turn the noodle cake over with a fish slice or metal spatula or invert on to a large plate and slide back into the wok.

6 Cook for 3 minutes more, then slide on to a heated plate. Keep warm.

7 Heat 30ml/2 tbsp of the remaining oil in the wok. Add the strips of leek, then the meat strips and stir-fry for 10–15 seconds.

8 Sprinkle over half the soy sauce and then add the bamboo shoots and mushrooms, with salt and pepper to taste. Toss over the heat for 1 minute, then transfer this mixture to a plate.

9 Heat the remaining oil in the wok and sauté the Chinese leaves for 1 minute. Return the meat and vegetable mixture to the wok and sauté with the leaves for 30 seconds.

10 Mix the cornflour with the reserved mushroom water. Stir into the wok along with the rice wine or sherry, sesame oil, sugar and remaining soy sauce. Cook for about 15 seconds until it has thickened.

11 Divide the noodles among 2–3 serving dishes and pile the meat and vegetables on top.

Pork Kebabs with BBQ Sauce

Use pork fillet for these kebabs because it is lean and tender and cooks quickly.

Serves 4

500g/1¼lb lean pork fillet
    (tenderloin)
8 large, thick spring onions
    (scallions)
120ml/4fl oz/½ cup
    barbecue sauce
1 lemon, cut into wedges,
    to garnish

Preparation: 3–4 minutes; Cooking: 10 minutes

1 Cut the pork into 2.5cm/1in cubes. Cut the spring onions into 2.5cm/1in-long sticks.

2 Preheat the grill (broiler) to high. Oil the wire rack and spread out the pork cubes on it. Grill (broil) the pork until the juices drip, then dip the pieces in the barbecue sauce and put back on the grill. Grill until cooked through, repeating the dipping process twice more. Set aside and keep warm.

3 Trim the spring onions and gently grill until soft and slightly brown on the outside. Do not dip in the barbecue sauce. Thread about four pieces of pork and three spring onion pieces on to each of eight bamboo skewers.

4 Arrange the skewers on a platter. Squeeze a little lemon juice over each skewer. Serve immediately, offering the remaining lemon wedges separately, so that guests can squeeze the juice over their meat.

Variation

This is an unusual kebab recipe, in that the cubes of pork are threaded on to the skewers only after cooking. This is because the meat is regularly dipped in glaze, and it is easier to get an all-round coating if the cubes of pork are free. If you prefer to assemble the skewers first and cook them on the barbecue, do so. Use metal skewers, which will not char, and baste frequently with the sauce.

Fried Noodles Energy 695kcal/2894kJ; Protein 35.3g; Carbohydrate 38.7g, of which sugars 7.7g; Fat 45.3g, of which saturates 8.5g; Cholesterol 79mg; Calcium 79mg; Fibre 4.6g; Sodium 1185mg.
Pork Kebabs Energy 192kcal/806kJ; Protein 27.6g; Carbohydrate 9.2g, of which sugars 8.8g; Fat 5.1g, of which saturates 1.8g; Cholesterol 79mg; Calcium 21mg; Fibre 0.6g; Sodium 578mg.

Lemon Grass & Ginger Pork Burgers

Lemon grass lends a fragrant citrus flavour to pork and is enhanced by the fresh zing of ginger. Serve the burgers in burger buns with tomato, crisp lettuce and some chilli sauce. Apricot chutney would also go well with the burgers, or use smooth or chunky apple sauce. Alternatively, dispense with sauce and instead add slices of fried fresh pineapple or canned pineapple rings.

Serves 4
450g/1lb/2 cups minced (ground) pork
15ml/1 tbsp grated fresh root ginger
1 lemon grass stalk, outer layers discarded and centre part chopped finely
30ml/2 tbsp sunflower oil
salt and ground black pepper

To serve
juicy tomatoes, thickly sliced
crisp lettuce leaves
chilli sauce

Preparation: 5 minutes; Cooking: 6–8 minutes

1 Put the pork in a bowl and stir in the ginger and chopped lemon grass. Season with salt and pepper. Shape the mixture into four burgers and ideally chill for about 20 minutes.

2 Heat the oil in a large, non-stick frying pan and add the burgers. Fry for 3–4 minutes on each side over a gentle heat, until cooked through.

3 Remove from the pan with a metal spatula and drain on kitchen paper.

4 Serve in burger buns with the sliced tomato, lettuce and chilli sauce, if you like.

Variation
Omit the ginger and lemon grass and add 60ml/4 tbsp grated apple to the pork to make tasty apple-flavoured burgers.

Pork with Cream & Apple Sauce

Tender noisettes of pork in a creamy leek and apple sauce make a great dinner party dish. Use the same white wine as the one you plan to serve with the meal, or try cider.

Serves 4
30ml/2 tbsp plain (all-purpose) flour
4 noisettes of pork, firmly tied
25g/1oz/2 tbsp butter
4 baby leeks, finely sliced
5ml/1 tsp mustard seeds, coarsely crushed
150ml/¼ pint/⅔ cup dry white wine
2 eating apples
150ml/¼ pint/⅔ cup double (heavy) cream
30ml/2 tbsp chopped fresh parsley
salt and ground black pepper

To serve
red cabbage
fried polenta

Preparation: 2 minutes; Cooking: 18 minutes

1 Place the flour in a bowl and add plenty of seasoning. Turn the noisettes in the flour mixture to coat them lightly and evenly on both sides.

2 Melt the butter in a heavy frying pan and cook the noisettes for 1 minute on each side, turning them with tongs.

3 Add the sliced leeks to the pan and cook for 3 minutes. Stir in the mustard seeds. Pour in the wine. Cook gently for 10 minutes, turning the pork occasionally. Peel the apples, remove the cores, cut in half and slice thinly.

4 Add the sliced apples and double cream to the pan and simmer for 3 minutes, or until the pork is fully cooked and the sauce is thick, rich and creamy. Taste for seasoning, add salt and pepper if needed, then stir in the chopped parsley and serve the pork at once with red cabbage and fried polenta.

Variation
Use thin slices of pork fillet (tenderloin) for even faster cooking.

Pork Burgers Energy 234kcal/974kJ; Protein 21.6g; Carbohydrate 0g, of which sugars 0g; Fat 16.4g, of which saturates 4.7g; Cholesterol 74mg; Calcium 8mg; Fibre 0g; Sodium 74mg.
Pork with Cream Energy 415kcal/1724kJ; Protein 23.1g; Carbohydrate 8.8g, of which sugars 4.4g; Fat 29.5g, of which saturates 17.2g; Cholesterol 128mg; Calcium 45mg; Fibre 1.3g; Sodium 119mg.

Bacon Chops with Apple & Cider Sauce

Either thin bacon or pork chops could be used in this recipe, which brings the traditional ingredients of pork and apples together in an attractive dish.

Serves 4

15ml/1 tbsp oil
4 bacon chops
1 or 2 cooking apples, peeled, cored and sliced
knob (pat) of butter
1 or 2 garlic cloves, finely chopped
5ml/1 tsp sugar
150ml/¼ pint/⅔ cup dry (hard) cider
5ml/1 tsp cider vinegar
15ml/1 tbsp wholegrain mustard
10ml/2 tsp chopped fresh thyme
salt and ground black pepper
sprigs of thyme, to garnish

To serve

mashed potatoes
steamed buttered cabbage

Preparation: 5 minutes; Cooking: 15 minutes

1 Heat the oil in a large heavy frying pan over a medium heat, and cook the chops for 10 minutes, browning well on both sides. Remove the chops from the pan and keep warm.

2 Add the butter and apples to the frying pan and cook until the juices begin to turn brown.

3 Add the garlic and sugar, and cook for 1 minute, then stir in the cider, cider vinegar, mustard and chopped thyme. Boil for a few minutes until reduced to a saucy consistency. Season well.

4 Place the chops on warmed serving plates, spoon over the sauce, garnish with the thyme sprigs and serve.

Cook's Tip

For the chops to cook through in the time stated, they will need to be fairly thin. For thick pork or bacon chops, cook for about 10 minutes on each side.

Aromatic Pork with Basil

The combination of moist, juicy pork and mushrooms, crisp green mangetouts and fragrant basil in this ginger- and garlic-infused stir-fry is absolutely delicious. Served with simple steamed jasmine rice, it makes a perfect quick supper during the week.

Serves 4

40g/1½oz cornflour (cornstarch)
500g/1¼lb pork fillet (tenderloin), thinly sliced
15ml/1 tbsp sunflower oil
10ml/2 tsp sesame oil
15ml/1 tbsp very finely shredded fresh root ginger
3 garlic cloves, thinly sliced
200g/7oz mangetouts (snow peas), halved lengthways
300g/11oz/generous 4 cups mixed mushrooms, such as shiitake, button (white) or oyster, sliced if large
120ml/4fl oz/½ cup Chinese cooking wine
45ml/3 tbsp soy sauce
a small handful of sweet basil leaves
salt and ground black pepper
steamed jasmine rice, to serve

Preparation: 6 minutes; Cooking: 10–13 minutes

1 Place the cornflour in a strong plastic bag. Season well and add the sliced pork. Shake the bag to coat the pork in flour and then remove the pork and shake off any excess flour. Set aside.

2 Preheat the wok over a high heat and add the oils. When very hot, stir in the ginger and garlic and cook for 30 seconds. Add the pork and cook over a high heat for about 5 minutes, stirring often, until sealed.

3 Add the mangetouts and mushrooms to the wok and stir-fry for 2–3 minutes. Add the Chinese cooking wine and soy sauce, stir-fry for 2–3 minutes and remove from the heat.

4 Just before serving, stir the sweet basil leaves into the pork. Serve with steamed jasmine rice.

Cook's Tip

When adding the oils to the hot wok, dribble them around the inner rim so that the oil flows down to coat the surface evenly.

Bacon Chops Energy 1140kcal/4760kJ; Protein 105.6g; Carbohydrate 26g, of which sugars 26gg; Fat 64.4g, of which saturates 21.6g; Cholesterol 160mg; Calcium 68mg; Fibre 3.2g; Sodium 536mg.
Aromatic Pork Energy 298kcal/1248kJ; Protein 30.4g; Carbohydrate 14.6g, of which sugars 4.8g; Fat 9.8g, of which saturates 2.4g; Cholesterol 79mg; Calcium 41mg; Fibre 2g; Sodium 903mg.

Pork & Pineapple Coconut Curry

The heat of this curry balances out its sweetness to make a fragrant dish.

Serves 4
400ml/14fl oz coconut milk
10ml/2 tsp Thai red curry paste
400g/14oz pork loin steaks, trimmed and thinly sliced
15ml/1 tbsp Thai fish sauce
5ml/1 tsp palm sugar (jaggery) or light muscovado (brown) sugar
15ml/1 tbsp tamarind juice, made by mixing tamarind paste with warm water
2 kaffir lime leaves, torn
1/2 medium pineapple
1 fresh red chilli, seeded and finely chopped
lime rind, to garnish

Preparation: 3 minutes; Cooking: 17 minutes

1 Pour the coconut milk into a bowl and let it settle, so that the cream rises to the surface. Scoop the cream into a measuring jug (cup). You should have about 250ml/8fl oz/1 cup. If necessary, add a little of the coconut milk.

2 Pour the coconut cream into a large pan and bring it to the boil over high heat, stirring once or twice.

3 Cook the coconut cream for about 8 minutes, until the cream separates, stirring frequently to prevent it from sticking to the base of the pan. Peel and chop the pineapple.

4 Ladle a little of the coconut cream into a bowl and stir in the red curry paste. Return the mixture to the pan and stir until well mixed. Cook, stirring occasionally, for about 3 minutes, until the paste is fragrant.

5 Add the sliced pork and stir in the fish sauce, sugar and tamarind juice. Cook, stirring constantly, for 2–3 minutes, until the sugar has dissolved and the pork is no longer pink.

6 Add the remaining coconut milk and the lime leaves. Bring to the boil, then stir in the pineapple. Reduce the heat and simmer gently for 3 minutes, or until the pork is fully cooked. Spoon into a large heated bowl or four individual bowls and sprinkle the chilli and strips of lime rind over. Serve immediately.

Sweet & Sour Pork Thai-style

It was the Chinese who originally created sweet and sour cooking, but the Thais also do it very well. This version has a fresher and cleaner flavour than the Chinese version.

Serves 4
350g/12oz lean pork
30ml/2 tbsp vegetable oil
4 garlic cloves, thinly sliced
1 small red onion, sliced
30ml/2 tbsp Thai fish sauce
15ml/1 tbsp sugar
1 red (bell) pepper, seeded and diced
1/2 cucumber, seeded and very thinly sliced
2 plum tomatoes, cut into wedges
115g/4oz piece fresh pineapple, cut into small chunks
2 spring onions (scallions), cut into short lengths
ground black pepper

To garnish
coriander (cilantro) leaves
spring onions (scallions), shredded

Preparation: 6 minutes; Cooking: 13 minutes

1 Cut the pork into thin strips. This is easier to do if you freeze it for 30 minutes first.

2 Heat the oil in a wok or large frying pan. Add the garlic. Cook over a medium heat until golden, then add the pork and stir-fry for 4–5 minutes. Add the onion slices and toss to mix.

3 Add the fish sauce, sugar and ground black pepper to taste. Toss the mixture over the heat for 3–4 minutes more.

4 Stir in the red pepper, cucumber, tomatoes, pineapple and spring onions. Stir-fry for 3–4 minutes more, then spoon into a bowl. Garnish with the coriander and spring onions and serve.

Cook's Tip
Also known as nam pla, Thai fish sauce is one of the most important ingredients in Thai cuisine. It is made from salted fish, usually anchovies, which are fermented to create the thin liquid that is the base of the sauce. The strong aroma and intense flavour becomes less pronounced with cooking.

Pork Curry Energy 187kcal/790kJ; Protein 22.2g; Carbohydrate 15.3g, of which sugars 15.3g; Fat 4.5g, of which saturates 1.6g; Cholesterol 63mg; Calcium 55mg; Fibre 1.2g; Sodium 449mg.
Sweet and Sour Pork Energy 211kcal/885kJ; Protein 20g; Carbohydrate 12.4g, of which sugars 11.8g; Fat 9.4g, of which saturates 2g; Cholesterol 55mg; Calcium 29mg; Fibre 1.8g; Sodium 68mg.

Pork with Marsala & Juniper

Although most frequently used in desserts, Sicilian Marsala gives savoury dishes a rich, fruity and alcoholic tang, bringing out the flavour of the pork perfectly.

Serves 4
25g/1oz/1/2 cup dried cep or
  porcini mushrooms

4 pork escalopes (US scallops)
10ml/2 tsp balsamic vinegar
8 garlic cloves
15g/1/2 oz/1 tbsp butter
45ml/3 tbsp Marsala
several fresh rosemary sprigs
10 juniper berries, crushed
salt and ground black pepper
noodles and green vegetables,
  to serve

Preparation: 4 minutes; Cooking: 15 minutes

1 Put the dried mushrooms in a bowl and just cover with hot water. Leave to stand. Bring a small pan of water to the boil and add the garlic cloves. Cook for 10 minutes until soft. Drain, put the garlic in a bowl and set aside.

2 Meanwhile, place the pork escalopes on a board, brush with 5ml/1 tsp of the vinegar and add a generous and even grinding of salt and black pepper.

3 Melt the butter in a large frying pan. Add the pork and fry quickly until browned on the underside. Turn the meat over and cook for another minute.

4 Add the Marsala and rosemary to the pan. Drain the dried mushrooms, saving the juices, and add them to the mixture. Stir in 60ml/4 tbsp of the mushroom juices, then add the garlic cloves, juniper berries and remaining vinegar. Simmer for 3 minutes, season and serve with noodles and vegetables.

Cook's Tips
• Use good quality butcher's pork, which won't be overwhelmed by the intense flavour of the sauce.
• Juniper berries are the principal flavouring for gin. When added to meat, they impart a gamey flavour.

Pork in Sweet & Sour Sauce

The combination of sweet and sour flavours makes this a popular dish. Crushed mixed peppercorns add extra bite.

Serves 2
1 whole pork fillet (tenderloin),
  about 350g/12oz
25ml/1 1/2 tbsp plain
  (all-purpose) flour

30–45ml/2–3 tbsp olive oil
250ml/8fl oz/1 cup dry white wine
30ml/2 tbsp white wine vinegar
10ml/2 tsp sugar
15ml/1 tbsp mixed peppercorns,
  coarsely ground
salt and ground black pepper
cooked broad (fava) beans tossed
  with grilled (broiled) bacon, to
  serve

Preparation: 2–3 minutes; Cooking: 6 minutes

1 Using a sharp knife, cut the pork diagonally into thin slices. Place between two sheets of baking parchment or clear film (plastic wrap) and pound lightly with a meat mallet or rolling pin to flatten them.

2 Spread out the flour in a shallow bowl. Season generously with salt and pepper, add the meat and turn it in the seasoned flour until coated evenly. Alternatively, put the seasoned flour in a strong plastic bag, add the pork and shake to coat.

3 Heat 15ml/1 tbsp of the oil in a wide heavy pan or frying pan and add as many slices of pork as the pan will hold. Fry over a medium to high heat for 2–3 minutes on each side until the pork is crisp and tender. Remove with a fish slice or metal spatula and place on a plate. Keep warm, either by tenting foil over the pork or in a low oven. Fry the remaining pork in the same way, adding more oil to the pan as necessary.

4 Mix the wine, vinegar and sugar in a measuring jug (cup). Pour into the pan and stir over a high heat until reduced.

5 Stir in the peppercorns and return the pork to the pan. Spoon the sauce over the pork until it is evenly coated and heated through. Serve with cooked broad beans tossed with grilled (broiled) bacon.

Pork with Marsala Energy 282kcal/1176kJ; Protein 32.2g; Carbohydrate 0.9g, of which sugars 0.9g; Fat 15.3g, of which saturates 8g; Cholesterol 118mg; Calcium 13mg; Fibre 0g; Sodium 175mg.
Pork in Sweet and Sour Energy 440kcal/1839kJ; Protein 38.3g; Carbohydrate 11.8g, of which sugars 6.1g; Fat 18.1g, of which saturates 4.1g; Cholesterol 110mg; Calcium 37mg; Fibre 0.3g; Sodium 128mg.

Five-flavour Noodles

The Japanese name for this dish is gomoku yakisoba, meaning five different ingredients; however, you can add as many different ingredients as you wish to make an exciting and tasty noodle stir-fry.

Serves 4

300g/11oz dried Chinese thin egg noodles or 500g/1¼lb fresh soba noodles
200g/7oz lean boneless pork, thinly sliced
22.5ml/4½ tsp sunflower oil
10g/¼oz grated fresh root ginger
1 garlic clove, crushed
200g/7oz green cabbage, roughly chopped
115g/4oz/2 cups beansprouts
1 green (bell) pepper, seeded and cut into fine strips
1 red (bell) pepper, seeded and cut into fine strips
salt and ground black pepper
20ml/4 tsp ao-nori seaweed, to garnish (optional)

For the seasoning mix

60ml/4 tbsp Worcestershire sauce
15ml/1 tbsp Japanese soy sauce
15ml/1 tbsp oyster sauce
15ml/1 tbsp sugar
2.5ml/½ tsp salt
ground white pepper

Preparation: 7–9 minutes; Cooking: 11–13 minutes

1 Cook the noodles according to the instructions on the packet. Drain well and set aside.

2 Cut the pork into 3–4cm/1¼–1½in strips and lay these on a board. Season with plenty of salt and pepper.

3 Heat 7.5ml/1½ tsp of the oil in a large wok or frying pan. Add the seasoned pork strips, stir-fry the pork until just cooked, then remove it from the wok or pan.

4 Wipe the wok or pan with kitchen paper, and heat the remaining oil in it. Add the ginger, garlic and cabbage and stir-fry for 1 minute. Add the beansprouts, stir until softened, then add the peppers and stir-fry for 1 minute more.

5 Return the pork to the pan and add the noodles. Stir in all the ingredients for the seasoning mix and stir-fry for 2–3 minutes. Serve immediately, sprinkled with ao-nori seaweed (if using).

Fried Pork with Scrambled Egg

When you need a tasty meal before going out for the evening, this quick-to-prepare and easy rice dish, with just a little meat, is the answer. Use regular rice, if you like, but that will take longer.

Serves 4

2 x 250g/9oz sachets quick-cook rice
45ml/3 tbsp vegetable oil
1 onion, chopped
15ml/1 tbsp chopped garlic
115g/4oz pork, cut into small cubes
2 eggs, beaten
30ml/2 tbsp Thai fish sauce
15ml/1 tbsp dark soy sauce
2.5ml/½ tsp caster (superfine) sugar

For the garnish

4 spring onions (scallions), finely sliced
2 fresh red chillies, sliced
1 lime, cut into wedges

Preparation: 5 minutes; Cooking: 12 minutes

1 Cook the rice according to the instructions on the packet. Spread out and leave to cool.

2 Heat the oil in a wok or large frying pan. Add the onion and garlic and cook for about 2 minutes, until softened.

3 Add the pork to the softened onion and garlic. Stir-fry until the pork changes colour and is cooked.

4 Add the eggs and cook until scrambled into small lumps.

5 Add the rice and continue to stir and toss, to coat it with the oil and prevent it from sticking.

6 Stir in the fish sauce, soy sauce and sugar and mix well. Continue to fry until the rice is thoroughly heated. Spoon into warmed individual bowls and serve, garnished with sliced spring onions, chillies and lime wedges.

Variation
Substitute sliced field (portabello) mushrooms for the pork.

Five-flavour Noodles Energy 425kcal/1799kJ; Protein 28.2g; Carbohydrate 62.6g, of which sugars 9.4g; Fat 8.6g, of which saturates 2.6g; Cholesterol 67mg; Calcium 82mg; Fibre 4.4g; Sodium 844mg.
Fried Pork Energy 602kcal/2512kJ; Protein 18.8g; Carbohydrate 101.3g, of which sugars 1.1g; Fat 12.8g, of which saturates 2.2g; Cholesterol 113mg; Calcium 45mg; Fibre 0.2g; Sodium 323mg.

Fusilli with Sausage

Getting sausages, pasta and tomato sauce ready at the right moment takes a bit of juggling, but the result is a delicious dish that every member of the family is bound to love.

Serves 4

400g/14oz spicy pork sausages
30ml/2 tbsp olive oil
1 small onion, finely chopped
2 garlic cloves, crushed
5ml/1 tsp paprika
5ml/1 tsp dried mixed herbs
5–10ml/1–2 tsp chilli sauce
1 large yellow (bell) pepper,
  seeded and cut into strips
400g/14oz can Italian
  plum tomatoes
250ml/8fl oz/1 cup
  vegetable stock
300g/11oz/2¾ cups dried fusilli
salt and ground black pepper
freshly grated Pecorino or
  Parmesan cheese, to serve

Preparation: 4–5 minutes; Cooking: 12–15 minutes

1 Grill (broil) the sausages for 10–12 minutes until they are browned on all sides.

2 Meanwhile, heat the oil in a large pan, add the onion and garlic and cook for 3 minutes. Add the paprika, herbs and chilli sauce to taste, then the yellow pepper. Cook for 3 minutes more, stirring occasionally.

3 Pour in the canned tomatoes, breaking them up with a wooden spoon, then add salt and pepper to taste and stir well. Cook over a medium heat for 10–12 minutes, adding the vegetable stock gradually. At the same time, add the pasta to a large pan of lightly salted boiling water and cook for 10–12 minutes, until *al dente*.

4 While the tomato sauce and pasta are cooking, drain the cooked sausages on kitchen paper, and, when cool enough to touch, cut each one diagonally into 1cm/½in pieces.

5 Add the sausage pieces to the sauce and mix well. Drain the pasta and add it to the pan of sauce. Toss well, then divide among four warmed bowls, sprinkled with the grated Pecorino or Parmesan cheese.

Spaghetti Carbonara

This Italian classic, flavoured with pancetta and a garlic-and-egg sauce that cooks around the hot spaghetti, is popular worldwide. It makes a great last-minute supper.

Serves 4

30ml/2 tbsp olive oil
1 small onion, finely chopped
1 large garlic clove, crushed
8 slices pancetta or rindless
  smoked streaky (fatty) bacon,
  cut into 1cm/½in pieces
350g/12oz dried spaghetti
4 eggs
90–120ml/6–8 tbsp
  crème fraîche
60ml/4 tbsp freshly grated
  Parmesan cheese, plus extra
  to serve
salt and ground black pepper

Preparation: 3 minutes; Cooking: 15–17 minutes

1 Heat the oil in a large pan, add the onion and garlic and fry gently for about 5 minutes until softened. Add the pancetta or bacon to the pan. Cook for 10 minutes, stirring often.

2 Meanwhile, cook the spaghetti in a large pan of lightly salted boiling water for 10–12 minutes.

3 Put the eggs, crème fraîche and grated Parmesan in a bowl. Stir in plenty of black pepper, then beat together well.

4 Drain the pasta thoroughly, tip it into the pan with the pancetta or bacon and toss well to mix. Turn off the heat under the pan, then immediately add the egg mixture and toss thoroughly so that it cooks lightly and coats the pasta.

5 Season to taste, then divide the pasta among four warmed bowls and sprinkle with ground black pepper. Serve immediately, with extra grated Parmesan handed around separately in a bowl.

> **Variation**
> *Instead of beating the eggs with crème fraîche, use double (heavy) cream or sour cream, if you prefer.*

Fusilli Energy 709kcal/2970kJ; Protein 20.9g; Carbohydrate 72.2g, of which sugars 10.5g; Fat 39.5g, of which saturates 13.3g; Cholesterol 47mg; Calcium 74mg; Fibre 4.6g; Sodium 774mg.
Spaghetti Energy 708kcal/2966kJ; Protein 30.7g; Carbohydrate 66.6g, of which sugars 4.2g; Fat 37.5g, of which saturates 15.5g; Cholesterol 261mg; Calcium 250mg; Fibre 2.8g; Sodium 824mg.

Tortellini with Ham

This is a very easy recipe that can be made quickly from store-cupboard ingredients. It is therefore ideal for an after-work supper or a casual lunch for friends.

Serves 4
2 tbsp olive oil
1 small onion, finely chopped
115g/4oz cooked ham, diced
150ml/1/4 pint/2/3 cup passata (strained tomatoes)
100ml/3 1/2 fl oz/scant 1/2 cup panna da cucina or double (heavy) cream
250g/9oz fresh tortellini alla carne (meat-filled tortellini)
75g/3oz/1 cup freshly grated Parmesan cheese
salt and ground black pepper

Preparation: 5 minutes; Cooking: 12 minutes

1 Heat the oil in a large pan, add the onion and cook over low heat, stirring frequently, for about 5 minutes, until softened. Add the ham and cook, stirring occasionally, until it darkens.

2 Add the passata to the pan along with 150ml/1/4 pint/2/3 cup water. Stir well, then add salt and pepper to taste. Bring to the boil, lower the heat and simmer the sauce for a few minutes, stirring occasionally, until it has reduced slightly. Stir the cream into the sauce and heat gently without boiling.

3 Meanwhile, bring a large pan of lightly salted water to the boil. Add the meat-filled tortellini, stir and cook for about 3 minutes, until it is tender.

4 Drain the pasta well and add it to the sauce. Add a handful of grated Parmesan to the pan. Stir, toss well and taste for seasoning. Serve in warmed bowls, topped with the remaining Parmesan cheese.

Cook's Tip
Keep a couple of cans of passata in the storecupboard and some vacuum-packed tortellini in the refrigerator and this dish is a doddle.

Fettuccine with Ham & Peas

This simple dish makes a very good first course for six people, or a main course for three to four. Despite its simplicity, it makes an ideal impromptu supper.

Serves 3–6
50g/2oz/1/4 cup butter
1 small onion, finely chopped
200g/7oz/1 3/4 cups fresh or frozen peas
100ml/3 1/2 fl oz/scant 1/2 cup chicken stock
2.5ml/1/2 tsp sugar
175ml/6fl oz/3/4 cup dry white wine
350g/12oz fresh fettuccine
75g/3oz piece cooked ham, cut into bitesize chunks
115g/4oz/1 1/3 cups freshly grated Parmesan cheese
salt and ground black pepper

Preparation: 4 minutes; Cooking: 8–10 minutes

1 Melt the butter in a medium frying pan, add the onion and cook over a low heat for about 5 minutes until softened but not coloured. Add the peas, stock and sugar, then stir in salt and freshly ground pepper to taste.

2 Bring the mixture to the boil, then lower the heat and simmer for 3–5 minutes or until the peas are tender. Add the wine, increase the heat and boil until the wine has reduced.

3 Meanwhile, cook the pasta in a large pan of lightly salted boiling water for about 3 minutes. When it is almost ready, add the ham to the sauce, with about a third of the Parmesan. Heat through, stirring, then taste for seasoning.

4 Drain the pasta and tip it into a large warmed bowl. Pour the sauce over the pasta and toss well. Serve immediately, sprinkled with the remaining Parmesan.

Cook's Tip
If you want to make this with dried pasta it will take a little longer, but if you start cooking the pasta before making the sauce, it won't take too much more time.

Tortellini Energy 509kcal/2118kJ; Protein 19.9g; Carbohydrate 26.2g, of which sugars 4.1g; Fat 36.8g, of which saturates 17.5g; Cholesterol 85mg; Calcium 353mg; Fibre 1.9g; Sodium 696mg.
Fettuccine Energy 414kcal/1738kJ; Protein 19.4g; Carbohydrate 48.6g, of which sugars 4g; Fat 15.1g, of which saturates 8.6g; Cholesterol 44mg; Calcium 259mg; Fibre 3.4g; Sodium 413mg.

Pasta with Ham & Asparagus

Tagliatelle dressed with a creamy asparagus sauce is the basis for this sustaining salad. If you've spent the morning gardening or playing sport, this is a great lunch you won't have to wait for.

Serves 4
450g/1lb asparagus
450g/1lb dried tagliatelle
225g/8oz cooked ham, in 5mm/
  ¼ in-thick slices, cut into fingers
2 hard-boiled eggs, sliced
50g/2oz Parmesan cheese
salt and ground black pepper

For the dressing
50g/2oz cooked potato
75ml/5 tbsp olive oil
15ml/1 tbsp lemon juice
10ml/2 tsp Dijon or
  wholegrain mustard
120ml/4fl oz/½ cup
  vegetable stock

Preparation: 5 minutes; Cooking: 12 minutes

1 Snap the asparagus spears; they will break naturally at the point where the tender top meets the base. Discard the tough woody ends. Cut the spears in half.

2 Bring a pan of salted water to the boil and cook the thicker halves for 12 minutes, adding the tips after 6 minutes.

3 Meanwhile, cook the pasta in a large pan of lightly salted boiling water for 10–12 minutes.

4 Drain the asparagus. Reserve the tips. Purée the remainder of the asparagus with the potato, olive oil, lemon juice, mustard and vegetable stock to make a smooth dressing.

5 Drain the pasta, toss with the asparagus sauce and cool slightly. Divide among four pasta plates. Top with the ham, hard-boiled eggs and asparagus tips. Shave Parmesan cheese over the top.

Variation
Use sliced chicken instead of the ham, or thin slices of softer Italian cheese, such as Fontina or Asiago.

Pan-fried Gammon with Cider

Gammon and cider are a delicious combination, since the sweet, tangy flavour of cider complements the gammon perfectly. Serve with mustard mashed potatoes and a dark green vegetable, such as steamed Savoy cabbage, green beans or lightly cooked Brussels sprouts.

Serves 4
4 gammon (smoked or cured
  ham) steaks, 225g/8oz each
150ml/¼ pint/⅔ cup dry
  (hard) cider
45ml/3 tbsp double (heavy) cream
30ml/2 tbsp sunflower oil
salt and ground black pepper
flat leaf parsley, to garnish
mustard mashed potatoes,
  to serve

Preparation: 1 minute; Cooking: 7–10 minutes

1 Heat the oil in a large frying pan until hot. Neatly snip the rind on the gammon steaks to stop them curling up and add them to the pan.

2 Cook the steaks for 3–4 minutes on each side, then pour in the cider. Allow to boil for a couple of minutes, then stir in the cream and cook for 1–2 minutes, or until thickened. Season with salt and pepper, and serve immediately.

Variation
The Irish dish, champ, makes a great alternative to mustard mashed potatoes: Cook 900g/2lb peeled potatoes in boiling salted water until tender. Meanwhile heat 120ml/4fl oz/½ cup creamy milk with 6 finely chopped spring onions (scallions). Mash the potatoes with the milk and onions and 50g/2oz/ ¼ cup butter. Pile the champ in a dish, make a well in the middle, and place another 50g/2oz/¼ cup butter in the well.

Cook's Tip
Cooking gammon (smoked or cured ham) in a liquid is a good way of ensuring it stays moist and soft-textured.

Ham and Pasta Energy 699kcal/2941kJ; Protein 35.4g; Carbohydrate 88.2g, of which sugars 6.6g; Fat 25.2g, of which saturates 6.3g; Cholesterol 140mg; Calcium 228mg; Fibre 5.3g; Sodium 852mg.
Gammon Energy 429kcal/1784kJ; Protein 39.6g; Carbohydrate 1.2g, of which sugars 1.2g; Fat 28.4g, of which saturates 10.1g; Cholesterol 67mg; Calcium 24mg; Fibre 0g; Sodium 1985mg.

Bacon, Pumpkin & Parmesan Pasta

The sweet flavour of pumpkin is nicely balanced by the Parmesan in this creamy pasta sauce, while fried garlic breadcrumbs provide a welcome crunch.

Serves 4
800g/1¾lb fresh pumpkin flesh, cut into small cubes
300g/11oz dried tagliatelle
65g/2½oz/5 tbsp butter
1 onion, sliced
115g/4oz rindless smoked back bacon, diced
15ml/1 tbsp olive oil
2 garlic cloves, crushed
75g/3oz/1½ cups fresh white breadcrumbs
150ml/¼ pint/⅔ cup single (light) cream
50g/2oz/⅔ cup freshly grated Parmesan cheese
freshly grated nutmeg
30ml/2 tbsp chopped fresh parsley
15ml/1 tbsp chopped fresh chives
salt and ground black pepper
sprigs of flat leaf parsley, to garnish

Preparation: 4 minutes; Cooking: 14 minutes

1 Bring two pans of lightly salted water to the boil. Place the pumpkin cubes in one pan and the pasta in the other. Cook for 10–12 minutes, stirring both pans several times.

2 Meanwhile, heat one-third of the butter in a separate large pan. Fry the onion and bacon for 5 minutes.

3 Melt the remaining butter with the oil in a frying pan. Add the garlic and breadcrumbs. Fry gently until the crumbs are golden brown and crisp. Drain on kitchen paper, spoon into a dish and keep warm for topping the pasta.

4 Drain the pumpkin and add it to the onion and bacon mixture, with the cream. Heat without stirring until bubbles appear on the surface and the cream is just below boiling point.

5 Drain the pasta, add to the pan and heat through. Stir in the Parmesan, nutmeg, chopped parsley, chives and seasoning. Spoon into a warmed bowl or individual pasta bowls, sprinkle with the garlic breadcrumbs and garnish with the sprigs of flat leaf parsley. Serve immediately.

Chorizo & Egg Bake

This adaptable dish is a swirl of red, green, yellow and white. You can use different vegetables, but should always include the chorizo for its flavour.

Serves 4
30ml/2 tbsp olive oil
115g/4oz diced smoked bacon or pancetta
2 chorizos, cubed
1 onion, chopped
2 garlic cloves, finely chopped
1 red and 1 green (bell) pepper, seeded and chopped
500g/1¼lb tomatoes, chopped
15–30ml/1–2 tbsp fino sherry
45ml/3 tbsp chopped parsley
8 large (US extra large) eggs
salt, paprika and cayenne pepper

For the garlic crumbs
4 thick slices stale bread
oil, for frying
2 garlic cloves, bruised

Preparation: 4–5 minutes; Cooking: 15 minutes

1 Preheat the oven to 180°C/350°F/Gas 4. Heat the oil in a large pan and fry the diced bacon and chorizo until they yield their fat. Add the onion and garlic and cook gently until softened, stirring.

2 Add the peppers and tomatoes and cook to reduce, stirring occasionally. Add some paprika and stir in the sherry.

3 Divide the mixture among four individual baking dishes. Sprinkle with parsley. Swirl the eggs with a fork, season with salt and cayenne, and pour over the vegetable mixture.

4 Bake the eggs and vegetables for 8 minutes, or until the eggs are just set.

5 Meanwhile make the garlic crumbs. Crumb the bread in a food processor. Heat plenty of oil in a large frying pan, add the garlic cloves for a few moments to flavour it, then remove and discard them. Throw in the breadcrumbs and brown quickly, scooping them out on to kitchen paper with a slotted spoon.

6 Season with a little salt and paprika, then sprinkle the crumbs around the edge of the eggs, when ready to serve.

Bacon Pasta Energy 691kcal/2897kJ; Protein 23.8g; Carbohydrate 76.6g, of which sugars 8.1g; Fat 34.2g, of which saturates 18.1g; Cholesterol 83mg; Calcium 293mg; Fibre 4.8g; Sodium 834mg.
Chorizo Bake Energy 597kcal/2485kJ; Protein 27.3g; Carbohydrate 28g, of which sugars 11.1g; Fat 42.4g, of which saturates 11.7g; Cholesterol 429mg; Calcium 163mg; Fibre 3.2g; Sodium 1116mg.

Shanghai Noodles with Lap Cheong

Lap cheong are firm, cured waxy pork sausages, available from Chinese food markets. Sweet and savoury, they can be steamed with rice, chicken or pork, added to an omelette or stir-fried with vegetables.

Serves 4
30ml/2 tbsp vegetable oil
115g/4oz rindless back (lean) bacon, cut into bitesize pieces
2 lap cheong, rinsed in warm water, drained and finely sliced
2 garlic cloves, finely chopped
2 spring onions (scallions), roughly chopped
225g/8oz Chinese greens or fresh spinach leaves, cut into 5cm/2in pieces
450g/1lb fresh Shanghai noodles
30ml/2 tbsp oyster sauce
30ml/2 tbsp soy sauce
ground black pepper

Preparation: 8 minutes; Cooking: 8 minutes

1 Heat half the oil in a wok or large frying pan. Add the bacon and lap cheong with the garlic and spring onions. Stir-fry for a few minutes until golden. Using a slotted spoon, remove the mixture from the wok or pan and keep warm.

2 Add the remaining oil to the wok or pan. When hot, stir-fry the Chinese greens or spinach over a high heat for about 3 minutes until it just starts to wilt.

3 Add the noodles and return the lap cheong mixture to the wok or pan. Season with oyster sauce, soy sauce and pepper. Stir-fry until the noodles are heated through.

Variation
Use chipolata sausages instead of the lap cheong.

Cook's Tip
You can buy rindless bacon already cut into bitesize pieces. To remove the rind from bacon rashers (strips) cut it off with sharp kitchen scissors, occasionally dipping them in hot water.

Pittas with Spiced Lamb Koftas

When you are eating *al fresco*, a bite in the hand is worth two on the plate. Harissa gives the lamb koftas a mildly fiery flavour, easily tamed by a drizzle of yogurt, some cucumber and tomato, and a little mint.

Serves 4
450g/1lb/2 cups minced (ground) lamb
1 small onion, finely chopped
10ml/2 tsp harissa paste
8 pitta breads, salad vegetables, mint and yogurt, to serve
salt and ground black pepper

Preparation: 10 minutes; Cooking: 10 minutes

1 Prepare a barbecue. Soak eight wooden skewers in cold water for 10 minutes.

2 Meanwhile, put the minced lamb in a large bowl and add the finely chopped onion and harissa paste. Mix well to combine, and season with plenty of salt and pepper.

3 Drain the skewers. Divide the spiced lamb mixture into eight equal pieces and mould each piece around a skewer in a sausage shape to make the koftas.

4 Cook the skewered koftas on the barbecue for about 10 minutes, turning occasionally, until cooked through.

5 Warm the pitta breads on the barbecue grill, then split them and open them out to make pitta pockets. Place a kofta in each one, and remove the skewer.

6 Add some cucumber and tomato slices, mint leaves and a drizzle of yogurt to each filled pocket, and serve immediately.

Variation
Instead of adding mint leaves and yogurt separately to the pittas, spoon in some tzatziki, made by mixing finely diced cucumber, spring onions (scallions) and crushed garlic with Greek (US strained plain) yogurt.

Shanghai Noodles Energy 485kcal/2043kJ; Protein 30.5g; Carbohydrate 60.7g, of which sugars 5.3g; Fat 14.9g, of which saturates 2.8g; Cholesterol 63mg; Calcium 47mg; Fibre 3.2g; Sodium 440mg.
Pittas Energy 609kcal/2568kJ; Protein 35.3g; Carbohydrate 83.8g, of which sugars 5.4g; Fat 17g, of which saturates 7.3g; Cholesterol 87mg; Calcium 230mg; Fibre 3.8g; Sodium 737mg.

Kofta Lamb Burgers

For a quick and easy supper, simply slide these spicy little burgers into cones made by rolling warmed tortillas. A dollop of thick yogurt or crème fraîche wouldn't go amiss either.

Serves 4
450g/1lb minced (ground) lamb
1–2 large slices French bread, very finely crumbed
½ bunch fresh coriander (cilantro), finely chopped
5 garlic cloves, chopped
1 onion, finely chopped
juice of ½ lemon
5ml/1 tsp ground cumin
5ml/1 tsp paprika
15ml/1 tbsp curry powder
a pinch each of ground cardamom, turmeric and cinnamon
15ml/1 tbsp tomato purée (paste)
cayenne pepper or chopped fresh chillies (optional)
1 egg, beaten (optional)
salt and ground black pepper
flat bread and salads, to serve

Preparation: 8 minutes; Cooking: 10 minutes

1 Put the lamb, crumbed bread, coriander, garlic, onion, lemon juice, spices, tomato purée, cayenne pepper or chillies and seasoning in a large bowl. Mix well. If the mixture does not bind together, add the beaten egg and a little more bread.

2 Divide the mixture into four large or eight small rounds. With wet hands, shape into burgers.

3 Heat a heavy non-stick frying pan, add the burgers and cook for about 10 minutes, until browned. Turn carefully once or twice, but make sure that they do not fall apart. Serve hot with flat bread and salads.

Variations
• *Mix a handful of raisins or sultanas (golden raisins) into the meat mixture before shaping it into burgers.*
• *Serve in conventional burger buns, splitting them and toasting them under a hot grill (broiler) before filling.*
• *Try these with coleslaw for a substantial snack.*

Pan-fried Mediterranean Lamb

This Mediterranean dish makes a simple weekday meal.

Serves 4
8 lean lamb cutlets (US rib chops)
1 onion, thinly sliced
2 red (bell) peppers, seeded and sliced
400g/14oz can plum tomatoes
1 garlic clove, crushed
45ml/3 tbsp chopped fresh basil
30ml/2 tbsp chopped pitted black olives
salt and ground black pepper
pasta, to serve (optional)

Preparation: 2 minutes; Cooking: 18 minutes

1 Trim any excess fat from the lamb, then cook in a non-stick frying pan, without any added fat, turning frequently, for 2 minutes, until golden brown all over. Add the onion and red peppers to the pan. Cook, stirring, for 1 minute to soften, then add the plum tomatoes, garlic and fresh basil leaves.

2 Cover and simmer for 15 minutes, or until the lamb is tender. Stir in the olives, season to taste and serve hot.

Cumin- & Coriander-rubbed Lamb

When summer sizzles, turn up the heat a little more with these spicy lamb chops. If you have time, marinate the chops for an hour – they will taste even better.

Serves 4
30ml/2 tbsp ground cumin
30ml/2 tbsp ground coriander
30ml/2 tbsp olive oil
8 lamb chops
salt and ground black pepper

Preparation: 3 minutes; Cooking: 10 minutes.

1 Prepare a barbecue or preheat the grill (broiler). Mix the cumin, coriander and oil in a bowl, beating with a spoon until a smooth paste is formed. Season with salt and pepper. Rub the mixture all over the lamb chops. Cook the chops for 5 minutes on each side, until lightly charred on the outside but still pink in the centre. Serve immediately.

Kofta Lamb Burgers Energy 298kcal/1249kJ; Protein 24.2g; Carbohydrate 16.5g, of which sugars 2.6g; Fat 15.5g, of which saturates 7.1g; Cholesterol 87mg; Calcium 57mg; Fibre 1.1g; Sodium 242mg.
Pan-Fried Lamb Energy 637kcal/2634kJ; Protein 23.9g; Carbohydrate 9.9g, of which sugars 9.3g; Fat 56g, of which saturates 27.3g; Cholesterol 117mg; Calcium 33mg; Fibre 2.8g; Sodium 272mg.
Cumin Lamb Energy 494kcal/2059kJ; Protein 55.6g; Carbohydrate 0g, of which sugars 0g; Fat 30.1g, of which saturates 12.6g; Cholesterol 220mg; Calcium 18mg; Fibre 0g; Sodium 150mg.

Lamb with Red Pepper Salsa

Vibrant red pepper salsa brings out the best in succulent lamb steaks to make a dish that looks as good as it tastes. Serve a selection of salads and crusty bread with the lamb.

Serves 6
6 lamb steaks
about 15g/½oz/½ cup fresh rosemary sprigs
2 garlic cloves, sliced

60ml/4 tbsp olive oil
30ml/2 tbsp maple syrup
salt and ground black pepper

For the salsa
200g/7oz red (bell) peppers, roasted, peeled, seeded and chopped
1 garlic clove, crushed
15ml/1 tbsp chopped chives
30ml/2 tbsp extra virgin olive oil
fresh flat leaf parsley, to garnish

Preparation: 3 minutes; Cooking: 4–10 minutes

1 Place the lamb steaks in a shallow dish that will hold them all in one layer. Season with salt and pepper. Pull the leaves off the rosemary and sprinkle them over the meat.

2 Add the slices of garlic, then drizzle the olive oil and maple syrup over the top. Cover and chill until ready to cook. If you have time, the lamb steaks can be left to marinate in the refrigerator for 12 hours or up to 24 hours.

3 Prepare a barbecue or preheat the grill (broiler). Make sure the steaks are liberally coated with the marinating ingredients, then cook them over the hot barbecue or under the grill for 2–5 minutes on each side. The cooking time willl depend on the heat of the barbecue coals and the thickness of the steaks as well as the result required – rare, medium or well cooked.

4 While the lamb steaks are cooking, mix together all the ingredients for the salsa in a bowl.

5 Serve the salsa spooned on to the plates with the meat or in a small serving dish on the side. Garnish the lamb with sprigs of flat leaf parsley and pass around a cool, crisp salad – iceberg lettuce would be ideal.

Sweet & Sour Lamb

Buy lamb loin chops from your butcher and ask him to French trim them for you. Serve the chops with a hot sauce based on their marinade and with steamed carrots and green beans on the side.

Serves 4
8 French-trimmed lamb loin chops
90ml/6 tbsp balsamic vinegar
30ml/2 tbsp caster (superfine) sugar
30ml/2 tbsp olive oil
salt and ground black pepper

Preparation: 3 minutes; Cooking: 8–10 minutes

1 Put the lamb chops in a shallow, non-metallic dish and drizzle over the balsamic vinegar.

2 Sprinkle with the sugar and season with salt and black pepper. Turn the chops to coat in the mixture, then cover with clear film (plastic wrap) and chill for 10 minutes.

3 Heat the olive oil in a large frying pan and add the chops, reserving the marinade. Cook for 3–4 minutes on each side.

4 Pour the marinade into the pan and leave to bubble for about 2 minutes, or until reduced slightly. Remove from the pan and serve immediately.

Variations
Use sherry vinegar instead of balsamic in the marinade. Mint and lamb are good companions, and adding a little chopped fresh mint to the marinade will also give good results.

Cook's Tip
Lamb loin chops are sold as a rack of lamb, which is also known as a guard of honour, but they are chined (have the backbone removed) to leave cutlets that can be easily separated. French-trimmed chops are those that have had the skin removed as well as the backbone.

Barbecued Lamb Energy 390kcal/1627kJ; Protein 44.1g; Carbohydrate 2.1g, of which sugars 2g; Fat 22.8g, of which saturates 6.8g; Cholesterol 158mg; Calcium 33mg; Fibre 0.5g; Sodium 106mg.
Sweet and Sour Lamb Energy 258kcal/1077kJ; Protein 19.7g; Carbohydrate 7.9g, of which sugars 7.9g; Fat 16.7g, of which saturates 6g; Cholesterol 76mg; Calcium 12mg; Fibre 0g; Sodium 87mg.

Lamb Steaks with Redcurrant Glaze

Good and meaty, but thin enough to cook quickly, lamb leg steaks are a good choice for the cook short on time. The redcurrant and rosemary glaze looks gorgeous especially with a fresh redcurrant garnish.

Serves 4

4 large fresh rosemary sprigs
4 lamb leg steaks
75ml/5 tbsp redcurrant jelly
30ml/2 tbsp raspberry or
* red wine vinegar*

Preparation: 2–3 minutes; Cooking: 10 minutes

1 Reserve the tips of the rosemary sprigs and finely chop the remaining leaves. Rub the chopped rosemary, salt and pepper all over the lamb to infuse it with flavour.

2 Preheat the grill (broiler). Heat the redcurrant jelly gently in a small pan with 30ml/2 tbsp water and a little seasoning. Stir in the raspberry or red wine vinegar.

3 Place the lamb steaks on a foil-lined grill (broiling) rack and brush with a little of the redcurrant glaze. Cook under the grill for about 5 minutes on each side, until deep golden, brushing frequently with more redcurrant glaze.

4 Transfer the lamb to warmed plates. Tip any juices from the foil into the remaining glaze and heat through gently. Pour the glaze over the lamb and serve with peas and new potatoes, garnished with the reserved rosemary sprigs.

Cook's Tip
This is a good recipe for the barbecue. Wait until the fierce heat has subsided and the coals are dusted with white ash, then place the rosemary-rubbed steaks directly on the grill rack. Brush frequently with the glaze as they cook. If you grow your own rosemary, try sprinkling some over the coals. As the oil in the herb warms, the scent of rosemary will perfume the air and stimulate the appetite.

Fried Lamb Meatballs

Meatballs cook quickly; the only fiddly bit is shaping them. Mixing everything together with your hands is very satisfying and also the most efficient way of preparing them.

Serves 4

2 medium slices of bread,
* crusts removed*
500g/1¼lb minced (ground)
* lamb or beef*
1 onion

5ml/1 tsp each dried thyme
* and oregano*
45ml/3 tbsp chopped fresh
* flat leaf parsley, plus extra*
* to garnish*
1 egg, lightly beaten
salt and ground black pepper
lemon wedges, to serve (optional)

For frying

25g/1oz/¼ cup plain
* (all-purpose) flour*
30–45ml/2–3 tbsp vegetable or
* light olive oil*

Preparation: 10–15 minutes; Cooking: 5 minutes

1 Soak the slices of bread in a shallow bowl of water for 5 minutes or until softened. While the bread is soaking, grate or very finely chop the onion.

2 Drain the bread in a colander. Using clean hands, squeeze it dry and put it in a large bowl. Add the meat, onion, dried herbs, parsley, egg, salt and pepper to the bread. Mix together, preferably using your hands, until well blended.

3 Shape the meat mixture into individual balls about the size of a walnut, and roll them in the flour to give them a light dusting, shaking off any excess coating.

4 Heat the oil in a large frying pan. When it is hot, add the meatballs and fry for about 5 minutes, shaking the pan, turning them frequently, until they are cooked through and look crisp and brown.

5 Using a slotted spoon, lift out the meatballs and drain on a double sheet of kitchen paper, to get rid of the excess oil. Sprinkle with the remaining chopped parsley and serve with lemon wedges, if you like.

Lamb Steaks Energy 362kcal/1518kJ; Protein 34.4g; Carbohydrate 13g, of which sugars 13g; Fat 19.6g, of which saturates 9.1g; Cholesterol 133mg; Calcium 16mg; Fibre 0g; Sodium 156mg.
Lamb Meatballs Energy 411kcal/1710kJ; Protein 28.4g; Carbohydrate 13g, of which sugars 1.5g; Fat 27.6g, of which saturates 9.7g; Cholesterol 123mg; Calcium 66mg; Fibre 1.1g; Sodium 192mg.

Devilled Kidneys on Brioche Croûtes

The trick with lamb's kidneys is not to overcook them, so this recipe is a gift for the quick cook. Cream tames the fiery sauce, making a mixture that tastes great on croûtes or as a filling for tartlets.

Serves 4
8 mini brioche slices
25g/1oz/2 tbsp butter

1 shallot, finely chopped
2 garlic cloves, finely chopped
115g/4oz/1½ cups mushrooms, halved
1.5ml/¼ tsp cayenne pepper
15ml/1 tbsp Worcestershire sauce
8 lamb's kidneys, halved and trimmed
150ml/¼ pint/⅔ cup double (heavy) cream
30ml/2 tbsp chopped fresh parsley

Preparation: 5 minutes; Cooking: 12–14 minutes

1 Preheat the grill (broiler) and toast the brioche slices until golden brown on both sides. Keep warm.

2 Melt the butter in a frying pan. Add the shallot, garlic and mushrooms and cook for 5 minutes, or until the shallot has softened. Stir in the cayenne pepper and Worcestershire sauce and simmer for 1 minute.

3 Add the kidneys to the pan and cook for 3–5 minutes on each side. Finally, stir in the cream and simmer for about 2 minutes, or until the sauce has heated through.

4 Remove the brioche croûtes from the wire rack and place on warmed plates. Top with the kidneys. Sprinkle with chopped parsley and serve with salad.

> **Cook's Tip**
> If you can't find mini brioches, you can use a large brioche instead. Slice it thickly and stamp out croûtes using a 5cm/2in round cutter. If you prefer, the brioche croûtes can be fried rather than toasted. Melt 25g/1oz/2 tbsp butter in a frying pan and fry the croûtes until crisp and golden on both sides.

Warm Lamb & Noodle Salad

This Thai-inspired salad combines thin slices of lamb with lightly cooked fresh vegetables and rice noodles, all tossed together with a deliciously fragrant dressing.

Serves 4
30ml/2 tbsp red Thai curry paste
60ml/4 tbsp sunflower oil
750g/1lb 11oz lamb neck (US shoulder or breast) fillets, thinly sliced
250g/9oz sugar snap peas
500g/1¼lb medium or thick fresh rice noodles

1 red (bell) pepper, seeded and very thinly sliced
1 cucumber, cut into very thin slices with a vegetable peeler
6–7 spring onions (scallions), sliced diagonally
a large handful of fresh mint leaves

For the dressing
15ml/1 tbsp sunflower oil
juice of 2 limes
1 garlic clove, crushed
15ml/1 tbsp golden caster (superfine) sugar
15ml/1 tbsp fish sauce
30ml/2 tbsp soy sauce

Preparation: 10 minutes plus marinating; Cooking: 7–9 minutes

1 In a shallow dish, mix together the red curry paste and half the oil. Add the lamb slices and toss to coat. Cover and leave to marinate in the refrigerator for up to 24 hours.

2 Blanch the sugar snap peas in a wok of lightly salted boiling water for 1–2 minutes. Drain, refresh under cold water, drain again thoroughly and transfer to a large bowl.

3 Put the noodles in a separate bowl and pour over boiling water to cover. Soak for 5–10 minutes, until tender, then drain well and separate. Add the noodles to the sugar snap peas, then add the red pepper, cucumber and spring onions.

4 Heat a wok over a high heat and add the remaining sunflower oil. Stir-fry the lamb in two batches for 3–4 minutes, or until cooked through, then add to the bowl of salad ingredients.

5 Place all the dressing ingredients in a screw-top jar, screw on the lid and shake well. Pour over the warm salad, sprinkle over the mint and toss to combine. Serve immediately.

Warm Lamb Salad Energy 820kcal/3418kJ; Protein 46g; Carbohydrate 76.4g, of which sugars 9.4g; Fat 36g, of which saturates 11.7g; Cholesterol 143mg; Calcium 55mg; Fibre 4.1g; Sodium 709mg.
Devilled Kidneys Energy 575kcal/2412kJ; Protein 37.7g; Carbohydrate 40.7g, of which sugars 13.2g; Fat 30.3g, of which saturates 16.3g; Cholesterol 623mg; Calcium 122mg; Fibre 2g; Sodium 599mg.

Lamb's Kidneys with Mustard Sauce

This piquant recipe is simple and flexible, so the exact amounts of any one ingredient are unimportant. It makes a tasty first course but would be equally suitable as a supper dish.

Serves 4
4–6 lamb's kidneys
butter, for frying

Dijon mustard or other mild
    mustard, to taste
250ml/8fl oz/1 cup white wine
5ml/1 tsp chopped fresh mixed
    herbs, such as rosemary, thyme,
    parsley and chives
1 small garlic clove, crushed
about 30ml/2 tbsp single
    (light) cream
salt and ground black pepper
fresh parsley, to garnish

Preparation: 5 minutes; Cooking: 5 minutes

1 Skin the kidneys and slice them horizontally. Remove the cores with scissors, and then wash them thoroughly in plenty of cold water. Drain and pat dry with kitchen paper.

2 Heat a little butter in a heavy frying pan and cook the kidneys for about 1½ minutes on each side. Be careful not to overcook. Remove the kidneys from the pan and keep warm.

3 Add a spoonful of mustard to the pan with the wine, herbs and garlic. Simmer gently to reduce the liquid by about half, then add enough cream to make a smooth sauce.

4 Return the kidneys to the pan and reheat gently in the sauce. Don't let them cook any further, or the kidneys will be tough. Serve on individual warmed plates, garnished with parsley. Rice and a green salad are ideal accompaniments, or serve with mashed potato and broccoli or cabbage.

Cook's Tip
Look for kidneys that are firm, with a rich, even colour. Avoid those with dry spots or a dull surface. Lamb's kidneys are milder in flavour than pig's or calf's kidneys, and are suitable for grilling (broiling), braising or frying.

Riñones al Jerez

Kidneys cooked in sherry are extremely popular. They are often on the menu in tapas bars, both in Spain and in the world's major cities. Quick and easy, they make an excellent family supper. As a first course, partner the dish with fried toast triangles or crusty bread. A fino montilla wine, less well known than sherry but with the same dry qualities, could replace the sherry. C.B. Montilla is often the choice in Andalusia for this tasty and satisfying dish.

Serves 4
12 plump lamb's kidneys
60ml/4 tbsp olive oil
115g/4oz smoked bacon lardons,
    or diced pancetta
1 large onion, chopped
2 garlic cloves, finely chopped
30ml/2 tbsp plain
    (all-purpose) flour
150ml/¼ pint/⅔ cup fino sherry
    or C.B. Montilla wine
15ml/1 tbsp tomato purée (paste)
30ml/2 tbsp chopped fresh
    parsley
salt and ground black pepper
new potatoes, boiled and
    buttered, to serve (optional)

Preparation: 5 minutes; Cooking: 9–10 minutes

1 Halve and skin the kidneys, then remove the cores. Cut the kidneys into cubes.

2 Heat half the oil in a large frying pan and fry the bacon or pancetta until the fat starts to run. Add the onion and garlic and fry until softened. Remove the mixture from the pan and put it on a plate.

3 Add the remaining oil to the pan and divide the kidneys into four batches. Put in one handful, and stir-fry over a high heat until sealed. (They should not give off any juice.) Remove to a plate and repeat with a second handful and remove to the plate. Continue until they are all cooked.

4 Return the onion and bacon mixture to the pan. Sprinkle with flour and cook, stirring gently. Add the sherry or Montilla wine and stir until thickened. Add the tomato purée and parsley. Return the kidneys to the pan, and heat through. Season well and serve hot with buttered new potatoes.

Lamb's Kidneys Energy 154kcal/640kJ; Protein 13.6g; Carbohydrate 0.9g, of which sugars 0.8g; Fat 6.2g, of which saturates 3.5g; Cholesterol 211mg; Calcium 44mg; Fibre 0.6g; Sodium 159mg.
Riñones al Jerez Energy 496Kcal/2074kJ; Protein 48.6g; Carbohydrate 10.8g, of which sugars 4g; Fat 24.5g, of which saturates 6.2g; Cholesterol 806mg; Calcium 49mg; Fibre 1.1g; Sodium 752mg.

Home-made Venison Sausages

Venison sausages have an excellent flavour, a much lower fat content than most sausages and they're easy to make if you forget about sausage skins and just shape the mixture.

10ml/2 tsp ground black pepper
1 garlic clove, crushed
5ml/1 tsp dried thyme
1 egg, beaten
plain (all-purpose) flour,
    for dusting
oil, for frying

Makes 1.4kg/3lb
900g/2lb finely minced
    (ground) venison
450g/1lb finely minced
    (ground) belly of pork
15ml/1 tbsp salt

To serve
fried onions
grilled (broiled) tomatoes
grilled (broiled) field (portabello)
    mushrooms

Preparation: 5 minutes; Cooking: 12 minutes

1 Combine all the sausage ingredients, except the flour and oil, in a bowl. Take a small piece of the mixture and fry it in a little oil in a heavy frying pan, then taste to check the seasoning for the batch. Adjust if necessary.

2 Pinch off small balls of the mixture and form into chipolata-size sausages, using floured hands.

3 Heat the oil in a large, heavy frying pan and shallow-fry the sausages for 10 minutes or until they are golden brown and cooked right through.

4 If you use a large pan, you'll be able to fry some onion rings alongside the sausages. At the same time, grill (broil) mushrooms and halved tomatoes to serve on the side.

> **Cook's Tip**
> *If you find yourself with more sausages than you need for one meal, freeze the surplus in a container for no more than a month. Be sure to thaw the sausages before cooking.*

Venison Steaks with Celeriac

This stylish dish is quick and simple to make. The sauce is superb and celeriac chips are delicious.

300ml/½ pint/1¼ cups game
    or chicken stock
salt and ground black pepper

Serves 4
4 venison steaks, 115–175g/
    4–6oz each
1 small celeriac, thinly sliced
oil, for deep-fat frying
25g/1oz/2 tbsp plain
    (all-purpose) flour

For the marinade
45ml/3 tbsp Drambuie
45ml/3 tbsp oil
30ml/2 tbsp apple juice
1 bay leaf
2 fresh thyme sprigs, plus extra
    thyme sprigs to garnish
2 juniper berries, crushed

Preparation: 3 minutes; Cooking: 15 minutes

1 Make the marinade. Mix the Drambuie, oil, apple juice, bay leaf, thyme sprigs and juniper berries in a large bowl. Season to taste. Add the venison steaks and coat them in the mixture.

2 Fry the celeriac slices in hot oil until crisp. Remove with a slotted spoon and drain on kitchen paper.

3 Lift the steaks out of the marinade and dry them with kitchen paper. Carefully pour off most of the oil from the frying pan. Add them to the pan and fry for 4 minutes on each side. Transfer the cooked steaks to a platter and keep them hot.

4 Strain the marinade into a jug (pitcher) and blend with the flour to a smooth paste. Stir into the pan with the stock and season with salt and pepper. Bring to the boil, stirring constantly, and cook for 2 minutes. Pour the sauce over the venison steaks, garnish with thyme and serve with the celeriac chips.

> **Cook's Tip**
> *Farmed venison steaks are young, so can be cooked very quickly. Wild venison can be considerably older and should be simmered in the marinade for 45 minutes.*

Venison Sausages Energy 1747kcal/7356kJ; Protein 302.4g; Carbohydrate 0g, of which sugars 0g; Fat 65.3g, of which saturates 17.6g; Cholesterol 924mg; Calcium 105mg; Fibre 0g; Sodium 880mg.
Venison Steaks Energy 383kcal/1596kJ; Protein 28.9g; Carbohydrate 6.5g, of which sugars 1.7g; Fat 25g, of which saturates 3.6g; Cholesterol 63mg; Calcium 57mg; Fibre 1.3g; Sodium 129mg.

Chicken Wings with Blood Oranges

This is a great recipe for the barbecue – it is quick and easy, and best eaten with the fingers. The oranges can be cooked separately or with the wings. Their flavour is great with chicken.

Serves 4
60ml/4 tbsp fiery harissa
30ml/2 tbsp olive oil
16–20 chicken wings
4 blood oranges, quartered
icing (confectioners') sugar
a small bunch of fresh coriander
   (cilantro), chopped
salt

Preparation: 3 minutes; Cooking: 10 minutes

1 Mix the harissa with the olive oil in a small bowl, or, if using home-made harissa (see Cook's Tip below), simply measure the required amount into a bowl.

2 Add a little salt and stir to combine. Brush this mixture over the chicken wings so that they are well coated.

3 Cook the wings on a hot barbecue or under a hot grill (broiler) for 5 minutes on each side, turning them over with tongs.

4 Once the wings begin to cook, dip the orange quarters lightly in icing sugar and grill (broil) them for a few minutes, until they are slightly burnt but not blackened. If you thread them on to skewers, it will be easier to turn them under the heat.

5 Serve the chicken wings immediately with the oranges, sprinkled with a little chopped fresh coriander.

> **Cook's Tip**
> *Try making your own harissa if you have a blender. You will need 6–8 dried red chillies, 2 crushed garlic cloves, 2.5ml/½ tsp salt, 5ml/1 tsp ground cumin, 2.5ml/½ tsp ground coriander and 120ml/4fl oz/1 cup olive oil. Blend to a paste. To store, spoon into a jar and cover with olive oil. It will keep for 1 month.*

Chicken Omelette Dippers

Have you got a reluctant eater in the family? Not any more. Children love these protein-packed chicken omelette rolls. You might have to ration the ketchup dip, however.

Serves 4
1 skinless chicken thigh, about
   115g/4oz, boned and cubed
40ml/8 tsp butter
1 small onion, chopped
½ carrot, diced
2 shiitake mushrooms,
   stems removed and
   caps chopped finely
15ml/1 tbsp finely chopped
   fresh parsley
225g/8oz/2 cups cooked long
   grain white rice
30ml/2 tbsp tomato ketchup,
   plus extra to serve
6 eggs, lightly beaten
60ml/4 tbsp milk
2.5ml/½ tsp salt, plus extra
   to season
ground black pepper

Preparation: 3 minutes; Cooking: 16 minutes

1 Season the chicken. Melt 10ml/2 tsp butter in a frying pan. Fry the onion for 1 minute, then add the chicken and fry until cooked. Add the mushrooms and carrot, stir-fry over a medium heat until soft, then add the parsley. Set aside. Wipe the pan with a wad of kitchen paper.

2 Melt 10ml/2 tsp butter in the frying pan, add the rice and stir well. Mix in the fried ingredients, ketchup and black pepper. Stir well, adding salt to taste. Keep the mixture warm.

3 Beat the eggs with the milk in a bowl. Stir in the salt, and add pepper. Melt 5ml/1 tsp of the remaining butter in an omelette pan. Pour in a quarter of the egg mixture and stir it briefly with a fork, then allow it to set for 1 minute. Top with a quarter of the rice mixture, spreading it evenly over the omelette.

4 There are two ways of shaping the omelette. Either just flip it over the filling, then cut in half to make wedges, or roll the omelette around the filling and cut in half. Keep the filled omelette hot in a low oven while cooking three more. Serve two wedges or rolls per person, on individual plates, with a bowl of ketchup for dipping.

Dippers Energy 316kcal/1322kJ; Protein 18g; Carbohydrate 21.5g, of which sugars 3.7g; Fat 18.4g, of which saturates 8.1g; Cholesterol 338mg; Calcium 80mg; Fibre 0.5g; Sodium 322mg.
Chicken Wings Energy 658kcal/2758kJ; Protein 61.9g; Carbohydrate 21.8g, of which sugars 20.7g; Fat 36.7g, of which saturates 10.1g; Cholesterol 264mg; Calcium 163mg; Fibre 2.6g; Sodium 866mg.

Chicken with Lemon & Garlic

These chicken strips make an unusual first course for four, and only need to be cooked at the last moment. Serve them as a main course for two with fried or baked potatoes.

Serves 2–4
2 skinless chicken breast fillets

30ml/2 tbsp olive oil
1 shallot, finely chopped
4 garlic cloves, finely chopped
5ml/1 tsp paprika
juice of 1 lemon
30ml/2 tbsp chopped fresh
    parsley
salt and ground black pepper
fresh flat leaf parsley, to garnish
lemon wedges, to serve

Preparation: 3 minutes; Cooking: 3–5 minutes

1 Remove the little fillet from the back of each breast portion. If the breast still looks fatter than a finger, bat it with a rolling pin to make it thinner. Slice all the chicken meat into strips.

2 Heat the oil in a large frying pan. Stir-fry the chicken strips with the shallot, garlic and paprika over a high heat for about 3 minutes until cooked through.

3 Add the lemon juice and parsley and season with salt and pepper to taste. Serve immediately on warmed plates, with lemon wedges. Garnish with flat leaf parsley.

> **Variation**
> For a variation on this dish, try using strips of turkey breast or pork fillet. They need slightly longer cooking. The whites of spring onions (scallions) can replace shallots, and the chopped green tops can be used instead of parsley.

> **Cook's Tip**
> Chicken breast fillets have a little fillet strip that easily becomes detached. Collect these in a bag or container in the freezer. You won't miss them and will soon have sufficient for this dish.

Chicken Croquettes

Croquettes are very popular snacks and there are many different variations. This one is based on béchamel sauce, which is perfect for taking on different flavours such as ham or chopped peppers.

Serves 4
25g/1oz/2 tbsp butter
25g/1oz/¼ cup plain
    (all-purpose) flour
150ml/¼ pint/⅔ cup milk

15ml/1 tbsp olive oil, plus extra
    for deep-frying
1 boneless chicken breast portion
    with skin, diced
1 garlic clove, finely chopped
1 small egg, beaten
50g/2oz/1 cup stale white
    breadcrumbs
salt and ground black pepper
fresh flat leaf parsley,
    to garnish
lemon wedges, to serve

Preparation: 2 minutes; Cooking: 12 minutes

1 Melt the butter in a pan. Add the flour and cook gently, stirring, for 1 minute. Gradually stir in the milk and cook until smooth and thick. Cover the surface closely to prevent the formation of a skin, and set aside.

2 Heat the oil in a medium frying pan and fry the piece of chicken with the garlic for 5 minutes.

3 When the chicken is lightly browned and cooked through, tip the contents of the frying pan into a food processor and process until finely chopped. Tip the mixture into the sauce and stir to combine. Season with plenty of salt and pepper to taste, then set aside to cool completely.

4 Once cooled and firm, shape the mixture into eight small sausage shapes. Dip each one in beaten egg, then roll in breadcrumbs to coat.

5 Heat the oil in a large pan, until a cube of bread dropped in the oil browns in 1 minute. Lower the croquettes into the oil and cook for 4 minutes until crisp and golden. Lift out using a slotted spoon and drain on kitchen paper. Serve with lemon wedges and garnish with fresh flat leaf parsley.

Chicken with Lemon Energy 139kcal/580kJ; Protein 18.6g; Carbohydrate 1.5g, of which sugars 1.1g; Fat 6.5g, of which saturates 1g; Cholesterol 53mg; Calcium 33mg; Fibre 0.8g; Sodium 50mg.
Chicken Croquettes Energy 286kcal/1195kJ; Protein 13.9g; Carbohydrate 16.4g, of which sugars 2.2g; Fat 18.9g, of which saturates 5.8g; Cholesterol 89mg; Calcium 80mg; Fibre 0.5g; Sodium 189mg.

Caramelized Chicken Wings

These caramelized chicken wings are irresistible.

Serves 2–4
75ml/5 tbsp sugar

30ml/2 tbsp vegetable oil
25g/1oz fresh root ginger, grated
12 chicken wings, split in two
chilli oil, for drizzling
mixed pickled vegetables, to serve

Preparation: 0 minutes; Cooking: 18 minutes

1 Heat the sugar with 60ml/4 tbsp water in a heavy pan until it forms a golden syrup. Heat the oil in a wok and stir-fry the ginger until fragrant. Add the chicken wings, brown them and continue to stir-fry for 5–6 minutes. Pour in the syrup and coat the chicken.

2 Cover and cook for 12 minutes, until the chicken is tender. Drizzle chilli oil over and serve with the mixed pickled vegetables.

Chicken Livers in Sherry

This delicious little tapas dish is particularly good eaten with bread or toast.

Serves 4
225g/8oz chicken livers, thawed
    if frozen
15ml/1 tbsp olive oil
1 small onion, finely chopped

2 small garlic cloves,
    finely chopped
5ml/1 tsp fresh thyme leaves
30ml/2 tbsp sweet oloroso sherry
30ml/2 tbsp crème fraîche or
    double (heavy) cream
2.5ml/½ tsp paprika
salt and ground black pepper
fresh thyme, to garnish

Preparation: 3–4 minutes; Cooking: 5 minutes

1 Trim any green spots and sinews from the chicken livers. Heat the oil in a frying pan and fry the onion, garlic, chicken livers and thyme for 3 minutes.

2 Stir the sherry into the livers, add the crème fraîche and cook briefly. Season with salt, pepper and paprika, garnish with thyme and serve immediately.

Crispy Five-spice Chicken

Strips of chicken fillet, with a spiced rice flour coating, become deliciously crisp and golden when fried. They make a great meal when served on stir-fried vegetable noodles.

Serves 4
200g/7oz thin egg noodles
30ml/2 tbsp sunflower oil
2 garlic cloves, very thinly sliced
1 fresh red chilli, seeded
    and sliced
½ red (bell) pepper, very
    thinly sliced

2 carrots, peeled and cut into
    thin strips
300g/11oz Chinese broccoli or
    Chinese greens, roughly sliced
45ml/3 tbsp hoisin sauce
45ml/3 tbsp soy sauce
5ml/1 tsp caster (superfine) sugar
4 skinless chicken breast fillets,
    cut into strips
2 egg whites, lightly beaten
115g/4oz/1 cup rice flour
15ml/1 tbsp five-spice powder
salt and ground black pepper
vegetable oil, for frying

Preparation: 5 minutes; Cooking: 10–12 minutes

1 Cook the noodles in a pan of salted boiling water according to the packet instructions, drain and set aside.

2 Heat the sunflower oil in a wok, then add the garlic, chilli, red pepper, carrots and broccoli or greens and stir-fry over a high heat for 2–3 minutes.

3 Add the sauces and sugar to the wok and cook for a further 2–3 minutes. Add the drained noodles, toss to combine, then remove from the heat, cover and keep warm.

4 Dip the chicken strips into the egg white. Combine the rice flour and five-spice powder in a shallow dish and season. Add the chicken strips to the flour mixture and toss to coat.

5 Heat about 2.5cm/1½in oil in a clean wok. When hot, shallow-fry the chicken for 3–4 minutes until crisp and golden.

6 To serve, divide the noodle mixture between warmed plates or bowls and top each serving with the chicken.

Chicken Wings Energy 393kcal/1641kJ; Protein 30.5g; Carbohydrate 14.4g, of which sugars 14.4g; Fat 24.1g, of which saturates 6.3g; Cholesterol 134mg; Calcium 16mg; Fibre 0g; Sodium 91mg.
Chicken Livers Energy 119kcal/494kJ; Protein 10.3g; Carbohydrate 1.5g, of which sugars 1.1g; Fat 7.1g, of which saturates 2.8g; Cholesterol 222mg; Calcium 13mg; Fibre 0.2g; Sodium 46mg.
Five-spice Chicken Energy 574kcal/2419kJ; Protein 49.6g; Carbohydrate 68g, of which sugars 9.4g; Fat 12.3g, of which saturates 2.5g; Cholesterol 120mg; Calcium 83mg; Fibre 5.1g; Sodium 1210mg.

Spicy Fried Noodles with Chicken

This is a wonderfully versatile dish as you can adjust it to include your favourite ingredients.

Serves 4

225g/8oz egg thread noodles
60ml/4 tbsp vegetable oil
2 garlic cloves, finely chopped
175g/6oz pork fillet (tenderloin),
   sliced into thin strips
1 skinless chicken breast fillet,
   sliced into thin strips
115g/4oz/1 cup peeled cooked
   prawns (shrimp)
45ml/3 tbsp fresh lemon juice
45ml/3 tbsp Thai fish sauce
30ml/2 tbsp soft light
   brown sugar
2 eggs, beaten
1/2 fresh red chilli, seeded and
   finely chopped
50g/2oz/2/3 cup beansprouts
60ml/4 tbsp roasted peanuts,
   chopped
3 spring onions (scallions), cut into
   5cm/2in lengths and shredded
45ml/3 tbsp chopped fresh
   coriander (cilantro)

Preparation: 6 minutes; Cooking: 8–10 minutes

1 Bring a large pan of lightly salted water to the boil, add the noodles and cook, then leave for 5 minutes.

2 Meanwhile, heat 45ml/3 tbsp of the oil in a wok or large frying pan, add the garlic and cook for 30 seconds. Add the pork and chicken and stir-fry until lightly browned, then add the prawns and stir-fry for 2 minutes. Stir in the lemon juice, then add the fish sauce and sugar. Stir-fry until the sugar has dissolved.

3 Drain the noodles and add to the wok or pan with the remaining 15ml/1 tbsp oil. Toss all the ingredients together. Pour the beaten eggs over the noodles and stir-fry until almost set, then add the chilli and beansprouts.

4 Divide the roasted peanuts, spring onions and coriander leaves into two equal portions, add one portion to the pan and stir-fry for about 2 minutes.

5 Transfer the noodles to a serving platter. Sprinkle on the remaining roasted peanuts, spring onions and chopped coriander and serve immediately.

Orange Chicken Salad

With their tangy flavour, orange segments are the perfect partner for tender chicken in this tasty rice salad. To appreciate all the flavours fully, serve the salad at room temperature. It makes the perfect dish for a hot summer day and could even be packed for a picnic. Keep the toasted nuts separate and add them at the last minute, or they will become soft.

Serves 4

3 large seedless oranges
175g/6oz/scant 1 cup long
   grain rice
10ml/2 tsp strong Dijon mustard
2.5ml/1/2 tsp caster
   (superfine) sugar
175ml/6fl oz/3/4 cup vinaigrette
450g/1lb cooked chicken, diced
45ml/3 tbsp chopped fresh chives
75g/3oz/3/4 cup almonds or
   cashew nuts, toasted
salt and ground black pepper
mixed salad leaves, to serve

Preparation: 5 minutes; Cooking: 15 minutes

1 Pare one of the oranges thinly, removing only the rind, not the white pith. Put the pieces of orange rind in a pan and add the rice.

2 Pour in 475ml/16fl oz/2 cups water, add salt and bring to the boil. Cover and cook over very low heat for 15 minutes, until the rice is tender and the water has been absorbed.

3 Meanwhile, peel the oranges, removing all the white pith. Working over a plate to catch the juices, separate them into segments. Tip in the orange juice from the plate and add to the vinaigrette with the mustard and sugar, whisking to combine. Check the seasoning.

4 When the rice is cooked, remove it from the heat and discard the pieces of orange rind. Spoon the rice into a bowl, let it cool slightly, then add half the dressing. Toss well, then set aside to cool completely.

5 Add the chicken, chives, toasted nuts and orange segments to the cooled rice. Pour over the remaining dressing and toss gently to combine. Serve on a bed of mixed salad leaves.

Spicy Fried Noodles Energy 605kcal/2537kJ; Protein 39.8g; Carbohydrate 52.1g, of which sugars 11.5g; Fat 27.9g, of which saturates 5.5g; Cholesterol 226mg; Calcium 83mg; Fibre 3.1g; Sodium 1052mg.
Orange Chicken Salad Energy 642kcal/2679kJ; Protein 35.6g; Carbohydrate 49.5g, of which sugars 14.1g; Fat 33.7g, of which saturates 4.7g; Cholesterol 79mg; Calcium 118mg; Fibre 3.5g; Sodium 278mg.

Pan-fried Chicken with Pesto

Warm pesto accompanying pan-fried chicken makes a deliciously quick meal. Serve with baby carrots and celery, braised in stock in a separate pan while the chicken is cooking. Mashed potato makes the most of the delicious sauce. For a lighter meal, serve the pan-fried chicken with couscous and a salad of baby spinach leaves with lemon dressing.

Serves 4
15ml/1 tbsp olive oil
4 chicken breast portions, skinned
fresh basil leaves, to garnish

For the pesto
90ml/6 tbsp olive oil
50g/2oz/^{1}/$_2$ cup pine nuts
50g/2oz/^{2}/$_3$ cup freshly grated
*   Parmesan cheese*
50g/2oz/1 cup fresh basil leaves
15g/^{1}/$_2$oz/^{1}/$_4$ cup fresh parsley
2 garlic cloves, crushed
salt and ground black pepper

Preparation: 2–3 minutes; Cooking: 18 minutes

1 Heat the 15ml/1 tbsp oil in a frying pan. Add the chicken breasts and cook gently for about 15 minutes, turning several times with tongs until they are tender, lightly browned and thoroughly cooked.

2 Meanwhile, to make the pesto, place all the ingredients in a food processor and process until smooth and well mixed.

3 Remove the chicken from the pan, cover and keep hot. Reduce the heat slightly, then add the pesto to the pan and cook gently, stirring constantly, for a few minutes, or until the pesto has warmed through.

4 Put the cooked chicken on a warmed platter or individual plates, pour the warm pesto over the top, then garnish with basil leaves and serve immediately.

> **Cook's Tip**
> *Save time by using bought pesto instead of fresh, or use a prepared bruschetta topping. An Italian tomato and herb one would be delicious, or try a French onion and garlic blend.*

Greek-style Chicken

The sauce for the chicken is based on avogolemono, an exquisite egg and lemon mixture which is one of Greece's gifts to good cooks everywhere. It tastes great with the fennel.

Serves 4
4 skinless chicken breast fillets
plain (all-purpose) flour,
*   for dusting*
30–45ml/2–3 tbsp olive oil
1–2 onions, chopped
^{1}/$_4$ fennel bulb, chopped (optional)
15ml/1 tbsp chopped fresh
*   parsley, plus extra to garnish*
7.5ml/1^1/$_2$ tsp fennel seeds
75ml/5 tbsp dry Marsala
120ml/4fl oz/^{1}/$_2$ cup
*   chicken stock*
300g/11oz/2^1/$_4$ cups petits pois
*   (baby peas)*
juice of 1^1/$_2$ lemons
2 egg yolks
salt and ground black pepper

Preparation: 3–4 minutes; Cooking: 15 minutes

1 Season the chicken with salt and pepper, then dust generously with flour. Shake off the excess flour; set aside.

2 Heat 15ml/1 tbsp oil in a pan, add the onions, fennel (if using), parsley and fennel seeds. Cook for 3 minutes, then add the remaining oil and the chicken to the pan and cook over a high heat for 5–6 minutes on each side, until lightly browned and cooked through. Remove from the pan and set aside.

3 Deglaze the pan by pouring in the Marsala and cooking over a high heat until reduced to about 30ml/2 tbsp, then pour in the stock. Add the peas and return the chicken and onion mixture to the pan. Cook over a very low heat while you prepare the egg mixture.

4 In a bowl, beat the lemon juice and egg yolks together, then slowly add about 120ml/4fl oz/^{1}/$_2$ cup of the hot liquid from the chicken and peas, stirring well to combine. Return the mixture to the pan and cook over a low heat, stirring, until the mixture thickens slightly. (Do not allow the mixture to boil or the eggs will curdle and spoil the sauce.) Serve the chicken immediately, sprinkled with a little extra chopped fresh parsley.

Pan-fried Chicken Energy 480kcal/1998kJ; Protein 43.2g; Carbohydrate 1g, of which sugars 0.9g; Fat 33.8g, of which saturates 6.4g; Cholesterol 118mg; Calcium 192mg; Fibre 1.1g; Sodium 232mg.
Greek-style Chicken Energy 301kcal/1260kJ; Protein 41.6g; Carbohydrate 10.4g, of which sugars 3.3g; Fat 8.4g, of which saturates 1.5g; Cholesterol 105mg; Calcium 34mg; Fibre 4.3g; Sodium 96mg.

Chicken Stuffed with Ham & Cheese

Breasts of chicken stuffed with smoked ham and Gruyère, coated in egg and breadcrumbs, make a tasty treat few can resist.

Serves 4

4 skinless, boneless chicken
   breast portions, about 130g/
   4½oz each
4 very thin smoked ham slices,
   halved and rind removed

about 90g/3½oz Gruyère cheese,
   thinly sliced
plain (all-purpose) flour,
   for coating
2 eggs, beaten
75g/3oz/¾ cup natural-coloured
   dried breadcrumbs
5ml/1 tsp dried thyme
75g/3oz/6 tbsp butter
60ml/4 tbsp olive oil
salt and ground black pepper
mixed leaf salad, to serve

Preparation: 6–8 minutes; Cooking: 10–12 minutes

1 Slit the chicken breasts about three-quarters of the way through, then open them up and lay them flat. Place a slice of ham on each cut side of the chicken, trimming to fit if necessary so that the ham does not hang over the edge.

2 Top with the Gruyère slices, making sure that they are well within the ham slices. Fold over the chicken and reshape, pressing well to seal and ensuring that no cheese is visible.

3 Spoon the flour for coating into a shallow bowl. Pour the beaten eggs into another shallow bowl and mix the breadcrumbs with the thyme and seasoning in a third bowl.

4 Toss each stuffed breast in the flour, then coat in egg and breadcrumbs, shaking off any excess.

5 Place half the butter and half the oil in one pan, and the remaining half measures in the other, and heat separately.

6 When the fat stops foaming, gently slide in the coated breasts, two in each pan. Shallow fry over a low to medium heat for about 5 minutes each side, turning over carefully with a spatula. Drain on kitchen paper for a few seconds to soak up the excess fat. Serve immediately with the mixed leaf salad.

Soy Sauce & Star Anise Chicken

Although the chicken cooks quickly, it does benefit from being marinated first. This only takes a moment and ensures that there is no last-minute work to do when guests arrive.

Serves 4

4 skinless chicken breast portions
2 whole star anise
45ml/3 tbsp olive oil
30ml/2 tbsp soy sauce
ground black pepper

Preparation: 3–4 minutes plus marinating; Cooking: 16 minutes

1 Put the chicken breast fillets in a shallow, non-metallic dish and add the star anise.

2 In a small bowl, whisk together the oil and soy sauce and season with black pepper to make a marinade.

3 Pour the marinade over the chicken and stir to coat each breast fillet all over. Cover the dish with clear film (plastic wrap) and set aside for as much time as you have. If you are able to make it ahead, leave the chicken in the marinade for around 6–8 hours as the flavour will be improved. Place the covered dish in the refrigerator.

4 Cook the chicken under a hot grill (broiler), turning occasionally. It will need about 8 minutes on each side. Place each piece of chicken on a warmed plate and serve immediately.

Variation
If you prefer, cook on a barbecue. When the coals are dusted with ash, spread them out evenly. Remove the chicken breasts from the marinade and cook for 8 minutes on each side, spooning over the marinade from time to time, until the chicken is cooked through. The chicken can also be cooked on top of the stove on a ridged grill (broiler) pan or griddle. Get the pan very hot first, add the chicken and turn the pieces after a few minutes so that they are branded in a criss-cross fashion.

Chicken Stuffed Energy 599kcal/2496kJ; Protein 41.8g; Carbohydrate 14.8g, of which sugars 0.8g; Fat 41.5g, of which saturates 18.4g; Cholesterol 220mg; Calcium 222mg; Fibre 0.4g; Sodium 698mg.
Star Anise Chicken Energy 237kcal/992kJ; Protein 36.2g; Carbohydrate 0.6g, of which sugars 0.6g; Fat 9.9g, of which saturates 1.6g; Cholesterol 105mg; Calcium 9mg; Fibre 0g; Sodium 624mg.

Chicken with Cashew Nuts

This popular Chinese dish is quick and easy to make and can be enjoyed to the full by using good-quality organic products that are full of flavour.

Serves 4

350g/12oz skinless chicken breast fillets
pinch of ground white pepper
15ml/1 tbsp dry sherry
300ml/½ pint/1¼ cups chicken stock

15ml/1 tbsp sunflower oil
1 garlic clove, finely chopped
1 small carrot, cut into cubes
½ cucumber, about 75g/3oz, cut into 1cm/½in cubes
50g/2oz/½ cup drained canned bamboo shoots, cut into 1cm/½in cubes (optional)
5ml/1 tsp cornflour (cornstarch)
15ml/1 tbsp soy sauce
25g/1oz/¼ cup dry-roasted cashew nuts
2.5ml/½ tsp sesame oil
noodles, to serve

Preparation: 10 minutes; Cooking: 7–8 minutes

1 Cut the chicken into 2cm/¾in cubes. Place the cubes in a bowl, stir in the white pepper and sherry, cover with clear film (plastic wrap) and marinate for 10 minutes.

2 Bring the stock to the boil in a large pan. Add the chicken and cook, stirring, for 3 minutes. Drain, reserving 90ml/6 tbsp of the stock, and set the chicken aside on a plate.

3 Heat the sunflower oil in a large non-stick frying pan until it is very hot, add the finely chopped garlic and stir-fry for a few seconds.

4 Add the cubed carrot and cucumber to the frying pan with the bamboo shoots, if using, and continue to stir-fry the vegetables over a medium heat for 2 minutes.

5 Stir in the chicken and reserved stock. Put the cornflour in a cup or small bowl and stir in the soy sauce. Add the mixture to the pan. Cook, stirring, until the sauce thickens slightly.

6 Finally, add the cashew nuts and sesame oil. Toss to mix thoroughly, then serve with noodles.

Chicken & Lemon Grass Curry

Quick-cook curries work well in a wok, especially if you use an electric one.

Serves 4

45ml/3 tbsp vegetable oil
2 garlic cloves, crushed
500g/1¼lb skinless chicken thighs, boned and chopped into small pieces
45ml/3 tbsp Thai fish sauce
120ml/4fl oz/½ cup chicken stock
5ml/1 tsp granulated (white) sugar
1 lemon grass stalk, chopped into 4 sticks and lightly crushed
5 kaffir lime leaves, rolled into cylinders and thinly sliced across, plus extra to garnish

chopped roasted peanuts and chopped fresh coriander (cilantro), to garnish

For the curry paste
1 lemon grass stalk, coarsely chopped
2.5cm/1in piece fresh galangal, peeled and coarsely chopped
2 kaffir lime leaves, chopped
3 shallots, coarsely chopped
6 coriander (cilantro) roots, coarsely chopped
2 garlic cloves
2 fresh green chillies, seeded and coarsely chopped
5ml/1 tsp shrimp paste
5ml/1 tsp ground turmeric

Preparation: 5 minutes; Cooking: 14 minutes

1 Make the curry paste. Place all the ingredients in a large mortar, or food processor. Pound or process to a paste.

2 Heat the vegetable oil in a wok or large, heavy frying pan, add the garlic and cook over a low heat, stirring frequently, until golden brown. Add the curry paste and stir-fry with the garlic for about 30 seconds more.

3 Add the chicken pieces to the pan and stir until thoroughly coated with the curry paste. Stir in the Thai fish sauce and chicken stock, with the sugar, and cook for 2 minutes more.

4 Add the lemon grass and lime leaves, reduce the heat and simmer for 10 minutes. If the mixture begins to dry out, add a little more stock or water.

5 Spoon the curry into four dishes, garnish with the lime leaves, peanuts and coriander and serve immediately.

Chicken with Cashews Energy 153kcal/645kJ; Protein 22.9g; Carbohydrate 5.1g, of which sugars 2.8g; Fat 4.3g, of which saturates 0.9g; Cholesterol 61mg; Calcium 14mg; Fibre 0.7g; Sodium 342mg.
Chicken Curry Energy 229Kcal/959kJ; Protein 31.3g; Carbohydrate 4.3g, of which sugars 3.4g; Fat 9.7g, of which saturates 1.4g; Cholesterol 94mg; Calcium 32mg; Fibre 0.5g; Sodium 397mg.

Curried Chicken Noodles

Chicken or pork can be used to provide the protein in this tasty dish. It is so quick and easy to prepare and cook, it makes the perfect snack for busy people who find themselves with little spare time.

Serves 2
30ml/2 tbsp vegetable oil
10ml/2 tsp magic paste
1 lemon grass stalk, finely chopped
5ml/1 tsp Thai red curry paste
90g/3½oz skinless chicken breast fillet or pork fillet (tenderloin), sliced into slivers
30ml/2 tbsp light soy sauce
400ml/14fl oz/1⅔ cups coconut milk
2 kaffir lime leaves, rolled into cylinders and thinly sliced
250g/9oz medium egg noodles
90g/3½oz Chinese leaves (Chinese cabbage), shredded
90g/3½oz spinach or watercress (leaves), shredded
juice of 1 lime
small bunch fresh coriander (cilantro), chopped

Preparation: 5 minutes; Cooking: 10 minutes

1 Heat the oil in a wok or large, heavy frying pan. Add the magic paste and lemon grass and stir-fry over a low to medium heat for 4–5 seconds, until they give off their aroma.

2 Stir in the curry paste, then add the chicken or pork. Stir-fry over a medium to high heat for 2 minutes, until the chicken or pork is coated in the paste and seared on all sides.

3 Add the soy sauce, coconut milk and sliced lime leaves. Bring to a simmer, then add the noodles. Simmer for 4 minutes. Add the Chinese leaves and watercress. Stir, then add the lime juice. Spoon into a warmed bowl and sprinkle with coriander.

Cook's Tip
Magic paste is a mixture of crushed garlic, coriander (cilantro) root and white pepper. It is extensively used in Thai cooking, and is available in jars from supermarkets and Asian stores.

Crème Fraîche & Coriander Chicken

This is an any-occasion main course dish that can be turned around in minutes. Be generous with the coriander leaves, as they have a wonderful flavour, and a fragrance all of their own.

Serves 4
6 skinless, boneless chicken thigh portions
60ml/4 tbsp crème fraîche
1 small bunch fresh coriander (cilantro), roughly chopped
15ml/1 tbsp sunflower oil
salt and ground black pepper

Preparation: 8 minutes; Cooking: 8 minutes

1 Using a sharp cook's knife or cleaver, cut each chicken thigh into three or four pieces.

2 Heat the oil in a large frying pan, add the chicken and cook for about 6 minutes, turning occasionally.

3 Add the crème fraîche to the pan and stir until melted, then allow the mixture to bubble for 1–2 minutes.

4 Add the chopped coriander to the chicken and stir to combine. Season with salt and ground black pepper to taste, spoon into a heated dish or onto individual plates and serve immediately.

Variations
• Cream cheese can be used instead of crème fraîche. Use the full-fat variety and mix it with a little cream or milk to thin it before adding it to the pan containing the cooked boneless chicken thighs. Stir constantly until it has melted.
• This recipe uses boneless chicken thighs, but boneless breast portions can be used instead. Simply cut into bitesize pieces and cook in the frying pan for 5–6 minutes, until just tender.

Cook's Tip
Make sure the chicken thighs are fully cooked before serving.

Curried Chicken Energy 702kcal/2965kJ; Protein 28.7g; Carbohydrate 101.6g, of which sugars 14.2g; Fat 23g, of which saturates 4.9g; Cholesterol 69mg; Calcium 187mg; Fibre 4.7g; Sodium 1564mg.
Coriander Chicken Energy 249kcal/1041kJ; Protein 32.1g; Carbohydrate 0.7g, of which sugars 0.6g; Fat 13.1g, of which saturates 5.6g; Cholesterol 174mg; Calcium 44mg; Fibre 0.6g; Sodium 143mg.

Penne with Chicken & Broccoli

Crisp-tender, lightly cooked broccoli gives this dish colour and crunch.

Serves 4

400g/14oz/3½ cups dried penne
115g/4oz/scant 1 cup broccoli
   florets, divided into tiny sprigs
50g/2oz/¼ cup butter
2 chicken breast portions, skinned
   and cut into thin strips
2 garlic cloves, crushed
120ml/4fl oz/½ cup dry
   white wine
200ml/7fl oz/scant 1 cup panna
   da cucina or double
   (heavy) cream
90g/3½oz Gorgonzola cheese,
   rind removed, finely diced
salt and ground black pepper
freshly grated Parmesan cheese,
   to serve

Preparation: 3–4 minutes; Cooking: 12–14 minutes

1 Bring two pans of lightly salted water to the boil. Add the penne to one pan and cook over a medium heat for 10–12 minutes or until tender.

2 Meanwhile, plunge the broccoli into the second pan of salted boiling water. Bring back to the boil and boil for 2 minutes, then drain in a colander and refresh under cold running water. Shake well to remove the surplus water and set aside to drain.

3 While the pasta is cooking, melt the butter in a large frying pan and add the chicken and garlic, with salt and pepper to taste. Stir well. Fry over a medium heat, stirring frequently, for 3 minutes, or until the chicken becomes white.

4 Pour the wine and cream over the chicken mixture in the pan, stir to mix, then simmer, stirring occasionally, for about 5 minutes, or until the sauce has reduced and thickened and the chicken is cooked through.

5 Add the broccoli, increase the heat and toss to heat it through and mix it with the chicken. Taste for seasoning.

6 Drain the pasta and add it to the sauce. Add the Gorgonzola and toss well. Serve in warmed bowls and sprinkle each portion with grated Parmesan.

Chicken Fried Rice

This stir-fry is based on cooked rice, so is ideal for using up yesterday's leftovers. Any rice will do, but jasmine has the best flavour, especially if cooked in coconut milk.

Serves 4

30ml/2 tbsp groundnut (peanut) oil
1 small onion, finely chopped
2 garlic cloves, chopped
2.5cm/1in piece fresh root ginger,
   peeled and grated
225g/8oz skinless chicken breast
   fillets, cut into 1cm/½in dice
450g/1lb/4 cups cold cooked
   white long grain rice
1 red (bell) pepper, seeded
   and sliced
115g/4oz/1 cup drained canned
   whole kernel corn
5ml/1 tsp chilli oil
5ml/1 tsp hot curry powder
2 eggs, beaten
salt
spring onion (scallion) shreds,
   to garnish

Preparation: 4–5 minutes; Cooking: 10–12 minutes

1 Heat the oil in a wok. Add the onion and stir-fry over a medium heat for 1 minute, then add the garlic and ginger and stir-fry for 2 minutes more.

2 Push the onion mixture to the sides of the wok, where it will keep warm but not cook, add the chicken to the centre and stir-fry for 2 minutes. Add the rice and toss well. Stir-fry over a high heat for about 3 minutes more, until the chicken is cooked through.

3 Stir in the sliced red pepper, corn, chilli oil and curry powder, with salt to taste. Toss over the heat for 1 minute. Stir in the beaten eggs and cook for 1 minute more, while the eggs lightly cook. Garnish with the spring onion shreds and serve.

Cook's Tip
If you don't have any cold cooked rice in the refrigerator, you can still make this stir-fry if you have a couple of pouches of instant or express long grain or basmati rice in the cupboard. This type of rice cooks in under 2 minutes. Cool it quickly.

Penne Energy 951kcal/3982kJ; Protein 47.8g; Carbohydrate 80.2g, of which sugars 8.6g; Fat 48.8g, of which saturates 28.5g; Cholesterol 165mg; Calcium 324mg; Fibre 10.2g; Sodium 433mg.
Fried Rice Energy 356kcal/1500kJ; Protein 21g; Carbohydrate 46.4g, of which sugars 6.3g; Fat 10.9g, of which saturates 2.5g; Cholesterol 135mg; Calcium 46mg; Fibre 1.4g; Sodium 150mg.

Spiced Chicken Risotto with Mint

A classic risotto must be stirred for around 20 minutes. This quick version is a good alternative.

Serves 4

250g/9oz skinless chicken breast fillets, diced
3 garlic cloves, chopped
5ml/1 tsp ground turmeric
30–45ml/2–3 tbsp olive oil
2 medium carrots, diced
seeds from 6–8 cardamom pods

500g/1¼ lb/2½ cups long grain rice
250g/9oz tomatoes, chopped
750ml/1¼ pints/3 cups chicken stock

For the lemon and mint relish

3 tomatoes, diced
1 bunch or large handful fresh mint, chopped
5–8 spring onions (scallions), thinly sliced
juice of 2 lemons

Preparation: 3–5 minutes; Cooking: 15–17 minutes

1 Mix the diced chicken with half the garlic and the turmeric. Heat a little of the oil in a pan, add the chicken and fry until the chicken has cooked through thoroughly. Remove from the pan and set aside.

2 Add the remaining oil, garlic and cardamom seeds with the carrots and rice. Stir-fry for 1–2 minutes.

3 Add the tomatoes and chicken stock to the pan and bring to the boil. Cover and simmer for about 10 minutes. Meanwhile, make the relish by mixing all the ingredients in a bowl.

4 When the rice is almost cooked, fork in the chicken and heat through. Serve with the relish.

Variations
• Use the same quantity of pumpkin or butternut squash in place of the carrots.
• To make a vegetarian version, omit the chicken and add a drained 400g/14oz can of chickpeas to the rice just before the end of cooking.

Chicken & Basil Coconut Rice

For this dish, the rice is partially boiled before being simmered with coconut so that it fully absorbs the flavour of the chillies, basil and spices.

Serves 4

350g/12oz/1¾ cups Thai fragrant rice, rinsed
30–45ml/2–3 tbsp groundnut (peanut) oil
1 large onion, finely sliced into rings
1 garlic clove, crushed

1 fresh red chilli, seeded and finely sliced
1 fresh green chilli, seeded and finely sliced
generous handful of basil leaves
3 skinless, boneless chicken breast fillets, about 350g/12oz, finely sliced
5mm/¼in piece of lemon grass, pounded or finely chopped
50g/2oz piece of creamed coconut dissolved in 600ml/ 1 pint/2½ cups boiling water
salt and ground black pepper

Preparation: 3–5 minutes; Cooking: 15–17 minutes

1 Bring a pan of lightly salted water to the boil. Add the rice to the pan and boil for about 6 minutes, until partially cooked. Tip into a colander and drain thoroughly.

2 Meanwhile, heat the oil in a frying pan and fry the onion rings for 5 minutes until golden and crisp. Lift out the rings with a slotted spoon, drain on kitchen paper and set aside.

3 Fry the garlic and chillies in the oil remaining in the pan for 2–3 minutes, then add the basil leaves and fry briefly until they begin to wilt. Remove a few leaves and set them aside for the garnish, then add the chicken slices with the lemon grass and fry for 2–3 minutes until golden.

4 Add the rice. Stir-fry for a few minutes to coat the grains, then pour in the coconut liquid. Cook for 4–5 minutes or until the rice is tender, adding a little more water if necessary.

5 Adjust the seasoning. Pile the rice into a warmed serving dish, scatter with the fried onion rings and basil leaves, and serve immediately.

Spiced Risotto Energy 600kcal/2511kJ; Protein 26g; Carbohydrate 105.9g, of which sugars 5.3g; Fat 7.4g, of which saturates 1.1g; Cholesterol 44mg; Calcium 73mg; Fibre 1.8g; Sodium 55mg.
Chicken Rice Energy 492kcal/2368kJ; Protein 16.1g; Carbohydrate 30.5g, of which sugars 8.7g; Fat 43.7g, of which saturates 18.2g; Cholesterol 95mg; Calcium 187mg; Fibre 8.5g; Sodium 1197mg.

Chicken & Pineapple Rice

This way of presenting rice not only looks spectacular, it also tastes so good that it can easily be served solo.

Serves 4

75g/3oz/³⁄₄ cup natural peanuts
1 large pineapple
45ml/3 tbsp groundnut (peanut) or sunflower oil
1 onion, chopped
1 garlic clove, crushed

2 chicken breast fillets, about 225g/8oz, cut into strips
225g/8oz/generous 1 cup Thai fragrant rice, rinsed
600ml/1 pint/2¹⁄₂ cups chicken stock
1 lemon grass stalk, bruised
2 thick slices of ham, cut into julienne strips
1 fresh red chilli, seeded and very finely sliced
salt

Preparation: 0 minutes; Cooking: 13–14 minutes

1 Dry-fry the peanuts by spreading them out in a non-stick frying pan and shaking over a medium heat until golden. When cool, grind one-sixth of them in a coffee or herb mill and chop the remainder.

2 Cut a lengthways slice of pineapple, slicing through the leaves, then cut out the flesh to leave a neat shell. Chop 115g/4oz of the pineapple into cubes, saving the remainder for another dish or for eating as a dessert.

3 Heat the oil in a pan and fry the onion and garlic for 3–4 minutes until soft. Add the chicken strips and stir-fry over a medium heat for a few minutes until evenly brown.

4 Add the rice to the pan. Toss with the chicken mixture for a few minutes, then pour in the stock, with the lemon grass and a little salt. Bring to just below boiling point, then lower the heat, cover the pan and simmer gently for 10 minutes until both the rice and the chicken pieces are tender.

5 Stir the chopped peanuts, the pineapple cubes and the ham into the rice, then spoon the mixture into the pineapple shell. Garnish by sprinkling the ground peanuts and the sliced chilli over the top and serve immediately.

Gingered Duck with Tamari

Duck takes very little time to cook on a griddle and tastes great with a tamari and mirin glaze.

Serves 4

4 large duck breast fillets, total weight about 675g/1¹⁄₂lb
5cm/2in piece fresh root ginger, finely grated

¹⁄₂ large cucumber, peeled
12 Chinese pancakes
6 spring onions (scallions), finely shredded

For the sauce

105ml/7 tbsp tamari
105ml/7 tbsp mirin
25g/1oz/2 tbsp sugar
salt and ground black pepper

Preparation: 4–5 minutes; Cooking: 13 minutes

1 Make four slashes in the skin of each duck breast fillet, then lay them skinside up on a plate. Squeeze the grated ginger over. Rub the juice all over the duck. Cut the cucumber in half, scoop out the seeds and chop the flesh. Set aside.

2 To make the sauce, mix the tamari, mirin and sugar in a heavy pan and heat gently together until the sugar has dissolved. Increase the heat and simmer for 4–5 minutes, or until the sauce has reduced by about one-third and become syrupy.

3 Heat a griddle on the stove over a high heat until a few drops of water sprinkled on to the surface evaporate instantly. Sear the duck breasts, placing them skinside down.

4 When the fat has been rendered, and the skin is nicely browned, remove the duck from the pan. Drain off the fat and wipe the pan clean. Reheat it, return the duck flesh side down, and cook over a medium heat for 3 minutes.

5 Brush on a little of the sauce, turn the duck over, brush the other side with sauce and turn again. This should take about 1 minute, by which time the duck should be cooked rare. Let the duck rest for a few minutes before slicing each breast across at an angle. Meanwhile, wrap the pancakes in foil and warm them in a steamer for about 3 minutes. Serve with the duck, sauce, spring onions and cucumber.

Chicken Rice Energy 124kcal/522kJ; Protein 12.6g; Carbohydrate 12.9g, of which sugars 11g; Fat 2.9g, of which saturates 0.5g; Cholesterol 32mg; Calcium 26mg; Fibre 1.8g; Sodium 32mg.
Gingered Duck Energy 436kcal/1829kJ; Protein 38g; Carbohydrate 23.3g, of which sugars 11g; Fat 21.6g, of which saturates 2.2g; Cholesterol 186mg; Calcium 113mg; Fibre 0.7g; Sodium 1615mg.

Skewered Duck with Poached Eggs

This combination of marinated duck, chanterelle mushrooms and poached eggs is quite delicious, and can easily be prepared within 20 minutes.

Serves 4

3 skinless duck breast fillets,
  thinly sliced
30ml/2 tbsp soy sauce

30ml/2 tbsp balsamic vinegar
30ml/2 tbsp groundnut (peanut) oil
25g/1oz/2 tbsp unsalted
  (sweet) butter
1 shallot, finely chopped
115g/4oz/1½ cups chanterelle
  mushrooms
4 eggs
50g/2oz mixed salad leaves
salt and ground black pepper
extra virgin olive oil, to serve

Preparation: 8 minutes; Cooking: 11 minutes

1 Toss the duck in the soy sauce and balsamic vinegar. Cover and marinate for 8–10 minutes. Soak 12 bamboo skewers in water to help prevent them from burning later.

2 Meanwhile, melt the butter in a frying pan and cook the finely chopped shallot until softened but not coloured. Add the chanterelle mushrooms and cook over a high heat for about 5 minutes, stirring occasionally. Leave the pan over a low heat while you cook the duck.

3 Preheat the grill (broiler). Thread the duck slices on to the skewers, pleating them neatly. Place on a grill pan and drizzle with half the oil. Grill (broil) for 3 minutes, then turn the skewers and drizzle with the remaining oil. Grill for 3 minutes more, or until the duck is cooked.

4 Poach the eggs while the duck is cooking. Half fill a frying pan with water, add salt and heat until simmering. Break the eggs one at a time into a cup before tipping carefully into the water. Poach the eggs gently for about 3 minutes, or until the whites are set. Use a slotted spoon to transfer the eggs to a plate.

5 Arrange the salad leaves on serving plates, then add the chanterelles, duck and poached eggs. Drizzle with olive oil, season and serve.

Stir-fried Duck with Pineapple

The fatty skin on duck makes it ideal for stir-frying: as soon as the duck is added to the hot pan the fat runs, creating delicious crisp skin and tender flesh when cooked.

Serves 4

250g/9oz fresh sesame noodles
2 duck breasts, thinly sliced

3 spring onions (scallions),
  cut into strips
2 celery sticks, cut into
  matchstick strips
1 fresh pineapple, peeled, cored
  and cut into strips
300g/11oz carrots, peppers,
  beansprouts and cabbage,
  shredded
90ml/6 tbsp plum sauce

Preparation: 5 minutes; Cooking: 10 minutes

1 Bring a pan of water to the boil and add the noodles. Cook for approximately 3 minutes, then drain and set aside.

2 Meanwhile, heat a wok. Add the duck and stir-fry for 2 minutes, until crisp. Drain off all but 30ml/2 tbsp of the fat. Add the spring onions and celery and stir-fry for 2 minutes. Remove the ingredients from the wok and set aside.

3 Add the pineapple strips and mixed vegetables to the wok and stir-fry for 2 minutes.

4 Add the cooked noodles to the wok with the plum sauce, then replace the duck mixture.

5 Stir-fry the duck mixture for about 2 minutes more, or until the noodles and vegetables are hot and the duck is cooked through. Serve at once.

> **Cook's Tip**
> Fresh sesame noodles can be bought from large supermarkets – you'll find them in the chiller cabinets alongside fresh pasta. If they aren't available use fresh egg noodles instead and cook according to the instructions on the packet. For extra flavour, add a little sesame oil to the cooking water.

Skewered Duck Energy 269kcal/1125kJ; Protein 29.3g; Carbohydrate 1.8g, of which sugars 1.3g; Fat 18.2g, of which saturates 6.3g; Cholesterol 327mg; Calcium 53mg; Fibre 0.7g; Sodium 412mg.
Stir-fried Duck Energy 455Kcal/1927kJ; Protein 28.3g; Carbohydrate 69g, of which sugars 22.6g; Fat 11g, of which saturates 1.4g; Cholesterol 110mg; Calcium 81mg; Fibre 5.7g; Sodium 143mg.

Duck & Sesame Stir-fry

For a special family meal that is a guaranteed success, this is ideal. It tastes fantastic and cooks fast, so you'll be eating in no time.

Serves 4
250g/9oz boneless duck meat
15ml/1 tbsp sesame oil
15ml/1 tbsp vegetable oil
4 garlic cloves, finely sliced
2.5ml/½ tsp dried chilli flakes
15ml/1 tbsp Thai fish sauce
15ml/1 tbsp light soy sauce
120ml/4fl oz/½ cup water
1 head broccoli, cut into small florets
coriander (cilantro) and 15ml/ 1 tbsp toasted sesame seeds, to garnish

Preparation: 3 minutes; Cooking: 5–7 minutes

1 Cut all the duck meat into bitesize pieces. Heat the oils in a wok or large, heavy frying pan and stir-fry the garlic over a medium heat until it is golden brown – do not let it burn. Add the duck to the pan and stir-fry for a further 2 minutes, until the meat begins to brown.

2 Stir in the chilli flakes, fish sauce, soy sauce and water. Add the broccoli and continue to stir-fry for about 2 minutes, until the duck is just cooked through.

3 Serve on warmed plates, garnished with coriander and the toasted sesame seeds.

Cook's Tip
Broccoli has excited interest recently since it is claimed that eating this dark green vegetable regularly can help to reduce the risk of some cancers. Broccoli is a source of protein, calcium, iron and magnesium, as well as vitamins A and C.

Variation
Pak choi (bok choy) or Chinese flowering cabbage can be used instead of broccoli.

Chinese Duck Curry

The duck is best marinated for as long as possible, although it tastes good even if you only have time to marinate it briefly.

Serves 4
4 duck breast portions, skin and bones removed
30ml/2 tbsp five-spice powder
30ml/2 tbsp sesame oil
grated rind and juice of 1 orange
1 medium butternut squash, peeled and cubed
10ml/2 tsp Thai red curry paste
30ml/2 tbsp Thai fish sauce
15ml/1 tbsp palm sugar or light muscovado (brown) sugar
300ml/½ pint/1¼ cups coconut milk
2 fresh red chillies, seeded
4 kaffir lime leaves, torn
small bunch coriander (cilantro), chopped, to garnish

Preparation: 3 minutes plus marinating; Cooking: 17 minutes

1 Cut the duck meat into bitesize pieces and place in a bowl with the five-spice powder, sesame oil and orange rind and juice. Stir well to mix all the ingredients and coat the duck in the marinade. Cover and marinate for at least 10 minutes.

2 Meanwhile, cook the squash in boiling water for 10 minutes, until just tender. Drain and set aside.

3 Pour the marinade from the duck into a wok and heat until boiling. Stir in the curry paste and cook for 1 minute, until well blended and fragrant. Add the duck and cook for 3 minutes, stirring constantly, until browned on all sides.

4 Add the fish sauce and palm sugar and cook for 1 minute more. Stir in the coconut milk until the mixture is smooth, then add the cooked squash, with the chillies and lime leaves. Simmer gently, stirring frequently, for 2 minutes, then spoon into a dish, sprinkle with the coriander and serve.

Cook's Tip
Save time by buying prepared butternut in bags from the supermarket. Small cubes are best, since they cook quickly.

Duck Stir-fry Energy 165kcal/686kJ; Protein 17.4g; Carbohydrate 2.3g, of which sugars 2g; Fat 10.6g, of which saturates 1.8g; Cholesterol 69mg; Calcium 72mg; Fibre 2.9g; Sodium 345mg.
Duck Curry Energy 295kcal/1241kJ; Protein 31.4g; Carbohydrate 13.3g, of which sugars 10g; Fat 10.5g, of which saturates 2.3g; Cholesterol 165mg; Calcium 65mg; Fibre 1.8g; Sodium 546mg.

Jungle Curry of Guinea Fowl

This is a traditional wild food country curry from the north-central region of Thailand.

Serves 4

1 guinea fowl or similar game bird
15ml/1 tbsp vegetable oil
10ml/2 tsp green curry paste
15ml/1 tbsp Thai fish sauce
2.5cm/1in piece fresh galangal, peeled and finely chopped
15ml/1 tbsp fresh green peppercorns
3 kaffir lime leaves, torn
15ml/1 tbsp whisky, preferably Mekhong
300ml/½ pint/1¼ cups chicken stock
50g/2oz snake beans or yard-long beans, cut into 2.5cm/1in lengths (about ½ cup)
225g/8oz/3¼ cups chestnut mushrooms, sliced
1 piece drained canned bamboo shoot, about 50g/2oz, shredded
5ml/1 tsp dried chilli flakes, to garnish (optional)

Preparation: 7 minutes; Cooking: 6–7 minutes

1 Cut up the guinea fowl, remove and discard the skin, then take all the meat off the bones. Chop the meat into bitesize pieces and set aside.

2 Heat the oil in a wok or frying pan and add the curry paste. Stir-fry over a medium heat for 30 seconds, until the paste gives off its aroma.

3 Add the fish sauce and the guinea fowl meat and stir-fry until the meat is browned all over. Add the galangal, peppercorns, lime leaves and whisky, then pour in the stock.

4 Bring to the boil. Add the vegetables, return to a simmer and cook gently for 2–3 minutes, until they are just cooked. Spoon into a dish, sprinkle with chilli flakes, if you like, and serve.

> **Cook's Tip**
> Fresh green peppercorns are simply unripe berries. They are sold on the stem and look rather like miniature Brussels sprout stalks. Look for them at Thai supermarkets.

Spiced Quail with Mushroom Salad

Quail is at its best when the breast meat is removed from the carcass, so that it cooks quickly and can be served rare.

Serves 4

8 quail breasts
50g/2oz/¼ cup butter
5ml/1 tsp paprika
salt and ground black pepper

For the salad

60ml/4 tbsp walnut oil
30ml/2 tbsp olive oil
45ml/3 tbsp balsamic vinegar
25g/1oz/2 tbsp butter
75g/3oz/generous 1 cup chanterelle mushrooms, sliced if large
25g/1oz/3 tbsp walnut halves, toasted
115g/4oz mixed salad leaves

Preparation: 5 minutes; Cooking: 9 minutes

1 Preheat the grill (broiler). Arrange the quail breasts on the grill rack, skin sides up. Dot with half the butter and sprinkle with half the paprika and a little salt.

2 Grill (broil) the quail breasts for 3 minutes, then turn them over and dot with the remaining butter, then sprinkle with the remaining paprika and a little salt.

3 Grill for a further 3 minutes, or until cooked. Transfer the quail breasts to a warmed dish, cover and leave them to stand while you prepare the salad.

4 Make the dressing first. Whisk the oils with the balsamic vinegar, then season and set aside.

5 Heat the butter in a medium pan until foaming and cook the chanterelles for about 3 minutes, or until just beginning to soften. Add the walnuts and heat through. Remove from the heat.

6 Thinly slice the cooked quail breasts and arrange them on four individual serving plates with the warmed chanterelle mushrooms and walnuts and mixed salad leaves.

7 Drizzle about half the oil and vinegar dressing over the salad and serve warm, with the remaining dressing served separately.

Guinea Fowl Energy 321kcal/1345kJ; Protein 42.2g; Carbohydrate 1.1g, of which sugars 0.7g; Fat 50.4g, of which saturates 12.8g; Cholesterol 240mg; Calcium 91mg; Fibre 1.5g; Sodium 305mg.
Quail Energy 443kcal/1837kJ; Protein 25.6g; Carbohydrate 0.9g, of which sugars 0.8g; Fat 37.5g, of which saturates 12.3g; Cholesterol 110mg; Calcium 24mg; Fibre 0.7g; Sodium 176mg.

Bean Salad with Tuna & Onion

This makes a great first course or even a light main meal if served with a green salad, some garlic mayonnaise and plenty of warm, crusty bread for mopping up the tasty tarragon dressing.

Serves 4

2 x 300g/11oz cans
  cannellini beans
200–250g/7–9oz fine French
  beans, trimmed
1 large red onion, very thinly sliced
45ml/3 tbsp chopped fresh flat
  leaf parsley

200–250g/7–9oz good-quality
  canned tuna in olive oil,
  drained
200g/7oz cherry tomatoes,
  halved
salt and ground black pepper
a few onion rings, to garnish

For the dressing

90ml/6 tbsp extra virgin olive oil
15ml/1 tbsp tarragon vinegar
5ml/1 tsp tarragon mustard
1 garlic clove, finely chopped
5ml/1 tsp grated lemon rind
a little lemon juice
pinch of caster sugar (optional)

Preparation: 6 minutes; Cooking: 3–4 minutes

1 Drain the cans of beans into a colander and rinse them under cold running water. Drain again and set aside.

2 Meanwhile, whisk all the dressing ingredients apart from the lemon juice and sugar in a bowl. Season to taste with salt, pepper, lemon juice and sugar, if liked.

3 Blanch the French beans in plenty of boiling water for 3–4 minutes. Drain, refresh under cold water and drain again.

4 Place both types of beans in a bowl. Add half the dressing and toss to mix. Stir in the onion and half the chopped parsley, then season to taste with salt and pepper. Flake the tuna into large chunks with a knife and toss it into the beans with the tomato halves.

5 Arrange the salad on four individual plates. Drizzle the remaining dressing over the salad and scatter the remaining chopped parsley on top. Garnish with a few onion rings and serve immediately, at room temperature.

Salad Niçoise

Made with the freshest of ingredients, this classic salad makes a simple yet unbeatable summer dish.

Serves 4

115g/4oz French beans, trimmed
  and cut in half
115g/4oz mixed salad leaves
1/2 small cucumber, thinly sliced
4 ripe tomatoes, quartered
50g/2oz can anchovies, drained

and halved lengthways
4 eggs, hard-boiled
1 tuna steak, about 175g/6oz
olive oil, for brushing
1/2 bunch small radishes, trimmed
50g/2oz/1/2 cup small black olives
salt and ground black pepper

For the dressing

90ml/6 tbsp extra virgin olive oil
2 garlic cloves, crushed
15ml/1 tbsp white wine vinegar

Preparation: 6 minutes; Cooking: 8–10 minutes

1 To make the dressing, whisk together the oil, garlic and vinegar and season to taste with salt and pepper. Set aside.

2 Cook the French beans in a pan of boiling water for 2 minutes until just tender, then drain.

3 Mix together the salad leaves, sliced cucumber, tomatoes and French beans in a large, shallow bowl. Halve the anchovies lengthways and shell and quarter the eggs.

4 Preheat the grill (broiler). Brush the tuna steak with olive oil and sprinkle with salt and black pepper. Grill (broil) for 3–4 minutes on each side until cooked through. Cool, then flake.

5 Scatter the flaked tuna, anchovies, quartered eggs, radishes and olives over the salad. Pour over the dressing and toss together lightly to combine. Serve at once.

Variation

Opinions vary on whether salad Niçoise should include potatoes but, if you like, include a few small cooked new potatoes and some chopped celery.

Bean Salad Energy 266kcal/1112kJ; Protein 27.3g; Carbohydrate 2.3g, of which sugars 2.3g; Fat 16.6g, of which saturates 3g; Cholesterol 32mg; Calcium 40mg; Fibre 0.7g; Sodium 55mg.
Salad Niçoise Energy 351kcal/1457kJ; Protein 21.7g; Carbohydrate 5.3g, of which sugars 5g; Fat 27.3g, of which saturates 5g; Cholesterol 210mg; Calcium 114mg; Fibre 2.6g; Sodium 876mg.

Olive, Tomato & Sardine Salad

The combination of ingredients in this salad – sardines, black olives, ripe tomatoes and acidic wine vinegar – brings a real burst of flavour to a delightful light summer dish. The sardines are best cooked under a preheated hot grill. They need very little cooking time so it is really quick to prepare; 2 minutes on each side will do it.

Serves 6
8 large firm ripe tomatoes
1 large red onion
60ml/4 tbsp white
   wine vinegar
90ml/6 tbsp good olive oil
18–24 small sardines, cooked
75g/3oz/¾ cup pitted black
   olives, well drained
salt and ground black pepper
45ml/3 tbsp chopped
   fresh flat leaf parsley,
   to garnish

Preparation: 4 minutes; Cooking: 0 minutes

1 Slice the tomatoes into 5mm/¼in slices. Using a sharp knife, slice the onion thinly.

2 Arrange the tomatoes on individual plates, overlapping the slices, then top with the red onion.

3 Mix together the wine vinegar, olive oil and seasoning, and spoon over each plate of salad.

4 Top each salad with 3–4 sardines and a few black olives. Sprinkle the chopped parsley over the top.

> **Cook's Tip**
> *You may not need all the vinegar as the juice from the tomatoes will contribute some acidity.*

> **Variation**
> *This recipe works equally well if the sardines are replaced with 6 shelled and halved hard-boiled eggs.*

Spicy Squid Salad

This tasty, colourful salad is a refreshing way of serving squid. The ginger and chilli dressing is added while the squid is still hot, and flavours the shellfish and beans.

Serves 4
450g/1lb squid
300ml/½ pint/1¼ cups fish stock
175g/6oz green beans, trimmed
   and halved

45ml/3 tbsp fresh coriander
   (cilantro) leaves
10ml/2 tsp granulated (white)
   sugar
30ml/2 tbsp rice vinegar
5ml/1 tsp sesame oil
15ml/1 tbsp light soy sauce
15ml/1 tbsp vegetable oil
2 garlic cloves, finely chopped
10ml/2 tbsp finely chopped fresh
   root ginger
1 fresh chilli, seeded and chopped

Preparation: 8–10 minutes; Cooking: 5–7 minutes

1 Prepare the squid. Holding the body in one hand, gently pull away the head and tentacles. Discard the head then trim and reserve the tentacles. Remove the transparent quill from inside the squid and peel off the purplish skin on the outside.

2 Cut the body of the squid open lengthways and wash thoroughly. Score criss-cross patterns on the inside, then cut into 7.5 x 5cm/3 x 2in pieces.

3 Bring the fish stock to the boil in a wok or pan. Add all the squid pieces, then lower the heat and cook for about 2 minutes until they are tender and have curled. Drain.

4 Bring a pan of lightly salted water to the boil. Cook the beans for 3–5 minutes, until they are crisp-tender. Drain, refresh under cold water, then drain again. Mix the squid and beans in a bowl.

5 In another bowl, mix the coriander leaves, sugar, rice vinegar, sesame oil and soy sauce. Pour the mixture over the squid and beans, and toss lightly, using a spoon, to coat.

6 Heat the vegetable oil in a wok or small pan. When it is very hot, stir-fry the garlic, ginger and chilli for a few seconds, then pour the dressing over the squid mixture. Toss gently and serve.

Black Olive Energy 94kcal/393kJ; Protein 7.7g; Carbohydrate 3.4g, of which sugars 3.2g; Fat 5.6g, of which saturates 1.4g; Cholesterol 21mg; Calcium 29mg; Fibre 0.1g; Sodium 52mg.
Spicy Squid Energy 143kcal/602kJ; Protein 18.2g; Carbohydrate 5.4g, of which sugars 3.6g; Fat 5.6g, of which saturates 0.9g; Cholesterol 253mg; Calcium 32mg; Fibre 1g; Sodium 124mg.

Seafood Salad

This is a very pretty arrangement of fresh mussels, prawns and squid rings served on a colourful bed of salad vegetables. Don't be tempted to chill the salad or the delicate flavours will be blunted.

Serves 6
115g/4oz prepared squid rings
12 fresh mussels, scrubbed and
   beards removed
1 large carrot
6 crisp lettuce leaves
10cm/4in piece cucumber,
   finely diced
115g/4oz cooked, peeled
   prawns (shrimp)
15ml/1 tbsp drained
   pickled capers

For the dressing
30ml/2 tbsp freshly squeezed
   lemon juice
45ml/3 tbsp virgin olive oil
15ml/1 tbsp chopped fresh parsley
salt and ground black pepper

Preparation: 3 minutes; Cooking: 4–6 minutes

1 Put the squid rings into a metal sieve (strainer) or vegetable steamer. Place the sieve or steamer over a pan of simmering water, cover with a lid and steam the squid for 2–3 minutes until it just turns white. Cool under cold running water and drain on kitchen paper.

2 Discard any open mussels that do not close when tapped. Cover the base of a large pan with water, add the mussels, then cover and steam for a few minutes until they open. Discard any mussels that stubbornly remain shut.

3 Using a swivel-style vegetable peeler, cut the carrot into wafer-thin ribbons. Tear the lettuce into pieces and arrange on a serving plate. Scatter the carrot ribbons on top, then sprinkle over the diced cucumber.

4 Arrange the mussels, prawns and squid rings over the salad and scatter the capers over the top.

5 Make the dressing. Put all the ingredients in a small bowl and whisk to combine. Drizzle half the dressing over the salad. Serve at room temperature with the remaining dressing.

Prawn & Rice Noodle Salad

The Thai-inspired dressing adds a superb flavour to the noodles and prawns. This delicious salad can be served warm or cold.

Serves 4
200g/7oz rice vermicelli or stir-fry
   rice noodles
8 baby corn cobs, halved
150g/5oz mangetouts (snow peas)
15ml/1 tbsp vegetable oil
2 garlic cloves, finely chopped
2.5cm/1in piece fresh root ginger,
   peeled and finely chopped
1 fresh red or green chilli, seeded
   and finely chopped
450g/1lb raw peeled tiger prawns
   (jumbo shrimp)
4 spring onions (scallions),
   very thinly sliced
15ml/1 tbsp sesame seeds,
   toasted
1 lemon grass stalk, thinly
   shredded, to garnish

For the dressing
15ml/1 tbsp chopped chives
15ml/1 tbsp Thai fish sauce
5ml/1 tsp soy sauce
45ml/3 tbsp groundnut (peanut) oil
5ml/1 tsp sesame oil
30ml/2 tbsp rice vinegar

Preparation: 10 minutes; Cooking: 7 minutes

1 Put the rice vermicelli or noodles in a wide heatproof bowl, pour over boiling water and leave for 5 minutes. Drain, refresh under cold water and drain again. Tip back into the bowl.

2 Boil or steam the corn cobs and mangetouts for about 3 minutes; they should still be crunchy. Refresh under cold water and drain. Now make the dressing. Mix all the ingredients in a screw-top jar, close tightly and shake well to combine.

3 Heat the oil in a large frying pan or wok. Add the garlic, ginger and red or green chilli and cook for 1 minute. Add the tiger prawns and stir-fry for about 3 minutes, until they have just turned pink. Stir in the spring onions, corn cobs, mangetouts and sesame seeds, and toss lightly to mix.

4 Tip the contents of the pan or wok over the rice vermicelli or noodles. Pour the dressing on top and toss well. Garnish with lemon grass and serve immediately.

Seafood Salad Energy 91kcal/379kJ; Protein 7.5g; Carbohydrate 1.5g, of which sugars 1g; Fat 6.2g, of which saturates 0.9g; Cholesterol 84mg; Calcium 29mg; Fibre 0.4g; Sodium 86mg.
Prawn Salad Energy 546kcal/2279kJ; Protein 25.2g; Carbohydrate 78.4g, of which sugars 6.8g; Fat 14.6g, of which saturates 1.7g; Cholesterol 110mg; Calcium 408mg; Fibre 3.3g; Sodium 665mg.

Prawn Noodle Salad

A refreshing salad with all the tangy flavour of the sea. Instead of prawns, try squid, scallops, mussels or crab.

Serves 4
115g/4oz cellophane noodles, soaked in hot water until soft
16 cooked prawns (shrimp), peeled
1 small green (bell) pepper, seeded and cut into strips
½ cucumber, cut into strips
1 tomato, cut into strips
2 shallots, finely sliced
salt and ground black pepper
coriander (cilantro) leaves, to garnish

For the dressing
15ml/1 tbsp rice vinegar
30ml/2 tbsp Thai fish sauce
30ml/2 tbsp fresh lime juice
pinch of salt
2.5ml/½ tsp grated fresh root ginger
1 lemon grass stalk, finely chopped
1 fresh red chilli, seeded and finely sliced
30ml/2 tbsp roughly chopped fresh mint
few fresh tarragon sprigs, roughly chopped
15ml/1 tbsp chopped chives

Preparation: 8–10 minutes; Cooking: 1 minute

1 Make the dressing by combining all the ingredients in a small bowl or jug (pitcher) and whisking well.

2 Drain the noodles, then plunge them in a pan of boiling water for 1 minute. Drain in a colander, rinse under cold running water, shake the colander and drain again well.

3 In a large bowl, combine the noodles with the prawns, pepper, cucumber, tomato and shallots. Lightly season with salt and pepper, then toss with the dressing.

4 Spoon the noodles on to individual plates, arranging the prawns on top. Garnish with a few coriander leaves and serve.

Cook's Tip
As the prawns (shrimp) are the prime ingredient of this salad, buy the largest and juiciest ones you can afford.

Roquefort & Salami Pasta Salad

This pasta dish is easy to make and would be perfect for a picnic or packed lunch.

Serves 4
225g/8oz/2 cups dried fusilli
275g/10oz jar charcoal-roasted peppers in oil
115g/4oz/1 cup pitted black olives
4 sun-dried tomatoes in oil, drained and quartered
115g/4oz Roquefort cheese, crumbled
10 slices peppered salami, cut into strips
115g/4oz packet mixed leaf salad
30ml/2 tbsp white wine vinegar
30ml/2 tbsp chopped fresh oregano
2 garlic cloves, crushed
salt and ground black pepper

Preparation: 3–4 minutes; Cooking: 10–12 minutes

1 Bring a large pan of lightly salted water to the boil and cook the pasta over high heat for 10–12 minutes.

2 Meanwhile, drain the peppers and reserve 60ml/4 tbsp of the oil for the dressing. Cut the peppers into long, fine strips and mix them with the olives, sun-dried tomatoes and Roquefort in a large bowl.

3 Drain the pasta thoroughly in a colander and rinse with cold water, then drain again. Stir it into the pepper mixture along with the strips of peppered salami.

4 Divide the salad leaves among four individual bowls and spoon the pasta salad on top.

5 Whisk the reserved oil with the vinegar, oregano, garlic and seasoning to taste. Spoon this dressing over the salad and serve at once.

Variation
Use slices of cold roast chicken instead of the salami and cubes of Brie in place of the Roquefort cheese.

Prawn Noodle Salad Energy 103kcal/438kJ; Protein 11g; Carbohydrate 15g, of which sugars 13g; Fat 0.5g, of which saturates 0.1g; Cholesterol 110mg; Calcium 54mg; Fibre 0.7g; Sodium 109mg.
Pasta Salad Energy 429kcal/1797kJ; Protein 17.8g; Carbohydrate 46.7g, of which sugars 6.6g; Fat 20.3g, of which saturates 8.9g; Cholesterol 37mg; Calcium 188mg; Fibre 3.9g; Sodium 1341mg.

Pan-fried Chicken Liver Salad

This Florentine salad uses vin santo, a delicious sweet dessert wine from Tuscany, but this is not essential – any dessert wine will do, or a sweet or cream sherry.

Serves 4

75g/3oz fresh baby spinach leaves, washed and dried
75g/3oz lollo rosso leaves, washed, dried and torn into pieces
75ml/5 tbsp olive oil
15g/½oz/1 tbsp butter
225g/8oz chicken livers, trimmed and thinly sliced
45ml/3 tbsp vin santo
50–75g/2–3oz fresh Parmesan cheese, shaved into curls
salt and ground black pepper

Preparation: 4 minutes; Cooking: 6 minutes

1 Put the spinach and lollo rosso leaves into a large bowl, season with salt and ground black pepper to taste and toss gently with salad servers or two spoons to mix.

2 Heat 30ml/2 tbsp of the oil with the butter in a large heavy frying pan. When foaming, add the chicken livers and toss over medium to high heat for 5 minutes, or until the livers are browned on the outside but still pink in the centre. Remove the pan from the heat.

3 Remove the livers from the pan with a slotted spoon, drain them on kitchen paper, then place them on top of the seasoned spinach and lollo rosso leaves.

4 Return the pan to medium heat, add the remaining oil and the vin santo and stir until sizzling. Pour the hot dressing over the leaves and livers and toss to coat. Put the salad in a serving bowl and sprinkle over the Parmesan shavings. Serve the salad at once, while the livers are still warm.

Cook's Tip
If you can't find baby spinach leaves, you can use older spinach, but discard any tough leaves along with the stalks and tear the remainder into pieces. Or use any other baby leaves.

Chicken, Vegetable & Chilli Salad

This Vietnamese salad is full of surprising textures and flavours. Serve as a light lunch dish or for supper with crusty French bread.

Serves 4

225g/8oz Chinese leaves (Chinese cabbage)
2 carrots, cut in matchsticks
½ cucumber, cut in matchsticks
2 fresh red chillies, seeded and cut into thin strips
1 small onion, sliced into fine rings
4 pickled gherkins, sliced into fine rings, plus 45ml/3 tbsp of the liquid from the jar
50g/2oz/½ cup peanuts, lightly ground
225g/8oz cooked chicken, sliced
1 garlic clove, crushed
5ml/1 tsp granulated (white) sugar
30ml/2 tbsp cider or white wine vinegar
salt

Preparation: 14 minutes; Cooking: 0 minutes

1 Discard any tough outer leaves from the Chinese leaves, then stack the remainder on a board. Using a sharp knife, cut them into shreds that are about the same width as the carrot matchsticks. Put the Chinese leaves and carrots in a bowl.

2 Spread out the cucumber matchsticks in a colander and sprinkle with salt. Stand the colander on a plate and set aside for 12–15 minutes, to extract the excess liquid.

3 Mix the chillies and onion rings in a small bowl. Add the sliced gherkins and peanuts. Rinse the salted cucumber thoroughly, drain well and pat dry with kitchen paper.

4 Add the cucumber matchsticks to the salad bowl and toss together lightly. Stir in the chilli mixture. Arrange the chicken on top. In a bowl, whisk the gherkin liquid with the garlic, sugar and vinegar. Pour over the salad, toss lightly and serve.

Cook's Tip
Add extra cider or white wine vinegar to the dressing for a sharper taste. If it is too tart, add extra sugar.

Pan-fried Chicken Energy 277kcal/1146kJ; Protein 16g; Carbohydrate 0.7g, of which sugars 0.6g; Fat 22.5g, of which saturates 6.9g; Cholesterol 234mg; Calcium 220mg; Fibre 0.8g; Sodium 255mg.
Chicken, Vegetable Energy 167kcal/700kJ; Protein 17.8g; Carbohydrate 9.1g, of which sugars 7.7g; Fat 6.9g, of which saturates 1.4g; Cholesterol 39mg; Calcium 47mg; Fibre 2.9g; Sodium 50mg.

Spicy Sichuan Noodle Salad

Subtly spiced but quite hot dishes are the keynote of western Chinese cuisine – fresh or dried chillies usually play a major role but are balanced.

Serves 4
350g/12oz thick noodles
175g/6oz cooked chicken, shredded
50g/2oz/½ cup roasted cashew nuts
salt and ground black pepper

For the dressing
4 spring onions (scallions), chopped
30ml/2 tbsp chopped coriander (cilantro)
2 garlic cloves, chopped
30ml/2 tbsp smooth peanut butter
30ml/2 tbsp sweet chilli sauce
15ml/1 tbsp soy sauce
15ml/1 tbsp sherry vinegar
15ml/1 tbsp sesame oil
30ml/2 tbsp olive oil
30ml/2 tbsp chicken stock or water
10 toasted Sichuan peppercorns, ground

Preparation: 6 minutes; Cooking: 4–6 minutes

1 Cook the noodles in a pan of boiling water until just tender, following the directions on the packet. Drain, rinse under cold running water and drain well.

2 While the noodles are cooking, combine all the ingredients for the dressing in a large bowl and whisk together well.

3 Add the noodles, shredded chicken and cashew nuts to the dressing, toss gently to coat.

4 Season to taste, and serve at once.

> **Variations**
> • *Substitute cooked turkey or pork for the chicken.*
> • *Make a vegetarian version of this noodle salad by dropping the cooked chicken in favour of baby corn cobs, halved lengthways, mangetouts (snow peas) cut in strips, and strips of red (bell) pepper. For extra crunch, drain some canned water chestnuts and slice them into the salad. Use vegetable stock instead of chicken stock in the dressing.*

Warm Chorizo & Spinach Salad

Spanish chorizo sausage contributes an intense spiciness to any ingredient with which it is cooked. In this hearty salad, spinach has sufficient flavour to compete with the chorizo and the combination works very well.

Serves 4
225g/8oz baby spinach leaves
90ml/6 tbsp extra virgin olive oil
150g/5oz chorizo sausage, very thinly sliced
30ml/2 tbsp sherry vinegar
salt and ground black pepper
warm crusty bread, to serve

Preparation: 2–3 minutes; Cooking: 3 minutes

1 Pour the oil into a large frying pan and add the sausage. Cook gently for 3 minutes, until the sausage slices start to shrivel slightly and colour.

2 Add the spinach leaves and remove the pan from the heat. Toss the spinach in the warm oil until it just starts to wilt. Add the sherry vinegar and a little seasoning. Toss all the ingredients together briefly, then serve the salad warm.

> **Cook's Tip**
> *Chorizos, of which there are over 50 varieties, are named after the choricero chilli that gives them both spiciness and colour. Red chorizos, made in links, contain minced (ground) meat, which is mottled with fat. They must be cooked and are usually fried or boiled. The longer varieties are usually sweeter, while some small round ones are hot and spicy. The second type of chorizo, and the one featured in the recipe above, is cured, so needs no further cooking.*

> **Variations**
> • *Watercress or rocket (arugula) could be used instead of the spinach, if you prefer.*
> • *For an added dimension, use a flavoured olive oil – rosemary, garlic or chilli oil would work perfectly.*

Spicy Sichuan Energy 536kcal/2256kJ; Protein 24.1g; Carbohydrate 71.3g, of which sugars 5.4g; Fat 19.1g, of which saturates 2.7g; Cholesterol 34mg; Calcium 57mg; Fibre 3.9g; Sodium 205mg.
Warm Chorizo Energy 273kcal/1127kJ; Protein 8g; Carbohydrate 2g, of which sugars 2g; Fat 26g, of which saturates 6g; Cholesterol 0mg; Calcium 96mg; Fibre 1.2g; Sodium 300mg.

Stir-fried Asparagus with Chilli, Galangal & Lemon Grass

Wherever it is grown, asparagus is popular and much sought after. This tasty recipe comes from Vietnam, where asparagus was introduced by French colonists.

Serves 2–4

30ml/2 tbsp groundnut (peanut) oil
2 garlic cloves, finely chopped
2 fresh red chillies, seeded and finely chopped
25g/1oz fresh galangal or root ginger, finely shredded
1 lemon grass stalk, trimmed and finely sliced
350g/12oz fresh asparagus stalks, trimmed
30ml/2 tbsp tuk trey or fish sauce
30ml/2 tbsp soy sauce
5ml/1 tsp sugar
30ml/2 tbsp unsalted roasted peanuts, finely chopped
1 small bunch fresh coriander (cilantro), finely chopped

Preparation: 8 minutes; Cooking: 3–5 minutes

1 Heat a large wok and add the oil. Stir in the garlic, chillies, galangal or ginger and lemon grass and stir-fry until golden.

2 Add the asparagus and stir-fry for a further 1–2 minutes, until it is just tender but not too soft.

3 Stir in the tuk trey or fish sauce with the soy sauce and sugar. Stir in the peanuts and coriander and serve immediately.

Cook's Tip
To prepare an asparagus stalk, snap the stem. It will break between the usable tender section and the woody base.

Variation
This recipe also works well with broccoli, green beans and courgettes (zucchini), cut into strips.

Caramelized Mushrooms with Allspice & Herbs

Button mushrooms caramelize beautifully in their own juice, but still keep their moistness and nutty flavour. They are usually served as a side dish for grilled lamb chops or liver, or as a hot or cold meze dish with chunks of bread to mop up the tasty cooking juices, but they are also good served on toasted bread as a light lunch with a salad. Use whatever herbs and spices you have available.

Serves 4

45ml/3 tbsp olive oil
15ml/1 tbsp butter
450g/1lb button (white) mushrooms, wiped clean
3–4 garlic cloves, finely chopped
10ml/2 tsp allspice berries, crushed
10ml/2 tsp coriander seeds
5ml/1 tsp dried mint
1 bunch each of fresh sage and flat leaf parsley, chopped
salt and ground black pepper
lemon wedges, to serve

Preparation: 2–3 minutes; Cooking: 15 minutes

1 Heat the oil and butter in a wide, heavy pan, then stir in the mushrooms with the garlic, allspice and coriander. Cover and cook for about 10 minutes, shaking the pan from time to time, until the mushrooms start to caramelize.

2 Remove the lid and toss in the mint with some of the sage and parsley. Cook for a further 5 minutes, until most of the liquid has evaporated, then season with salt and pepper.

3 Tip the mushrooms into a serving dish and sprinkle the rest of the sage and parsley over the top. Serve hot or at room temperature, with lemon wedges for squeezing.

Cook's Tip
Button (white) mushrooms are ideal for this recipe as they don't release much liquid into the pan and caramelize beautifully. Don't wash the mushrooms before cooking, just wipe with a clean dish towel and keep them whole.

Stir-fried Asparagus Energy 117kcal/482kJ; Protein 5g; Carbohydrate 3.3g, of which sugars 2.7g; Fat 9g, of which saturates 1g; Cholesterol 0mg; Calcium 30mg; Fibre 2g; Sodium 535mg.
Caramelized Mushrooms Energy 125kcal/517kJ; Protein 2.8g; Carbohydrate 1.2g, of which sugars 0.8g; Fat 12.2g, of which saturates 3.3g; Cholesterol 8mg; Calcium 58mg; Fibre 2.5g; Sodium 37mg.

Sautéed Herb Salad with Chilli & Lemon

Firm-leafed fresh herbs, such as flat leaf parsley and mint, tossed in a little olive oil and seasoned with salt, are fabulous with spicy kebabs or beef steaks.

Serves 4
1 large bunch of flat leaf parsley
1 large bunch of mint
1 large bunch of fresh coriander (cilantro)
1 bunch of rocket (arugula)
1 large bunch of spinach leaves, about 115g/4oz
60–75ml/4–5 tbsp olive oil
2 garlic cloves, finely chopped
1 fresh green or red chilli, seeded and finely chopped
1/2 preserved lemon, finely chopped
salt and ground black pepper
45–60ml/3–4 tbsp Greek (US strained plain) yogurt, to serve

Preparation: 4–5 minutes; Cooking: 2 minutes

1 Roughly chop the herbs and put them in a bowl. Trim the rocket and spinach, discarding any tough stems or tattered leaves. Add them to the herbs and mix well.

2 Heat the olive oil in a wide, heavy pan. Stir in the garlic and chilli, and fry until they begin to colour. Toss in the herbs and leaves and cook gently, until they begin to wilt.

3 Spoon into a serving bowl, add the preserved lemon and season to taste. Serve warm with yogurt.

> **Cook's Tip**
> This is the perfect recipe for anyone with a herb garden. Pick the herbs immediately before preparing them, if possible. If you must pick them sooner, stand the stems in a jar of water.

> **Variation**
> Flavour the yogurt with crushed garlic, if you like.

Broccoli with Soy Sauce & Sesame Seeds

The best way to cook broccoli is to fry it quickly in a wok, so that the rich colour and crunchy texture are retained. Soy sauce and sesame seeds add to the flavour of this tasty dish.

Serves 2
225g/8oz purple-sprouting broccoli
15ml/1 tbsp sesame seeds
15ml/1 tbsp olive oil
15ml/1 tbsp soy sauce
salt and ground black pepper

Preparation: 2 minutes; Cooking: 3–4 minutes

1 Using a sharp knife, cut off and discard any thick stems from the broccoli and cut the broccoli into long, thin florets.

2 Spread out the sesame seeds in a small frying pan and dry-fry over a medium heat until toasted. Do not leave them unattended as they will readily burn and acquire a nasty, bitter taste if left just a fraction too long.

3 Heat the olive oil in a wok or large frying pan and add the broccoli. Stir-fry for 3–4 minutes, or until tender, adding a splash of water if the pan becomes too dry.

4 Add the soy sauce to the broccoli, then season with salt and ground black pepper to taste. Add the sesame seeds and toss to combine. Tip the broccoli mixture into a warmed serving bowl or individual bowls and serve immediately.

> **Variation**
> Purple-sprouting broccoli has been used for this recipe. This vegetable is at its best when in season during early spring, so finding a good crop may not always be easy during the rest of the year. When it is not available, an ordinary variety of broccoli, such as calabrese, will also work very well. Or you could substitute the broccoli altogether with Chinese leaves, which offer just as much crunch.

Sautéed Herb Salad Energy 142kcal/585kJ; Protein 3.6g; Carbohydrate 3.1g, of which sugars 2.7g; Fat 12.9g, of which saturates 2.1g; Cholesterol 2mg; Calcium 216mg; Fibre 4.4g; Sodium 82mg.
Broccoli with Soy Sauce Energy 135kcal/558kJ; Protein 6.6g; Carbohydrate 2.7g, of which sugars 2.3g; Fat 10.9g, of which saturates 1.7g; Cholesterol 0mg; Calcium 115mg; Fibre 3.5g; Sodium 545mg.

Crispy Cabbage

Like so many brassicas, cabbage is lovely when crisp and horrible when soggy. In this recipe the balance is just right.

Serves 4–6
1 medium green or small white cabbage
30–45ml/2–3 tbsp oil
salt and ground black pepper

Preparation: 2–3 minutes; Cooking: 2–3 minutes

1 Remove the central core from the cabbage as well as any coarse outside leaves and the central rib from the larger remaining leaves.

2 Place the cabbage on a board and shred the leaves finely. Wash under cold running water, drain in a colander, shake well and blot on kitchen paper to dry thoroughly.

3 Heat a wok or wide-based flameproof casserole over a fairly high heat. Heat the oil and add the cabbage. Stir-fry for 2–3 minutes, using one or two wooden spoons to keep the cabbage moving so that it cooks evenly but is still crunchy. Season with salt and pepper and serve immediately.

Cook's Tip
Don't throw away the coarse outer leaves and central rib from the cabbage. They can be used with other vegetables such as onions and carrots to make vegetable stock. As long as the cabbage doesn't dominate, the flavour will be very good.

Variation
For cabbage with a bacon dressing, fry 225g/8oz diced streaky (fatty) bacon in a pan. Set aside while cooking the cabbage. Remove the cabbage from the pan and keep warm with the bacon. Boil 15ml/1 tbsp wine or cider vinegar with the juices remaining in the pan. Bring to the boil and season with ground black pepper. Pour over the cabbage and bacon. This makes a versatile side dish, and is especially good with chicken.

Cabbage with Onions, Bacon & Garlic

Serve this quick, easy and flavoursome dish with goose, turkey or pork, or try it with sausages or chops and creamy mashed potatoes with chives.

Serves 4
25g/1oz/2 tbsp butter or bacon fat or pork fat, or 30ml/2 tbsp olive oil
115g/4oz bacon or pancetta, chopped
1 onion, halved and thinly sliced
5ml/1 tsp caraway seeds or cumin seeds (optional)
2 garlic cloves, finely chopped
1 green cabbage (such as Savoy cabbage), thick stalks removed and leaves shredded
105ml/7 tbsp water
salt and ground black pepper

Preparation: 5 minutes; Cooking: 11–12 minutes

1 Melt the butter or fat or heat the oil in a large frying pan over a gentle heat. Cook the bacon or pancetta and onion gently, until the onion is soft.

2 Increase the heat slightly to medium-low and scatter over the caraway seeds or cumin seeds, if using, then cook, stirring occasionally, until the onion begins to brown.

3 Add the chopped garlic and stir-fry for 2 minutes.

4 Add the cabbage and turn it in the juices to coat, then stir in 5ml/1 tsp salt and the water. Cover tightly and cook over a high heat for 5–6 minutes, stirring once. The cabbage should be tender, but still retain a little crispness. Season to taste with black pepper and serve immediately.

Variations
• *Substitute a large leek for the onion and use shredded Brussels sprouts instead of the green cabbage. Omit the seeds.*
• *For vegetarians, leave out the bacon or pancetta and use strips of sun-dried tomato instead.*

Crispy Cabbage Energy 56kcal/230kJ; Protein 1.2g; Carbohydrate 4.2g, of which sugars 4.1g; Fat 3.8g, of which saturates 0.5g; Cholesterol 0mg; Calcium 41mg; Fibre 1.8g; Sodium 6mg.
Cabbage with Onions Energy 151kcal/623kJ; Protein 6.7g; Carbohydrate 7.4g, of which sugars 7g; Fat 10.5g, of which saturates 2.6g; Cholesterol 15mg; Calcium 67mg; Fibre 2.8g; Sodium 452mg.

Green Beans with Tomatoes

This recipe is full of the flavours of summer. It relies on first-class ingredients, so use only the best ripe plum tomatoes and green beans that you can buy.

Serves 4
30ml/2 tbsp olive oil
1 large onion, finely sliced
2 garlic cloves, finely chopped
6 large ripe plum tomatoes, peeled, seeded and coarsely chopped
150ml/¼ pint/⅔ cup dry white wine
450g/1lb green beans, sliced in half lengthways
16 pitted black olives
10ml/2 tsp lemon juice
salt and ground black pepper

Preparation: 3–4 minutes; Cooking: 15 minutes

1 Heat the oil in a large frying pan. Add the finely sliced onion and chopped garlic. Cook over a medium heat for about 5 minutes, stirring frequently and lowering the heat if necessary, until the onion has softened but not browned.

2 Add the chopped tomatoes, white wine, beans, olives and lemon juice, and cook over a gentle heat for a further 10 minutes, stirring occasionally, until the sauce has thickened and the beans are tender. Season with salt and pepper to taste and serve immediately.

Variation
The best tomatoes for this recipe are those you harvest from your own garden, with the warmth of the sun still on the fruit. However, when tomatoes are out of season, and the only ones available in the shops have little flavour, it is better to use good quality canned plum tomatoes, either plain or with herbs such as oregano or marjoram. Add a pinch of sugar if necessary.

Cook's Tip
Green beans need little preparation and now that they are grown without the string, you simply trim either end.

Stir-fried Brussels Sprouts with Bacon

This is a great way of cooking Brussels sprouts, helping to retain their sweet flavour and crunchy texture. Stir-frying guarantees that there will not be a single soggy sprout. Children who turn up their noses when offered sprouts often enjoy this.

Serves 4
450g/1lb Brussels sprouts, trimmed and washed
30ml/2 tbsp sunflower oil
2 streaky (fatty) bacon rashers (strips), finely chopped
10ml/2 tsp caraway seeds, lightly crushed
salt and ground black pepper

Preparation: 4 minutes; Cooking: 5 minutes

1 Using a sharp knife, carefully cut all the Brussels sprouts into fine shreds.

2 Heat the oil in a wok or large frying pan. Add the shredded sprouts and turn quickly over the heat, season with salt and ground black pepper, then remove and set aside.

3 Use the same wok or pan to cook the chopped bacon. Stir-fry for 1–2 minutes until golden.

4 Return the seasoned sprouts to the pan containing the bacon and stir in the caraway seeds. Cook for a further 1–2 minutes, then serve immediately.

Variation
Instead of seasoning the Brussels sprouts with salt and pepper, add a little soy sauce or mushroom ketchup.

Cook's Tip
Save time on preparation by buying diced bacon or diced pancetta, available ready packaged at the supermarket.

Green Beans Energy 162kcal/672kJ; Protein 4.2g; Carbohydrate 14.4g, of which sugars 11.6g; Fat 8g, of which saturates 1.3g; Cholesterol 0mg; Calcium 80mg; Fibre 5.4g; Sodium 298mg.
Brussels Sprouts Energy 131kcal/545kJ; Protein 5.9g; Carbohydrate 4.6g, of which sugars 3.5g; Fat 10g, of which saturates 2g; Cholesterol 8mg; Calcium 30mg; Fibre 4.6g; Sodium 164mg.

Broad Beans with Bacon

This dish is particularly associated with Ronda, in southern Spain, the home of bull fighting, where broad beans are fed to fighting bulls to build them up. It is also found elsewhere in Spain, where it is known as habas españolas. If you have time, remove the dull skins from the broad beans to reveal the bright green beans beneath.

Serves 4
30ml/2 tbsp olive oil
1 small onion, finely chopped
1 garlic clove, finely chopped
50g/2oz rindless smoked streaky (fatty) bacon, roughly chopped
225g/8oz podded broad (fava) beans, thawed if frozen
5ml/1 tsp paprika
15ml/1 tbsp sweet sherry
salt and ground black pepper

Preparation: 5 minutes; Cooking: 12 minutes

1 Heat the olive oil in a large frying pan or sauté pan. Add the chopped onion, garlic and bacon and fry over a high heat for about 4 minutes, stirring frequently, until the onion is softened and the bacon browned.

2 Add the beans and paprika to the pan and stir-fry for 1 minute. Add the sherry, lower the heat, cover and cook for 7 minutes until tender. Season with salt and pepper to taste and serve hot.

Cook's Tip
Also known as horse beans or fava beans, broad beans are delicious, especially when young. Podding them is a satisfying job, but nature provides an extraordinary amount of packaging, and you will end up with a big bag of fleshy pods. Put these on the compost heap, as they are a good source of nitrogen.

Variation
For a vegetarian version of this dish, fry sun-dried tomatoes with the onion and garlic instead of the chopped bacon.

Carrot, Mango & Ginger Stir-fry

Ripe, sweet mango tastes wonderful with carrots and ginger in this spicy vegetable dish, which is good enough to serve on its own with plain yogurt and boiled new potatoes or chunks of wholemeal or rustic white bread.

Serves 4–6
15–30ml/1–2 tbsp olive oil
2–3 garlic cloves, chopped
1 onion, chopped
25g/1oz fresh root ginger, peeled and chopped
5–6 carrots, sliced
30–45ml/2–3 tbsp shelled pistachio nuts, roasted
5ml/1 tsp ground cinnamon
5–10ml/1–2 tsp ras el hanout
1 small firm, ripe mango, peeled and roughly diced
a small bunch of fresh coriander (cilantro), finely chopped
juice of ½ lemon
salt

Preparation: 6 minutes; Cooking: 4–5 minutes

1 Heat the olive oil in a heavy frying pan or wok. Stir in the garlic, then the onion and ginger. Fry for 1 minute.

2 Add the carrots, tossing them in the pan to make sure that they are mixed with the flavouring ingredients, and cook until they begin to brown.

3 Roughly chop the roasted pistachio nuts. Add to the pan with the ground cinnamon and ras el hanout, then gently mix in the diced mango.

4 Sprinkle with the chopped coriander, season with salt and pour over the lemon juice.

5 Toss with two spoons to mix, then spoon into a heated dish and serve immediately.

Cook's Tip
Ras el hanout is a traditional spice mix that is widely used across the Middle East and North Africa. It is available in most North African and Arab food stores.

Stir-fried Carrots Energy 89kcal/371kJ; Protein 1.7g; Carbohydrate 8.2g, of which sugars 7.5g; Fat 5.7g, of which saturates 0.8g; Cholesterol 0mg; Calcium 23mg; Fibre 2.2g; Sodium 47mg.
Broad Beans Energy 140kcal/583kJ; Protein 6.6g; Carbohydrate 8g, of which sugars 1.8g; Fat 8.8g, of which saturates 1.9g; Cholesterol 8mg; Calcium 36mg; Fibre 3.9g; Sodium 163mg.

Carrot & Parsnip Purée

Puréed vegetables aren't just for the under-fives. Their creaminess appeals to all ages, and they are ideal partners for crisp vegetables such as lightly cooked green beans. If serving the purée directly on to plates, mould it by using two spoons, taking a scoop with one and sliding it off with the other.

Serves 6–8
350g/12oz carrots
450g/1lb parsnips
a pinch of freshly grated nutmeg
  or ground mace
15g/½oz/1 tbsp butter
about 15ml/1 tbsp single (light)
  cream or crème fraîche
a small bunch of parsley,
  chopped, plus extra to garnish
salt and ground black pepper

Preparation: 3 minutes; Cooking: 15–17 minutes

1 Peel the carrots and slice fairly thinly. Peel the parsnips and cut into bitesize chunks.

2 Boil the carrots and parsnips in separate pans of lightly salted water until tender. Drain them well, then purée them together in a food processor, with the grated nutmeg or mace, a generous seasoning of salt and ground black pepper, and the butter. Whizz until smooth.

3 Transfer the purée to a bowl and beat in the cream or crème fraîche. Add the chopped parsley for extra flavour.

4 Transfer the carrot and parsnip purée to a warmed serving bowl, sprinkle with the remaining chopped parsley to garnish, and serve immediately, as vegetable purées lose heat rapidly.

Cook's Tips
• Any leftover purée can be thinned to taste with good-quality chicken or vegetable stock and heated to make a quick home-made soup. Add more seasoning if needed.
• The carrots can be replaced by a small sweet potato. Peel and dice finely. Boil the sweet potato a little ahead of the parsnips, if possible.

Cauliflower Cheese

The use of flour to thicken sauces began in France in the 17th century – hence the name 'roux' for the mixture of flour and fat that forms the basis of a white sauce – but cheese sauce made in this way has become a staple of English cookery.

Serves 4
1 medium cauliflower
25g/1oz/2 tbsp butter
25g/1oz/4 tbsp plain
  (all-purpose) flour
300ml/½ pint/1¼ cups milk
115g/4oz mature Cheddar or
  Cheshire cheese, grated
salt and ground black pepper

Preparation: 2 minutes; Cooking: 10 minutes

1 Trim the cauliflower and cut it into florets. Bring a pan of lightly salted water to the boil, drop in the cauliflower and cook for 5–8 minutes or until just tender. Drain and tip the florets into an ovenproof dish.

2 To make the sauce, melt the butter in a pan, stir in the flour and cook gently, stirring constantly, for about 1 minute (do not allow it to brown). Remove from the heat and gradually stir in the milk.

3 Return the pan to the heat and cook, stirring, until the mixture thickens and comes to the boil. Simmer for 1–2 minutes.

4 Stir in three-quarters of the cheese and season to taste. Spoon the sauce over the cauliflower and scatter the remaining cheese on top. Put under a hot grill (broiler) until the cheese topping bubbles and turns golden brown.

Variations
• Boost the cheese flavour by adding a little English (hot) mustard to the cheese sauce.
• As an alternative to Cheddar or Cheshire cheese, use a blue cheese such as Stilton. You will not need as much.
• Cauliflower cheese is delicious with strips of crisp fried bacon, either served on the side or crumbled into the sauce.

Carrot and Parsnip Purée Energy 71kcal/298kJ; Protein 1.5g; Carbohydrate 10.7g, of which sugars 6.6g; Fat 2.7g, of which saturates 1.4g; Cholesterol 5mg; Calcium 49mg; Fibre 4g; Sodium 31mg.
Cauliflower Cheese Energy 318kcal/1318kJ; Protein 17.4g; Carbohydrate 4.4g, of which sugars 3.9g; Fat 25.8g, of which saturates 16.3g; Cholesterol 71mg; Calcium 371mg; Fibre 1.8g; Sodium 453mg.

Colcannon

This traditional Irish dish is especially associated with Halloween, when it is likely to be made with curly kale and would have a ring hidden in it – predicting marriage during the coming year for the person who found it. At other times during the winter green cabbage is more often used.

Serves 3–4

450g/1lb potatoes, peeled and boiled
450g/1lb curly kale or cabbage, cooked
milk, if necessary
50g/2oz/¼ cup butter, plus extra for serving
1 large onion, finely chopped
salt and ground black pepper

Preparation: 5 minutes; Cooking: 10 minutes

1 Mash the potatoes and spoon them into a large bowl. Chop the kale or cabbage, add it to the potatoes and mix. Stir in a little milk if the mash is too stiff, and season with salt and ground black pepper.

2 Melt a little butter in a frying pan over a medium heat and add the onion. Cook for 3–4 minutes until softened. Remove and mix well with the potato and kale or cabbage.

3 Add the remainder of the butter to the hot pan. When it is very hot, turn the potato mixture on to the pan and spread it out in an even layer.

4 Fry the potato mixture until golden brown, then cut it roughly into pieces and continue frying until these are crisp and brown.

5 Spoon the colcannon into a large bowl or individual bowls, and add a generous knob of butter to each. Serve immediately. As the butter melts, guests fork it in to the cabbage mixture.

> **Cook's Tip**
> *It is delicious with pork chops or sausages or can simply be served with fried eggs.*

Patatas Bravas

There are several variations on this chilli and potato dish, but the most important thing is the spicing, which is made hotter still by adding vinegar. The classic version is made with fresh tomato sauce flavoured with garlic and chilli. The name bravas implies that the potatoes are so hot that it is manly to eat them. Patatas bravas often appear on tapas menus and are good with drinks.

Serves 4

675g/1½lb small new potatoes
75ml/5 tbsp olive oil
2 garlic cloves, sliced
3 dried chillies, seeded and chopped
2.5ml/½ tsp ground cumin
10ml/2 tsp paprika
30ml/2 tbsp red or white wine vinegar
1 red or green (bell) pepper, seeded and sliced
coarse sea salt, for sprinkling (optional)

Preparation: 4 minutes; Cooking: 15 minutes

1 Scrub the potatoes and put them into a pan of lightly salted water. Bring to the boil and cook for 10 minutes, or until almost tender. Drain and leave to cool slightly. Peel, if you like, then cut the potatoes into neat, even-sized chunks.

2 Heat the oil in a large frying or sauté pan and fry the potatoes, turning them frequently, until golden.

3 Meanwhile, crush together the garlic, chillies and cumin using a mortar and pestle. Mix the paste with the paprika and wine vinegar, then add to the potatoes with the sliced pepper and cook, stirring, for 2 minutes. Scatter with salt, if using, and serve hot as a tapas dish or cold as a side dish.

> **Variations**
> *Patatas bravas means fierce potatoes. They are meant to be fiery but the flavour can be moderated by reducing the amount of chilli. Although classically vegetarian, they are often served with chorizo or with chunks of roast pork. Try making them with sweet potatoes for a tasty change.*

Patatas Bravas Energy 256kcal/1070kJ; Protein 3.3g; Carbohydrate 30g, of which sugars 4.9g; Fat 14.4g, of which saturates 2.2g; Cholesterol 0mg; Calcium 14mg; Fibre 2.4g; Sodium 20mg.
Colcannon Energy 1224kcal/5124kJ; Protein 21.6g; Carbohydrate 162.4g, of which sugars 54.4g; Fat 58.4g, of which saturates 35.2; Cholesterol 144mg; Calcium 416mg; Fibre 23.6g; Sodium 508mg.

Fried Plantains

These simple and tasty treats from the Caribbean are the perfect accompaniment to highly spiced and seasoned foods. Their sweet flavour provides an interesting contrast.

Serves 4

4 ripe plantains
75g/3oz/6 tbsp butter
10ml/2 tsp vegetable oil
strips of spring onion (scallion)
 and red (bell) pepper,
 to garnish

Preparation: 2 minutes; Cooking: 10–12 minutes

1 Peel the plantains, cut them in half lengthways, then cut them in half again. Melt the butter with the oil in a large frying pan.

2 Add the plantains to the pan in a single layer and fry for 8–10 minutes, turning halfway through. Drain on kitchen paper. Spoon into a heated dish and garnish with strips of spring onion and red pepper. Serve immediately.

Variation
Fried plantains are very good on their own, or with a generous scoop of sour cream, crème fraîche or thick yogurt, but also taste great with black beans. Soak 450g/1lb/2½ cups black turtle beans in water overnight. Next day, drain the beans and put them in a pan. Cover with cold water. Add a 115g/4oz piece of gammon or uncooked ham and a bay leaf. Bring to the boil, then simmer and cook for 1 hour or until the beans are tender. In a separate pan, fry 2 crushed garlic cloves in 30ml/2 tbsp oil until aromatic. Add two ladles of cooked beans and fry for 2–3 minutes, breaking up the beans. Tip the refried beans back into the pan and season. Simmer gently for 10 minutes, then serve.

Cook's Tip
Ripe plantains have dark, almost black skins. Do not use green, under-ripe plantains, which are very hard and which will not soften, no matter how long you cook them for.

Corn with Cream

In Mexico, this would be made with heavy cream, the American equivalent of double cream, but the sauce has a better consistency when made with full-fat soft cheese. The jalapeños give the somewhat bland corn kernels a bit of a kick, but could be omitted in favour of diced sweet pepper or even peppadews.

Serves 6

4 corn cobs
50g/2oz/¼ cup butter
1 small onion, finely chopped
115g/4oz/⅔ cup drained pickled
 jalapeño chilli slices
130g/4½ oz/⅔ cup full-fat
 soft cheese
25g/1oz/⅓ cup freshly grated
 Parmesan cheese, plus
 shavings, to garnish
salt and ground black pepper

Preparation: 2 minutes; Cooking: 11–13 minutes

1 Strip off the husks from the corn and pull off the silks. Place the cobs in a bowl of water and use a vegetable brush to remove any remaining silks. Stand each cob in turn on a board and slice off the kernels, cutting as close to the cob as possible.

2 Melt the butter in a pan, add the chopped onion and fry for 4–5 minutes, stirring occasionally, until the onion has softened.

3 Add the corn kernels and cook for 4–5 minutes, until they are just tender. Chop the jalapeños finely and stir them into the corn mixture until evenly distributed.

4 Stir in the soft cheese and the grated Parmesan. Cook over a low heat until both cheeses have melted and the corn kernels are coated in the mixture. Season to taste, tip into a heated dish and serve, topped with Parmesan shavings.

Cook's Tip
To save time, use 350g/12oz/2 cups frozen corn kernels. Thaw before adding to the fried onion mixture. Alternatively, use canned whole kernel corn. Drain it well and just let it heat up in the onion mixture before adding the cheese.

Fried Plantains Energy 205kcal/861kJ; Protein 1.2g; Carbohydrate 29.5g, of which sugars 5.8g; Fat 10g, of which saturates 5.5g; Cholesterol 21mg; Calcium 11mg; Fibre 1.3g; Sodium 65mg.
Corn with Cream Energy 328kcal/1367kJ; Protein 7.6g; Carbohydrate 27.7g, of which sugars 10.4g; Fat 21.6g, of which saturates 12.8g; Cholesterol 45mg; Calcium 126mg; Fibre 1.5g; Sodium 463mg.

Wilted Spinach with Rice & Dill

This is a delicious dish that can be made in little time and with little effort.

Serves 5

675g/1½lb fresh spinach, trimmed of any hard stalks
105ml/7 tbsp extra virgin olive oil
1 large onion, chopped
juice of ½ lemon
150ml/¼ pint/⅔ cup water
115g/4oz/generous ½ cup long grain rice
45ml/3 tbsp chopped fresh dill, plus extra sprigs to garnish
salt and ground black pepper

Preparation: 5 minutes; Cooking: 15 minutes

1 Thoroughly wash the spinach in cold water and drain. Repeat four or five times until the spinach is completely clean and free of grit, then drain it completely in a colander. Brush off the excess water with kitchen paper.

2 Heat the olive oil in a large pan and sauté the onion until translucent. Add the spinach and stir for a few minutes to coat all the leaves with the olive oil. As soon as the spinach looks wilted, add the lemon juice and the measured water and bring to the boil.

3 Add the rice and half of the dill, then cover and cook gently for about 10 minutes, or until the rice is cooked to your taste. If it looks too dry, add a little hot water.

4 Spoon into a serving dish and sprinkle the sprigs of dill over the top. Serve hot or at room temperature.

Variation
This is equally good with chard or spring greens.

Cook's Tip
This dish is ideal to accompany fried or barbecued fish or chickpea rissoles. It can also be eaten as a first course.

Saffron Rice with Cardamoms

The addition of aromatic green cardamom pods, cloves, milk and saffron gives this dish both a delicate flavour and colour. It is the perfect dish to accompany a simple chicken or lamb curry and would also go well with a spicy vegetable dish or dhal.

Serves 6

450g/1lb/2⅓ cups basmati rice, soaked
750ml/1¼ pints/3 cups water
3 green cardamom pods
2 cloves
5ml/1 tsp salt
45ml/3 tbsp semi-skimmed (low-fat) milk
2.5ml/½ tsp saffron strands, crushed

Preparation: 6 minutes; Cooking: 10 minutes

1 Drain the rice and place it in a pan. Pour in the water.

2 Add the cardamoms, cloves and salt. Stir, then bring to the boil. Lower the heat, cover the pan tightly and simmer the rice for about 5 minutes so that it starts to cook.

3 Meanwhile, place the milk in a small pan. Add the saffron strands and heat gently.

4 Add the saffron milk to the rice and stir. Cover again and continue cooking over a low heat for 5–6 minutes. Remove from the heat without lifting the lid. Leave the rice to stand for 5 minutes before serving.

Cook's Tips
• The saffron milk can be heated in the microwave. Mix the milk and saffron strands in a suitable jug (pitcher) or bowl and warm them for 1 minute on Low.
• The rice can be coloured and flavoured with a generous pinch of ground turmeric instead of saffron. The effect will not be as subtle, but the results will still be very satisfactory.
• Just before serving the rice, remove the cardamom pods and whole cloves, or warn guests to look out for them.

Wilted Spinach Energy 325Kcal/1,343kJ; Protein 7.8g; Carbohydrate 29.9g, of which sugars 5.6g; Fat 19.2g, of which saturates 2.7g; Cholesterol 0mg; Calcium 327mg; Fibre 4.8g; Sodium 242mg.
Saffron Rice Energy 348kcal/1452kJ; Protein 6.7g; Carbohydrate 71g, of which sugars 0.9g; Fat 3.6g, of which saturates 2g; Cholesterol 8mg; Calcium 21mg; Fibre 0.2g; Sodium 515mg.

Pilau Rice with Whole Spices

This fragrant rice dish makes an excellent accompaniment to any Indian meal.

Serves 4

generous pinch of saffron
  strands
600ml/1 pint/2½ cups
  chicken stock
50g/2oz/¼ cup butter
1 onion, chopped
1 garlic clove, crushed
½ cinnamon stick
6 green cardamom pods
1 bay leaf
250g/9oz/1⅓ cups basmati rice
50g/2oz/⅓ cup sultanas
  (golden raisins)
15ml/1 tbsp sunflower oil
50g/2oz/½ cup cashew nuts

Preparation: 2 minutes; Cooking: 17 minutes

1 Add the saffron strands to a jug (pitcher) of hot chicken stock. Stir well to release the colour, and set aside.

2 Heat the butter in a pan and fry the chopped onion and crushed garlic for 5 minutes. Stir in the cinnamon stick, cardamoms and bay leaf and cook for a further 2 minutes.

3 Add the rice and cook, stirring, for 2 minutes more. Pour in the saffron-flavoured stock and add the sultanas. Bring to the boil, stir, then lower the heat, cover with a tight-fitting lid and cook gently for about 8 minutes or until the rice is tender and all the liquid has been absorbed.

4 Meanwhile, heat the oil in a frying pan and fry the cashew nuts until browned. Drain on kitchen paper. Scatter the browned cashew nuts evenly over the rice.

Cook's Tip
Don't be tempted to use black cardamoms in this dish. They are coarser and more strongly flavoured than green cardamoms and are only used in highly spiced dishes that are cooked for a long time. When using cardamoms of any colour, make sure they are fresh or the dish will taste musty.

Special Fried Rice

More colourful and elaborate than other fried rice dishes, special fried rice is almost a meal in itself and is ideal for a midweek supper. It is satisfying without being stodgy.

Serves 4

50g/2oz/⅓ cup cooked peeled
  prawns (shrimp)
3 eggs
5ml/1 tsp salt
2 spring onions (scallions),
  finely chopped
60ml/4 tbsp vegetable oil
115g/4oz lean pork, finely diced
15ml/1 tbsp light soy sauce
15ml/1 tbsp Chinese rice wine
  or dry sherry
450g/1lb/6 cups cooked rice
115g/4oz green peas

Preparation: 3 minutes; Cooking: 7 minutes

1 Pat the prawns dry with kitchen paper. Put the eggs in a bowl with a pinch of the salt and a few pieces of spring onion. Beat well.

2 Heat half the oil in a wok, add the pork and stir-fry until golden. Add the prawns and cook for 1 minute, then add the soy sauce and rice wine or sherry. Remove the mixture from the wok, cover with foil and keep warm.

3 Heat the remaining oil in the wok and lightly scramble the eggs. Add the rice and stir with chopsticks to make sure that each grain of rice is separated.

4 Add the remaining salt and spring onions, the stir-fried prawns, pork and peas. Toss well over the heat to combine, spoon into a bowl and serve either hot or cold.

Cook's Tips
• The weight of rice increases about two and a half times after cooking. When a recipe calls for cooked rice, use just under half the weight in uncooked rice to achieve the desired amount.
• This is a good way of using up leftover roast pork or chicken. Add it with the prawns as it will only need to be heated through, unlike the raw pork, which must be fully cooked.

Pilau Rice Energy 302kcal/1258kJ; Protein 5.8g; Carbohydrate 46.4g, of which sugars 1g; Fat 10.1g, of which saturates 1.1g; Cholesterol 0mg; Calcium 49mg; Fibre 0.8g; Sodium 2mg.
Fried Rice Energy 343kcal/1872kJ; Protein 14.5g; Carbohydrate 51g, of which sugars 4.4g; Fat 20.9g, of which saturates 3.1g; Cholesterol 113mg; Calcium 48mg; Fibre 1.1g; Sodium 58mg.

Chilli Bean Dip

Substantial enough to serve for supper on a baked potato, this creamy bean dip also tastes great with triangles of lightly toasted pitta bread or a bowl of crunchy tortilla chips. Serve it warm to enjoy it at its best. If the flavours are too fiery, use sweet peppers instead of green chillies and omit the red chilli strips.

Serves 4
2 fresh green chillies
2 garlic cloves
1 onion
30ml/2 tbsp vegetable oil
5–10ml/1–2 tsp hot chilli powder
400g/14oz can kidney beans
75g/3oz/³⁄₄ cup grated
  (shredded) mature (sharp)
  Cheddar cheese
1 fresh red chilli, seeded
salt and ground black pepper

Preparation: 2–3 minutes; Cooking: 9–10 minutes

1 Slit the green chillies and use a sharp knife to scrape out and discard the seeds. Chop the chilli flesh finely, then crush the garlic and finely chop the onion.

2 Heat the oil in a large pan or wok and add the garlic, onion and green chilli mixture. Stir in the chilli powder. Cook gently for 5 minutes, stirring, until the onions have softened and are transparent, but not browned.

3 Drain the kidney beans, reserving the liquid in which they were canned. Set aside 30ml/2 tbsp of the beans and purée the remainder in a food processor or blender.

4 Spoon the puréed beans into the pan or wok and stir in 30–45ml/2–3 tbsp of the reserved can liquid. Heat gently, stirring to mix all the ingredients well.

5 Stir in the reserved whole kidney beans and the Cheddar cheese. Cook gently for 2–3 minutes, stirring regularly until the cheese melts. Add salt and pepper to taste.

6 Cut the red chilli into tiny strips. Spoon the dip into four individual serving bowls and sprinkle the chilli strips over the top. Serve warm.

Melting Cheese Dip

This is a classic fondue in true Swiss style. It should be served with cubes of crusty, day-old bread, speared on long-handled forks, but it is also good with chunks of spicy, cured sausage such as chorizo, or with batons of carrot or celery.

Serves 2
1 garlic clove, finely chopped
150ml/¼ pint/²⁄₃ cup dry
  white wine
150g/5oz Gruyère cheese
5ml/1 tsp cornflour (cornstarch)
15ml/1 tbsp Kirsch
salt and ground black pepper
bread or chorizo cubes, to serve

Preparation: 3 minutes; Cooking: 7 minutes

1 Place the garlic and wine in a small pan and bring gently to the boil. Lower the heat and simmer for 3–4 minutes.

2 Coarsely grate the cheese and stir it into the wine. Continue to stir as the cheese melts.

3 Blend the cornflour to a smooth paste with the Kirsch and pour into the pan, stirring. Bring to the boil, stirring continuously until the sauce is smooth and thickened.

4 Add salt and pepper to taste. Serve immediately in heated bowls or transfer to a fondue pan and keep hot over a spirit burner. Garnish with black pepper and serve with bread or chorizo cubes.

Cook's Tips
• *In the 1960s this was a favourite centrepiece for a dinner party, usually kept warm in a pottery pot set over a burner. Using long-handled forks, guests speared cubes of bread and dunked them in the cheese, twirling the forks until the bread was thoroughly coated. This activity could be hazardous and cubes of bread were often lost. When this happened, the individual concerned had to pay a forfeit.*
• *Gruyère is a tasty cheese that melts incredibly well. Don't substitute other cheeses in this dip.*

Chilli Bean Dip Energy 240kcal/1002kJ; Protein 12.3g; Carbohydrate 20.3g, of which sugars 5.4g; Fat 12.3g, of which saturates 4.8g; Cholesterol 18mg; Calcium 219mg; Fibre 6.6g; Sodium 527mg.
Melting Cheese Dip Energy 390kcal/1617kJ; Protein 19.4g; Carbohydrate 3.3g, of which sugars 0.6g; Fat 24.6g, of which saturates 16.3g; Cholesterol 73mg; Calcium 562mg; Fibre 0.1g; Sodium 547mg.

Orange, Tomato & Chive Salsa

Fresh chives and sweet oranges provide a very cheerful combination of flavours. An unusual salsa, this is a very good accompaniment for grilled meats, such as lamb or pork kebabs. It also tastes good with grilled halloumi.

Serves 4

2 large, sweet oranges
1 ripe beefsteak tomato, or 2 plum tomatoes
bunch of fresh chives
1 garlic clove
30ml/2 tbsp extra virgin olive oil or grapeseed oil
sea salt

Preparation: 6–8 minutes; Cooking: 0 minutes

1 Slice the base off one orange so that it will stand firmly on a chopping board. Using a large sharp knife, remove the peel by slicing from the top to the bottom of the orange. Prepare the second orange in the same way.

2 Working over a bowl, segment each orange in turn. Slice towards the middle of the fruit, and slightly to one side of a segment, and then gently twist the knife to release the orange segment. Repeat. Squeeze any juice from the remaining membrane so that it falls into the bowl.

3 Roughly chop the orange segments and add them to the bowl with the collected orange juice.

4 Halve the tomato and use a teaspoon to scoop the seeds into the bowl. With a sharp knife, finely dice the flesh and add to the oranges and juice in the bowl.

5 Hold the bunch of chives neatly together and use a pair of kitchen scissors to snip them into the bowl.

6 Thinly slice the garlic and stir it into the orange mixture. Pour over the olive oil, season with sea salt and stir well to mix. Serve the salsa in the bowl in which it was made, or spoon into four individual bowls. It can also be spooned into the empty orange shells for serving. This involves slightly more difficult preparation but looks very effective.

Thousand Island Dip

This variation on the classic Thousand Island Dressing is far removed from the original version, but can be served in the same way – with shellfish laced on to bamboo skewers for dipping or with a simple mixed salad.

Serves 4

4 sun-dried tomatoes in oil
4 plum tomatoes, or 2 beefsteak tomatoes
150g/5oz/²⁄₃ cup mild soft cheese, or mascarpone or fromage frais
60ml/4 tbsp mayonnaise
30ml/2 tbsp tomato purée (paste)
30ml/2 tbsp chopped fresh parsley
1 lemon
Tabasco sauce, to taste
5ml/1 tsp Worcestershire sauce or soy sauce
salt and ground black pepper

Preparation: 6 minutes; Cooking: 0 minutes

1 Drain the sun-dried tomatoes and cut them into small pieces. Cut a cross in the blossom end of each fresh tomato, place them in a heatproof bowl and pour over boiling water. Leave for 1–2 minutes, then lift them out and peel off the skins. Chop the flesh finely. Put the sun-dried tomatoes and chopped fresh tomatoes in separate bowls and set aside.

2 Put the soft cheese in a bowl. Beat it until it is creamy, then gradually beat in the mayonnaise. Add the tomato purée in the same way.

3 Stir in the parsley and sun-dried tomatoes, then the fresh tomatoes. Mix well so that the dip is evenly coloured.

4 Grate (shred) the lemon finely and add the rind to the dip. Mix well. Squeeze the lemon and add the juice to the bowl, with Tabasco sauce to taste. Stir in the Worcestershire sauce or soy sauce, and salt and pepper to taste.

5 Spoon the dip into a serving bowl, swirling the surface attractively. Cover with clear film (plastic wrap) and chill in the refrigerator until ready to serve.

Orange Salsa Energy 91kcal/380kJ; Protein 1.3g; Carbohydrate 9.3g, of which sugars 9.3g; Fat 5.7g, of which saturates 0.8g; Cholesterol 0mg; Calcium 49mg; Fibre 2g; Sodium 7mg.
Thousand Island Dip Energy 194kcal/805kJ; Protein 4.7g; Carbohydrate 5.7g, of which sugars 5.6g; Fat 17.1g, of which saturates 5.2g; Cholesterol 27mg; Calcium 11mg; Fibre 1.2g; Sodium 184mg.

Citrus Fruit Flambé

A fruit flambé makes a dramatic finale for a dinner party. Topping this refreshing citrus fruit dessert with crunchy pistachio praline makes it extra special.

Serves 4
4 oranges
2 ruby grapefruit
2 limes

50g/2oz/¼ cup butter
50g/2oz/⅓ cup light muscovado (brown) sugar
45ml/3 tbsp Cointreau
fresh mint sprigs, to decorate

For the praline
oil, for greasing
115g/4oz/½ cup caster (superfine) sugar
50g/2oz/½ cup pistachio nuts

Preparation: 5 minutes; Cooking: 8–10 minutes; Make ahead

1 First, make the pistachio praline. Brush a baking sheet lightly with oil. Place the caster sugar and nuts in a small heavy pan and cook over a low heat, swirling the pan occasionally until all the sugar has melted completely.

2 Continue to cook over a fairly low heat until the nuts start to pop and the sugar has turned a dark golden colour. Pour on to the oiled baking sheet and set aside to cool. Using a sharp knife, chop the praline into rough chunks.

3 Cut all the rind and pith from the citrus fruits. Holding each fruit in turn over a large bowl, cut between the membranes so that the segments fall into the bowl, with any juice.

4 Heat the butter and muscovado sugar together in a heavy frying pan until the sugar has melted and the mixture is golden. Strain the citrus juices into the pan and continue to cook, stirring occasionally with a wooden spoon, until the juice has reduced and is fairly thick and syrupy.

5 Add the fruit segments and warm through without stirring. Pour over the Cointreau and set it alight. As soon as the flames die down, spoon the fruit flambé into serving dishes. Scatter some praline over each portion and decorate with sprigs of fresh mint.

Mango Stacks with Raspberry Coulis

This makes a very healthy yet stunning dessert – it is low in fat and contains no added sugar. However, if the raspberries are a little sharp, add a pinch of sugar to the purée to sweeten it.

Serves 4
3 filo pastry sheets, thawed if frozen
50g/2oz/¼ cup butter, melted
2 small ripe mangoes
115g/4oz/⅔ raspberries, thawed if frozen

Preparation: 10 minutes; Cooking: 5 minutes

1 Preheat the oven to 200°C/400°F/Gas 6. Lay the filo sheets on a clean work surface and cut out four 10cm/4in rounds from each.

2 Brush each round with the melted butter and lay the rounds on two baking sheets. Bake for 5 minutes, or until crisp and golden. Place on wire racks to cool.

3 Peel the mangoes, remove the stones and cut the flesh into thin slices. Put the raspberries in a food processor with 45ml/3 tbsp water and process to a purée.

4 Place a pastry round on each of four serving plates. Top with a quarter of the mango and drizzle with a little of the raspberry purée. Repeat until all the ingredients have been used, ending with a layer of mango and a drizzle of raspberry purée.

Variation
Use sliced nectarines or peaches instead of the mangoes.

Cook's Tip
Always place a dish towel or some clear film (plastic wrap) over the filo sheets you are not working with to prevent them from drying out, becoming brittle and cracking.

Fruit Flambé Energy 446kcal/1872kJ; Protein 4.8g; Carbohydrate 65.2g, of which sugars 64.8g; Fat 17.4g, of which saturates 7.4g; Cholesterol 27mg; Calcium 127mg; Fibre 4.4g; Sodium 155mg.
Mango Stacks Energy 186kcal/779kJ; Protein 2.2g; Carbohydrate 21.7g, of which sugars 11.9g; Fat 10.7g, of which saturates 6.7g; Cholesterol 27mg; Calcium 36mg; Fibre 3.1g; Sodium 79mg.

Fresh Fig Compote

Lightly poaching figs in a vanilla and coffee syrup brings out their wonderful flavour, especially if the dessert is left to stand for an hour or so before being served. Do not put the compote in the refrigerator.

Serves 4–6

400ml/14fl oz/1²/₃ cups brewed coffee
115g/4oz/¹/₂ cup clear honey
1 vanilla pod
12 slightly under-ripe fresh figs
Greek (US strained plain) yogurt, to serve (optional)

Preparation: 3 minutes; Cooking: 8 minutes; Make ahead

1 Choose a frying pan with a lid, large enough to hold the figs in a single layer. Pour in the coffee and add the honey.

2 Split the vanilla pod lengthways and scrape the seeds into the pan. Add the vanilla pod, then bring to the boil over high heat. Continue to boil the syrup until it has reduced to about 175ml/6fl oz/³/₄ cup. Pour into a bowl and cool quickly.

3 Wash the figs and pierce the skins several times with a sharp skewer. Cut in half and add to the syrup. Lower the heat, cover and simmer for 5 minutes. Remove the figs from the syrup with a slotted spoon and set aside to cool.

4 Strain the syrup over the figs. Allow to stand at room temperature for 1 hour before serving with yogurt, if liked.

Cook's Tips
• *Rinse and dry the vanilla pod; it can be used several times. If placed in a jar of sugar, it will impart a delightful flavour.*
• *Figs come in three main varieties – red, white and black – and all three are suitable for cooking. Naturally high in sugar, they are sweet and succulent and complement well the stronger flavours contributed by the freshly brewed coffee and vanilla.*
• *To cool the syrup quickly, place the bowl in a larger bowl filled with iced water. Stirring speeds the cooling process.*

Grapefruit in Honey & Whisky

Create a simple yet elegant dessert by arranging a colourful fan of pink, red and white grapefruit segments on a plate and pouring over a sweet whisky sauce. This dessert is perfect after a rich meal.

Serves 4

1 pink grapefruit
1 red grapefruit
1 white grapefruit
50g/2oz/¹/₄ cup sugar
60ml/4 tbsp clear honey
45ml/3 tbsp whisky
mint leaves, to decorate

Preparation: 4 minutes; Cooking: 14 minutes; Make ahead

1 Cut a thin slice of peel and pith from each end of the grapefruit. Place the cut side down on a plate and cut off the peel and pith in strips. Remove any remaining pith. Cut out each segment leaving the membrane behind. Put the grapefruit segments into a shallow bowl and set aside.

2 Put the sugar and 150ml/¹/₄ pint/²/₃ cup water into a heavy pan. Bring to the boil, stirring constantly, until the sugar has completely dissolved, then reduce the heat and simmer, without stirring, for 10 minutes, until thickened and syrupy. Do not cover the pan.

3 Heat the honey in a small pan and boil until it becomes a slightly deeper colour and begins to caramelize. Remove the pan from the heat and carefully add the whisky, standing back in case the mixture spits. Using a match or taper, carefully ignite, if you like, then pour the mixture into the sugar syrup.

4 Bring the syrup to the boil, and pour over the grapefruit segments. Cover and leave until cold. To serve, put the grapefruit segments on to four serving plates, alternating the colours. Pour over some of the syrup and decorate with the mint leaves.

Variation
The whisky can be replaced with brandy or an orange liqueur such as Cointreau, Grand Marnier or Van der Hum.

Fresh Fig Compote Energy 147kcal/628kJ; Protein 1.7g; Carbohydrate 36g, of which sugars 35.8g; Fat 0.6g, of which saturates 0g; Cholesterol 0mg; Calcium 103mg; Fibre 3g; Sodium 27mg.
Grapefruit in Honey Energy 154kcal/649kJ; Protein 1.1g; Carbohydrate 32.7g, of which sugars 32.7g; Fat 0.1g, of which saturates 0g; Cholesterol 0mg; Calcium 35mg; Fibre 1.6g; Sodium 6mg.

Cool Chocolate Float

Chocolate milkshake and scoops of chocolate and vanilla ice cream are combined here to make the most meltingly delicious dessert drink ever.

Serves 2
115g/4oz plain (semisweet) chocolate, broken into pieces

250ml/8fl oz/1 cup milk
15ml/1 tbsp caster (superfine) sugar
4 large scoops classic vanilla ice cream
4 large scoops dark (bittersweet) chocolate ice cream
a little lightly whipped cream
grated chocolate or chocolate curls, to decorate

Preparation: 6 minutes; Cooking: 2 minutes

1 Put the chocolate in a heavy pan and add the milk and sugar. Heat gently, stirring with a wooden spoon until the chocolate has melted and the mixture is smooth. Pour into a bowl and set in a larger bowl of iced water to cool quickly.

2 Blend the cooled chocolate mixture with half of both ice creams in a blender or food processor until the mixture resembles chocolate milk.

3 Scoop the remaining ice cream alternately into two tall glasses: vanilla then chocolate.

4 Using a dessertspoon, drizzle the chocolate milk over and around the ice cream in each glass, so that it dribbles down in swirls. Top with lightly whipped cream and sprinkle over a little grated plain chocolate or some chocolate curls to decorate. Serve the floats immediately.

> **Variations**
> • *You can experiment with all kinds of flavours of ice cream. Try substituting banana, coconut or toffee flavours for the chocolate and vanilla ice cream if you prefer.*
> • *The health-conscious cook might prefer to substitute frozen yogurt, but for best results, make sure it is a creamy variety.*

Blackcurrant Fool

The strong flavour and deep colour of this fruit makes it especially suitable for fools and ices, although this adaptable recipe can be made using other soft fruits too. Try it with raspberries, redcurrants or loganberries.

Serves 6
350g/12oz/3 cups blackcurrants
45ml/3 tbsp water
about 175g/6oz/scant 1 cup caster (superfine) sugar
5ml/1 tsp lemon juice
300ml/½ pint/1¼ cups double (heavy) cream

Preparation: 5 minutes; Cooking: 5 minutes; Make ahead

1 Put the blackcurrants into a small pan with the measured water and cook over a low heat until soft. Remove from the heat, add the sugar according to taste and stir until dissolved.

2 Cool slightly, then liquidize (blend) to make a purée. Leave to cool completely. Add the lemon juice and stir well.

3 Whip the double cream until it is fairly stiff and, using a metal spoon, carefully fold it into the blackcurrant purée, losing as little volume as possible.

4 Turn the mixture into a serving dish or six individual serving glasses, smooth the surface and leave to set. Cover with clear film (plastic wrap). Chill in the refrigerator until ready to serve.

> **Cook's Tip**
> *Freeze blackcurrants on the stalks and they will come off easily.*

> **Variation**
> *To make an easy no-stir blackcurrant ice cream, turn the completed fool into a freezerproof container. Cover and freeze (preferably at the lowest setting). Transfer from the freezer to the refrigerator 10–15 minutes before serving to allow the ice cream to soften. Serve with whipped cream and biscuits.*

Fool Energy 253kcal/1054kJ; Protein 1g; Carbohydrate 23.5g, of which sugars 23.5g; Fat 17.9g, of which saturates 11.1g; Cholesterol 46mg; Calcium 50mg; Fibre 1.4g; Sodium 10mg.
Float Energy 990kcal/4149kJ; Protein 17.7g; Carbohydrate 115.4g, of which sugars 110.4g; Fat 52.3g, of which saturates 32g; Cholesterol 83mg; Calcium 518mg; Fibre 1.5g; Sodium 262mg.

Whisky Trifle

This luxuriously rich trifle is made the old-fashioned way, with real sponge cake, fresh fruit and rich egg custard, but with whisky rather than the usual sherry flavouring.

Serves 6–8
1 x 15–18cm/6–7in sponge cake
225g/8oz raspberry jam
150ml/¼ pint/⅔ cup whisky
450g/1lb ripe fruit, such as
   pears, bananas and
   strawberries

300ml/½ pint/1¼ cups
   whipping cream
flaked almonds, to decorate

For the custard
450ml/¾ pint/scant 2 cups
   full cream (whole) milk
1 vanilla pod (bean) or a few
   drops of vanilla essence
   (extract) (optional)
3 eggs
25g/1oz/2 tbsp caster
   (superfine) sugar

Preparation: 12 minutes; Cooking: 5 minutes

1 To make the custard, put the milk into a pan with the vanilla pod, if using, and bring almost to the boil. Remove the pan from the heat. Whisk the eggs and sugar together lightly. Remove the pod. Gradually whisk the milk into the egg mixture.

2 Rinse out the pan with cold water, return the mixture to it and stir over low heat until it thickens enough to cover the back of a wooden spoon; do not allow the custard to boil.

3 Turn the custard into a mixing bowl and add the vanilla essence, if using. Cover the custard and set aside.

4 Halve the sponge cake horizontally, spread with the raspberry jam and make a sandwich. Using a sharp knife, cut it into slices and use them to line a large glass serving bowl.

5 Sprinkle with the whisky. Peel and slice the fruit, then spread it out over the sponge to make an even layer. Pour the custard on top, cover with clear film (plastic wrap) to prevent a skin forming, and leave to cool and set. Chill until required. Before serving, whip the cream and spread it over the set custard. Decorate with the almonds.

Pineapple & Rum Cream

When pineapple is heated, the flavour intensifies and the gorgeous sweet juices caramelize. Add rum and cream and you have a dream of a summer dessert for the grown-ups.

Serves 4
25g/1oz/2 tbsp butter
115g/4oz pineapple,
   roughly chopped
45ml/3 tbsp dark rum
300ml/½ pint/1¼ cups double
   (heavy) cream

Preparation: 4 minutes; Cooking: 4 minutes

1 Heat the butter in a frying pan and add the pineapple. Cook over a moderate to high heat until the pineapple is starting to turn golden at the edges.

2 Add the rum and allow to bubble for 1–2 minutes, then remove from the heat and set aside.

3 Pour the cream into a bowl and beat until soft. Fold the pineapple and rum mixture evenly through the cream, then spoon carefully into four glasses and serve immediately.

Cook's Tip
A ripe pineapple has a lovely perfume. The leaves on top should be glossy and healthy-looking, and the skin should be free from bruising. To prepare the pineapple, cut off the plume, then cut a slice off the base so the fruit will stand upright. Cut off the skin in wide diagonal strips, removing the black eyes, which have a peppery taste. Any that remain should be gouged out. Slice or dice the fruit, removing the hard central core if necessary.

Variation
Although a sumptuous dessert in its own right, this fruity alcoholic cream also works very well as a topping. Spoon over vanilla or rum-and-raisin ice cream for an extra special touch to a simple dessert.

Whisky Trifle Energy 533kcal/2219kJ; Protein 9.1g; Carbohydrate 43.5g, of which sugars 32g; Fat 32.4g, of which saturates 10.8g; Cholesterol 128.3mg; Calcium 146mg; Fibre 1.7g; Sodium 252mg.
Pineapple Cream Energy 455kcal/1876kJ; Protein 1.4g; Carbohydrate 4.2g, of which sugars 4.2g; Fat 45.5g, of which saturates 28.3g; Cholesterol 116mg; Calcium 43mg; Fibre 0.4g; Sodium 55mg.

Hot Chocolate Zabaglione

Once you've tasted this slinky, sensuous dessert, you'll never look at cocoa in quite the same way again. The Marsala makes it rather expensive – and fairly alcoholic – so this is an indulgence that is strictly adults only. Make it when the children are safely tucked up in bed.

Serves 6
6 egg yolks
150g/5oz/⅔ cup caster
  (superfine) sugar
45ml/3 tbsp unsweetened
  cocoa powder
200ml/7fl oz/scant 1 cup
  Marsala
unsweetened cocoa powder or
  icing (confectioners') sugar,
  for dusting

Preparation: 2 minutes; Cooking: 5–7 minutes

1 Half fill a medium pan with water and bring to simmering point. Select a heatproof bowl which will fit over the pan, place the egg yolks and sugar in it, and whisk until the mixture is pale and all the sugar has dissolved.

2 Add the cocoa and Marsala, then place the bowl over the simmering water. Whisk with a hand-held electric mixer until the mixture is smooth, thick and foamy.

3 Pour quickly into tall heatproof glasses, dust lightly with cocoa or icing sugar and serve immediately, with chocolate cinnamon tuiles or amaretti biscuits.

Cook's Tips
Use the best cocoa powder you can find. There are a couple of Fairtrade products that are particularly good, and it is worth paying a little extra. Cocoa powder is made from cocoa solids, the residue when chocolate liquor is pressed to extract the cocoa butter. To neutralize the acids, some cocoa is treated with alkali. The cocoa that results is called Dutch-processed. If this is used for cakes, it is important to use baking powder as a raising agent, since bicarbonate of soda (baking soda) will not react unless one of the other ingredients is sufficiently acidic.

Honey Figs with Hazelnut Ice Cream

Figs baked in a lemon grass-scented honey syrup have the most wonderful flavour, especially when served with a good-quality ice cream dotted with roasted hazelnuts. If you prefer to avoid nuts, because you don't like them or because a guest has an allergy, use plain rich vanilla or toffee ice cream instead.

Serves 4
1 lemon grass stalk,
  finely chopped
1 cinnamon stick, roughly broken
60ml/4 tbsp clear honey
200ml/7fl oz/scant 1 cup water
75g/3oz/¾ cup hazelnuts
8 large ripe dessert figs
400ml/14fl oz/1⅔ cups
  good-quality vanilla ice cream
30ml/2 tbsp hazelnut
  liqueur (optional)

Preparation: 4 minutes; Cooking: 16 minutes

1 Preheat the oven to 190°C/375°F/Gas 5. Make the syrup by mixing the lemon grass, cinnamon stick, honey and measured water in a small pan. Heat gently, stirring until the honey has dissolved, then bring to the boil. Simmer for 2 minutes.

2 Meanwhile, spread out the hazelnuts on a baking sheet and grill (broil) under a medium heat until golden brown. Shake the sheet occasionally, so that they are evenly toasted.

3 Cut the figs into quarters, leaving them intact at the bases.

4 Stand the fig quarters in a baking dish, pour the syrup over, cover tightly with foil and bake for 13–15 minutes until the figs are tender.

5 While the figs are baking, remove the ice cream from the freezer and let it soften slightly. Chop the hazelnuts roughly and beat the softened ice cream briefly with an electric beater, then fold in the toasted hazelnuts until evenly distributed.

6 To serve, puddle a little of the syrup from the figs on to each dessert plate. Arrange the figs on top and add a spoonful of ice cream. At the very last moment before serving, spoon a little hazelnut liqueur over the ice cream, if you like.

Hot Zabaglione Energy 627kcal/2635kJ; Protein 11.9g; Carbohydrate 82.6g, of which sugars 80.3g; Fat 19g, of which saturates 6.7g; Cholesterol 537mg; Calcium 127mg; Fibre 2.4g; Sodium 222mg.
Honey Baked Figs Energy 433kcal/1816kJ; Protein 7.8g; Carbohydrate 53.6g, of which sugars 52.1g; Fat 21.2g, of which saturates 7g; Cholesterol 24mg; Calcium 227mg; Fibre 4.2g; Sodium 88mg.

Coffee Crêpes with Peaches

Juicy golden organic peaches and cream conjure up the sweet taste of summer. Here they are delicious as the filling for these light buckwheat crêpes.

Serves 6
75g/3oz/²⁄₃ cup plain (all-purpose) flour
25g/1oz/¹⁄₄ cup buckwheat flour
1 egg, beaten
200ml/7fl oz/scant 1 cup milk

15g/¹⁄₂ oz/1 tbsp butter, melted
100ml/3¹⁄₂ fl oz/scant ¹⁄₂ cup brewed coffee, cooled
sunflower oil, for frying

For the filling
6 ripe peaches
300ml/¹⁄₂ pint/1¹⁄₄ cups double (heavy) cream
15ml/1 tbsp brandy
225g/8oz/1 cup crème fraîche
65g/2¹⁄₂ oz/generous ¹⁄₄ cup caster (superfine) sugar

Preparation: 5 minutes; Cooking: 15 minutes

1 Sift the flours into a mixing bowl. Make a well in the middle and add the beaten egg, half the milk and the melted butter. Gradually mix in the flour, beating until the mixture is smooth, then beat in the remaining milk and the coffee.

2 Heat a drizzle of sunflower oil in a 15–20cm/6–8in crêpe pan. Pour in just enough batter to cover the base of the pan thinly, swirling the pan to spread the mixture evenly. Cook for 2 minutes, then flip the crêpe over and cook the other side.

3 Slide the crêpe out of the pan on to a plate. Continue making crêpes until all the mixture is used, stacking and interleaving them with baking parchment.

4 To make the filling, slice the peaches thickly. Whip the cream and brandy together until soft peaks form. Beat the crème fraîche with the sugar until smooth. Beat 30ml/2 tbsp of the cream into the crème fraîche, then fold in the remainder.

5 Place six of the crêpes on individual serving plates. Spoon a little of the brandy cream on to one half of each crêpe and top with peach slices. Gently fold the crêpe over and dust with a little sifted icing sugar, if you like. Serve immediately.

Fruit-filled Soufflé Omelette

This impressive dish is surprisingly quick and easy to make. The creamy omelette fluffs up in the pan, is flopped over to envelop its fruit filling and then slid out on to the plate.

Serves 2
75g/3oz/³⁄₄ cup strawberries, hulled

45ml/3 tbsp Kirsch, brandy or Cointreau
3 eggs, separated
30ml/2 tbsp caster (superfine) sugar
45ml/3 tbsp double (heavy) cream, whipped
a few drops of vanilla extract
25g/1oz/2 tbsp butter
icing (confectioners') sugar, sifted

Preparation: 5 minutes; Cooking: 4–5 minutes

1 Cut the strawberries in half and place in a bowl. Pour over 30ml/2 tbsp of the liqueur and set aside to macerate.

2 Beat the egg yolks and sugar together until pale and fluffy, then fold in the whipped cream and vanilla extract. Whisk the egg whites until stiff, then carefully fold in the yolks.

3 Melt the butter in an omelette pan. When sizzling, pour in the egg mixture and cook until set underneath, shaking occasionally. Spoon on the strawberries and liqueur and, tilting the pan, slide the omelette so that it folds over.

4 Carefully slide the omelette on to a warm serving plate, spoon over the remaining liqueur, and serve dredged with icing sugar. Cut the omelette in half, place on plates and serve.

Cook's Tip
You can give your omelette a professional look by marking sizzling grill lines on top. Protecting your hand with an oven glove, hold a long, wooden-handled skewer directly over a gas flame until it becomes very hot and changes colour. Sprinkle the top of the omelette with icing (confectioners') sugar, then place the hot skewer on the sugar, which will caramelize very quickly.

Soufflé Omelette Energy 434kcal/1802kJ; Protein 10.2g; Carbohydrate 18.4g, of which sugars 18.4g; Fat 30.7g, of which saturates 16.4g; Cholesterol 343mg; Calcium 70mg; Fibre 0.4g; Sodium 189mg.
Coffee Crêpes Energy 578kcal/2403kJ; Protein 6.5g; Carbohydrate 36.3g, of which sugars 23.1g; Fat 45.7g, of which saturates 28.8g; Cholesterol 150mg; Calcium 123mg; Fibre 2.1g; Sodium 63mg.

Hot Mocha Rum Soufflés

These superb hot mocha soufflés always rise beautifully. Serve them as soon as they are cooked for a fantastic finale to a dinner party.

Serves 6
25g/1oz/2 tbsp unsalted (sweet) butter, melted
65g/2½oz/generous ½ cup unsweetened cocoa powder
75g/3oz/⅓ cup caster (superfine) sugar
60ml/4 tbsp strong black coffee
30ml/2 tbsp dark rum
6 egg whites
icing (confectioners') sugar, for dusting

Preparation: 3–4 minutes; Cooking: 12–15 minutes

1 Preheat the oven with a baking sheet inside to 190°/375°F/ Gas 5. Grease six 250ml/8fl oz/1 cup soufflé dishes by brushing the interiors all over with melted butter.

2 Mix 15ml/1 tbsp of the cocoa with 15ml/1 tbsp of the caster sugar in a bowl. Tip the mixture into each of the dishes in turn, rotating them so that they are evenly coated.

3 Put the remaining cocoa in a bowl. Add the strong black coffee and then stir in the dark rum.

4 Whisk the egg whites in a clean, grease-free bowl until they form firm peaks. Whisk in the remaining caster sugar. Stir a generous spoonful of the whites into the cocoa mixture to lighten it, then fold in the remaining whites.

5 Spoon the mixture into the prepared dishes, smoothing the tops. Place on the hot baking sheet, and bake in the hot oven for 12–15 minutes or until well risen. Serve the soufflés immediately, dusted with icing sugar.

> **Cook's Tip**
> When serving the soufflés at the end of a dinner party, prepare them just before the meal is served. Pop in the oven as soon as the main course is finished and serve freshly baked.

Fried Bananas with Sugar & Rum

Children love fried bananas, but this Caribbean version with rum delivers an extra kick and is strictly for grown-ups. Fried bananas can be incredibly sweet, but the lime juice cuts through the sweetness with delicious and satisfying results.

Serves 4
50g/2oz/¼ cup caster (superfine) sugar
45ml/3 tbsp rum
65g/2½oz/5 tbsp unsalted (sweet) butter
grated rind and juice of 1 lime
4 bananas, peeled
vanilla ice cream, to serve

Preparation: 2–3 minutes; Cooking: 12 minutes

1 Place the sugar, rum, butter, grated lime rind and lime juice in a large heavy frying pan over a low heat. Cook for a few minutes, stirring occasionally with a wooden spoon, until the sugar has completely dissolved.

2 Add the bananas to the pan, turning to coat them in the sauce. Cook over a medium heat for 5 minutes on each side, or until the bananas are golden. Remove from the heat and cut the bananas in half. Serve two pieces of banana per person with a scoop of vanilla ice cream and a generous drizzle of the hot sauce.

> **Variations**
> • Rum is the traditional spirit for this delicious dessert, but brandy can be used instead. Alternatively, try this with an orange liqueur such as Grand Marnier or Cointreau, and substitute grated orange rind and juice for the lime.
> • Use half a pineapple instead of bananas. Peel a fresh pineapple, quarter it, then slice each quarter into wedges.

> **Cook's Tip**
> Avoid using bananas that are too ripe, otherwise they may break apart in the pan before they get a chance to colour.

Rum Soufflés Energy 148kcal/619kJ; Protein 5g; Carbohydrate 14.3g, of which sugars 13.1g; Fat 5.8g, of which saturates 3.6g; Cholesterol 9mg; Calcium 23mg; Fibre 1.3g; Sodium 190mg.
Fried Bananas Energy 385kcal/1616kJ; Protein 5.9g; Carbohydrate 53.9g, of which sugars 29.7g; Fat 17.7g, of which saturates 5.8g; Cholesterol 48mg; Calcium 59mg; Fibre 3g; Sodium 22mg.

Flambéed Bananas with Coffee Sauce

This dessert has all the flavour of the Caribbean: bananas, dark sugar, coffee and rum. The bananas become beautifully tender, with a sweet, sticky sauce that is delicious, whether you enjoy it alone or with ice cream.

Serves 4–6

6 bananas

40g/1 ½ oz/3 tbsp butter

50g/2oz/¼ cup soft dark brown sugar

50ml/2fl oz/¼ cup strong brewed coffee

60ml/4 tbsp dark rum

vanilla ice cream, to serve

Preparation: 3–4 minutes; Cooking: 7–8 minutes

1 Peel the bananas and cut in half lengthways. Melt the butter in a large frying pan over a medium heat. Add the bananas and cook for 3 minutes, turning halfway through cooking time, taking care not to break them. They will be quite soft.

2 Sprinkle the sugar over the bananas, then add the coffee. Continue cooking, stirring occasionally, for 2–3 minutes, or until the bananas are tender and covered in the sticky sauce.

3 Pour the rum into the pan and bring to the boil. Using a long match or taper, and tilting the pan, ignite the rum. As soon as the flames subside, remove the bananas and serve them with vanilla ice cream.

Variation
Espresso is the best coffee for this intensely flavoured sauce. Partner it with a coffee liqueur instead of rum, if you like. Toussaint is a good choice. Not as sweet as some of the other coffee liqueurs, it gives the sauce impressive depth.

Cook's Tip
These hot bananas taste equally good served with coconut or coffee ice cream. Alternatively, try them with thick, creamy yogurt.

Steamed Custard in Nectarines

Steaming nectarines or peaches brings out their natural colour and sweetness, so this is a good way of making the most of underripe or less flavourful fruit from the market.

Serves 6

6 nectarines

1 large (US extra large) egg

45ml/3 tbsp light muscovado (brown) sugar or palm sugar

30ml/2 tbsp reduced-fat coconut milk

Preparation: 4–5 minutes; Cooking: 5–10 minutes; Make ahead

1 Cut the nectarines in half. Using a teaspoon, scoop out the stones (pits) and a little of the surrounding flesh.

2 Lightly beat the egg, then add the sugar and the coconut milk. Beat until the sugar has dissolved.

3 Transfer the nectarines to a steamer and carefully fill the cavities three-quarters full with the custard mixture. Steam over a pan of simmering water for 5–10 minutes. Remove from the heat and leave to cool completely before transferring to plates and serving.

Variations
• *Instead of nectarines, use peaches, skinning them first by dunking them in boiling water until the skins peel back and can easily be removed.*
• *An alternative method of preparation is to chop 3 nectarines and spoon the fruit into six ramekins. Divide the custard among them and steam until set.*
• *Use full-fat coconut milk if you prefer.*

Cook's Tip
Palm sugar, also known as jaggery, is made from the sap of certain Asian palm trees, such as coconut and palmyrah. It is available from Asian food stores. If you buy it as a cake or large lump, grate it before use, so it will dissolve easily.

Flambéed Bananas Energy 200kcal/839kJ; Protein 1.3g; Carbohydrate 32g, of which sugars 29.7g; Fat 5.8g, of which saturates 3.6g; Cholesterol 14mg; Calcium 12mg; Fibre 1.1g; Sodium 42mg.
Steamed Custard Energy 119kcal/507kJ; Protein 3.8g; Carbohydrate 25.2g, of which sugars 25.2g; Fat 1.1g, of which saturates 0.3g; Cholesterol 32mg; Calcium 24mg; Fibre 2.3g; Sodium 20mg.

Index

almonds: trout with almonds 61
anchovies: anchovy and quail's egg
    bruschetta 45
    scrambled eggs with anchovies 15
asparagus: pasta with ham and asparagus 109
    Scrambled Eggs with Asparagus and
        Mangetout 14
    stir-fried asparagus with chilli, galangal and
        lemon grass 138
aubergine: grilled aubergine 41
avocados: avocado soup 18
avgolemono 18

bacon: American pancakes with bacon 12
    bacon and egg muffins hollandaise 13
    bacon chops with apple and cider sauce 103
    bacon, pumpkin and parmesan pasta 110
    bacon sandwich 9
    broad beans with bacon 142
    cabbage with onions, bacon and garlic 140
    oatmeal pancakes with bacon 11
    scallops with bacon 85
    scallops with bacon and sage 33
    stir-fried Brussels sprouts with bacon 141
bananas: flambéed bananas with coffee sauce
    157
    fried bananas with sugar and rum 156
beef: beef strips with orange and ginger 94
    beef stroganoff 94
    beef with blue cheese sauce 95
    beef with chanterelle mushrooms 98
    beef with peppers and black bean sauce 97
    collops of beef with shallots 96
    corned beef and egg hash 93
    green beef curry 97
    home-made burgers with relish 92
    pan-fried steaks with whisky and cream 96
    steak with pickled walnut sauce 94
    steak with warm tomato salsa 95
    Thai-style beef and mango salad 92
black bean sauce, beef with peppers and 97
black pudding: fried black pudding 29
blackcurrant fool 152
blood oranges, chicken wings with 118
brill: fillets of brill in red wine sauce 74
brioche: chive scrambled eggs in brioches 14
    devilled kidneys on brioche croûtes 115
broad beans: broad beans with bacon 142
broccoli: broccoli with soy sauce and sesame
    seeds 139
    penne with chicken and broccoli 126

Brussels sprouts: stir-fried Brussels sprouts
    with bacon 141
buckwheat noodles: noodles with smoked
    salmon 60
burgers: home-made burgers with relish 92
    kofta lamb burgers 112
    lemon grass and ginger pork burgers 102
    Russian hamburgers 93
burritos, red snapper 52
butter bean and tomato soup 19

cabbage: cabbage with onions, bacon and
    garlic 140
    crispy cabbage 140
cajun blackened fish with salsa 64
calf's liver with crisp onions 98
cardamom, saffron rice with 146
carrots: carrot and parsnip purée 143
    carrot, mango and ginger stir-fry 142
cashew nuts: chicken with cashew nuts 124
cauliflower: cauliflower cheese 143
celeriac, venison steaks with 117
cheese: bacon, pumpkin and Parmesan pasta
    110
    cauliflower cheese 143
    cheese fritters in wonton wrappers 28
    cheese toasties 8
    chicken stuffed with ham and cheese 123
    croque monsieur 8
    egg and cheese soup 20
    figs with prosciutto and Roquefort 38
    rice balls stuffed with mozzarella 30
    goat's cheese and trout toasties 40
    melting cheese dip 148
    pasta salad with Roquefort and peppered
        salami 135
    pears with blue cheese and walnuts 24
    salad leaves with Gorgonzola 25
    steak and blue cheese on ciabatta 49
    tuna melt muffins 44
    walnut and goat's cheese bruschetta 29
    Welsh rarebit 40
chicken: caramelized chicken wings 120
    chicken and basil coconut rice 127
    chicken and lemon grass curry 124
    chicken and pineapple rice 128
    chicken and soba noodle soup 23
    chicken croquettes 119
    chicken fried rice 126
    chicken lettuce parcels 39
    chicken liver and brandy pâté 38
    chicken omelette dippers 118
    chicken stuffed with ham and cheese 123
    chicken, vegetable and chilli salad 136
    chicken wings with blood oranges 118
    chicken with cashew nuts 124
    chicken with lemon and garlic 119
    crème fraîche and coriander chicken 125
    crispy five-spice chicken 120
    curried chicken noodles 125
    Greek-style chicken 122
    orange chicken salad 121
    pan-fried chicken with pesto 122
    penne with chicken and broccoli 126
    roast chicken pitta pockets 46
    soy sauce and star anise chicken 123
    spiced chicken risotto with mint 127
    spicy fried noodles with chicken 121
chicken livers: chicken livers in sherry 120
    pan-fried chicken liver salad 136
chillies: chicken, vegetable and chilli salad 136
    chilli bean dip 148
    grilled hake with lemon and chilli 67
    sautéed herb salad with chilli and lemon 139

stir-fried asparagus with chilli, galangal and
    lemon grass 138
chocolate: cool chocolate float 152
    hot chocolate zabaglione 154
chorizo: chorizo and egg bake 110
    chorizo in olive oil 39
    dates stuffed with chorizo 47
    warm chorizo and spinach salad 137
clams: lemon, chilli and herb steamed razor
    clams 89
    mussels and clams with lemon grass 88
    seafood risotto 82
    spiced clams 89
cod: roasted cod with tomato sauce 63
coffee: coffee crêpes with peaches 155
    flambéed bananas with coffee sauce 157
    hot mocha rum soufflés 156
corn: Chinese crab and corn soup 20
    corn with cream 145
    tuna and corn fish cakes 36
crab: Chinese crab and corn soup 20
    crab dim sum with Chinese chives 43
    crab meat in vinegar 90
    crab salad with rocket 26
    soft-shell crabs with chilli and salt 91
cream cheese, lox with bagels and 12
crème fraîche and coriander chicken 125
crêpes: coffee crêpes with peaches 155
croque monsieur 8
cucumber: cucumber and salmon soup with
    salsa 21
    sweet and sour cucumber with dill 24

dates stuffed with chorizo 47
duck: Chinese duck curry 130
    duck and sesame stir-fry 130
    gingered duck with tamari 128
    skewered duck with poached eggs 129
    stir-fried duck with pineapple 129

eggs: anchovy and quail's egg bruschetta 45
    avgolemono 18
    bacon and egg muffins hollandaise 13
    chive scrambled eggs in brioches 14
    chorizo and egg bake 110
    corned beef and egg hash 93
    egg and cheese soup 20
    egg crostini with rouille 13
    eggs Benedict 12
    fried pork with scrambled egg 106
    fruit-filled soufflé omelette 155
    omelette Arnold Bennett 17
    scrambled eggs with anchovies 15
    Scrambled Eggs with Asparagus and
        Mangetout 14
    scrambled eggs with prawns 16
    scrambled eggs with smoked salmon and
        roe 15
    skewered duck with poached eggs 129
    smoked salmon and chive omelette 16
    sweet breakfast omelette 17
eggplant see aubergine

figs: figs with prosciutto and Roquefort 38
    fresh fig compote 151
    honey figs with hazelnut ice cream 154
fish: Cajun blackened fish with salsa 64
    classic fish and chips 62
    escabeche 66
    fish moolie 65
    fish cakes 35
    kedgeree 68
    Mediterranean fish cutlets with aniseed
        tomato sauce 64

poached fish in spicy tomato sauce 65
seafood pancakes 82
smoked fish platter 27
surtido de pescado 37
Thai-style fish cakes 35
see also anchovies; brill; cod; haddock;
    hake; halibut; herring; hoki; kippers;
    mackerel; monkfish; plaice; salmon;
    sardines; skate; smoked mackerel; smoked
    salmon; smoked trout; snapper; sole;
    swordfish; trout; tuna; whitebait; whitefish

galangal: stir-fried asparagus with chilli,
    galangal and lemon grass 138
gammon: pan-fried gammon with cider 109
garlic: cabbage with onions, bacon and garlic
    140
ginger: carrot, mango and ginger stir-fry 142
    gingered duck with tamari 128
grapefruit: citrus fruit flambé 150
    grapefruit in honey and whisky 151
green beans: green beans with tomatoes 141
guava sauce, baked salmon with a 56
guinea fowl, jungle curry of 131

haddock in cider sauce 68
hake: grilled hake with lemon and chilli 67
    hake and potato salad 67
halibut with sauce vierge 70
    griddled halibut 71
ham: chicken stuffed with ham and cheese 123
    fettucine with ham and peas 108
    ham-wrapped trout 62
    pasta with ham and asparagus 109
    tortellini with ham 108
herring fillets in oatmeal with apples 73
hoki stir-fry 66
honey and whisky, grapefruit in 151
hummus: steak ciabatta with hummus 48

ice cream: honey figs with hazelnut ice
    cream 154

kebabs: pork kebabs with bbq sauce 101
kedgeree 68
kidneys: devilled kidneys on brioche croûtes
    115
    kidney and mushroom toasts 9
    lamb's kidneys with mustard sauce 116
    riñones al Jerez 116
kippers, jugged 17

lamb: cumin- and coriander-rubbed lamb 112
    fried lamb meatballs 114
    kofta lamb burgers 112
    lamb steaks with redcurrant glaze 114
    lamb with red pepper salsa 113

lamb's kidneys with mustard sauce 116
pan-fried Mediterranean lamb 112
pittas with spiced lamb koftas 111
sweet and sour lamb 113
warm lamb and noodle salad 115
leeks: lemon grass: chicken and lemon grass
    curry 124
lemon grass and ginger pork burgers 102
stir-fried asparagus with chilli, galangal and
    lemon grass 138
lemons: chicken with lemon and garlic 119
    grilled hake with lemon and chilli 67
    lemon and salmon pappardelle 58
    mackerel with mustard and lemon 73
    pan-fried sole with lemon butter sauce 72
    salmon with lemon and tofu sauce 56
    sautéed herb salad with chilli and lemon 139
limes: fried sole with lime 63
    scallops with lime butter 85
    sea bass with parsley and lime butter 69
lox with bagels and cream cheese 12

mackerel with mustard and lemon 73
mangoes: carrot, mango and ginger stir-fry 142
    mango stacks with raspberry coulis 150
    Thai-style beef and mango salad 92
meatballs, fried lamb 114
monkfish with pimiento and cream 74
muffins: bacon and egg muffins hollandaise 13
    tuna melt muffins 44
mushrooms: beef with chanterelle
    mushrooms 98
    caramelized mushrooms with allspice and
    herbs 138
    kidney and mushroom toasts 9
    spiced quail with mixed leaf and mushroom
    salad 131
    spinach and mushroom salad 24
mussels: mouclade of mussels 88
    mussels and clams with lemon grass 88
    mussels in cider 87
    mussels in garlic butter 86
    sautéed mussels with garlic and herbs 34
    seafood risotto 82
    seafood salad 134
    Thai steamed mussels in coconut milk 87

nectarines, steamed custard in 157
noodles: noodles with smoked salmon 60
    Cantonese fried noodles 101
    chiang mai noodle soup 23
    chicken and soba noodle soup 23
    chilled soba noodles with nori 28
    curried chicken noodles 125
    five-flavour noodles 106
    pork and Sichuan pickle noodle soup 22
    prawn and rice noodle salad 134
    prawn noodle salad 135
    prawn rice vermicelli 81
    prawns on crisp noodle cake 80
    Shanghai noodles with lap cheong 111
    snapper, tamarind and noodle soup 22
    spicy fried noodles with chicken 121
    spicy Sichuan noodle salad 137
    stir-fried noodles in seafood sauce 91
    sun-dried tomato and prawn stir-fry 81
    warm lamb and noodle salad 115
nori, chilled soba noodles with 28

oatmeal: herring fillets in oatmeal with
    apples 73
    oatmeal pancakes with bacon 11
olives: black olive, sliced tomato and sardine
    salad 133

omelettes: chicken omelette dippers 118
    fruit-filled soufflé omelette 155
    omelette Arnold Bennett 17
    smoked salmon and chive omelette 16
    sweet breakfast omelette 17
onions: bean salad with tuna and onion 132
    cabbage with onions, bacon and garlic 140
oranges: chicken wings with blood oranges
    118
    citrus fruit flambé 150
    orange chicken salad 121
    orange, tomato and chive salsa 149
oysters: oysters on the half-shell 33
    oysters Rockefeller 90

pancakes: American pancakes with bacon 12
    buttermilk pancakes 11
    light pancakes 10
    oatmeal pancakes with bacon 11
    pancakes with caramelized pears 10
    seafood pancakes 82
parsnips: carrot and parsnip purée 143
pasta: bacon, pumpkin and Parmesan pasta 110
    creamy penne with smoked salmon 58
    farfalle with smoked salmon and dill 59
    fettucine with ham and peas 108
    fusilli with sausage 107
    fusilli with smoked trout 61
    lemon and salmon pappardelle 58
    pasta salad with Roquefort and peppered
    salami 135
    pasta with ham and asparagus 109
    pasta with smoked salmon 59
    penne with chicken and broccoli 126
    seafood conchiglie 83
    smoked trout pasta salad 60
    spaghetti carbonara 107
    tortellini with ham 108
pâté: chicken liver and brandy pâté 38
    smoked mackerel pâté 38
peaches, coffee crêpes with 155
pears: pancakes with caramelized pears 10
    pears with blue cheese and walnuts 24
peas: fettucine with ham and peas 108
    pea soup with garlic 19
peppers: beef with peppers and black bean
    sauce 97
pineapple: chicken and pineapple rice 128
    pineapple and rum cream 153
    pork and pineapple coconut curry 104
    stir-fried duck with pineapple 129
pittas with spiced lamb koftas 111
pizza: courgette and chèvre pizza 181
    fiorentina pizza 180
plaice: fried plaice with tomato sauce 72
plantain: fried plantains 145
pork: aromatic pork with basil 103
    five-flavour noodles 106
    fried pork with scrambled egg 106
    fusilli with sausage 107
    lemon grass and ginger pork burgers 102
    pork and pineapple coconut curry 104
    pork and Sichuan pickle noodle soup 22
    pork in sweet and sour sauce 105
    pork kebabs with bbq sauce 101
    pork on lemon grass sticks 47
    pork with cream and apple sauce 102
    pork with Marsala and juniper 105
    sweet and sour pork Thai-style 104
potatoes: colcannon 144
    hake and potato salad 67
    patatas bravas 144
prawns: aromatic tiger prawns 31
    butterflied prawns in hot chocolate sauce 79

INDEX

Chinese-steamed prawns 31
fragrant tiger prawns with dill 78
garlic prawns 31
garlicky scallops and prawns 83
hot and spicy prawns with coriander 80
king prawns in crispy batter 79
prawn and rice noodle salad 134
prawn and sesame toasts 32
prawn cocktail 25
prawn noodle salad 135
prawn rice vermicelli 81
prawn salad 76
prawns in garlic butter 77
prawns on crisp noodle cake 80
pumpkin and prawn cakes 32
salt and pepper prawns 76
scrambled eggs with prawns 16
seafood pancakes 82
seafood risotto 82
sizzling prawns 77
special fried rice 147
stir-fried prawns with tamarind 78
sun-dried tomato and prawn stir-fry 81
prosciutto: figs with prosciutto and
    Roquefort 38
pumpkins: bacon, pumpkin and Parmesan
    pasta 110
    pumpkin and prawn cakes 32

quail: spiced quail with mixed leaf and
    mushroom salad 131

raspberries: mango stacks with raspberry
    coulis 150
redcurrants: lamb steaks with redcurrant
    glaze 114
refried beans: Mexican tortas 48
rice: chicken and basil coconut rice 127
    chicken and pineapple rice 128
    chicken fried rice 126
    rice balls stuffed with mozzarella 30
    kedgeree 68
    pilau rice with whole spices 147
    rice triangles 27
    saffron rice with cardamoms 146
    special fried rice 147
    wilted spinach with rice and dill 146
risotto: seafood risotto 82
    spiced chicken risotto with mint 127
rocket: crab salad with rocket 26
    warm swordfish and rocket salad 51
rum: fried bananas with sugar and rum 156
    hot mocha rum soufflés 156
    pineapple and rum cream 153

saffron rice with cardamoms 146
salad: bean salad with tuna and onion 132

black olive, sliced tomato and sardine salad
    133
chicken, vegetable and chilli salad 136
crab salad with rocket 26
hake and potato salad 67
pan-fried chicken liver salad 136
pasta salad with Roquefort and peppered
    salami 135
prawn and rice noodle salad 134
prawn noodle salad 135
prawn salad 76
salad leaves with Gorgonzola 25
salad Niçoise 132
sautéed herb salad with chilli and lemon 139
seafood salad 134
seared tuna steaks with watercress salad 53
smoked trout pasta salad 60
Spanish salad 26
spiced quail with mixed leaf and mushroom
    salad 131
spicy Sichuan noodles salad 137
spicy squid salad 133
spinach and mushroom salad 24
Thai-style beef and mango salad 92
warm chorizo and spinach salad 137
warm lamb and noodle salad 115
warm swordfish and rocket salad 51
whitefish salad with toasted bagels 44
salmon: baked salmon with a guava sauce 56
cucumber and salmon soup with salsa 21
filo-wrapped salmon 57
hot smoked salmon 57
salmon and scallop brochettes 43
salmon and tuna parcels 54
salmon fish cakes 54
salmon tortilla cones 45
salmon with green peppercorns 55
salmon with lemon and tofu sauce 56
salmon with whisky and cream 55
sardines: black olive, sliced tomato and
    sardine salad 133
sardines and tomatoes on focaccia 46
sausages: fusilli with sausage 107
    home-made venison sausages 117
scallops: garlicky scallops and prawns 83
    herb- and chilli-seared scallops 84
    salmon and scallop brochettes 43
    sautéed scallops 86
    scallops with bacon 85
    scallops with bacon and sage 33
    scallops with garlic and coriander 84
    scallops with lime butter 85
    seafood conchiglie 83
scrambled eggs see eggs
sea bass with parsley and lime butter 69
shellfish see clams; mussels; oysters; scallops
shrimp see prawns
skate: skate with bitter salad leaves 69
    skate with black butter 70
smoked mackerel pâté 38
smoked salmon: noodles with smoked
    salmon 60
    creamy penne with smoked salmon 58
    farfalle with smoked salmon and dill 59
    lemon and salmon pappardelle 58
    pasta with smoked salmon 59
    scrambled eggs with smoked salmon and
    roe 15
    smoked salmon and chive omelette 16
smoked trout: fusilli with smoked trout 61
    smoked trout pasta salad 60
snapper: red snapper burritos 52
    red snapper with fresh coriander and
    almonds 52

sole: breaded sole batons 42
    fried sole with lime 63
    grilled sole with chive butter 71
    pan-fried sole with lemon butter sauce 72
soufflés: hot mocha rum soufflés 156
spinach: spinach and mushroom salad 24
    warm chorizo and spinach salad 137
    wilted spinach with rice and dill 146
squid: fried squid with salt and pepper 34
    seafood risotto 82
    seafood salad 134
    spicy squid 75
    spicy squid salad 133
    stir-fried squid with ginger 75
steak see beef
stroganoff: beef stroganoff 94
swordfish: griddled swordfish with tomatoes
    50
    grilled swordfish skewers 50
    swordfish tacos 51
    warm swordfish and rocket salad 51

tacos: Mexican tacos 49
    Swordfish Tacos 51
thousand island dip 149
tofu: salmon with lemon and tofu sauce 56
tomatoes: black olive, sliced tomato and
    sardine salad 133
    sardines and tomatoes on focaccia 46
    fresh tuna and tomato stew 53
    fried plaice with tomato sauce 72
    green beans with tomatoes 141
    griddled swordfish with tomatoes 50
    mozzarella and tomato skewers 30
    orange, tomato and chive salsa 149
    poached fish in spicy tomato sauce 65
    roasted cod with tomato sauce 63
    steak with warm tomato salsa 95
tortillas: salmon tortilla cones 45
trifle: whisky trifle 153
trout: goat's cheese and trout toasties 40
    ham-wrapped trout 62
    trout with almonds 61
tuna: bean salad with tuna and onion 132
    fresh tuna and tomato stew 53
    salad Niçoise 132
    salmon and tuna parcels 54
    seared tuna steaks with watercress salad 53
    tuna and corn fish cakes 36
    tuna melt muffins 44

veal: escalopes of veal with cream sauce 100
    pan-fried veal chops 99
    veal escalopes with lemon 100
    veal escalopes with tarragon 99
venison: home-made venison sausages 117
    venison steaks with celeriac 117

walnuts: pears with blue cheese and walnuts
    24
    walnut and goat's cheese bruschetta 29
watercress: seared tuna steaks with
    watercress salad 53
whisky: grapefruit in honey and whisky 151
    pan-fried steaks with whisky and cream 96
    salmon with whisky and cream 55
    whisky trifle 153
whitebait: devilled whitebait 37
    fried whitebait with sherry salsa 36
whitefish salad with toasted bagels 44
wontons: cheese fritters in wonton
    wrappers 28

zabaglione: hot chocolate zabaglione 154